Sambia Sexual Culture

Sambia Sexua

Gilbert Herdt

WORLDS OF DESIRE
THE CHICAGO SERIES ON SEXUALITY, GENDER, AND CULTURE
A Series Edited by Gilbert Herdt

Culture

Essays from the Field

The University of Chicago Press
Chicago & London

GILBERT HERDT is director of the Human Sexuality Studies program
and professor of human sexuality and anthropology at San Fancisco
State University. He is the author or editor of many books,
including *Guardians of the Flutes: Idioms of Masculinity*
and *Third Sex, Third Gender.*

The University of Chicago Press, Chicago 60637
The University of Chicago Press, Ltd., London
© 1999 by The University of Chicago
All rights reserved. Published 1999
08 07 06 05 04 03 02 01 00 99   5 4 3 2 1

ISBN (cloth): 0-226-32751-5
ISBN (paper): 0-226-32752-3

Library of Congress Cataloging-in-Publication Data

Herdt, Gilbert H., 1949–
    Sambia sexual culture : essays from the field / Gilbert Herdt.
        p.   cm. — (Worlds of desire)
    Includes bibliographical references (p.   ) and index.
    ISBN 0-226-32751-5. — ISBN 0-226-32752-3 (pbk.)
        1. Sambia (Papua New Guinea people) — Rites and ceremonies.
    2. Sambia (Papua New Guinea people) — Sexual behavior.
    3. Initiation rites — Papua New Guinea.   4. Sex customs — Papua
    New Guinea.   5. Sex symbolism — Papua New Guinea.
    6. Homosexuality, Male — Papua New Guinea.   7. Masculinity —
    Papua New Guinea.   8. Papua New Guinea — Social life and
    customs.   I. Title.   II. Series.
    du740.42.h46   1999
    306.7'089'9912 — dc21   98-54692
                                                                        CIP

To the memory of
Robert J. Stoller, M.D.
Mentor and friend

CONTENTS

A gallery of photographs follows page 162

These essays, in their original forms, appeared in disparate journals and books, and while the core is essentially unchanged, all of the papers have been shortened to eliminate redundancy and overlap. The introduction is new and previously unpublished.

The inspiration and support for my original field work among the Sambia of Papua New Guinea, while acknowledged in print before, deserves recognition again because of the debt owed to many. First and foremost were my Ph.D. supervisors at the Australian National University, J. Derek Freeman and the late Roger Keesing, to both of whom I remain greatly indebted. And again I wish to pay deepest tribute to the memory of the two most important professional influences of my life: the late Kenneth E. "Mick" Read, my teacher and long-time friend, who shared many insights on New Guinea over the years; and the late Robert J. Stoller, mentor and collaborator, for his guidance and support over a period of many years.

Original funding for the field research among the Sambia came primarily from my 1974–77 Predoctoral Fulbright Fellowship to Australia, and from the Research School of Pacific Studies, the Australian National University. Additional funding in 1979–81 derived from an Individual NIMH Postdoctoral Fellowship and the Department of Psychiatry at UCLA. Subsequently the Wenner-Gren Foundation for Anthropological Research, Stanford University, and the University of Chicago provided occasional research support. I offer my gratitude to all these institutions for their generosity. The writing of the introduction to this book was made possible by a William Simon Henry Guggenheim Memorial Fellowship and support from the Robert Penn Warren Center for the Humanities at Vanderbilt University, where I was Robert S. Vaughn Fellow and Visiting Professor of Anthropology in 1997–98. I would especially like to thank Tom Gregor, Volney Gay, and Mona Frederick for their kindness.

Many persons have read and commented on various chapters of this book in their original form, but I should most like to thank once more my *ix* colleagues and friends Donald F. Tuzin, Michele Stephen, Bruce Knauft, Andrew Boxer, and the late Robert J. Stoller. I would also like to express my thanks to three great scholars whose influence on these essays, as well as their support and friendship, is not always apparent but was critical: Melford E. Spiro, Robert A. LeVine, and the late George Devereux.

Chapters 1, 2, and 4 owe much to the late Robert J. Stoller, who read and commented on them. Chapter 1 was originally dedicated to Derek Freeman. Chapter 3 was originally dedicated to Kenneth E. Read. I am grateful to Derek Freeman, Michael Young, Inge Riebe, the late Robert J. Stoller, Leonard B. Glick, Shirley Lindenbaum, the late Michelle Z. Rosaldo, and Marilyn Strathern, Joseph Carrier, Terence E. Hays, the late Roger M. Keesing, Fitz J. P. Poole, the late K. E. Read, and Donald F. Tuzin for their comments on the original versions of chapters 2, 3, or 4.

Chapter 5 owes much to a detailed reading by the late George Devereux.

Chapter 6 was originally presented to the International Workshop on New Guinea, convened by the Center for Australian and Oceanic Studies, Catholic University, Nijmegen, the Netherlands, in February 1987, and I am grateful to my colleagues there, especially Laurent Serpenti, Marilyn Strathern, Eric Schwimmer, and Donald Tuzin, for their comments. Special thanks go to the late Jan Van Baal for his ethnological help. I am also grateful to the Boston Psychoanalytic Society for the invitation to deliver the William Binstock lectures for 1987, where an earlier version of this chapter was presented. For their helpful comments there I am indebted to Bennett Simon and Robert A. LeVine. I wish to thank Andrew Boxer, Mark Busse, Bertram Cohler, Bruce Knauft, Julia Targ, and Donald Tuzin for comments on the published form.

Chapters 7 and 8 were commented on by the following colleagues, to whom I am grateful: Andrew Boxer, Norman Bradburn, Joseph Carrier, Julian Davidson, John DeCecco, Daniel Freedman, Paul Friedrich, Martha McClintock, John Money, Steven Murray, Robert LeVine, Bennett Simon, the late Robert J. Stoller, Richard Shweder and Donald Tuzin.

I would like to thank John Fout for the encouragement to write the original of chapter 9.

My editor, Doug Mitchell, is a key person in my work and my life, and I wish to thank him again for his patience, guidance, and friendship.

It is a pleasure to acknowledge the help of Heather Lindquist, Andrew Hostetler, and Eleonora Bartoli for their organizational and editorial assistance in the preparation of this book.

Lastly, I dedicate the book to Bob Stoller, a loving mentor and steadfast friend, who was killed by a speeding car in September 1991. I am thankful that his wife, Sybil, survived. Bob touched the lives of everyone who knew him. I can never repay his lasting gifts of friendship, knowledge, and insight. I honor his memory in this small way, and I think he might have liked it, for it was because of Bob's interest in the Sambia that we first made contact, exchanged ideas, and eventually worked together in New Guinea and in the United States, a string of rare memories to last a lifetime.

Sexual Cultures, Strange and Familiar

In the Cold War days of my tender youth it still was taught that our culture was superior to others, most of all, the East. In that time of armed camps, no matter how much we compared Them with Us, we always came out ahead. Sex was no different: the Others were either hypersexual or castrated, as the case may be, making their sexual cultures monstrous. But then the idea of cultural relativism was reintroduced to the middle class and was surging by the 1960s. As culture study popularized the glory of other lands, and political opinion grew skeptical of the Cold War institutions, Western customs looked not only less familiar but also less appealing, even the sexual ones, and this was reflected in that special meditation on modernity known as anthropology. To go off to the ends of the world in search of something different, perhaps better, in the human condition, was the spirit of the times. I still believe in the old-time religion of fieldwork in other cultures. I saw the Sambia as an island out of time and practiced fieldwork that way. Others came to see Sambia "homosexuality" as proof of the universality of same-gender desires. Years later, after completing a study of sexuality and gays and lesbians in the United States, I discovered how much Sambia sex and homoeroticism in my account had depended upon the categories and meanings of American sexual culture, which I had also carried with me to the hot tropics. Relativism had relativized so much; but no matter how the Cold War had ossified it and the social resistance of baby boomers had destabilized our own and other cultures, sex was unmoved: untouched, natural, timeless.

This was long before the sad swan song of postmodernism, when in 1949 Margaret Mead warned that ethnography at home must fail unless the   *1* field-worker first studied in two other cultures.[1] Mead's feminist standard helped promote the idea in subsequent generations of gender as a "social construction." Gender, but not sexuality; today, however, the distinction is all but forgotten. All notions of "foreign" fieldwork are typically relegated to the dustbin of colonialism, and their aspirations of "objectivity"—the method of cross-cultural comparison—seem not only suspect but simply wrong to the trenchant skeptics of relativist anthropology. They question the merit of Westerners studying another country. Generally they reject as a fetish of Orientalism the old-time fieldwork. They prefer instead that convenient and not altogether imperfect fiction that cultures are texts whose constructions the ethnographer might just as well read in the pages of the *National Geographic,* as eyewitness in the tropics. The practice of culture study, once immortalized in faraway Samoa, the Trobriand Islands, and Azande-land, had fallen prey to the dissection of anthropology. Is it not curious that the demise of the Cold War had ushered in this failed romanticism?

There is merit in some of these epistemological changes and the cynical charges against fieldwork in other cultures, and I will not attempt to dispute them except in the one area that concerns this book: sexuality. Sex was seldom dissected, either at home or abroad, and the radical comparison—their sex versus ours, East not as feminized and castrated but as divergent, even better—was never attempted until recently. Much had first to change in the world, in society, in science. The postmortem of postmodernism thus does not apply, for Mead's formula—study first the strange, then the familiar—was never applied (the word "faithfully" sticks to applied) to the anthropology of sexuality. Now we can study the reasons why.

When sex was found across the seas, and none found it grander than Malinowski's *Sexual Life of Savages* (1929) or more famously than Margaret Mead's (1927) polemicized *Coming of Age in Samoa,* these ethnographies served not to test the water but rather to reinforce the popular prejudice that "sex was sex," whether in Greenland or the tropics. That was not, of course, what their authors had intended. Their classic studies did not de-

1. Two generations ago, Margaret Mead wrote: "But so far, in seeking to make anthropological accounts useful to the sophisticated reader, who may be psychiatrist or biologist or geologist, judge or pediatrician or banker or mother of five children, we have tried to do only two things: either to convey that some aspect of human behavior could be organized differently—such as adolescence, or a proneness to heavy drinking, or a sensitivity to art—or to convey the extent to which cultures differ from one another" (1949:31). One generation ago Geertz's (1973) essay on thick description awakened the social sciences again to the place of anthropology in the academy through a similar but fresher rhetoric. Today, under the flag of postmodernism, our ship is adrift.

naturalize sex or relativize it; sex as biology was still needed to procreate and make babies, Malinowski advised. The pleasure of sex (tabooed between Trobriand siblings, whose night dreams revealed wishes for the forbidden sex) was unanalyzed. The fact that the culmination of sexual excitement among Trobriand lovers was achieved through the biting of each other's eyelashes was quaint and cute, a divergent erotics, more fun, but unexplained in its particulars. The procreative focus (notice that its discourse has been dominated by men in anthropology and demography [Herdt 1997b]) made the topic more respectable and polite, and perhaps less policed (Foucault 1980). Female emancipation through the gender studies of the times was promoted in the same way (Rosaldo and Lamphere 1974a). However, the more subversive topics, such as homosexuality, were avoided, and both Malinowski and Mead treated homoeroticism as "deviant" biology, typically absent in the cultures studies, which applied the same tropes (i.e., "invert") as did psychiatrists back home.

Western meanings were thus projected onto many areas of sexual life, completing the naturalization of Western realities in the other sexual cultures. This was true even though the manifestations of these other sex/gender systems were insinuated to be less personal than they were in the West, hemmed in by taboos and biology. This was because whole persons, in the Western sense, were typically felt not to inhabit these local notions of "desire" and "pleasure," for the absence of "individualism" and "privacy" created unfathomable obstacles to desire and made pleasure largely irrelevant, in the sense of its joys and pains of a Western sort. Neither "marriage" nor "love" was uncoupled from reproductivity; the South Seas cultures did not inflect the anchored truths of these historical Judeo-Christian traditions. The peculiar American notion of "sex hormones" driving rebelliousness against parents was not countered by the image of lovely Samoan girls at peace with their families. Indeed, it remains a popular conflict which American parents still credit today. Sex, in short, remained sex: in desire, the genes, raging hormones, sex drives, mothering, and especially procreation—inhabiting the nature land of sex, outside the laws of culture.

That sex eluded the relativists and remained a black hole, an empty space understudied and underanalyzed in anthropology, as much as in the other social sciences, is no news. Surely Malinowski and Mead, and, in his twilight years, Evans-Pritchard (1970), had hoped for more: they had shown how the Other was, if not superior to Us, then at least less conflicted, experiencing more pleasure, equality between the genders, bisexuality, and fewer hang-ups in sexual life. But since sex was more natural, and underanalyzed by the social scientists—much as it had been overanalyzed by Freud and his too-faithful followers, who saw sex as mostly natural, with domestication added for a topping—what was socially distinctive or culturally unique about sexuality was left out. When cultural claims were established for sexual Otherness, or sexual difference, whether in China (where men were spontaneously aroused by women's bound feet) or Azande (where men took boys as their lovers for some years) or Amazonia (where they stole sex with one another's wives every day [Gregor 1985]) they were so often couched in the only language available: the tropes and metaphors of Western European/North American cultures. The trouble was: Our traditions treated sex as medicalized and problematical, even punitive, not at all like the liberated cultural reality (ontology) of the fabled sexual Other.

Sex in the Anglo-American tradition was like a scab that would occasionally itch and which society had to scratch, as John Gagnon has said; whether the scratch was the seduction of innocent girls in the Jacksonian age, masturbation in the Victorian period, the crisis of masculinity at the turn-of-the century, the steamy closet of burgeoning homosexuality after the trial of Oscar Wilde, the proverbial rebelliousness of adolescence in the twenties, unwanted adolescent pregnancy in the sixties, gay liberation, or AIDS/STDs of late. Sex was a problem to be gotten rid of. Not much was learned from each attempt at eradication; once the irritant was removed, society went back to its puritanical business.

Sex was simply too physical to theorize, so much a part of Malinowski's (1927) functional theory of biological needs, which led far away from the marketplace of sociality into the private or even unconscious (Freud 1962) recesses of "drives" and "desires." And how very often sex has been conflated with marriage and kinship, as if the cultural ideal or norm explained sexual practice, in Lévi-Strauss (1949) no less than David Schneider (1968)! Sex, in the sociocentric paradigm of social anthropology, could never exist save in the intercourse of the social contract and "heteronormativity." (We can be grateful to queer theorists for the invention of this latter concept, which strikes at the core of social theory's obsession with social and biological reproduction, and the norms that fashion its reality inside and outside the person [Herdt 1997a].)

Much of the problem can be explained by the absence of a general concept of sexual culture. By default, we have treated sexuality as part of nature, but not part of culture: as apart from the rules and beliefs and institutional practices which surround and bind all else. This is not to deny the biology of sexuality, which is as biological, and as socially regulated, as anything else, even the kiss. But the kiss, among humans at least, is renowned for its rainbow of meanings, its spectrum of social observances, from respect and filial deference, to lust and romantic diversion, and on to the kiss of God, by proxy of the bishop's ring. The kiss is for culture as much as it is for nature; but it cannot be a substitute for nature, as witness those cultures, such as the Sambia, in which the kiss is completely unknown and absent, while sex is so omnipresent.

The kiss is too easy, some would say; the orgasm is harder to separate from biology; and heterosexuality is the most "biological" of all. True to their histories, these claims are borne out. The closer to sexual action the orgasm is imagined, the less analytical (and the more biological) sex becomes. If sex were a drive (Geoffrey Gorer [1955] once called Alfred Kinsey's sex-drive theory too orgasm oriented, by analogy to a sneeze: blow the nose, and the physical event was done), then it had nothing to do with meanings, with culture; if sex were intimate, it belonged to the private matters of bedroom reproduction (and now tabloid television); if sex were homosexual, it provoked a general disgust and disregard for why it was institutionalized in some places and persecuted in others. Homosexuality, so much trouble in the Cold War (for the Russians, Igor Kon [1995] has mused, homosexuality was a capitalist plot, and for the Americans it was the great communist plot) the whipping boy for all time, hardly studied until so very late (Corber 1997). While the Kinsey et al. (1948) study of American male sexuality was enormously influential in changing attitudes about sex and, indeed, in paving the way for the baby boomers' gender and sexual studies a generation later, it left intact the idea of sex as a natural development, with no fits and starts, or disjunctions in society (see chapter 7).

Sexual theory, at least in anthropology, followed n the entry of gays and lesbians into the academy, but ever so slowly. In the social sciences, with few exceptions, sexuality study in general and homosexuality study in particular in the United States up to the mid-1980s remained impoverished (Gagnon and Simon 1973; Greenberg 1988; Mead 1961; Laumann et al. 1994; Vance 1991). A hundred years of classical study (Halperin 1990) or of anthropological reports on boy-inseminating rites in Melanesia (Herdt 1984b) hardly dented either the classics or anthropology, or even popular-culture ideas about "homosexual inversion." Only with the rise of third-wave feminism and first-wave gay and lesbian studies, and the emergence of the anthropology of sexuality, did these matters change (Herdt and Boxer 1992; Stimpson 1996; Weston 1993). And that had to await the coming of a new generation, especially those who studied other cultures, fortunately before postmodernism had denigrated the task (Newton 1972). These were children of the sexual and social revolution which typified the liberal reform era—led by feminists and then gay and lesbian anthropologists find-

ing their way out of an increasingly crowded closet—who were idealistic
and adventuresome enough to think they might change the attitudes of society (Rubin 1975; Duberman 1996). Their work critically examined some
of the norms and institutions and gender roles, East and West, and went so
far as to question the policing of sex and the prejudice against homosexuality by establishing the existence of strange and "superior" sexual customs in
other cultures (Williams 1986). The baby-boom generation of feminist and
gay or lesbian anthropologists, much like myself, were thus to step up and
wager their careers on the gamble that sexual meanings are made into culture, in that deliberate bundle of social regulations and intimate liberties
known as sexual culture.

• ◆ •

While neither Sambia culture study nor my own self-analysis was a trans-
parent process I believe that the key barriers to conceptualizing the issues
studied in this book were fundamentally political. The history of my own
work among the Sambia, while it reflected the particulars of their historical
society and my own personality, typified the problems of social scientists in
the past two decades who helped to pioneer the new anthropology of sexual
cultures. The initial two years of my fieldwork (1974–76) among the Sambia amounted to an accidental study of their sexuality, since it never was my
intention to study sex in the field. Field study of Sambia initiation rites and
male identities was not meant to unearth the sexual; that was incidental to
my study of ritual initiation in boys. It was only after having conducted
fieldwork for some months that I learned that younger initiates, before puberty (ages seven to fourteen) were routinely inseminated orally, in secret,
by older adolescent warriors—the pride of the men's house. The men regarded this insemination as the royal road to their social performance of
manhood and, as they believe, the younger boys' physical growth and inculcation into the secret society.

Subsequent field studies, in 1979 and later, increasingly focused my attention on male adolescent sexual development and behavior, on men's and
women's marital relations, sexual practices, and reproduction. This convinced me that to better understood the tropes and practices through which
I had implicitly (and unconsciously) been writing about Sambia, I must
study sexuality in the United States. How different from Mead's advice!
Having studied the Sambia for two years, I felt that deeper understanding
awaited analysis of my own sexual culture, on matters such as "desire" and
"sexual subjectivity," little discussed by the Sambia, but of great importance

to analyzing the meanings of their sexual culture. For example: How to explain the peculiar objectification of the male body as the focus of desire in Sambia culture? Such a notion—virtually unknown to the modernist Western tradition—has led to new insights in the Sambia ethnography (chapter 9).

My knowledge of sexuality from my own culture, the United States, was originally too puny to meet the formidable demands of analyzing Sambia sexual culture. Procreation was too natural and homosexuality too unnatural to dissect it all, at least at first. Anthropological theory was of limited help, because anthropologists had not critically understood as of then what homosociality and homoeroticism in sexual cultures were all about (Weston 1993). Psychoanalysis—the next tool of my work—colored my early essays of the 1980s and was both a help and a hindrance. Ultimately it would prove insufficient to complete the project. I had to go back to America to rethink and study, close up, sexuality and homosexuality, leading me into places unfamiliar or even strange (Herdt 1992), the better to know the categories and desires of Sambia sexual conduct. And no doubt my own process of "coming out" as a gay man in the 1970s and 1980s, first in personal relationships and then professionally, was part of the "cultural" as well as the "personal" work that influenced my own approach to studying sexual culture.

In 1986 I thus began (with the critical help of developmental psychologist Andrew Boxer) a long-term study of gay and lesbian youth (fourteen to nineteen years old), their families, and gay "culture" in Chicago, published as *Children of Horizons* (1993). While gay and lesbian teens may seem far removed from Sambia sexual culture, I wanted to identify a set of ideas and practices of equal cultural and psychological power to those surrounding the richly ceremonialized practices of male initiation of the Sambia boys. The "master narrative" of Sambia men left no stone unturned in their effort to "resocialize" the boys' interiority, social status, and sexuality. Male initiation rhetoric regarded the boys' sexual and gender development explicitly as products of ritual, in opposition to their bodies or the influences of the "natural products" (e.g., menstrual blood) of their mothers' bodies and sexuality. Sambia sexual culture fundamentally split apart desires, gendered them, and made sexual practices and sociosexual objects the instrumentalities of their culture and power structures. This unalterably changed my views—of sexual theory, of homosexuality, heterosexuality, bisexuality, and of desire—among the Sambia.

The rise of the gay and lesbian political movement fitted a divergent concept of human nature to a new sexual culture. "Coming out" in the United

States-the idiomatic folk idea of a boy or girl growing up assumptively categorized as "heterosexual," but feeling his or her desires diverge in the direction of the same gender—enabled teens and young adults to live openly
as gay. Their developmental process was thus disjunctive, since they questioned the self, family, and nation. They pioneered an alternative idea of
sexual citizenship (Weeks 1985). But as with the Sambia, this developmental process is not linear, or smooth, but highly disruptive (chapter 8). As
Boxer and I found in our Chicago study, young, self-identified gay men and
lesbians clung to an idea of essential, secret, or "true" self (as they referred to
it themselves), hidden from society, immutable, and in opposition to the
hegemonic "double standards" of sexual morality in American society
(Herdt and Boxer 1993). Parents said, Be truthful and open, but when their
children revealed their same-sex desires or relationships, the parents treated
this as "confusion," "denial," "mental illness," "rebelliousness," and so on;
truth was least desired. Gay youth, we countered, were not confused or
untruthful about their identities; their only confusion was political: how
to express their identities and self-truths in a homophobic and punitive
society.

The study of gay and lesbian sexual culture in Chicago thus enabled
me to see around the edges of the profound obstacles to anthropological
study of sexuality, strange and familiar. By coming out of the closet, self-
identified gay/lesbian adolescents challenged some of the most deeply held
cultural postulates about sexual nature and human development in the
Western tradition. These included the notions that all human nature can
only be "heterosexual," while "homosexuality" can only be perverse, dis-
eased, or insane. Secret processes of passing and coming out—the twin ve-
hicles of ritual presentations and performances—directed these teenagers
into sexual citizenship, as when they are encouraged to march proudly in
the public Gay and Lesbian Pride Day parades now characteristic of this
sexual culture (Herrell 1992). Of course, these narratives were in keeping
with the tropes and rhetoric of this new social movement, and in opposition to the dominant culture, even among parents of these youth (Boxer,
Cook, and Herdt 1991; Herdt and Boxer 1992, 1995; Herdt and Koff, in
press). Sexual cultures are not invented overnight; they are not capricious
and without grounding in the bodies and ontologies of people, any less
than their desires and dreams. But the lesson of this decade of study was
clear: Sexual cultures can rise and fall with the social politics of the
times, they are not dependent upon procreation in any simple sense, and
their meanings can rather quickly be spun into "traditional" customs and
lifeways.

By the time of my last field trip in 1993 to the Sambia, when I helped to make the film *Guardians of the Flutes* (produced by the British Broadcasting Corporation), I had in mind a new slate of questions. Do the male desires for women and boys exist in sequence or are they parallel? Should we conceptualize Sambia as one or two gendered sexual cultures? Can desires be achieved by different but complementary developmental lines? How is desire for the male object the same and different for Americans and Sambians? What desires and objects are distinctive in both? Of course, Sambia society had also undergone a dramatic change in gender roles and sexual behavior during the ensuring period of approximately twenty years. The Sambia film ends with stories of how the men's secret society is largely gone, a historical reality, and new forms of sexual relations between men and women have opened up. Though people do not say so on the film, Sambia imply that boy-inseminating as social and sexual practice is a thing of the past. The strange was more familiar, but no less difficult to explain (Spiro 1989).

Whatever the answers to these interrogations and the resulting interpretations of them in culture and desires, neither the ethnographer nor his or her culture or background, including each one's sexuality, can be left out of the equation (Herdt and Stoller 1990). But this does not make the ethnographer's subjectivity anything special or his or her authority particularly interesting; it only provides a modus operandi for the greater project of making ethnography out of the all-too-frequent but delicious ambiguities of sexual lives, strange and familiar.

•◆•

Much of the importance of the Sambia in cross-cultural study has hinged upon whether we consider male homosocial and homoerotic practices to be cultural or natural. Readers of my work will know that I consider this a false dichotomy, but the answers rest in exactly how we study "sexual culture." I define "sexual culture" to include the classification of sexual beliefs and behaviors, the range and extent of people's desires and the subjectivities that express them in action, and their ideologies of sexual nature and gender difference, reproduction, and pleasure in human development. The local ontology of sexuality is also quite critical; that is, how the Sambia conceptualize reality, which inflects or "naturalizes" their categories, seeing, for instance, the cassowary as only one sex ("female"), women as having more sexual heat than men, or the human male as especially vulnerable to pollution by menstrual blood. In all these matters, ritual "socializes" their norms, and leads socialization and the development of subjectivities into distinctive "morally proper" desires. Generally, sexual culture, and its subject positions and approved cultural desires and objects, are all aimed at securing social control, and thus an analysis of power and legitimacy in public as well as in intimate relationships is a necessary part of the total study of sexuality.

The Sambia did not allow me automatically to attend their initiations. They had never before allowed outsiders to witness their secret performances. Ritual secrecy and homoerotic relations between younger and older males were the main reasons, though there were plenty of other secrets of ritual hidden in the men's house. The Sambia elders and great men had no intention of changing the situation when I came to live with them in 1974. They have told me many times in retrospect that they thought I could be deceived—as were the missionaries. In fact, I was; there were numerous attempts to conceal the existence of same-sex erotic contacts from me, to throw me off the track, as I have described before (Herdt 1981, 1987a). And this was true in spite of my having lived for weeks in the great discomfort of the men's house of my village upon arrival. But I had friends and age-cohort chums. Some of them from day one befriended me and allowed me to see more and hear their life stories until, in February 1975, two of them, an older married man (Nilutwo, the cassowary hunter, described in Herdt [1981]) and an older adolescent (Moondi; see his portrait in Herdt and Stoller [1990]), began to reveal secrets to me privately. Why they chose to do so at precisely that time and independently of each other still remains a mystery. Indeed, I had already concluded that Sambia "homosexuality"—as I mistakenly thought of it in those days—did not exist. Moreover, I eventually felt that the insinuation of it constituted a slanderous attribution by outsiders who read into the close affectionate ties of Sambia men with men or women with women an eroticism that was not there: projections of their own sexual chauvinism. I was wrong, but the larger view was right (chapter 9).

My subsequent journey into the men's secret world changed many of these preconceptions, and startled me in a way that still remains as fresh and remarkable as the experience of Sambia initiation (chapter 3). Once it was revealed that homoerotic relations were mandatory for all males in growing up, I began to realize the enormity of the strangeness of Sambia sexual culture. But then I was also put on the spot: There were days of intense pressure and even hostility directed toward me, and the men who revealed the secrets to me, until I promised to become like them a secret sharer who could never broach the topics with Sambia women and children. How else were the elders to contain the explosive and morally dangerous threat of a man having free access to their secrets—one who had never been initiated? Only after my promise and the intervention of friends in the village was I permitted to witness the initiations and resume a normal life.

My empathy for and closeness to these men facilitated their "confession" to me. I was in turn deeply grateful to them, and felt the desire to "confess" my own secrets too. These friends knew that I could be trusted to keep my word, and over the years I have been true to this promise. When Moondi asked me whether I knew of this practice and had ever done it before, I could say yes; and my own revelation sealed a pact that has endured many years. And yet I felt that I was skating on thin ice; there were no precedents in my anthropological training. The narrative of these formative days opens chapter 1.

Here I found myself, thousands of miles away from home, at the green and conflicted age of twenty-five and during the terrible travails of the Viet Nam holocaust, having left behind an unfinished sexual history. The reader does not need my intellectual biography or personal autobiography to know why my own sexual orientation and cultural identity as a gay American are constitutive of my study of Sambia sexual culture. In the Sambia village I came to love I discovered a strange mirror of my homoerotic feelings (about men my own age) that were as unfamiliar to the Sambia (who only allow men to inseminate boys) as theirs were to mine. I began to see the strange become familiar, but still not a part of me. During this time (1975) I entered into correspondence with the American psychoanalyst Robert J. Stoller, professor at UCLA. As the years went by, Stoller's influence in helping me to understand sexuality was profound. Those familiar with my earlier work in the United States already know that of my sexual orientation, since Andrew Boxer and I revealed our gay identities in a key book (Herdt and Boxer 1993). Nonetheless, I never explicitly stated that I was gay in the Sambia work, as I began writing these essays in 1980 while still professionally "in the closet." In fact, the publishers of my first Sambia books were more concerned than was I regarding the effect of my self-disclosure on the audience.

It was thus in dialogue with Bob Stoller (who died in a tragic car accident in 1991) that many of these early essays were written.[2] Following the award

---

2. I conducted twenty-two months of initial fieldwork among the Sambia in the years 1974–76, when I was completing my dissertation as a Fulbright Scholar and Ph.D. student in the Department of Anthropology (Research School of Pacific Studies) of the Australian National University. I was supervised by Professors J. Derek Freeman and the late Roger Keesing, both of whom took an active but divergent interest in the project. Derek was interested in my ethnography of subjectivity and cultural reality, while Roger was more concerned with the ritual and pol-

of my Ph.D., I went to UCLA (with the support of an Individual Postdoctoral NIMH Fellowship) to train in sexual and gender-identity research with Stoller, in an intensive apprenticeship that resulted in collaborative research publications (Stoller and Herdt 1982, 1985; Herdt and Stoller 1990). I also continued fieldwork among the Sambia in 1979 (for six months), 1981 (for three months), 1983 (for two months), and 1985, 1987, 1988, 1989, and 1990 for a month each year, capped by the 1993 BBC film shoot and final trip.[3] During all of this period, as my publications reflect, and as substantiated in many of the essays during the 1980s, I was influenced by psychoanalysis, albeit in the particular mode practiced by Stoller (more context sensitive and concerned with conscious subjectivity and culture). Some critics have argued that I was too heavily psychoanalytic in my representations of the Sambia; there are times when I would agree with them. However, in those days, before sexuality study was accepted in anthropology, and homophobia rode high in the academy, it would have been impossible for me to pursue my research without the protections and mentoring of Bob Stoller, and I am forever indebted to him for that.

Through the combination of these influences, at home and abroad, a new understanding of Sambia sexual culture took shape in three important ways. First, this work precipitated my effort to construct a general theory of sexual culture, offering a more detailed developmental view of how culture influences the ontology of individual sexual desires and behaviors. Second, I realized that my own experiences and gay identity were a means of reincorporating the necessary personal insights into anthropology rather than treating these as marginal to the project (see Lewin and Leap 1996). Sexual behavior, formerly on the periphery, became the central focus. Finally, then, I was led back to complete the larger description of Sambia sexual culture, which aims to explain how Sambia desires, subjectivities, and power take their particular forms across the life course.

But let us come full circle: After the village leaders of the men's cult house accepted my promise of confidence, I spent the remainder of the two years' research observing the initiation rites, and then talking with my inter

---

lution rules of gender and initiation rites. Work with the Sambia was generally easy, if not in fact fun, except for when I was momentarily depressed or suffering from malaria, which was mercifully limited. In 1975, moreover, I began an intensive correspondence with the American psychoanalyst Robert J. Stoller, who was referred to me through a colleague of ours at UCLA. Stoller served as the main source of my ideas about sexuality and gender for the next decade, and aside from my dear friend and teacher Kenneth E. Read and the anthropologist George Devereux, Stoller was my main intellectual correspondent during the second year of fieldwork.

3. I was infected with a new and deadly strain of malaria at the end of fieldwork in 1993 and nearly died. For medical reasons I am now advised not to return to New Guinea.

preters about the meanings of these events. My bonds of friendship grew with people such as Tali, Weiyu, Moondi, Kanteilo, Nilutwo, and Saku-lambei, among the significant others described in detail before (Herdt 1987a; Herdt and Stoller 1990). I still find these friendships as precious and loaded with the communal intimacies of Sambia sociality and eroticism, sans sex, as ever, but I leave it to the reader to pass judgment on their sub-stance.[4] By the time of the 1975 initiations I was permitted entry into and was involved to a minor extent in the performances. I served, for instance, as ritual guardian for one initiate of my village in the second-stage initiation of 1975, when his previously assigned guardian was unable to fulfill this re-sponsibility (described in Herdt 1987a). I was empathically engaged in the ceremonies, even if I did not participate personally in all the events. What-ever sticky array of meanings we must assign to that most unlikely of all approaches—participant observation—this much was true for me: My ability to apprehend and interpret Sambia sexuality depended upon accep-tance of my own sexuality and the intuitive use of myself to understand how homoerotic relations were built into the Sambia design for life.

• ◆ •

The lesson from my anthropological discovery narrative pertains to the in-vention of "sexual culture" as a concept, which backgrounds the remainder of what I have to say in this introduction. Anthropology is today more about the discovery of the strange in what is familiar in our own traditions. Having renounced its colonial past, many seek the sources of Orientalism in the societies of Western Europe and North America from which it was invented and exported. Dissertation students are working in their own imagined or real communities, neighborhoods, and institutions, simulta-neously strange and familiar. Backyard anthropology brings formidable challenges as yet unchallenged: judgments about the ethnographer, favors expected in return for knowledge, the misappropriation of identities, au-thority threatened by the disruptions of local politics as much as by the dis-ruptions of empathy that arise from ethnographers mixing with fellow citizens and power brokers. None of these things, in principle, are absent from Orientalism and anthropology in exotic communities, to be sure.

However, sexual behavior study poses a special challenge for students who would brave the ethnography of "sexual culture." Sexual encounters

4. As of this writing, Nilutwo died of a fatal accident in 1979, Moondi died of tuberculosis in 1996, Tali suffers from terminal stomach cancer, and Kanteilo is extremely aged and infirm. The others all live in the village area in which I originally worked.

are often, perhaps always and everywhere, more private than public in nature, as Mead (1961) and later Friedl (1994) have argued. To describe and interrogate differences between the real and imagined, between the ideal norm and the actual sex, entails intimacies and involvements of a totally unprecedented kind in participant observation. To vest oneself as a shareholder in a sexual culture, to be at ease with local actors familiar to its cultural scenes, and to participate with them (individually or otherwise) in erotic encounters raise methodological and ethical issues never imagined by Malinowski, Mead, and our intellectual ancestors. The blend of strange and familiar desires and relationships of power in this context undermines the fiction of "objectivity," and is never as unsettling as when an anthropologist enters into sexual encounters with local people to such an extent that the boundary called Other is erased in part or whole (see, e.g., Bolton 1996; Kulick and Willson 1995; Murray 1996).

The study of sexual cultures, through acts of comparison inscribed in erotic ethnographies, invites meditations on "difference" and "similarity/ sameness," at home and abroad (Weeks and Holland 1996). Our closely hovering American folk theory of sexuality regards the area of sexual/gender "difference" far too uncritically in this respect: "Desire" and "orientation" and "drive," as well as "love" and "romantic behavior," are heavily "essentialized," like genes, hormones, brain, and desire, which seem miraculously to precede culture in the creation of sexuality. Gender difference between men and women ethnographers (argued long ago, in Golde 1970) is probably instrumental in viewing difference/similarity (Butler 1992), just as sexual orientation likely influences what is desired and disliked in social and erotic encounters (Bem 1996). A claim may be made for an "essential desire" or a "natural behavior" on the part of men, especially heterosexual men, while a contrary claim may be made for the "social construction" of desires, narratives, and emotional expressions in women (Fine 1992). Likewise the differences between men and women, straight and gay, critically inflect ethnography (Kulick and Willson 1995; Weston 1993; see also Lewin and Leap 1996). When the sexual has been so heavily essentialized, as in the Western tradition, a particularly large obstacle is imposed on study at home.

Consider homosexuality. Merely referring to two different acts, or traditions, of "homosexual contacts" is, of course, a comparison, but for the purposes of cultural comparison, it is one in rhetoric only. It seemingly invokes the ontological claims already spelled out but without the necessary understanding of person, time, conduct, and meaning requisite to comparing either cultural practices or their subjective worlds. Perhaps it was historically necessary to broach comparisons of precolonial New Guinea with modern Western ontological models in order to legitimize the authority of the ethnographer. Homosexuality, which was supposed to occur only in the abnormal or perverse, was found in simple societies and then rediscovered in archaic civilizations, and not only was it found to be a cultural practice but it also seemed to be at the very center of these antique and quaint primitive places. The Victorians, and then anthropologists, could not reconcile this apparent "contradiction": that is, their own cultural ontology had no room for the conception of the homoerotic as institutionalized or ritualized in the life course of the person and culture. We can appreciate their difficulty; I dare say we have not escaped the ontological morass in our culture and cultural sciences.

What is at stake, as argued in chapter 9, is thus the very idea of "sexuality" as represented in comparative study. If comparison is a form of symbolic assimilation (in the Piagetian sense of an entity being incorporated into another, causing transformation in the original entity), then it is critical to begin the analysis with the familiar, not with what is strange (Devereux 1967). But this poses a paradox: We cannot analytically know what is unconscious unless we know what is conscious first; that has been the signal function of exotic anthropology for decades (Geertz 1990). By studying the familiar, and the categories and concepts applied to transform these into the unfamiliar, we find that our personal and cultural preconceptions are revealed.

To counter the heritage of colonial domination of non-Western societies involves two critical procedures. First, ethnographers inscribe other cultures' local theories of "sexuality" and "human nature," often based in myth and ritual, kinship and sociality, rendering sexuality in cultural sociality. These categories and tropes represent major symbols and codes for how sexual love and lust, in private and public, are enacted, subjectified, and empowered in social practice. I call this the premise of "translatability": Any form of sexuality can be translated into an account that we Westerners can understand. Nevertheless, special conditions (usually of prejudice) may render the native form monstrous or weird, as when the concept of "two-spirit" was appropriated to the pejorative colonial category "berdache" (Jacobs et al. 1997), and this was further corrupted as "berdachehood" (Whitehead 1981). Misappropriation and disruption of empathy and identities occur within our own culture as a result of mistranslations too, since the "imported materials" ("berdache") may (as they always have from anthropology) challenge authority, local convention, and even the ethnographer's role.

Second, ethnographers back-translate the insights of other cultures—especially their ideas and sensibilities about "sexual nature," their kernels of historical truth about sex and the human condition—into Western texts and practice (reviewed in Herdt 1997a). This "experimentability" principle, in which the "social experiment" begins with the discovery and explorations of other cultures, may lead to superior analysis, amelioration, or liberation of what was disparaged as strange (e.g., two-spirits, transgendered people, third sexes; Herdt 1994; Williams 1986). Selecting the best trope and using this to describe another's lifeway are the critical challenge. Increasingly, however, experimentability goes further to render what is familiar, but formerly disliked as Other, for example, transgendered, into strange and, by currents of relativism, more liked and respected (Jacobs et al. 1997). This second process, obviously more activist or explicitly "ideological," as in the case of gay, lesbian, bisexual, or transgendered ethnographers who employ their findings to change Otherness, brings postmodern projects into relief (Roscoe 1998). What is thus rendered familiar and canonical, such as marriage, is then translated and experimented back into the strange (gay and lesbian marriage), through a series of disruptions of what is good and beautiful in the reclaimed Other (Lewin 1998).

In the translatability of Sambia homoerotics, for example, they were more familiar than strange, but the reader will now understand this statement much differently than before. Thus, the Sambia ethnography suggests the lesson that humans can create, enjoy, and socially manage sexual relations with both genders under certain historical conditions. But we should not call this homosexuality, which in the West is an explicit and largely irreversible social identity among adults, exclusive of sexual relations with the other gender, a condition unknown to the Sambia. Many years are spent in pursuit of the semen of other males, but Sambia men do not become fetishists (the condition Freud required of Western homosexuality). That they go on to develop desires for females suggests how profoundly Sambia erotics are conditioned by social and historical influence. These simple descriptive points can be amplified: We might say that "homosexuality" occurs only in modern or premodern Western capitalist states, that cunnilingus is not a universal sexual custom, that repression can be so complete that masturbation to orgasm is unknown, and so on (Tuzin 1994). From this ever-widening account emerges the general aim of the study of sexual culture: to reveal the immense diversity of sexual practices and lifeways across time and space without making any of these into the strange or familiar, but rather using the sexual as a means to understand the nearly infinite possibilities of culture and the human condition.

•◆•

To back-translate Sambia sexual culture is to reexamine the basic principles of late modern sexuality in the West. To understand Sambia sexual subjectivities, for instance, we have to deconstruct the meanings of "homosexuality" as a Western category. While it is true that Sambia practice homoerotic insemination, they lack the category "homosexual" and have no "homosexuals" to fill the category even if they did! This is why I have backed away from the use of "ritual homosexuality" as an inclusive category (Herdt 1993) in favor of the more particular but accurate term "boy-inseminating rites." The Sambia pattern of age-structured homoerotic relations made the boy the first object of erotic desire; the older boy who inseminated him graduated in social maturity to marriage and women as an object. This structure of homoerotic and heteroerotic relations has become a prime example of what postmodernists like to call the "destabilization" of traditional Western desires, identities, and sexual subjects (Bech 1997). Indeed, it helps us rethink bisexuality (Herdt and Boxer 1995). Sociosexual theory has exploited ethnographic cases like that of the Sambia in shaking up the hitherto imperturbable relationship between "identity," "gender," and "sexual behavior" (Vance 1991). What formerly seemed either "biological" or "socially constructed" now seems more complex, interactive, and emergent.

Consider the most striking manifestations of the belief that semen is not natural, does not naturally occur in the male (or female) body, and must be introduced through oral sex: (1) The cultural purpose of physically "growing" boys by substituting insemination for mother's milk. (2) The "masculinizing" of boys' bodies, especially culminating at puberty in the magical birth of the glans penis, icon of adult maleness, promoting ordeals meant to prepare for warrior life. However, insemination of girls' bodies by their husbands prior to menarche also feminized the girls by supposedly converting semen into breast milk for lactation. (3) The provision of "homoerotic play" or pleasure for the older youths, who took younger boys as their only sexual partners prior to marriage. (4) The transmission through semen from one generation to another of spiritual substance, which was believed vital for a clan's rituals to achieve jural and religious ends in social reproduction (outlined in chapter 2).

How typical were these predicates of an age-structured homoerotic system in the region of precolonial Melanesia? Only a generation ago it was common to find assertions that "homosexuality" did not occur in Melanesia, as Kenneth Read (1980) long ago complained. Compared with then, the traditional social geography of boy-inseminating practices and the postcolonial history of "homosexuality" are now well known, having been historically located in more than fifty societies of Melanesia and Aboriginal Australia (reviewed in Herdt 1984a and updated in Herdt 1993). Among the Papuans of the Trans-fly River (Willliams 1936a), the Marind-anim of Southwest New Guinea (van Baal 966), the Big Nambas tribe of the New Hebrides (Deacon 1934), or the Etoro and Kaluli tribes (Kelly 1976 and Schieffelin 1976, respectively) on the Great Papua Plateau of New Guinea, semen was used to "grow boys up"—to strengthen or masculinize their bodies. Indeed, their ritual insemination was a social fact and foundation of religious life.

No example of precolonial practice is known in which egalitarian relations between two males of same social status were institutionalized. The two exceptions in the anthropological archives are both instances of social change and Westernization (Herdt 1993). Is it not curious that these highly egalitarian societies of precolonial Melanesia fostered homoerotic relationships that were inherently unequal in power status? These and other curiosities are argued throughout this book, especially in chapter 9.

Why this absence of adult egalitarian homoerotic relationships in precolonial societies matters is that, as David Halperin (1990) has argued, anthropological concepts—especially "homosexuality" itself—contain marked categories and implicit assumptions about sex and social status, gender and power. These ideas preoccupied the Western discourse on homosexuality until very late, beginning in the later nineteenth century, when these identity categories were institutionalized in peculiar ways that provide a signature of their historical times (Weeks 1985). Until the emergence of the social idea of "individual identity," and particularly with the late modern construct "sexual identity," social status and sexual desires and objects had a very different composition (Greenberg 1988; Herdt 1997a). Like the Ancient Greeks and, indeed, many non-Western cultures today (Herdt 1997a), precolonial New Guinea cultures never emphasized "identities," and they lacked a concept of "essential sexual orientation" in person and self-conceptions (chapter 5).

Among the Sambia, sex is always a relationship between unequals. Explicit homoerotic relationships between younger and older males in the course of growing up created sexual subjectivity and secrecy as part of the social and political condition of learning how to operate power and male agency in male-female relations (chapter 3). Their sexual culture emphasized not the individual acts but rather the sociosexual practices of the person and place. Sexual customs created social control not through institutionalization of norms and categories of sex, which separate individuals—or through "identities"—but rather through control of social and sexual relationships, including marriage contracts for reproduction, all of which appealed to the sanctity of spiritual and ritual authority for their social reproduction. As New Guineasts have long known, colonial domination tended to usurp traditional sex and gender hierarchies in these societies, under the Pax Australiana (Brown 1995; Godelier 1986). Subsequent messianic movements tended also to destroy precolonial ideas of the relationship between the body, secret knowledge, power, and sexual meanings (Tuzin 1997; see below, chapter 4). Perhaps the end of war and the outbreak of peace have had the dual effect in Melanesia of making life safer while also undermining local sexual cultures in the course of regional migrations into global market economies (Herdt 1997a; Knauft 1996).

The role of religion in sexual culture remains obscure and unanalyzed here. Western culture has long treated religion and sex as antithetical at least in the more recent modern period of Western European history (Greenberg 1988). Sambia sexual culture challenges this historical trend. Ritual insemination is the means of incorporation of the Sambia person into the religious culture, and without the act of coition or insemination, as the case may be, the gods do not bless the proceedings, and the product is not a person. Sambia are not alone in this practice; indeed, in Melanesia the practice is surely the rule and not the exception, as we learned long ago from the great work of van Baal (1966), and as we have recently been reminded by the regional analysis of Knauft (1993). The sexual cultures of Attic Greece were closer to Melanesia, it is now argued (Dover 1978; reviewed in Herdt 1993), though their ethics and meanings differ. As Freud (1962) puzzled in *The Three Essays*, the "sex instinct" and its "erotic aim" seemed disconnected among the Ancient Greeks, as Desire seemed unconcerned with the gender of the object (Trumbach 1994). How could a masculine man desire another male, Freud wondered? The strange, not the familiar, provides the solution.

It is a remarkable fact of Sambia sexual culture that overt desire and romance (but without necessary erotic expression) were everywhere present, in public and private relationships, but only between the same sex. What threatened the social order was to gaze into the eyes of the other sex. Same-gender relations existed within what we would today describe as intensely homosocial settings, women with women, and men with men. Indeed, we might agree with Godelier (1986), who suggests that only men can make men, and only women can make women. As the male homosocial culture, centered in the secretive men's house, also promoted ideals of male desire and beauty, homoerotic feelings and meanings were constitutive of exclusive, even secret sexual ontologies, but not without obstacles and resistance, because it was Sambia men who were the primary agents of desire in traditional Sambia sexual culture. Indeed, they idealized the male body, and made the boys their first objects of sexual desire, just as they later made men their primary objects of social attraction. Close bondedness between males became the royal road to the development of social cognition, notions of desired objects, and subjective masculinity.

Sexual lifeways in Melanesia and among the Sambia in particular thus created social identities and personal networks of relationships generative of multiple desires in sexual relations across the total course of life, from childhood to old age. Sambia sexual lifeways required that men engage in same-sex relations before marriage, with exclusive relations with their wife afterward, creating multiple desired person-objects. Thus, Sambia sexuality and cultural reality are based upon a capacity to experience multiple sexual desires and social relations. It must be remembered, of course, that "love" and "romance" and "marriage" are very different envelopes of experience in this worldview, compared with their counterparts in sexual cultures of the late modern period in the West. Marriage was, after all, a political contract for Sambia men and women over which they had little control (women almost none). Romantic love in the heteronormative sense was typically unknown in precolonial Sambia. However, when romantic infatuations and attachments occurred, especially in adolescence, these companionships and other signatures of romance-like desires were always between persons of the same gender.

•◆•

In the modernist view, one gender desires only the other gender, because of the differences in anatomy and hence of sexual nature, making the "opposite" sex an object of attraction. How could the Sambia male function so differently—both as an object (prepubertal boy) and then as a subject (postpubertal man) of sexual desire? For, according to the Western formula, the subject/object must be separated by gender, and typically divided between two distinct persons, that is, a male subject who desires a female, and a female object who desires to be desired and possessed. We have come to think of this binarism as Truth—in biology, in culture, not to mention in religion. Like other non-Western cultures throughout the world, however, the Sambia would disagree with the formula primarily because they would see it as inimical to culture, not to nature. While "man" and "woman" are regarded as polarized, these gender ideals are a product of culture. They do not share the binarism that sexualities are polarized natures: "natural" (heterosexual) or "unnatural" and subversive (homosexual: the desire of a woman to be a subject, the desire of a man to be an object). Such a formulaic of heterosexuality sits surprisingly cozily on the ladder of evolutionary tropes of Western sexuality left over from the nineteenth century (Herdt 1994). However, the Sambia sexual culture diverges from this natural linear sexual development. They would not agree with the late modern American view that a person has but one sexual preference, learned or acquired once, making everyone into either a sexual object or subject but never both (chapter 8). Instead, the Sambia would offer that sexual desires and practices can be learned and unlearned; they are as detachable from nature as the famed floating gardens of Mexico once perplexed the distinction between land and water before the conquest.

The Sambia system of desires appears contrary to the received theories of psychology and psychoanalysis, as well, which motivate Western folk models of sexuality and human nature. Indeed, is not all of desire ultimately "sexual? (Freud thought so.) I would say no.(Kinsey and other social theorists, including Foucault, would agree [Plummer 1996].) The Sambia example suggests the interdependence of sex and sociality in the production of desire. But how do sexual cultures "stimulate" and "regulate" desires, in the broad sense of what is "socially valued" and may enter into the symbolic capitol of personhood? There are other rights and duties constitutive of sexual citizenship: demands to conform and adapt to communities and social roles, to be married and rear children. These desires are of great import to the internal creation of desires of the erotic, not just of the social (Plummer 1996). Desire as an ontological reality is highly dependent upon cultural processes, such as Sambia rituals, which validate experience, and stipulate public and secret subjects and objects within the male life course. Such a view suggests that we cannot reduce desire to brain, biology, or the body, as theorists in the past, Freud and Alfred Kinsey, for example, were wont to do. Conceptions of desire are closer to what anthropologists have called "values—the general disposition to merit something and want to possess that "object" or a culturally valued social role (to be a warrior, a wife, a husband, a chief) or aim(to be brave, virtuous, rich, powerful) in life. Power is obviously crucial to the interpretation of many desires and to cultures of desire.

Sexual cultures provide intentional ontological realities through discursive local values, beliefs, and desires we could summarize as "human nature." To desire the toys of Santa Claus as a child or the muscles of Arnold Schwarzenegger as an adult is to participate in a collective system of valued objects that lies half-way between the social and the erotic. Non-Western cultural ontologies stake a claim, a plan for life, or what I like to call a lifeway: a way to achieve full personhood, connecting interior with social goals and desired objects, human and material (Herdt 1997b). In the microscopic cultural situations of everyday life, as a mother nurses her child, a boy approaches his father to play sports, or a girl contemplates routines in the company of her favorite peer, the roles and social practices of growing up distill personal tastes, objectify the demands made upon children and then adults, subjectify the objects we are drawn into wanting or needing, and habituate us to systems of erotic and social desires. We thus come to have instantiated—in our private parts, and even in the whispers of the self—sociosexual lifeways that signify membership in the sexual culture.

One of the virtues of this approach is to understand that what is learned can be unlearned in a sexual culture, a point that runs counter to the sexual psychology of Western modernist notions (chapter 8). Cultures that introduce discontinuities into the life course as a socially institutionalized part of growing up (Mead 1930; Benedict 1938) have long suggested the rule that it is not just what is learned as sexual habit that matters; it is what we unlearn that may count more. Sambia boys are socialized into powerful and prescribed secret homoerotic relations, practiced for the long years leading up to their fatherhood; these duties are revoked and new rights are introduced as they achieve full personhood. To unlearn sexual patterns is as important to their development as what originally signified their advancement into the men's secret society (chapter 5). We cannot rely upon simple learning principles to describe culturally prescribed sexual development in such cases, whether they pertain to the homoerotic or the heteroerotic (Stoller and Herdt 1985). Taboo and other obstacles of desire thus enter the equation of sexual culture.

Prohibitions suggest the regulation of desires, as well as the generation of powerful goals to achieve and avoid on the horizon of development. The Sambia prescriptive rule allows youths, aged fifteen and older, to inseminate younger initiates for years, which sacred lore describes as the bachelors' being "married" to the boys. Ritual symbolizes this by secret ritual flutes, themselves empowered by female spirits, a combined image of man/woman, breast and penis (chapter 3). When a youth's wife reaches the menarche, he should deescalate his involvement in boy-inseminating practices, and, with the achievement of fatherhood, the vast majority of Sambia men stop inseminating boys (though perhaps their desires for boys continue). The taboo usually sticks, but not always. Among the most powerful pieces of male sexual culture are the rules and violations of homoerotic relationships. Incest-avoidance taboos come into effect, preventing man-boy sexual relations between father and son and all closely related kin. However, cousins of adjacent generations sometimes have sex in defiance of this taboo. They risk scandal to do so.

That equals can never be lovers is a paramount social fact in all sexual relations among the Sambia. Boy-inseminating practices among the Sambia were typically matters of sexual relations between unrelated kin and must be seen in the same light as the semen exchanges of delayed sister-exchange marriage: hamlets of potential enemies exchange women and participate in the semen exchange of boys, which are necessary for the production of children and the maturation of new warriors. In point of fact, as noted in these essays, a few Sambia men do not complete this life-course transition. Indeed, equality serves as the chief obstacle to desire among the Sambia, since the calculations of who is older and younger, bigger and smaller, male and female, hover about the erotic encounter. As part of their sexual ethic of power and excitement introduced through the social/gender/physical difference, we begin to understand how sociality is merged with sexuality. Perhaps in Melanesia more widely, the contrast in social age and status is transferred into same- and opposite-sex relations, which make complete the Other (Strathern 1988). The premise of insemination thus is to make what was smaller, larger; less, more; child- or girl-like more boy-like, but never equal, in the same frame of time. While it is hard to judge the extent to which these generational and age variations were formative of desires and relational practices in all cases, the evidence presented in chapter 5 (the strange case of Kalutwo, who greatly feared semen depletion, and desired boys all the more) suggests that Sambia taboos against boy insemination in adulthood were not only barriers to but perhaps instigators of sexual excitement and transgression.

•◆•

The subjectivities of these desires and attachments were laid down beginning in first-stage initiation, and they were indivisible from the emergence of self-awareness and masculinity in Sambia boys. Since the sexual culture of men privileges desire for the male, and later social attachments between men, it is only plausible to assume a deeply situated social and power relationship between these areas of cultural reality. My original arguments here, largely reflective of pre-Oedipal psychoanalytic theory, are still valid (chapters 3). The subjectivity of the rites, particularly the primary process thinking which surrounds the flutes and erodes the boundary between "reality" and "fantasy," produces a new identity and personhood in the development of the boy.

The boy's luxurious relationship with his mother prior to initiation will never find its equal in subsequent relations; perhaps this is implied by the notion that all relations with sexual partners to follow are unequal. Mother is a signifier of all that was past: the women's world, the women's sexual culture, visits to the menstrual hut now considered horrendous and terrifying to the initiated boy, the close and semi-erotic relationship he enjoyed with his mother's body. These become iconic of what the boy once desired but now is forbidden, indeed, unthinkable in social discourse. The icons, especially the flutes, are for a period of the boy's developmental time, the equivalent of what Winnicott (1971) called "transitional objects," carrying the meaning and comfort of mother/object (Herdt 1987b). They are bidden away, that is, repressed, but they are not gone; they remain permanent fixtures of desire throughout later adult life, as suggested by chapters 3, 4, and 6. Indeed, their desires are subsumed within ritual frames of flutes and penises, semen for mother's milk, and the ritual guardian for mother, all on behalf of seducing the boy into the men's sexual culture.

Initiation thus served as the bridge into male homosocial life as it simultaneously provided the entree into all male sexual life. The ideology of the transition was facilitated by a mythological creature, an Ideal Man, Warrior, Powerful, Feared, and Desired. This bundle of notions is not unlike Godelier's (1986) concept of the "great man," which argues for a series of social and cultural productions that romanticize and exaggerate the characteristics of charismatic masculinity. Notably, the Ideal or Great Man was irreplaceable, a fixture of charismatic leadership, and was highly sexual in his social and aggressive actions. The complex of sexual culture, desire, and social practice mythologized in this image is puzzling, because it surely involved a major split in subjectivity between the public world of village politics and the secret world of male ritual practice. The social practices of adulthood, as these mythologized the warrior role, were largely public. Ritual practices among the Sambia that took the boy as their desired sexual object were fiercely secret. Early on, a split was introduced into the subjectivity of the boy: between being a budding member of the powerful men's house, which gave the boy agency or at least the promise of it some day, and being a sexual object, to be inseminated and filled up in the manner of a receptacle, not agentic at all. No wonder the boys fantasized that they might become pregnant; their objectified status as being "married to the bachelors" engendered the liminal sense of being born again, as well as giving birth. Paradoxically, however, this subject-object position is what anointed the boy as a sexual agent in future sociality.

If a sexual practice is collective and supported by religious rituals, as are Sambia boy-inseminating rites, we would like to say that they define the form that desire will take, for individual males and for the men's house. A perfect kind of social construction of desire would seem to apply in this case, until we notice the secrecy. Why does the desired object—Ideal Man—require hiding if it is so ideal and socially important? Must the hidden nature of the practice change our definition of desire or of sexual culture? Of course it must. Otherwise the desire would be fully public, not secret, and such a cultural detail is extremely important in defining the meaning and action of sociosexual practice and its perturbations in power relations.

The genius of the Sambia is in how they maneuvered through their public social order into a utopian homosocial sexual culture out of time and space. They created through secret ritual a system of subject-object relationships which obey the signs of a secret internal discourse, where flutes are penises and breasts, in order to reproduce a hidden cultural reality. What was their social aim? In its simplest forms we might say that they sought to create homosocial trust, and to evade the dangers and pitfalls of the time-and-space world, especially the disruptions of warfare. Their desires, in short, are for Ideal Man, a utopian object that outlives themselves. This is their special cultural fetishism. It invites utopian fantasies, mystification, forms of manipulations of sexual partners, rebellion on the part of boys or men who do not like it, and the possibility (ideally forbidden) of loving boys in secret long past the proper time for the men who so much desire boys (Herdt and Stoller 1990). In such a tradition the cultural practice cannot define desire, not completely; and yet for many persons the very heart of their *gemeinschaften* is based upon conformity to the practice, the desire to desire a homosocial sexual culture.

Does the younger boy thus desire to be inseminated? Yes, virtually always, we know from the narratives of boys themselves (Herdt and Stoller 1990). But the motivations differ from those we might expect of our own sexual psychology. The younger boy's motive is not for the sexual pleasure, which goes by the name *chemonyi* (erotic play), a domain reserved for the postpubertal bachelor. The younger boy experiences none (or very little, until he is older). Rather, he has social desires that substitute for erotic pleasure: to be the object of physical growth through insemination, to be selected by an admired member of the men's house as the one to receive the gift of sperm, and the desire to grow big, to be strong, and to become an inseminator-father in time. For the second-stage initiates, however, and particularly as they approach puberty, they express a homoerotic yearning not unlike the feelings for emotional and physical closeness reported by Gagnon (1971) in his famous study of the development of American adolescent boys. The crossover comes at third-stage initiation, when the boy is able to serve as an inseminator himself, by which point he has begun to be the agent of his own desires and will—following initiation—begin to put them in action. This does not mean that the younger initiate experiences no erotic pleasure in his recipient role; that is a matter of individual subjectivity. It simply means that the sexual culture assigns this prerogative not to the boy but to the man.

And what of the older male? Yes, he nearly always desires the boy as his opportunistic sexual object. And contrary to the boy, we might say that it is for the pleasure, but that is not all. Why? The bachelor gains prestige by the donor sexual role that he takes, his gift of semen validates his manhood, and he seeks the sister of the boy that may come to him. He gains sexual pleasure, the arousal of his own penis: "He is such an independent-minded bugger," the men say. "You cannot control him!" And thus in local cultural knowledge the penis is seen as an organ of the body that has its own will and desires, displaced onto the social person of the actor. Desire here represents a combination of erotic feeling and social ambition as the older male operates increasingly by intentional will and aggression in such a cultural system. Let me emphasize, however, particularly for those whose cultural hygiene inclines them to deodorize accounts of the sexual (Elliston 1995), that without sexual excitement and arousal (whatever the sources of this in the individual case) there will be no opportunity for this sexual culture to do its work.

But where is the boy's father in this complicated circle of sociosexual dramas? I pose the question, in chapter 7, against the seemingly orthodox Freudian angle of father absence. What is the relationship between ritualized boy-inseminating practices and the presence of the boy's father when he is growing up? I wanted not only to counter the psychoanalytic influence of my earlier writings but also to contest what I saw as a fundamental precept of Western sexual psychology, that father absence creates homosexuality. The counterintuitive indeed emerges: Wherever we find boy-inseminating practices in New Guinea, there the father has lived not in absence but close by his son, at least during part of child development. Contrast that with the social fact, virtually universal in New Guinea, that boys who sleep close to their mothers and apart from their fathers never participate in ritualized

boy-insemination. This is all the more remarkable, since gender segregation is perhaps more finely developed, and more readily apparent, in "absence" cultures than in their cousins, the Sambia.

Again, the notion of desire is at fault. Do we desire something simply because it is absent? The desire is not, as the Freudians once imagined, a mere
Oedipal longing to be followed by homosexual triumph over the (unconscious) father. For in these Melanesian cultures, shared reality acknowledges the prime role of taking in as well as giving semen in order to complete
manhood. The imaginal of the Ideal Man, with an iconic flute-phallus
symbolized in many rituals and sacred myths, is surely related to the practice of boy insemination. I rethink in chapter 6 why the unusual presence of
the father in childhood might compel the men's sexual culture to make the
male the desired sexual object.

The identity of the inseminator is, for this and several other social and
political reasons, linked to the symbolic role of the father in the boy's initiation. Wherever the father's presence in childhood was marked, there too
we find that the ritual inseminator will play a large part in the creation of
masculinity in the boy, though his mythic and ritual status involves symbolic features both of mothers and fathers. Here we should remember how
sexual intercourse functions to strengthen and "grow" the boys, in the manner of a symbolic reproduction necessary for clans and tribes to prevail
across social time. And we can appreciate that the boy-inseminating practice is often referred to as a "marriage" between the older and younger
males. It is not just that these are "man-admiring societies that place extreme emphasis upon the phallus," as the British anthropologist John Layard (1942) once wrote. Insemination is a social right and duty: It is a form
of exchange, the semen going from one kin group to another, in the opposite direction of the marriageable woman the boy is to marry. The gift of semen is a form of bride-wealth to the other clan, to "grow" their sons in
return for the daughters they have given up (chapter 2). The sexual culture
of these practices thus combines relationships with desired boy-objects and
then with women betrothed as wives, to create a sexual subjectivity
uniquely Sambian.

•◆•

The ethnography of sexual cultures, old and new, is a discovery narrative,
leading from strange to familiar, and then back home again. It preserves the
record of translations and experiments that have been made in the effort to
defetishize the Other. Sad to say that much of this history of anthropologi-

cal sexuality is partial, incomplete, and even prejudicial. But we have no special purchase on sexual chauvinism. Nor are these characteristics missing from the history of sexuality study in Western culture. Yet interpretive anthropology offers the possibility of making scholarship out of this uneven and crude mosaic of the past. To do so, it commends us to reflect upon the meanings of the sexual traditions of East as well as West, and to ask about our own motives in the discovery process. Did I have to work in New Guinea to understand this? Yes, I think so. Could I have made the leap back into Western sexual ontologies without having come back to the United States to do anthropology here? No, I do not think so. Of course my own ethnographies are not a looking glass, and Mead was right to urge us on in understanding other cultures before we tackled the intricacies of our own. Anthropology may be an impossible dream (which may die, if not nurtured), but in the study of sexuality across time and space, it still holds the promise of delivering to us what is most precious: a mirror of the Other in which we recognize ourselves for what we are, and are not, as well as what we might better become.

ONE

Songs in the Key of Life

It still surprises me, the memory of that first time I saw a gruff older warrior openly sob in a songfest. It was during a crowded gathering in our hamlet, Nilangu, amid his male comrades—when the last thing a man should do is cry, especially when he was a great man, and the lead singer. His name was Soluwulu. And while his story may seem an unlikely place to begin the ethnography of Sambia sexual culture, in fact, its implications for the sexuality and social identities of Sambia men in general open a special window of anthropological understanding. Indeed, the wondrous thing is not the exoticness but the ordinariness with which such performances privilege us to see how the sexual is a part of the whole—culture, psyche, and sexual development in context.[1]

The singing arose spontaneously in the men's house early that evening. It was cool outside, one of those crisp, brilliant nights of the dry season, whose

1. The reader should know that I did not select the singing focus for its exotic interest. I am not a singer; most Sambia men are not much better. Nor does my love of song at all match that of Sambia, who wrap themselves in it. Indeed, these events, name songs, song-ropes, esoteric words, and singing contexts, depicted below, were marginal to my fieldwork and only later did I understand their importance. Nor do these topics figure prominently in the writings of other New Guineasts. Ethnomusicologists seldom study the symbolic meaning of such phenomena. However, see the marvelous work of Feld (1982).

There are scattered references in the literature to similar phenomena, like those of Malinowski (1929) on Trobriand love songs, Nilles (1950) on the songs of Chimbu courting parties, and many references on ceremonial singing (e.g., Williams 1936a, 1940). A. J. Strathern (1974) has added a piece on Melpa love songs, and in a series of studies, Schieffelin has written well on the ceremonial singing of Kaluli (1976, 1979). But, as far as I know, there is little on the interpersonal meanings of singing or song systems, the latter of which are scarcely reported for Melanesia, but are common in Australia (see Berndt and Berndt 1951). While I am at it, I cannot help wondering aloud what was at issue in Malinowski's fieldwork that led to his being called "The Man of Songs" by Trobrianders?

days had been sunny—as only Sambia, who annually see nine months of miserable rain, can appreciate. A stiff north wind had swept away the sunset fog, revealing a drape of diamonds. Children were still playing outside in the dazzling moonlight when the singing began. I stepped out on my verandah; in the hamlet, slightly below, an orange glow shone here and there from doorways of the other, thirty-odd huts. Past them, far beyond the hamlet's sharp ridge, one could dimly see, a mile off in the darkness, the faint outlines of our neighbor hamlets, brooding on their own shadowy mountainside. The singing rang through this stillness. While songfests are ordinary, they were new to me, for after two months I still felt like a tourist. I was a bit curious, besides having had enough of that disciplined aloneness called "writing notes" for the night. Duty called, and I was glad for the distraction.

The men's house was just a minute's walk away from my house, and it was already alive with an assortment of its inhabitants, most of them older bachelors and younger initiates. Singing, like other social activities, is age graded; it has a ritual hierarchy based on the authority of the elders, which inhibits boys till they are older and excludes women and children. A few married men had also joined in, as usual, having left their women to take a place in the all-male quarters. The igloo-shaped men's house was warm from a blazing hearth.

After only a few weeks' fieldwork the men's house already seemed familiar: the smoky smell of burning oak, the dirty bamboo walls, brown and tan bark cloth and feathers on brown and black bodies, bows and arrows, sweet potatoes and sugarcane peelings strewn on the floor or ready to be cooked. But what gripped you was the friendly faces: bright and wide open, with hungry smiles around teeth stained red from chewing betel nut, raised voices and laughter, and looks that embraced, and did not draw back—in this safe refuge—in young and old alike; the old ones, taut and weather-beaten, proud of having made it so far against life's dangers and their enemies, and prouder still of being in charge of their destinies. A couple of youths smiled at me, and I sat down in a place which my friends, Weiyu and Moondi, cleared for me, glad for their company. More men arrived. Then unceremoniously Soluwulu walked in, tall and stately—a near middle-aged fighter who later captured attention.

The crowd grew as more married men pushed in. The singing progressed until a little later (around 10:00 P.M.), when the great men and elders filed in. They arrived late, as befits their status. In Nilangu there were a half-dozen of these wizards, ranging in age from fifty to seventy years; all of them made it that night except old Bangeratwo, who was senile but sometimes came along. Their leader, Kanteilo, my sponsor, entered, not greeting me or anyone else, as was his fashion. He matter-of-factly plunged in. Having attended to the day's business and seen to it that their houses were in order, the elders always entered with aplomb. Younger men were moved to the back as the great men took the choice spots around the hearth fire, toward which the circle of eyes trained. Soluwulu sat among them. Greetings were exchanged. One of the elders leaned into the next, mumbling a confidence. Bamboo pipes and tobacco were passed around; betel nut was brought out and shared. The hut was fogged up with smoke. Meanwhile, the singing momentarily broke off, and then grew stronger.

There was a special intimacy in the crowd of singers that night. I don't think I am romanticizing their mood, for it cropped up again, from time to time, usually in response to the mingling and the liminal return to intimacy, though seldom did it radiate as strongly as it did that night. Perhaps it was a contagious effect of their own spontaneity, reflecting lucky providence—the bright weather, the general health and prosperity of the community, and their being safe together—blessings appreciated by those who had suffered long wars, epidemics, and even famine. The homogeneity helped, for only villagers were present: no need to stage a singing contest with competitive neighbors or to impress pompous visitors, since none were among us. And perhaps my own presence added more than a new audience. I was, after all, another sign of good fortune: a lifeline (money, medical care, a radio) previously lacking to an outside world that increasingly pushed inward. In that way I signified the outside, but one still controlled by the Sambia.

But whether for these reasons or not, no special event that night or on the morrow should have created the oneness which thickened their singing, and I doubt that we should search further for cause. Sambia love to sing, as individuals, and in groups. They will use most any excuse, aside from the ceremonial situations requiring it, to raise song, even fabricating a reason if necessary to stage a songfest—a noisy, smoked-up jam session made simply for the enjoyment of whiling away an evening in good company. By the time I had moved into the village in 1974, some things in traditional Sambia life had changed after pacification by the Australians—ending warfare, introducing rapid change—but the songfest was not one of them. The singers were still around.

That ancient song tradition was still foreign to me. I didn't understand the significance of the name songs or their words yet. I was especially green to their language. People knew that, and while at times it caused problems, they did their best to teach me. That was true even though there was safety for them in my ignorance; they were still hiding ritual secrets. Friends helped me out in the songfests, patiently pronouncing the words so I could parrot the phrases. Curiosity was my supporter in these frustrating lessons, but even that weakened after the long hours of monotonous chords seemed to merge, growing muddier from the men's slurred refrains. One grows positively saturated with it, this singing that goes on and on and seems timeless, the singers transfixed for long hours.

I never ceased to marvel at how the men (who rose at dawn) could fend off sleep with their paltry stimulants—tobacco and betel nut. The initiates, pushed back against the walls, grew bored and tired, dozing off while sitting up, knees pushed into their jaws.

Not so with the elders and men, who sang on: sometimes low, baritone, even drab; sometimes stronger, lighter, exuberant; sometimes stiff; sometimes with greater harmony, especially when the bachelors—who were still not manly enough and had to overcome embarrassment to sing in their elders' presence—would take the lead; and sometimes in lonely stillness, as a lead singer would raise solo chords to which his fellows responded in collective refrain. As the hours ticked by, it seemed the men would go on till dawn, oblivious to the body's need for sleep, the demands of their work tomorrow, their wives, or the rest of the world.

Sometime then—was it midnight or after?—another vocal quality, so unpredictable yet characteristic of the do-or-die stance of Sambia men, crept into their singing. On the surface this affect seems like dogged determination, an expression of their stoicism. The singing quickens, becoming pleasantly higher pitched. It grows more intense and steadier, and the singers more self-assured, smoking more and straightening up to stay awake. That high, late-night pitch has always seemed to me a sort of broadcasting—that one is master of, not slave to, the forces that challenge—inside and around. (But who or what is the audience for that signal? Peers? Women? The spirits? The other hamlets? Oneself? Now me? Or all of these resonating with one another?) Yes, bullheadedness. But waiting in the wings, backstage of this hard and fast endurance test, is a surprising guest at these nocturnal and very masculine parties that postpone dreams: displays of sorrow and sometimes weeping.

When first sensing the sorrow, I found myself moved by the thought that the songfest was not just a performance, that the men were sentimentally moved. What kind of sentiment involved the communal chanting or the sorrowful attentions of a lone lead singer who sang proudly alone, obviously connected to some inner images of the songs? In the following minutes I spontaneously fell in with this reverie, not consciously searching for the memories that returned of boys' nights spent singing by campfires in

Kansas when friendship was less complicated, of afternoons idled away at moody California concerts during the late sixties and early seventies. The singing shifted; the crowd's mood thickened. An hour had thus passed as if in moments. I had drifted and was drowsy. The singing turned melancholy. The mood was neither clearly apart from me nor in the others. Then a vague uneasiness grew and I shot awake.

It was then that I focused on Soluwulu—the lead singer—and became aware that something in his voice had minutes before sent me slumbering with the crowd, remembering boyhood and college as if they were yesterday, not a thousand years ago, until my drifting grew uneasy. Soluwulu's voice was fainter, though he still glared ahead. But as he continued singing, his face suddenly blazed two streaks of firelight reflecting the orange flames—like tiny streams of molten lava down a mountain. Tear tracks; he was crying. I could hardly believe my eyes. There in the Spartan men's house—its high ceiling rafters smoked filled, cold, and empty, looking down on walls beaming with the armaments of a proud warriorhood, the crowded audience unmoved and chanting round the hearth, Soluwulu broke off and bent slightly forward, silently sobbing amid his old cronies. Now a part of me stepped back, puzzled and disconcerted: Why was that man, alone—the one across the fire—crying?

The other men seemed merely to "ignore" Soluwulu. Though another elder spontaneously took the lead, and, in a moment, the singing actually picked up, as if to compensate for that one less voice. No one spoke; no one touched him or seemed to mind; no one (except me) looked around. (Two other times I have seen such crying in songfests. On one occasion at this moment, I did see a married man—the old shaman Gambakutu—say, "Oh cousin . . . ," and then reach out and warmly pat the man's side.) The two older men seated beside him, which included Kanteilo, raised their voices—staring straight ahead, with half-closed eyes drilling past the fire, and beyond us, fixed on the wall. They sang on. The elders' faces were in clear view, and I watched carefully, expecting some reaction—be it care, anger, or shame—to this utterly uncharacteristic and "unmanly" action. But to no avail; they were unchangingly calm. I wanted to ask why, what the crying meant, for that was the first time I had ever seen it in a Sambia man, who generally disguise their emotions in public. Certainly, wincing from pain and crying were considered shameful reactions by warriors. Since no one else moved, I adopted the "carry on" (not disinterested) posture of my hosts. In a minute, Soluwulu straightened up, and I realized that I had been privy to this fleeting outpouring until he resumed his lead.

Although I looked at my friends again, they stared ahead, and I wondered if they had even noticed. In a couple of minutes though, Moondi and Kwinko began a new tack. Again they began correcting my faulty singing. Moondi carefully enunciated words of refrains so I could try learning some more. Other initiates nearby, amused by my attempts, turned away to laugh so they wouldn't shame me and, hence, themselves. There was some relaxation in that quiet clowning, but no mention of Soluwulu. (Nor would there ever have been unless I had asked.) By now, Soluwulu was "himself" again, smoking and singing; things were back to normal. The crowd became expansive and carried on the singing.

Finally, at a fitting moment, I whispered to Weiyu, "Why was he crying?" "Who?" (as if he hadn't noticed). "Soluwulu." "Oh. He was singing his brother's song, who's dead." Weiyu continued, "It was his brother's song, he was crying for [the memory of] him." It was just a simple fact.

It would be a long time until I understood more about the songs, the sorrow in Soluwulu's singing, or Weiyu's words. Or about these male happenings—what they meant to Sambia—and how they are constructed around the "song-ropes" *(ndaat-oolu)* of men, as Sambia refer to them. Weiyu's remark seemed like all the answer necessary—at first—and it was enough to quell my curiosity. But it didn't tell what Soluwulu had felt, nor why his crying was so cozily accepted. It never occurred to me to realize that rather than shaming them, Soluwulu's grief actually brought the men secret pride, and marked a boundary around the men's sexual culture. However, I was not to guess this till later. Meanwhile, I had more pressing interests to attend to—such as the ritual initiations—and the singing seemed to require no explanation. But I could never quite forget that episode and the look on Soluwulu's face.

•◆•

Any visitor to a Sambia hamlet could not help noticing how much people enjoy singing. Those who stayed longer would learn that men love convening songfests—events that punctuate so much of daily and, especially, ceremonial life. Singing is a creative expression of joy, personal celebration, social achievement and triumph—feelings we associate with "happiness." My informant, Moondi, described the importance of the songfests: "We feel happy when we go. . . . Plenty of men have come together. They joke around; there's fun. They chew betel and there's lots of good tobacco. And they tell stories and the singing is strong. . . . We feel some excitement there: It's because many men have come together."

The songfest is a ceremonial event used to bring folks together, to encircle and solidify them, as it were—shutting out the cold, sickness, ghosts, strangers and enemies, and death. So it is used defensively, too, when the shamans conduct healing rites and at the mortuary wake. But whether in joy or with sorrow, Sambia songs are individually named and particularized: identified with real persons, entities, or things in the world. Songs are metaphors for the many ways of being Sambia. They link the living with the dead, society and nature, individual and group. Songs are pieces of identity.

From the start I sensed this special significance in the singing. For example, on initial reconnaissance patrols in the area—trying to locate a field site—I noticed how often the men spontaneously broke into song, sharing lyrics and refrains. Unknown and unnamed, the chants were strange to me, but they had good uses: to bolster their spirits when the men were tired and climbing that last mountain at the day's close, or when they were together, at nightfall, relaxing after dinner. Even on the first night of my arrival in Nilangu there was a festive songfest. Many other songfests followed in the coming months. I often joined in, and no other experience runs so much with the grain of Sambia life as do they—those cozy, sexually segregated male happenings.

My own house provided for change in those customary arrangements, but I didn't understand it until later. I was white and different; that's how people initially accepted me and my study of their "customs." My house was large, indeed huge, by Sambia standards, and I wanted it that way. The American in me needed space to spread out; the dismal weather makes one's dwelling a sanctuary for weeks on end; and it became, in time—without planning it that way—an object of interest for the whole village.[2] The result: My house soon became a gathering place for public songfests in which men, and later women, children, and initiates—none of whom otherwise mixed (and even in my house, the initiates covered themselves with their bark capes in the corner), owing to ritual taboos—would come together and sing. Even the women joined in, and the men would tolerate their singing, usually with good humor, though privately the men said the women's weak and disorganized choruses, sung only during female ceremonies, proved once and for all that women were inept, even in singing. In time, however, seasonal events pulled people away, and the novelty wore off.

2. My house was used for everything: for local council meetings; as neutral ground for dispute settlements, marriage negotiations, and ritual planning (by the men); for long afternoons of storytelling by elders among themselves, village cooking and feasting, baby-sitting, and gossiping; and as a way station and lodge for village visitors as well as songfests. I was also allowed to live there.

The men went back to their segregated men's house songfests. Occasionally, when the need arose, a healing ceremony would be performed in a family house. A shaman would officiate, and, of course, women and children joined in. Singing occurred in mixed company, then, but the women sang very little. I never again saw the same attempts as those in my house: women singing while males made up the audience.[3] The singing among individuals was just as impressive and intriguing. I'd see a man singing quietly to himself as he walked up the forest path for gardening. The small initiates, pushed out into the night to fetch water from the creek for their seniors, would bundle themselves up and carry a bamboo torch, loudly singing together—braving the ghosts and other evil powers in the darkness—and the men would traipse off at dawn on a hunt, singing till they entered the forest, where only silence reigned.

But none of the singers impressed me as much as old Kanteilo, who made me reluctantly recognize that singing had a personality of great depth. For the first weeks, when I usually lived alone, he'd come warm himself by the stomachless barrel that served as my stove, eating and sleeping there—away from his fourth wife—so I "wouldn't be alone." (He experienced this as a friendly, status-filled protective gesture, to let others know that he sponsored me. Yet at times it got too cold in my house, and it was a sacrifice, except when he wanted to be away from his wife, fearing that sleeping near her too much would "weaken" him quickly, while not wanting to admit that to her or to suffer the ordinary discomforts of sleeping in the plain old, flea-infested men's house.) He'd rise at dawn, as was his habit, but not quietly. He'd build a fire, noisily splitting logs, loudly yodeling (as do the most exhibitionist senior men), and then settle down to baking tubers. For an hour or so, he'd sit alone, ostentatiously singing the same chants, merrily self-contained. He amused and annoyed me: I never woke as early as he—until he moved in. In late afternoon, his gardening and visiting rounds complete—and no one his age could match him—he'd return again. He'd hand me some taro or choice sugarcane or similar morsel and

3. Perhaps we can see, in this example, one of the changes anthropologists unwittingly produce in their hosts. I could plead that I was at first innocent of the meaning of these mixed songfests in my house. But they were not an accident; something was propelling people together, overcoming traditional barriers, into the unprecedented arena of an alien's abode. That something was increasing social change—of which my presence was a major sign, indicating that "Here is an opportunity to try out a change we [Sambia] can control." It was their experiment. After several weeks I sensed that, and realized better what was occurring. Then I was not an innocent. I was complicit conspirator in their innovation. Scores of other examples—seemingly trivial, but taken together, they add up—could be adduced to underline the same point: Ethnographers do introduce or facilitate significant changes in their hosts.

then ask for coffee. Thus his singing would begin again at dusk, only it was quieter and more relaxed, hummed over and interspersed with news, until his low voice disappeared into a drowse by the stove.

Not until months later, during the collective initiation rites of 1975, did I see the grander version of singing in great dance-ground ceremonial sing-sings. Staged out-of-doors, in public, on important ceremonial occasions, these are not to be confused with the indoor songfests, where song-ropes are performed, segregated affairs.[4] Hundreds of men and women collect at the initiations, decked out in their finest ritual plumes and garb. Men circle in great clan groups on the dance ground, singing war-ritual chants. Those chants are different from other kinds of singing and belong to the clan group only by virtue of their harmonic style. But that singing also signifies proud, stampeding masculinity, powerful enough to frighten enemies and get things done—which every Sambia recalls from initiation events observed since childhood.

Somewhere in that early period, armed with a lengthy checklist of questions on subjects as diverse as pig herding, politics, and categories of pollution, I got around to a few glib queries about singing. What I wanted to know, but didn't yet even know how to ask, was what the devil Soluwulu had felt that night when his singing led to sobs. I thought no one (perhaps not even Soluwulu, whom I didn't know) could tell me that. And in those days anthropologists, including Malinowski's descendants, largely avoided such subjective matters. They were too "private." Besides, no one else, as far as I could see, ever talked about men crying. That wasn't what men did in singing, wasn't even what men did. So I followed my questionnaire, and Weiyu or Moondi obliged.

Their answers would have heartened Durkheim. Every Sambia male has not one but several "individual" songs that "belong" to his name and thereby mark off his social personhood. And every man has several names. The first, the childhood name, is bestowed sometime following birth. (Sambia wait until several months after birth to name a baby, for they say they fear its death; naming the baby makes people attached to it, and if it dies prematurely, they feel "so sad"—an attitude that gains plausibility from the high rate of infant mortality.) The second name, a sort of nickname used only by age mates, replaces the first, and this "initiate name" is

4. Men never sing in the forest, which is the preserve of the forest and hamlet spirits, even ghosts. Singing arouses their attention, inviting trouble: being struck with an invisible ghostly arrow, or having a tree pushed over on one. But Sambia are warriors, too. It is considered bad luck, even dangerous, to sing while out of the hamlet fortress, since one never knows who is waiting to attack.

bestowed at a boy's first initiation. The third and usually the last name—the adult, proper name—is also awarded then, but it is seldom used, except by women in formal reference at a distance, till the third-stage initiation at social maturity: pubescent bachelorhood, warrior status, and the marriage contract its status confers. Each name, even the baby name, has a song identified publicly with it. The song has a simple lyric and refrain, the refrain being repeated three and four times, harmoniously, whereupon the whole is repeated. Here is a simple example:

Oorumbiundunmo	—andumouwuno:
("Man's name"—"mine")	(He is there)
awei, awei	—awei, awei.
. . . (refrain)	. . . (repeat)

Most names are inherited. A boy may receive the name of a deceased (never living) father or uncle or brother, even a grandfather, usually patrilateral, but male matrilateral names are also chosen. Both the father and mother may have a hand in naming children, but others, like shamans, may play a part too. Sometimes, at the death of his father, a boy or youth will discard his adult name and assume his father's. If a man has several sons, however, the rule seems to be that a much older, already married, and established son will not change his name; instead, a younger son, usually but not always the last-born male, will adopt his father's name so long as that son has been initiated. This naming custom forms part of the Sambia kinship system, and it is born out of the respect for social heritage. One's name and therefore a piece of one's very selfhood are a social product that have a collective seal stamped into them.

Not only people but also most of the animals, important plants, and spiritual forces in the Sambia world are named, and thus identified with songs. It is a kind of musical totemism: songs for the cassowary and possum and other important animals; songs for the sun, moon, and stars; those for sugarcane and cordylines—red and green types—and for taro, yam, tobacco, betel nut, and banana; a song to scare away ghosts. Even the wind and some insects, like the preying mantis, ants, bees, and such, have songs. There are silly songs that make children laugh, like one about body lice. But there are formal and proud songs—like the one identified with the Harpy Eagle—great clan totem/spirit familiar of Nilangu hamlet. Nothing is too great or too insignificant to have escaped being hitched to the system of songs.

Each of a man's name songs is connected with the others by virtue of his self- and social identity as a particular Sambia person. Those songs are interconnected with many others that are inherited and handed down from father to son in what I call the song-rope. Sambia say that these "ropes"—the idiom conveys a sense of physical continuity, from past to present generations—have come down from their ancestors. A rope is made up of a long sequence of songs associated with a man, his father's clan, cognatic kin group, forest territory, property marks, and particular spirit familiars known and counted as integral to a family line for generations. The extensiveness of these ropes varies, some containing a score of songs, others hundreds. It is usually the eldest son who has the right to lead his father's song-rope during songfests in the men's house. There is a practical reason for this right. Each rope encompasses many songs, some of them esoteric, some of them full of archaic language, and the whole of which is sufficiently complex that a man must teach his son the sequence over a long period of time.[5] In plain terms there may be only several others—usually elders—who have heard the ropes over a lifetime and who correctly "know" a man's particular sequence of songs.

It took a long time to understand that these ropes are an invariable structure of songs, oriented in four ways: by tradition, by time, by geographic space, and by the particular singer's identity. Tradition dictates how the songs follow a certain order, rhythm, and musical pattern, inherited from the ancestors. Time is another dimension, for, in general, the songs are sung from present to past, from the living singer back to bygone, uncounted generations. Spatially, the songs also follow an imaginary course—the imaginary trajectory of the "rope" extending from the speaker's location to particular water courses, garden patches, groves of bamboo, especially liked groves of ritually efficacious trees, up to the peaks of the mountain ridges.[6] These special spots have their own place names (e.g., Tarowultangu, a taro patch growing near a high mountain pandanus grove). Thus, these local place names have songs too. Last, there is the personal singer—his own name songs, those of his father and direct ancestors, as well his and his

5. This archaic language is Sambia, but some of the morphemes and infinitives occur only in the songs and are probably survivals of a parent language, namely, Menyamya-area languages like those belonging to Sambia-like neighbors and their ancestors, whom Sambia say they are descended from.

6. In one of the few pieces on traditional singing in Melanesia, Schieffelin (1979:133) insightfully notes of the Kaluli, a people of the Southern Highlands: "In effect, as one moves along tracks and pathways through successive areas of different kinds of forest, one passes sites representing a history of houses and gardens and the people who made them over the previous fifty years. These sites mark to people the various contexts of their own past experience. The Kaluli identify themselves with their lands because they are reflected in them. And this, in turn, is in part the source of the nostalgia with which people react to place names in ceremonial songs." Here we see a striking parallel with Sambia use of geographical signs in their song system.

father's spirit familiars *(numelyu),* each of which has a name song gained through initiation ceremonies or his dreams (see Herdt 1977). So the song-ropes embody a wealth of information about oneself, the social network and genealogical ancestry, property and its jural boundary, and a sense of being centered in a universe the songs chart by time and space.

The act of singing, which on its surface appears so simple, thus bathes a man in the fullness of his existence. A Sambia man's songs carve out his social world and personal history, exhaustively demarcating—even beyond that of Lévi-Strauss's (1966) fictitious bricoleur—a circle of symbols we could appropriately gloss as his full personhood. Having learned this, however, I had learned nothing more of the topic that had initiated my probe and still stuck with me—Soluwulu's crying that night, a performance that hadn't recurred during the ensuing months of other songfests. But I came to realize how everything of importance in the Sambia world is named and everything has its own song—a certitude of identity signs. All, that is, except the aliens, Australian government (the former colonizer) patrol officers, for example—and that included me.

• ◆ •

I was almost disbelieving when I first heard others "singing" my name. My memory is of walking along the path in our hamlet, as usual, returning from a trip to another village. Some women greeted me as they sat outside making grass skirts and chatting, easily distracted because they were simply enjoying themselves. They welcomed me by breaking into a song as if they had sung it their whole lives. I didn't think much about it. Sambia commonly greet others, especially male kinsmen to whom they want to draw attention or who have been away, with a little demonstration like that. It is a fond greeting. "The women are just amusing themselves," I thought to myself with a smile. Still, in looking back, I realize that I felt a momentary combination of subtle embarrassment and pleasure; their song had hugged me.

The same kind of song greeting came later, but from a different group of women. Again, one afternoon, a while later, the initiates did it inside my house. It happened like this a few times: I discovered that someone had eaten all the taro in my larder, and when I showed my irritation, chiding them like their mothers but still half-faking, they turned away, chuckling. Whereupon they began "singing me," which drowned out my complaints, Moondi leading this beguiling ploy, which made me laugh.

So it went for another week or so, my drifting through the usual scenes with only subliminal awareness of the singing—until one afternoon, when another sense of their singing crystallized for me. Some young women passed my yard, quietly stepping but then halting to stare at me, giggling and singing.[7] Even then I smiled at the suspicion that they were flirting. But when I asked them, "What are you singing?" they ran off, noisily laughing, down the creek path. They were still "singing me," as if I were a Sambia bachelor.[8]

I found Weiyu and Moondi later and, intensely curious and with consternation, asked them: "Do people have a song for me?" They smiled yes rather matter-of-factly, and they seemed amused that I would ask. I was thrilled and honored, for I "knew" intuitively that people's singing signaled recognition of me as a social person and a "self" among themselves.

Yet, in an instant, my feeling changed back to puzzlement. How could I, a stranger without Sambia ancestry, have a name song? My two friends weren't of much help in that department. After I asked them where the song had come from, they vaguely replied that "some women" had started singing it. That is all they knew. It seemed a sufficient explanation. In fact, the "singing of me" occurred so subtly that I took little notice. It seemed to happen in situations as a spontaneous response to me. I did feel closer to them, intersubjectively, as a result of being sung. That idea is worth pondering.

After six months' of my living with Sambia, the singing, like so much else, was just another part of a great thick soup, as fascinatingly exotic and perplexing as were the language and rituals and feelings behind the names. But for me, the singing was insignificant: just singing, "having fun," musical entertainment, a minor part of ceremonies. Singing didn't seem serious

7. Such staring is considered a form of sexual looking among Sambia: if a woman had been alone and done that—winking both eyes at me—it would have been the signal men and women furtively use to communicate erotic desire. But in that case they would not have sung. Only women sing about men like this; men never sing about women. That is unheard of, and would be rude, like a man's patting a woman's behind in America. Nor do women, except rarely in groups, ever sing a lone bachelor's song. It is too risqué. I have only seen it happen a couple of times in recent years. It used to never happen. More commonly, sisters, mothers, cross-cousins may sing a man's song—a fleeting expression of fondness or of dramatic heroizing—such as upon his return from a successful hunt or trading party or a long patrol away. I think, now, that there was another reason for my embarrassment, aside from the teasing. That gentle, innocent singing was so naive, and awareness of that naïveté can make me feel awkward about my social power. But I consciously realized that six years later, not then.

8. I realized belatedly that women's gestures were the first sign of a change in my status, as is true of other social changes in Sambia hamlets. In ordinary, nonsecret discourse, it is the women (and less so children, who sometimes act as go-betweens for women) who may themselves serve as go-betweens for men (see Strathern 1972), and have license to move around informally and push the men into action on matters like arranging feasts, marriage prestations, or garden corvée work, and the disciplining of children or misbehaving men. In interpersonal relations between adults, women are sometimes "in the know" about domestic news before men.

enough to take seriously. Besides, who had ever said that song systems or interpersonal singing had had much importance in New Guinea? It was all too strange and humorous, and I had come to study serious things that books taught were important, like initiation rites. And another thing—and here I must confess an acceptance of the men's smug chauvinism on this score—it was the women and children who were "singing me," with their unserious smiles and giggles. I knew, at least I thought I knew, that it was the men who could teach me important things. It wasn't until later that the men lent weight to the women's and initiates' casual acts by singing my song with formality in a men's house songfest.

Ironically, it was my sociological checklist that impeded my understanding the significance of the interpersonal change that people were "singing me." The songs were a product of the group, a synthesis of its cultural heritage. No one, at least not the living, had created them, as they were a product of the ancestors. Yet their living effects were to categorize people, stereotyping them into age sets, status groups, persons and nonpersons (e.g., women). The songs were tied to a naming system that celebrated male maturity: being male, being initiated, having a family and estate—all the social trappings that solidified men as a clan group with property and politico-jural rights to defend. The song-ropes seemed to convey that fullness of male personhood in a closed system. Men were tagged with songs and counted in the songfests. Taken together, the songs were threaded into genealogical lines, and the ropes of clans crisscrossed to weave a larger rope for the community as a bounded, property-based, local descent group. This is the view I adopted; social theory had dictated it, and it was reassuring, at first. The group had taken me in. An unwitting, nonconscious group process had been responsible for what I had experienced. Of course, there were problems with this view. What was Soluwulu's anomalous crying? Why had the women—not the men—started my singing? Who had gotten it into their heads to do that to me, and why, in the first place?

The answers might lie in the structure of the song system itself, as if that object could reflect insights back to me. So that is where I next looked. For a few days—it stands out vividly because it was frustrating—I wedged questions into my conversations with the men and initiates. I searched for clues, some rule, a hidden cultural code, some kind of symbolic calculus that would clarify how the song-ropes assumed their general ordering. Beyond that, men would say, glibly, of course, that the songs were their "custom" and had been "made by the ancestors"—the last resort of consciousness in all such matters! All that work hadn't helped much in finding a social logic for unraveling the symbolic system in which the songs were wrapped.[9] Friends seemed perplexed by my perplexity. Several younger men, for example, said they could not understand the archaic words and obscure names in the lyrics of older songs. The elders were worse. When asked about the songs' root meanings (*kablu:* base, kernel)—which was appropriate to ask, though no one ever did so for songs—they gave me the same line. Even Moondi, my gifted younger translator, said on one occasion that the song-ropes were very hard to explain in everyday language, and he compared the difficulty to explaining the idea of *numelyu* (roughly, spirit familiar), which remains partially untranslatable because of its metaphysical meanings (Herdt 1989). He said the song-ropes would be as hard as learning the language. In despair I went back to the more productive study of ritual.

Meanwhile, I also became more adept at singing, listening to the words and refrains. I spontaneously fell into the Sambia style of singing my friends' names on occasion. I could do it with Kanteilo and several others. A couple of times, as I said, the men actually sang the song identified with me in the songfests, and someone would preface it with: "They all want to sing your song now." It seemed natural, another way of being with them.

By then I had lived in Nilangu a year, and I was to take a break, going back to Australia and America. The women began singing of me differently—this time sadly—and it was a little painful. People accused me of wanting to "go away and never coming back." Kanteilo got depressed and disappeared from my house. When I found him, he said he felt sad that I was leaving, so he didn't want to live with me now, for it would make him sadder to see me go. I kept saying that this fuss was unnecessary, that I would be back. But people said they had heard that story before.

I don't think anything I ever did in all the years of being with the Sambia had such an effect upon people in my village as when I did return two months later. Some were incredulous; others said, "I told you so." I chided Kanteilo that I hadn't lied to him after all, and he had seen for himself that my things—including field notes—had stayed behind (an assurance of my return). The shamans held a healing ceremony for me before and after I left, their way of magically protecting my person in transit, and then again welcoming me back. People were "singing me" more than ever.

9. I cannot take up the whole range of anthropological problems that are involved here, which would distract from the main argument. The symbolic interlinkages still perplex me, though. I believe that the individual creative element, as in the elaborate instance of the symbolic system Sambia use for dream interpretation, is sufficiently large and complex, and has been at work for generations, such that the song system has changed far beyond its original form, but retaining linguistic archaisms with it.

My relationships deepened. I began case studies of individuals—
Moondi, Weiyu, Nilutwo, and other men, like Tali, the ritual expert, and
some initiates (see Herdt and Stoller 1990). I went to work studying with
the shamans. I became more interested in sexuality. I began studying
Nilutwo's dreams. I also got to know Soluwulu, Tali's older half-brother.
Working with individuals was not entirely new to me. A few years earlier
I had studied social transactions, especially those of psychotherapy in a
California psychiatric ward. Sambia interviews were much different from
those, of course, but there were certain kinds of experiences—communications—that were like familiar faces. That work was, and still remains, more
exciting to me than is conventional ethnography focused on normative observations of social relationships and cultural institutions. This is still vital
and necessary as a baseline for individual subjectivities. But it lacks the personal involvement of one-on-one interchanges of awareness—wanting to
know what other persons see and feel and think, and not just what they
"think with"—that led me to anthropology. It was from this mosaic of
ethnographies of individual lives that I began to see the "singing of me" in a
different light. I saw how singing me had evolved my "Sambia" identity—
and presented an important change in people's feelings about being with
me. There is the rub: "important" in whose eyes, defined and compared as
a "change" in whom or in what? It was all too damn subjective—my embarrassment at being sung had told me that. But that was *my problem*. It
didn't explain at all what Soluwulu had felt the night he cried.

•◆•

To understand the cultural experience Soluwulu expressed that night, we
have to go back before my arrival on the scene (1974) to the period around
1939. Soluwulu was born in Nilangu about then. It was an important period
in Sambia history—a full generation before pacification reached the valley
in 1964–65.[10]
Only shortly before Soluwulu's birth, Nilangu had been founded, an
event that changed the political complexion of the Sambia Valley. Six generations before, ancestors of the first Sambia pioneers had left the Papuan
hinterland to the southwest and penetrated into the southeastern Kratke

10. What follows is ethnohistory, i.e., people's versions of social change as I have pieced them
together from oral traditions, elders' memories, legends, and genealogies, with special reference
to Soluwulu's history, elicited from him and Tali. No historical records exist before the 1960s,
when the first exploratory patrols reached the Sambia Valley, and even these reports are crude. My
most detailed account of these events can be found in Herdt (1987a).

Mountains. They were Papuans, fierce warriors, and most probably—if we are to judge by the intermediate Vailala people—cannibals. (Sambia, themselves, are not cannibals; and cannibalistic figures do not appear in Sambia stories, folklore, or myths either, except in the form of enemy tribes, animals [e.g., pythons] or spirits [e.g., ghosts, bogs]).

The vast stretches of Sambia territory were uninhabited save for scattered hunters and gatherers. Generations later, pioneers forged into the Sambia Valley itself, invading and overcoming the indigenous Kumundi people, one of these scattered groups. The whole belt of this territory is rugged and thinly populated. Even now Sambia are small in numbers and politically insignificant compared with the groups of the steaming Eastern Highlands that live just the other side of the Great River, a natural ecological barrier. Hamlets were established, settlers gradually moving northward till reaching present-day Nilangu, which was still being expanded into the roughest virgin rainforest in Soluwulu's youth.

Those pioneers had a hard life, for Sambia live in a hard land. Isolated, landlocked, amidst a broken landscape, high in elevation, the hamlets are virtual island fortresses, only recently unbarricaded after pacification, where one has a feeling of living in a windswept bird's nest that nature threatens to topple any day. One would have to search a good bit to find a more ruthlessly beautiful habitat, perfect for the stockading of a warrior band. In the short sunny season the weather is beyond perfection. But most of the year it is brooding with heavy to light rain that changes into dense fog—an Australian patrol officer once called it Frankenstein's country. One is chilled to the very bones by that cold damp fog, which seeps right into the huts. Subsistence is not easy. The rain forest was cleared with stone tools until the 1960s, when the Australians came. A single large tree took days to fell; a garden patch required months. Nature didn't yield easily; it still doesn't.

By 1940 the hamlet was settled. The total village was little more than 100 by 20 square yards, bounded by small creeks on either side of its ridge and, far below in the valley, by the stormy Sambia River. Gardens extended in many directions. This tight-knit fortress was virtually impenetrable to attack. It wasn't long before it was a political power in the whole valley, for it contained a group of ambitious men—young bucks, war leaders, a couple of shamans, and many young initiates—the present elders of Nilangu, including Kanteilo. Soluwulu's father was among them. He was a warrior, a minor shaman, and some say he was a great man. He also had three wives and many children. He was an outsider, as was his clan, which had splintered during a previous fight, years later settling in Nilangu. Nilangu's leaders took them in but never quite trusted them. Back in those days you could never completely trust anyone beyond the security circle. The deciding factor was the need for manpower, the need for hunting and gardening; but the needs for defense always came first.

Theirs was a warrior society; it had to be, for the world seemed at war with itself. It is hard for us to imagine this premodern social reality, to summon up its ghost without overdramatizing the harsh cruelty of war hammering into everyday existence, because man-to-man stone-age combat could cut, tear, and decapitate human bodies—men, women, children—the victims of quasi-enemies across the river, or true enemies in the next valley. The fear and horror and glory of war colored everything, shadowing everyone's way of gardening or playing or making love, because it was always so close and so possible, that ugly death. Dreaded warfare, more than anything else, moved Sambia social relationships and their other cultural institutions.

To understand how warfare inflected social practices, we can look at marriage, for instance. Incest taboos made the contracting for wives a trade between different hamlets, which could also fight with one another, and had. Marriage was a political arrangement, always. Personal choice could not be admitted. What woman would willingly leave hearth and home and loved ones to take up squatter's rights with a stranger in a hostile hamlet? The elders made the arrangements by infant betrothal or sister exchange. It was an awkward business, these marriages, and only ritual could make them work. The men were taught through ritual to fear women and their bodies, a gender antagonism that invaded sexual relationships, parenting, eating, gardening, along with just about everything into which spouses were drawn. At best, marriage was compatible; at worst, it was hell—arguments and beatings, anxieties about menstrual pollution, sorcery, or semen depletion, and suicide. The children were party to it; they were the reason marriage had to work, and they made it bearable. They were the inheritors.

And religion, too, reflected this deadly warfare, for religion is the soul of culture. For what else could weave together such a worldview and spirit system, with protective female hamlet spirits and fearsome male forest spirits, who were capricious, but not carnivorous or as angry as the hated ghosts of Sambia of both genders? The ghosts forever hover about, vengeful and envious, and must be formally cast out with screaming ritual bull-roarers (a sound instrument) and long, song-filled wakes, cast as far away as possible to ensure safety for the living. (Maurice Bowra was wrong; people don't always get the gods they deserve.)

Overseeing all of this plan for life was the men's secret society, a ritual cult that created initiations, age sets, status-ranked relationships between males, all wholly aimed at the production of warriors. They were needed to run a society that was based on the idea that "strength" *(jerungdu)* is the only means for surviving and winning in the battle and the hunt, in making babies, in being honorable.

Soluwulu was initiated into this warriorhood when he was seven or eight. Like his father, he was conscripted, for in such a small world, every individual is vital and is counted; a boy must count as a man. He left a household where he preferred his mother and was probably spoiled by her; he knew his father less, admired and feared him more. Good parents would have prepared and encouraged him for the fearsome ordeals that lay ahead. So he would have cried and possibly held on to them, but could stomach the hard rituals, fasts, beatings, and teachings, emerging more like a man— in the tradition of his father-warrior.

First-stage initiation lasted approximately seven months. Its greatest secret was that Soluwulu had to suck the bachelors' penises to take in their semen to grow strong. Those homoerotic activities were necessary, the elders said, because his body could not make its own semen, the only thing that could physically mature him. For semen is the elixir of life and a life force, the men think. So he did as his father said and had also done. Those inseminations, at first preceded by a moment of panic, and then filled with shame, would go on for years (see chapter 3). They were carefully hidden from his mother and all other women and children. To ensure that secrecy, the men entrusted the boys with another secret: that the strange sounds said to be the power-filled cries of the old female hamlet spirits, which the men could direct and the women feared, were really the flutes men blown at times of ritual. It was a great secret; death awaited any that revealed it.

By puberty—or bachelorhood—Soluwulu was stronger and was ready. More nosebleeding, endurance tests, and glory, too: dressing up in a true warrior's outfit, his own now; marching in public for the whole village. His parents had fed and clothed him his whole life; now it was his turn to help them. (In a year or so his father would die, and he would have to support his mother and younger siblings anyway.) He got to sing, too, could be addressed now by his adult name and be counted in the songfests. It was his right.

Coming of age at that initiation allowed, indeed forced him, to take the inseminator's role with younger initiates. He became the fellated; finally he was out from under the thumbs of the older males (at least sexually), and it was exciting and risky, too, for he would begin "losing" semen through sex with boys. He was still roped off from women. Even casual heteroerotic relations were forbidden, and sex with women was punished by death. The boys were his sexual outlet; they were available, wanted semen, and needed him and his age mates to get it, so homoerotic intercourse was easy and pleasurable. It could be rough, sometimes cruel, but that didn't matter: After all, his fellators were usually "strangers" from the other hamlets who were taking his semen, since only non-kin could engage in sex. It was manly, and was a duty. But there was far more to it than that (a part of him knew): He desired the boys, at least some of them, whom he could control and who were more like himself than the dangerous, mysterious women the men kept for themselves. He used the fellators; they used him. There was one who would even sing his name song, teasing and honoring, or was it to provoke him sexually? The initiate got away with it because Soluwulu favored him for awhile. Thus it went for years until marriage. After a while the novelty wore off, and he would tire of boys. And he worried that his semen was being drained too much, with no benefit for himself, except to "wash his penis."

His brothers were among the men's house gang. Tuvunu, his oldest brother, had helped initiate him. And Soluwulu had helped initiate Tali later. He and Tuvunu had not been very close for years. He never understood this until initiation. Before then, as it had been with his father, there were hidden areas—ritual secrets, the avoidance taboos (namely, women), the homoerotic play—that created awkwardness in their relationship. Even after initiation they belonged to different status age groups empowered by dominant/submissive rights and duties, as was true of men and women, who were even more walled off by secrecy and pollution taboos.

Soluwulu's biggest status change came when he was taken on war raids with the adults. Some of the treks were to far-off places, of which he had heard stories. After third-stage initiation, he was expected to earn his place by killing someone. At least that was the ideal. Whether or not he did, it was an honor just to be on the raid, returning with a new kind of experience the initiates and women lacked. He was a warrior; they would have to respect and even fear him now. Tuvunu respected him more, and they grew closer. There were other bow fights with the neighboring hamlets, too, yet they were more for show. War clubs and axes were not used with them, only bows and arrows, and usually from a distance. It was part of a contest: Who was the strongest? Who had grown up quickest? Who could outfight us or outdo us in masculinizing boys or producing babies? He was compared with his age mates as either a war leader or a "rubbish" man. His brother became a war leader and married. War was a game, but a deadly one.

There were other initiations, six in all, which directed and matured Soluwulu, from childhood to manhood, over some fifteen years. His life was lived as a warrior only in the Spartan men's house after initiation. Taboos hemmed in his daily life—eating, drinking, moving around—and especially he could never talk or be with women, including his mother and sisters, who remained in his father's household, a world apart. All the while, war was going on.

Several years later he got a wife from Kwoli hamlet. She had been marked for him at birth and had come of age. He was eager to marry, wanted his own house and children. They had no sex until her menarche, though he had heard rumors that some of his age mates had fellatio with their pre-menarchal brides. He still had homoerotic intercourse sometimes on the side. But that stopped soon, after his wife had her first menses and they initiated coitus, a totally different kind of sex from that with the boys: Genital-to-genital, more dangerous, more exciting, more uncontrollable—more adult. It was all a bit overwhelming at first, but he couldn't let his bride see that; the elders had told him to stay composed, in command, and not get too involved—by avoiding looking into her eyes during intercourse. He had to keep mint leaves in his nose and bitter bark in his mouth so he wouldn't smell her or swallow his saliva, for either would contaminate him. Soon a child came. Sex was now forbidden till the baby was weaned. Occasionally Soluwulu would coax a boy into sex, which was made easier when he slept in the men's house or forest houses, as he was expected to stay far away from his wife during the first months of her mothering. After the second child came, however, he knew he was forbidden to inseminate boys. It was a hard transition to make: no sexual contacts at all. The sacrifice hardened him more. He went on long hunts and a trading expedition; went on a war raid; had wet dreams; and remembered that Numboolyu, the ancestral culture hero, had had to endure all this too, so the elders had said in their secret myth (Herdt 1981).

Two years before (c. 1957) word reached Nilangu that strange and powerful "red-skinned" men (the Australians) in weird garb had entered Kaim hamlet over the mountains. They had crossed the Great River, passing over from Indoowi (Fore) country. They had strange, booming sticks that had killed a pig and could make booming sounds greater than the bull-roarer, people said. They stole food, too. The Kaim people fled into the forest, and some of the warriors later tried to ambush them but failed. It was a weird sound, the booms, like the ones the elders said were heard over the valley just after Soluwulu's birth (c. 1942) and came from the flying things—the elders called them "great white birds"—up there swooping around, booming at each other.[11] During that period another war began with the North-

11. Sambia memories and Australian reports from World War II campaigns indicate that Allied bombers flew over the Sambia territory several times, engaging Japanese planes in aerial combat at least once.

ern Wantuki'u tribe. It was over some stolen pandanus nuts on the same old disputed boundary up in the mountains. There were raids and counterattacks. Sporadic engagements went on for more than two years.

Soluwulu's parents had both died. He was now becoming a great man. Several more initiation cycles were staged. There had been a big sickness for awhile, especially over in the Green River hamlets, where many people died. That was their tough luck. Our shamans had blocked it out; only a couple of old people died over on the other side of the river. Tali was first initiated (c. 1955), and later initiated as a bachelor (c. 1962), a responsibility that fell upon Tuvunu and Soluwulu, because their father was dead. Arrangements had already been made to exchange their younger sisters for women from other hamlets to marry their youngest brothers, Tali and Yawutyu. After the next initiations, around 1960, a great songfest was held, for the men had decided to launch a large war raid against the Wantuki'u people and put their neighbor in their place, once and for all. The war leaders wanted blood. The new bachelors would be tested to see who among them would become the new fighters.

That songfest was special; it belonged to the all-night ceremony that preceded a war raid. There were hooting and dancing on the village dance ground. The shamans all came and purged the men, removing the traces of women from their bodies that attracted arrows like a magnet, magically blessing them for a safe journey. There were war chants. But the songs were brought out, too, the song-ropes of the ancient ones. After his father died, Soluwulu took his name, so he sang his father's rope. His brother Tuvunu was older and therefore did not take the name; he sat in the crowd and joined in. At dawn they all left for the mountains.

The raid was launched, and a Wantuki'u hamlet was attacked. There were no deaths, and the raid wasn't very successful. The party was chased back, their enemies counterattacked, and the war dragged on for months. Meanwhile another argument flared up, and bow fighting began with the Wunyu-Sambia phratry across the river. One bow fight lasted for days. The Wantuki'u could have attacked at any time, inflicting a heavy blow, for the valley was itself divided; but they didn't. The bow fighting dragged on.

In one of those bow fights Tuvunu was wounded. A few days later he died. He had led the fighting. Soluwulu wept, wanted blood revenge, and eventually Nilangu got it. Tuvunu's body was wailed over and put atop nearby trees in customary fashion. Wakes were held; the flutes and bullroarers mourned. At least it was a warrior's death. Soluwulu has kept the skull, as was customary, and hid it away to make sorcery with.

Wars and conflict went on like that; there were many battles. The "red skins" were sighted twice more. Rumor had it that "great white birds" (air-planes) had landed in the Baruya Valley.[12] The red men fought with the Baruya and won. This gladdened the Sambia, for the Baruya were the worst of enemies. Sambia never imagined they would suffer the same fate.

A few months later the "red skins" came again, this time invading the Sambia Valley. The women were terrified and fled to the forest and hid there. A couple of war leaders stood up though—from a distance—and launched arrows. Kanteilo was one. The trespassers left. Another battle flared up, this time between Nilangu and Moonunkwambi—a hamlet on a neighboring ridge.[13] Shortly before, around 1962–63, initiations were held again. Weiyu's age set was made a part of the cult. No sooner was it done than another battle began; this time Nilangu was itself torn apart because several men, actual blood brothers, took sides over an argument involving an eel stolen from a river trap.

That incident led to the last great battle the Sambia knew. Many men were wounded. It seemed as though it would turn into an all-out war when the "red skins"—lead by the Australian patrol officer—appeared. He seemed to ignore the fighting and went away. But in a few days he returned with a great line of black-skinned constabulary from the provincial capital. He built a hut near Kwoli hamlet and made a speech. A Kaimeru man— a Sambia—who lived far away served as the government interpreter. The Australian said he wanted to put the men's names in a book, so they were all to assemble the next day. But they were tricked; the police circled the men, took their weapons, and put them in handcuffs. It was terribly hu-miliating. Two score men, including Soluwulu, were marched off in chains to Mountain Patrol Station and jailed. They were treated as—what is the right term? Savages? Animals? In a few weeks they were released and warned never to fight again. That was in 1964. War was done with.

Two years later (1966) a missionary came. He settled not far from the vil-lage, down in the valley. He appeared strange to the Sambia, but said he wanted to learn the language. The missionaries lived down by the river, made a settlement of their own (Kwat-Sambia) in time. The missionary never suspected what went on in the initiations. Even twenty years later, the Sambia had still managed to keep him ignorant of the secrets. Meanwhile, more initiation cycles were held; Moondi's was the first. Two years later (1968) Mountain Patrol Station was built. Sambia helped clear the airstrip.

Six years later (1974), I arrived. Nilangu seemed idyllic; people were

---

12. See Godelier (1971); also Schieffelin and Crittenden (1991).

13. Moonunkwambi was abandoned in 1971. Its people, including Soluwulu's clan, then moved to Nilangu.

friendly. War was a living memory, and Sambia were glad it was gone, though sometimes the elders acted as though the glory days had been better. The next year, the last full initiation was performed, for the pace of change was increasing. New Guinea was decolonized that year and became Papua New Guinea, an independent state. I was to return many times over the ensuing twenty years.

What we call "Sambia culture" is the accumulated product of generations of change compressed into the story of Western "contact"—pacification drilling backward and forward unevenly and building this tiny outpost of a broader world itself divided. History has transmuted Sambia identities, which that convenient fiction the "ethnographic present" ignores. Any moment of it is "microdotted"[14]—in events like the night of Soluwulu's singing.

•◆•

It is precisely because Sambia men share in their knowledge and experience of this remarkable history that Soluwulu's crying that night made "sense" to them. Life is harsh; war could kill; it took Tuvunu. They knew all that; I did not. It is precisely because the songs celebrate male identity in songfests that Soluwulu could proudly sob in what becomes an intensely masculine performance. Take away the men's house and place women and children in the audience, and he might not have wept; that would be shameful. But the homosocial situation and the fact of his dead brother's song would still not have produced this rare performance were it not that Soluwulu was a great man.

Is it coincidence that I have only seen the most masculine of warriors weep—in this very noble manner—in songfests? No. A "quiet" man probably would not do that, and a rubbish man might be dismissed (or even scoffed at: "same old weakness") for it. Soluwulu could do this because he was Soluwulu, the fine and respected warrior people knew to be the embodiment of all that was idealized as Sambia manhood. By knowing this, we see a different side of Sambia men, richer and more complex, than their behavior "speaks" in public.

But what of my place in this? Sambia used my name (or versions of it) to interact with me. They gave me a song because they had to do so in order to absorb me into the group. Perhaps someone else could have been taken in but not given a song; I don't know. Perhaps if I had come later, during the throes of massive cultural change, it wouldn't have mattered. The songfests,

14. The concept is Stoller's (1979): it indicates intense meanings condensed into a single event or memory.

like the initiations, are now largely a thing of the past. But in 1974, I could not be admitted into the initiations and entrusted by Sambia without myself having a song they could keep inside themselves and hold on to, even when I was gone.

I didn't understand this fact until years later, when I was able to figure out how they named me: "Gilbert" was corrupted to "Gimbo" (pronounced "Geem-bo") or "Gimbatwo"; later on people called me "Gilberto," and my friends used "Gil."[15] In 1979 it came out—or so I thought—that my song had been borrowed from my friend Kokwai, a young married man in the village. But that was wrong: Our names, as modified in song, simply sound alike. Then I thought that perhaps the shamans had invented my song; they used to astonish me by coining new names and songs from their dreams and who knows what else. But that was wrong too. Someone or some group— I'll never know just who—created my song. It has three key phrases that go like this:

1. Weiyat'meilo . . . Weiyat'melio . . . Weiat'mei . . . (corruption of Weiyapu— "red-skinned one"?—mine . . . etc.)
2. Gimbat'meilo . . . Gimbat'meilo . . . Gimbatwo (Gilbert, mine . . . etc.)
3. Bwanjat'meilo . . . Bwanja'tmeilo . . . Bwanjat'wo (Harpy Eagle, mine . . . etc.). Awei, awei . . . Awei, awei . . . etc.

The order is then reversed, and the refrain sung again.

The etymology of "Weiyat'meilo" is vague, but it probably is a form of "Weiyaapu," which Sambia use for "White skin." *Bwanju*—the Harpy Eagle—is the great clan totem and spirit familiar of Nilangu, a highly prized protective symbol. It is forbidden to kill or eat this bird. For several reasons I was identified with it.[16] The three phrases rhyme and are harmonized. When sung, they sound similar to those of Kokwai's song, though the words are all different. When my song is sung in ordinary settings as a greeting, only the "Gimbat'meilo" chord is sung. Sometimes, *bwanju* was used as a metaphor for me, and people have said: "You've come to be with us, and you have the spirit familiar of the *bwanju;* that *bwanju* must stay here."

There is something intensely personal and remarkably assimilative in how the Sambia have constructed being with people by singing their songs. It took me many years to be conscious of it. Everything important in the known world is named and has a song. The songs are strung together to link

15. The old people still call me Gimbatwo; one old man calls me "Toopeikwi," a nonsense name he dreamed up, which people think ridiculous.

16. These include the politics of my belonging to Nilangu's clan group, dreams shamans reported in which they believed I was identified with the eagle, and an odd incident that occurred

past and present in so many ways. But men do not sing of women (although the reverse is true). Only older men have the status and self-esteem to sing their own songs in the songfests, and only the most masculine men have been seen to weep on rare occasions. What is in a song? The identity that Sambia "say" with their behavior: the full-blown identity of esteemed masculine personhood. I can add two other observations. First, of all that is named and has songs, none includes the body or body parts. Second, a strict taboo forbids anyone ever to say his own name—except when singing his own song. Likewise, it is forbidden ever to say one's childhood name or sing that song except in songfests. Obviously some older, and perhaps deeper, parts of selfhood are summoned up as guests to men's private songfests. Why should that be?

I note again that Sambia is a technologically simple society, without our electronics, buildings, bombs, and supermarkets. They have no mirrors, and nothing, not even water pools, in which to see their reflections. That means that Sambia never directly saw their own faces—images or reflections of their bodies—before recently. People now have mirrors from trading posts, and some Sambia, particularly the younger generation, enjoy looking at themselves.

What would it be like to have lived one's whole life without ever having seen your own face? Think on that a moment. One can see the products of one's labor in gardens or hunting, or see one's trappings—clothes, exuviae (fingernails, hair, spittle), and waste products (feces, urine). But one cannot see fully what we Westerners call the "self," the primary referent of which is our face. Sambia *see themselves only in the responses of others:* smiles, body posture, grimaces, gestures, interactions. In a society like America, the "me" society, a "culture of narcissism," as Lasch (1979) refers to it, we have surrounded ourselves with mirrors, photographs, portraits. We seem to be in love with ourselves.[17] Yet so many people seem alone, and diminished of self. Certainly, we Americans seldom sing together; our radios blast songs anonymously to anonymous selves. Sambia had none of that. Their world stopped at the top of their mountain ridges. Everyone was named, known, and sung. Their songs were mirrors, reflecting their selves to and from

---

in 1976 in which an eagle killed my pet cockatoo. Though I was sad about the last and felt people would see it as a bad omen, it was quite the contrary: they saw it as a protective sign of my power, for reasons that are too complex to describe here.

17. See Lasch (1979). Pardon my pseudophilosophical social criticism, for I do not mean to imply that Sambia are not in love with themselves, only that the way in which our industrialized, capitalist system, with its ideology (in many ways mystifying) of individualism, institutionalizes narcissism more, and in more atomistic ways, than do Sambia.

themselves and others. But because they are also songs taught, learned, and sung together with the only significant others there are, they define a social selfhood that seems to be equally public and private, and is in no way anonymous. Singing expresses the very life force of Sambia society, the existence of separate but interlocking selves.

• ◆ •

It will never be easy to translate experience between people, their cultures and discourses. Sexuality makes it harder still. But sex is not the only impediment, obviously. My initial avoidance of topics like singing, and my belief that it was trivial, were intellectualizations and rationalizations that kept me from understanding what was going on in me and in my friends. I see this now but didn't know it then. Sometimes insight, like age, grows slowly. For readers will have only words (rarely photographs or films) to know what the ethnographer knows—of Africa, New Guinea, South Carolina, southern France, or wherever—and had they been there, they would still not know what the ethnographer knows, for they did not see, feel, think, hear, and touch what he or she did. And the natives, being humans, would respond somewhat differently to anyone else.

Anthropology has afforded me the best of two worlds: a very privileged Western education and research training, and the wonderful experience of living with a non-Western people full and rich with life. It has also provided a lifestyle that well suits me: direct contact with the wholeness of people, which I need and enjoy; and, through my field data and thoughts about them, reflection upon another culture, hence reflecting about humankind, leading back to reflection upon myself. We anthropologists are largely a powerless and poorly paid lot. But we are lucky to have had that great intellectual experience—fieldwork—which, of all other training experiences, only psychoanalysis matches in depth and complexity and far-reaching discovery of self. Where the anthropologist works through another society back to cultural insight, the psychoanalyst works through past and present experience to personal insight (see Habermas 1971:228). The process of discovery in both is similar, but analysis is more focused on self-insight as its chief product. Cultural and personal insights must go together, for they are of a piece, and one is damaged without the other. Have those of us who study sexual cultures not concluded but merely begun the exploration of our true object: understanding the range of variation in the possibilities of human existence? The answers to that question create for each of us our own songs in the key of life.

TWO

Sambia Sexual Culture

The sexual and the social ultimately belong within the same framework of personal and cultural reality, and the main effort of my work among the Sambia has been to restore this holistic sense of things. Thus in this chapter I focus on how Sambia traditions of social practices and meanings, values, and beliefs regulate sexual behavior and, in turn, how these sexual transactions create a unique sexual culture.

In each instance, the concept of a particular "sexual culture" is meant to inflect relations between sexuality and meaning at the most fundamental level of the local cultural history, knowledge, power, sociality, the regulation of markets, and the development of the person and selfhood. This does not mean that the content of sexual culture is everywhere particularistic and diverse, since, in general, full personhood, in the Maussian sense of rights and duties, involves being married and parenting children. Thus every sexual culture must grapple with the norms and exigencies of marriage, sexual partnerships, parenting, childhood socialization, and the exceptions that depart from these norms. In this sense, the sexual is but one of many overlapping domains of shared meanings, which would include kinship, politics, religion, and economy in virtually all human communities.

Sambia sexual culture creates these sexual meanings—both at a symbolic level of representations and institutional discourses and at the level of practices of embodiment and subjectivity of the individual, the values and understandings, rights and duties, of being a sexual actor in the flood of social relations that exist among the Sambia. Sexual culture has an extremely wide scope, in this view, and is actually a window that opens onto the widest topography of cultural and social life. This includes the classification of sexual relationships, definitions of sexuality which impose norms (and resistance to norms), the creation and maintenance of local theories of "human nature," as well as a kind of local ontology of psychological types of sexual actors, according to folk concepts registered by social status, gender, age, personality, sexual proclivities, marital status, and so on. Beliefs about the nature of the genders and their difference or similarity are of significance as well, and of greater import in New Guinea than in certain other culture areas of the world. Of special importance to the Sambia are the variety of institutional forms of sexual transactions, and the beliefs and values relevant to the larger society which Sambia bring to their erotic encounters with one another. These can be studied as a kind of lexicon of forms because the Sambia have heavily ritualized and tabooed these sexual transactions.

But precisely how is the student of human society and history to go about describing a phenomenon, such as sexual culture, which seems all-encompassing? We can employ a variety of strategies in answering the question, though the answer of anthropology is different. Every anthropologist has certain choices when he or she sets out to write a particular ethnographic piece. In another era the answer would always have been staid, formal, impersonal (see Herdt and Stoller 1990). Today, however, the relentless battering of postmodernism has made accounts which omit the personal seem old-fashioned, passé. We cannot do without an account of the cultural environment, nevertheless. And we must pay special attention to the fact that many people tend to project their own "natural" meanings and assumptions onto what they read about "sex." The following symbolic and structural account of Sambia culture elucidates these matters by providing the key domains of sexual beliefs, their constraints upon semen transactions in same and opposite sexual relation, as these regulate social and sexual life.

Precolonial Society and Culture

The Sambia dwell on the fringe area of the Eastern Highlands of Papua New Guinea. Traditional society and economy revolve around small hamlets built atop high mountain ridges for defense. Gardening and hunting are the main economic pursuits. Sweet potatoes and taro are the chief staples. Women do most of the garden work. Men do all the hunting, primarily for possum, cassowary, birds, and eels. Pigs are few and are of little ceremonial importance. Descent is ideally organized on the basis of patriliny. Postmarital residence is patrivirilocal, so males grow up in their father's hamlet, inherit his land, and reside there. Marriage is by infant be-trothal or sister exchange; bride-wealth was introduced only in the mid-1970s. Some men, especially senior leaders, have several wives. All marriage is arranged by elders, women being traded between exogamous clans, which tend to be internally organized as an extended family. Inside ham-lets, nuclear (or polygamous) families live together in small, separate huts, but there are also one or two men's houses wherein all initiated, unmarried males over age seven live. The hamlet tends to function as a corporate group in warfare, subsistence activities, marriage, ritual, and dispute settlements.

Sambia society is comprised of six different population clusters of ham-lets in adjacent river valleys. These population clusters are divided, in turn, into subgroups (phratries) believed related by ancestry, ritual, and common geographic origin. Each phratry has between two and six hamlets, situated on ridges often within sight of one another. These local hamlet groups, known as confederacies, intermarry and engage in joint ritual initiations every three or four years.[1] But they sometimes fight among themselves. Warfare has indeed been rife throughout the entire area of the Sambia, tak-ing two forms: intertribal war raids to kill and loot and intratribal bow fights designed to bluster and get revenge for perceived wrongs. In other words, within the Sambia Valley, hamlets have intermarried, initiated, and fought—sociopolitical dynamics that are crucial for understanding social and sexual life.

Relationships between the sexes are highly polarized. One sees this gen-der polarization in virtually every social domain. A strict division of labor and ritual taboos forbids men and women from doing each other's tasks in hunting and gardening. Women are responsible for food preparation and child care. Authority rests in the hands of elders and war leaders. Men are in charge of public affairs. The hamlet itself is divided into male and female spaces and paths tabooed to the opposite sex after initiation. Men's rhetoric disparages older married women as oversexed or lecherous and younger women as prudish or shy. Men fear being contaminated and sapped of their strength *(jerungdu)* by marriageable women.

Furthermore, male-female sexual relationships are generally antagonis-tic, and many marital histories reveal arguments, fights, jealousies, sorcery fears, some wife beating, and even suicides, especially by women. Wives (more than female kin) are stigmatized as inferior, as polluting and deplet-ing to men, because of their menstrual and vaginal fluids. Sexual inter-

1. Confederacy here marks the same social unit as "parish" and "subtribe" in other New Guineast typologies.

course is supposed to be spaced to avoid depletion and premature aging or death. (Couples may have sex every three to five days, or as infrequently as once every two or three weeks, depending on their ages, length of marriage, personalities, etc.) Prolonged postpartum taboos prohibit couples from engaging in coitus for up to two-and-a-half years following the birth of a child. These generalizations indicate trends, but Sambia are generally highly sexually regulated compared with other Highlands groups (Langness 1967 [reviewed in Herdt and Poole 1982]; Strathern 1988).

How do Sambia understand the nature and functioning of the sexes? Male is the socially preferred and valued sex. Female is perceived by men as inferior, except reproductively. Infants are assigned to the male, female, or hermaphroditic sex, and sex typing of behaviors and gender traits is rigid. Females, however, are believed to mature quickly and without external aids, for their bodies contain a menstrual blood organ *(tingu)* that hastens physical and mental development, puberty, and eventually menarche—the key sign a woman is ready for marriage and procreation. (Menarche occurs late in New Guinea and in precolonial times was about age nineteen for Sambia.) At menarche a woman is initiated through secret ceremonies in the menstrual hut forbidden to all males (see Godelier 1986:74ff.). Males, by contrast, do not naturally mature as fast or as competently. Womb blood and maternal care not only hold them back but endanger their health. Males cannot reach puberty or acquire secondary sex traits (e.g., facial hair, mature penis) without semen; their bodies, their semen organs *(keriku-keriku)*, do not internally produce semen, Sambia believe. Therefore males require inseminations and magical ritual treatments over many years to "catch up" with females and become strong, manly men.

Male development and masculinization after childhood are the responsibility of the men's secret cult and its initiation system. This cult is organized and perpetuated by the confederacy of hamlets. Boys are initiated at seven to ten years of age, when they are separated from their mothers, natal households, older sisters, and younger siblings. Thereafter, they must avoid all females for many years while living in the men's house. Avoidance taboos are rigidly enforced with shaming, beatings, and ultimately death (the last used to keep boys from revealing ritual secrets).

Males undergo six initiations in all over the next ten or fifteen years. First initiation *(moku)* graduates are called *choowinoku;* second-stage initiation *(imbutu)* occurs between ages eleven and thirteen; and third-stage initiation *(ipmangwi),* bachelorhood puberty rites, is for youths fourteen to sixteen years of age. These initiations are all done in sequence on large groups of age-mate boys, who are from neighboring hamlets, thus making them members of a regional age grade. Initiates also become members of war-riorhoods, which as local units are responsible for defending their own hamlets. Fourth-stage initiation *(nuposha)* may occur anytime afterward. It is a public marriage ceremony associated with secret male rites and sexual teachings for youths to whom girls have been individually assigned for their marriage. But genital intercourse does not yet occur between the couple. Fifth-stage initiation *(taiketnyi)* occurs when a man's wife has her menarche, typically in her late teens. The bride then has her secret initiation in the menstrual hut. Afterward, the couple can engage in coitus. The final, sixth-stage initiation *(moondangu),* is held when a man's wife bears her first child. She then undergoes a final women's secret ceremony too. Two children bring full adult manhood *(aatmwunu)* for males and personhood for both sexes.

The men's secret cult is ideally organized in the men's house as a social hierarchical system according to ritual rank. Initiates are lumped into ritual categories: *kuwatni'u* is a category term for first- and second-stage prepubescent initiates (who may also be referred to as *choowinuku* or *imbutnuku,* ritual-grade titles); *ipmangwi* (or *moongenyu,* "new bamboo") bachelors are third-stage initiates of higher adolescent status. Pubescent bachelors dominate prepubescent initiates; older youths and young married men dominate bachelors; elders are seen as politically and spiritually superior to everyone (Herdt 1981). War leaders and shamans lead in fights and healing ceremonies, respectively. There is nothing unique about this ritual system, for many similar forms can be found in Eastern Highlands (e.g., Read 1952), Papuan Gulf (e.g., Williams 1936a), and Telefomin (e.g., Barth 1975) societies. What is special, and what links Sambia and their Anga neighbors with Papuan lowland systems (e.g., Keraki, Kiwai Island, Marind-anim), are the wide-scale institutionalization of age-graded homoerotic relations (see Herdt 1984a, for a review).

Sambia practice secret homoerotic fellatio, which is taught and instituted in first-stage initiation. Boys learn to ingest semen from older youths through oral sexual contacts. First- and second-stage initiates may only serve as fellators; they are forbidden to reverse erotic roles with older partners. Third-stage pubescent bachelors and older youths thus act as fellateds, inseminating prepubescent boys. All males pass through both erotic stages, being first fellators, then fellated; there are no exceptions, since all Sambia males are initiated into homoerotic insemination.

The symbolism of the first homoerotic teaching in initiation is elaborate and rich; the meaning of fellatio is related to secret bamboo flutes, and ritual equations are made between flutes, penis, and mother's breast, as between semen and breast milk (see chapter 4). Boys must drink semen to grow big and strong. At third-stage initiation, bachelors may experience personal difficulty in making the erotic switch in roles (see Herdt 1987a). Thereafter, they may continue having oral sex with boys until they father children. Essentially, youths pass from an exclusively homoerotic behavioral period to a briefer bisexual period, during which they may have both homoerotic and heteroerotic contacts in secret, and finally to exclusive heterosexual relationships. Social and sexual inadequacies in masculine personhood are regarded as individual failures to achieve these social transitions (see chapter 5).

Sexual Subjects and Objects

For the Sambia, who ritualize male obligatory homoerotic practices on a broad scale, it may be said that two forms of sexual behavior characterize their culture and developmental experience. For males, first sexual contacts are secret, transitional, male-male oral sexual behaviors. For adult males and females, the parallel form is initial male-female oral (the woman is fellator) sex in marriage. Later, heterosexual genital contacts occur. To my knowledge, no other customary form of sexual behavior occurs, including masturbation to orgasm or anal intercourse. The rules and norms surrounding these two sexual modes are parallel. But in both cases, semen acquisition is an imperative organizing principle of people's social interaction and sexual behavior. Its magical power does things to people, changing and rearranging them, as if it were a generator. They, however, can do little to affect this semen principle: it does not reflect on but merely passes through them—as an electrical current through a wire—winding its way into bodies, like generator coils, for temporary storage. Because it is instrumental to growth, reproduction, and regeneration, semen (and its substitutes, detailed below) is needed to spark and mature human life. Humans are its objects.

This strange view may seem upside-down to us, since it animates a body fluid with agency and life force in a way that seems "magical." However, this belief system is fundamental to the Sambia worldview, and such a parallel view was once common in premodern Europe as influenced by alchemy. By thus beginning with the novelty of Sambia sexual culture, we may hope to achieve a better understanding of the relationship between heteroerotic and homoerotic life, a subject about which we Westerners assume so much. I shall first examine cultural ideas about semen and then study how these ideas influence sociologic types of semen transactions between males and males and males and females. Taken together, these ideas and social trans-actions form a system of objects of the semen. Though these two per-spectives are conceptually distinct, their complementarity suggests how normative goals affect individual social action and the developmental cycle of the group. When viewed as a total system, all of these valuations structure the sexual interactions and subjectivities of Sambia participants.

Semen predicates two different sorts of relationships: direct sexual trans-actions between semen donors and recipients, on either the individual or group level (in the latter sense, I am speaking normatively); and indirect se-men transactions that affect changes in a third party via the semen recipi-ent, who is believed to serve as a transformer of semen (e.g., father to mother to baby). The concept "transformer" is analogous to Meig's (1976) use of "transmitter," in which she argues that a person's body may store or deliver fluids (e.g., blood or semen) or essences to someone else. "Trans-former" differs because of another dimension needed, transformation: that is, changing semen into something else, as medieval alchemists were thought to change lead into gold. I shall later disentangle these levels of de-scription and analysis.

Cultural Ideas of Semen Value

Sambia have five main cultural categories of semen valuation. These in-clude erotic play, procreation, growth, strength, and spirituality, all of which are connected with sexual behavior. The metaphoric and analogic uses in rhetoric and imagination of these categories can be found in other domains too (see Herdt 1981). Here, though, I shall explore their social sig-nificance for insemination.[2] The study of these categories will involve us in understanding how people (and in some ways, nonhuman entities) are rep-resented as potential semen donors or recipients, transformers, or trans-mitters of semen value in Sambia culture. This section is concerned with the cultural level of these concepts.[3]

There are two analytic senses in which I shall use the term "value." First, the anthropologic sense of conventional valuations in a culture: attributed or assumed meanings shared by and assigned to people, institutions, and sub-

2. These cultural categories cross-cut various symbolic domains and social arenas, such as taboo, ritual, food sharing, myth, etc. One certainly could abstract from action and rhetoric the normative and metaphoric operations of these categories (see Wagner 1972, 1975). As I indicate below, sexual interaction is a conscious, though not always marked, frame for acting and speaking among Sambia, but I cannot here provide a description of all its manifestations.

3. See Herdt (1981) for conceptual models. This chapter considers mainly the male view-point, and it is not meant to be an exhaustive cultural analysis.

stances. Thus we can speak of the cultural regard for semen and the social esteem with which it thus endows bodies and social relationships. (There is also a libidinal value, present in conscious and unconscious thought, which will not concern us.)[4] Second, there is the Marxist sense of the value of a commodity, such as gold, which "when impressed upon products, obtains fixity only by reason of their acting and reacting upon each other as quantities of value" (Marx 1977:248).[5] Hence, we can analyze semen as a scarce resource that can be consumed and produced, conserved, invested, or otherwise spent. Persons and relationships may be valuated (as a means to an end) in regard to their status as donors or recipients of the commodity semen.

There are several tacit assumptions underlying the relation between semen information and the categories examined below, and I begin with them. (1) Semen is the most precious human fluid. Because it is believed vital for procreation and growth and is in short supply, semen is more precious than even mother's milk, its closest cultural equivalent. But precious does not necessarily mean powerful. Menstrual blood is the logical antithesis of semen; it is dangerous and, in some rituals, is equally efficacious as semen (cf. Faithorn 1975). (2) Sambia are by character prudish people. (May

4. Sambia tend to treat and think of semen as an energy force, in individuals and society, that may be compared, by direct analogy, to Freud's concept of libido. The analogy is apt in several ways: This energy force circulates through others (e.g., as subjects), who may be taken in (e.g., as objects) via semen or its equivalents (mother's milk), and it can be dammed up or released—the imagery of the hydraulic model is apt (but cf. Heider [1976:78–79], who thinks otherwise). If these terms were translated into Freudian lingo, Federn (1952) would contrast subject-libido (energy available to self qua subject) and object-libido (energy available for investment in objects). Technically, I think, semen as a symbol among Sambia is used narcissistically (object libido invested in ego is narcissistic libido) in self-other interactions.

5. My use of the terms "commodity" and "fetishization" is not a homology with Marx's usage, which was tied, of course, to the specific analysis of capitalist production, characterized by the production of commodities that emerge in a market economy. By analogy, though, these terms are useful for my analysis. Marx argued that the results of human activity transform resources into items of use-value, which are assigned an exchange value by society; the worker's time is overshadowed by the supreme importance attached to the commodity, a process through which the capitalist extracts surplus labor as profit. The Sambia, however, acknowledge semen as a result of social relationships of production (e.g., as marriage bonds), and they tend also to stress the importance of semen as a fluid that can transform resources into more useful reproductive items or characteristics (e.g., babies, warrior strength). Nonetheless, the way that men value semen as a circulating commodity has a mystifying effect on these social relationships of production: They deny women's essential part in the reproductive process and claim that final biologic development in boys is achieved only through insemination. This mystification of the total reproductive process thus enables men to extract from others the resources needed to sustain and expand themselves and their clans and to control the related scarce resources in relation to women.

Finally, I do not imply by use of these terms that other Melanesian groups, or even all societies with ritualized homoeroticism, use semen as a key resource in the same way as Sambia or that they value it as a commodity in their systems of circulation in order to reproduce social entities. Elements or fluids such as semen and blood clearly have variable significance in Melanesian societies; our separable analyses of them must, in a sense, renegotiate their meaning in each cultural system.

I refer to them as "prudish lechers" [see Meggitt 1964]?) Semen, other body fluids, and sexuality are sensitive subjects: the data and viewpoints described below took years to accumulate, even though the presentation makes them seem obvious. (3) Sexual pleasure is seen by Sambia only in relation to another person; that is, there is no equivalent to the Western category "sex" (used in relation to masturbation, pornography, etc., as an indefinite noun; e.g., "Sex is . . . good, bad, fun, boring, etc."). Sex, in the Sambia sense, is only spoken of as *duvuno* (pushing or penetrating into) a boy's mouth or a woman's vagina, in the sense of a battle between one's erect penis (lit., *lakelu mulu*, "penis fight") and the sexual partner: "his bamboo orifice" (metaphor for boy's mouth) or "her thing down below" (euphemism for vagina). Again, the verb *duvuno* is not used for masturbation (which is not a cultural concept among the Sambia) and is only rarely applied to wet dreams, in which the dream images concern copulating with persons (e.g., always interpreted as spirits).[6] (4) When men refer to erotic desire (e.g., "I swallow my saliva [thinking about sex] with him/her"), they tend to refer to their sexual outlets as if their alter's orifice (mouth or vagina) were a fetishized object, like a commodity: "My penis is hungry" (i.e., they use "food" as a metaphor for their sexual needs). (5) All sexual intercourse may be defined as either work *(wumdu)* or play *(chemonyi),* but usually not both. For example, it is *wumdu* to produce a baby by copulating with a woman many times, but it is *chemonyi* to inseminate a boy once or twice, knowing he will not procreate. Insemination is also an action (e.g., like ritual, *pweiyu*) that mediates between work and play, sacred and profane. Let us examine each category in turn.

EROTIC PLAY

When Sambia use *chemonyi* (play) as a noun in relation to sexual intercourse, they normatively refer to sexual interaction as "erotic pleasure."[7] Semen is expended and orgasm *(imbimboogu)* achieved. I begin with this

6. By comparison, Sambia men do not use *duvono* in reference to what we would call "masturbation," which is not an explicit category in the Sambia language (the neo-Melanesian term for which means "peeling away the glans from penis"). Genital rubbing, in the limited sense (not necessarily erotic) of stimulation of the genitals, occurs. I have seen children do it, boys sometimes do it to bachelors (to produce erections for fellatio), and men sometimes report doing it to themselves in preparation for coitus with their wives. But what they mean is self-stimulation without ejaculation. This conceptual distinction is important and should not be misunderstood: spilling one's seed not only makes no sense to Sambia; it does not seem erotically exciting for them. Their fantasy life and erotic scripting have no place for it

7. There is no marked category for erotic play as such, but the English term "pleasure," as in sexual pleasure, would be an appropriate gloss. It is signified in ideology and social intercourse by

category not because it is most crucial—Sambia themselves would rank procreation first (Herdt 1981)—but because semen valuations are contingent upon orgasm, and anthropologists often ignore orgasm and its erotic manifestations, including erotic motivation, as native categories.

The most general cultural attributes of erotic play may be sketched as follows. First, the factor of the sex of one's partner: erotic play symbolically typifies male-male more than male-female erotic contacts. Male-male sexual transactions are culturally defined as behaviorally casual. Male-female contacts, normative only in marriage, are viewed (unless adulterous) as noncasual transactions aimed toward procreation. Erotic play is of course an aspect of all male-female sex, but it is not their most important one. Exclusive sexual access to a person seems in time to be inversely related to erotic play: a man's wife, as his sexual property, as Sambia see it, is less exciting than a boy or woman taken at first (i.e., as a virgin), or only once, on the sly. Age is a contributing factor here: sexual partners are perceived as having more "heat" and being more exciting the younger they are, especially females. A second factor is reciprocity: the more unequal the sexual partners (youth/boy), the more erotic play seems to define their contact culturally. (By contrast, the husband-wife dyad is the most symmetrical sexual relationship in Sambia culture [see chapter 4].) Third, sexual constancy, that is, greater frequency and permanence of sexual contacts, generally transforms sexual contacts from being erotic play into something else. Husband-wife contacts are the most constant, though not necessarily the most frequent, in Sambia sexual culture.

Erotic play may be defined also according to the social purpose of insemination. Erotic pleasure is attached to male-male and male-female sexual contacts and to both oral and vaginal intercourse.[8] But only heterosexual genital contacts result in procreation; all other sexual contacts fulfill other quasi-reproductive functions (e.g., growth of spouse) or are for erotic play. Since homoerotic fellatio cannot result in reproduction (marriage consummation), it becomes a demonstration of the older male's maturity, that is, of his power to masculinize a boy. But this valuation is significant only for donors; the boy-recipients value semen for their own growth.

---

chemonyi, "orgasm," and several conditions of sexual excitement (e.g., erection). "Sexual" has a wide range of physical and social connotations in English; erotic, however, refers specifically to that which stimulates sexual desire and arousal, so I prefer "erotic" in this context.

8. All sexual contacts are symbolically defined by the norm of penetration and ejaculation into an insertee's mouth (initiate or woman) or vagina, insemination resulting from (the belief that) the full seminal emission ingested/absorbed by the recipient's body (mouth or vagina as entrance).

What donors value also is the fellator's mouth as a sexual outlet: the social purpose is sexual release in appropriate relationships that demonstrate status.

Erotic play may be defined, lastly, according to the flow of a scarce commodity. Semen is viewed as a very scarce resource by Sambia, for, in reproduction, it is believed instrumental from conception to adulthood. It takes many inseminations to procreate: large expenditures of time, energy, semen. From this viewpoint, all male-female contacts may be construed as benefiting procreation (as we shall see next). Homoerotic play unevenly fits this paradigm. It is, after all, play, not work: procreative work is defined as producing babies. So how do homoerotic transactions benefit the donor? Essentially, homoerotic play is culturally defined as an unequal exchange of commodities: recipients acquire semen; donors get sexual services. This exchange is unequal because (as Sambia see it) a man's semen is being depleted, but he gets only erotic pleasure in return ("which is insubstantial"). Homoerotic activity thus creates a dilemma for bachelors, which is perhaps why some engage in it less frequently as they approach marriage. Homoerotic play is, however, less depleting than heterosexual intercourse (work), which is, in part, why bachelors are less worried about replenishing the semen lost during their early homoerotic activities compared with later sex with their wives.

PROCREATION

Procreation is defined as genital-to-genital heterosexual contacts that lead to the birth of offspring. Sambia regard vaginal intercourse as primarily focused on the production of babies. Oral insemination prepares a wife's body for making babies by strengthening her as well as by precipitating her menarche (if she has not already attained it). Fellatio also prepares her for lactation by semen's being transformed into breast milk. Oral sexual contacts are not believed to make babies in anyone; only vaginal intercourse does that. All heterosexual genital intercourse contributes directly to procreation in one's marriage, and all sexual contacts may be viewed as contributing directly to the recipients' procreative competence (wife or boy-fellator) or reproduction (wife).[9]

Procreation is jurally defined as resulting from genital-to-genital sexual contacts between formally married husband and wife. Since heterosexual

---

9. Oral heterosexual contacts indirectly help procreation; see below under section on growth.

contact is not morally or jurally allowed outside marriage, privilege of sexual access to a woman's body is restricted by marriage; exclusive sexual rights belong to her husband. Likewise, exclusive access to a husband's body and semen, after the birth of their first child, is his wife's right (which view is a key argument women use to resist polygyny). Traditionally, only infant betrothal and bride-service marriage (which was rare) required the transfer of goods or services to the donors bestowing a wife. Infant betrothal, though, required meat and small food prestations only, whereas bride-service required more wealth, in addition to the bridegroom's years-long work for his prospective affines. Sister exchange requires no exchange other than that of the women. Since infant betrothal is preferred and sister exchange marriages far outnumber those of bride-service, marriage transactions are largely unrelated to bride-wealth.

Genital-to-genital intercourse creates a fetus by successively "injecting" semen into a woman's womb. After initial oral sexual contacts, a woman's body is viewed as ready to procreate. One instance of vaginal intercourse does not a fetus make: Sambia have no notion of conception in our Western scientific sense. The womb is the container and transformer of semen. It changes semen into fetal tissue: primarily bone and skin but also muscle and internal organs. The semen coagulates inside the birth sac; this "biological" process is central to fetal development, and its imagery is important in social thought (Herdt 1981:167–72ff.). Womb and umbilical blood also become circulatory blood in the fetus; they do not produce any hard body parts of the child, which result only from semen. Social ideology thus defines procreation as productive work (not erotic play) in two senses: it is hard work to feed enough semen into a woman's womb to create a fetus; and it is hard work for the woman's body to change this semen into a whole baby, sapping her own blood and carrying the child in her body for so long.

Blood and semen also differentially contribute to the sex of the offspring and his or her gender differentiation. First, both parents can magically influence the fetus's sex by ingesting various plants. They do this both because Sambia ideally prefer a boy as the firstborn and because they want to make the infant more attractive. Second, it takes more semen to create a girl than a boy. Two other beliefs explain why, and they pertain to the procreative/economic productive capacities of males versus females (i.e., in social reproduction). The most important is that females do more hard work (i.e., garden work) all the time; therefore, the female fetus "pulls" more semen from the mother to make itself. (A magical elaboration of this idea is that since females think about garden work constantly, their fetal thought anticipates and drains more semen strength in preparation.) The other belief is that a female fetus has a *tingu* (menstrual-blood organ), which makes the mother's vagina hot and therefore drains off more semen from the father during sexual contacts that create the fetus. During womb life, the sexes receive blood in differential amounts too. Essentially, girls have some of their mother's menstrual blood transmitted to their own menstrual-blood organs in utero. Later, during postnatal growth, this blood stimulates girls' psychobiological feminization (sexual and gender differentiation). Boys, by contrast, have no blood transmitted to their inactive *tingus*. Nor do they receive their father's semen for use in their own semen organs; father's semen in both male and female offspring merely creates fetal tissue.

Marriage is fully consummated after the birth of a child. Procreation results in final but distinct initiation ceremonies for the husband-father and wife-mother alike. The new father and his clan bestow a meat prestation on the wife's cognatic kin, especially patrilateral female kin, and her ritual sponsor, in public village ceremonies. Because procreation defines full adulthood for men and women, childless adults are not perceived as full persons. Nonetheless, all childlessness in marriage is attributed to barrenness in the woman or contraceptive sorcery by other men (usually thought to be envious fellow villagers who wanted the woman for themselves). Sambia men dogmatically deny the possibility of sterility in a husband (see also Read 1955); indeed, such is never discussed in social discourse, and the only category for sterility is "barren woman" *(kwoliku)*. Childlessness is thus an acceptable reason for taking a second wife but not for divorce. Once a marriage is consummated, it is contracted for life; a woman is rarely taken back by the donor. When warfare occurs, a woman's ties with her natal group (i.e., enemies) are severed. Divorce is thus extremely rare and usually instigated by a husband over his wife's perceived adultery; their children become jural members of the father's clan. And so only death breaks the marital bond.

GROWTH

Sambia believe that biologic growth in humans results from ingesting semen and equivalent substances (mother's milk, pandanus nuts). Sexual intercourse for growth is described as *pinu pungooglumonjapi* ("pushing" to "grow" him or her, where *pinu* is an alternate verbal form of *duvuno*). This idiomatic form may be applied to both male-male and male-female sexual transactions.

The value of semen for human growth comes in successive stages, which differ according to the mode of semen transmission and one's sex. Initial growth for every fetus occurs through semen accumulations in the mother's womb. Postnatal growth in babies results mainly from breast-feeding. A woman's body is again treated as a biologic transformer of semen in this regard: a man's inseminations (especially oral) amass in and are transformed by his wife's breasts into mother's milk (*nu-tokeno,* breast food). After weaning, growth is aided by eating pandanus nuts, which are seasonal but are treated as nearly equal nourishment to that of mother's milk. (The productive source of this nut food is one's father's trees and his hard work in tending and scaling to procure the nuts.) Meat fed to children also contributes smaller increments to growth. Following weaning, though, girls continue to grow without further aids, whereas boys falter, staying weak and puny.

Male growth after weaning comes mostly from homoerotic inseminations following initiation. This semen-nourishment form is male *monjapi'u,* which men liken to breast-feeding (Herdt 1981:234–36).[10] Oral sexual contacts feed semen into a boy's body, distributing semen to his maturing skin, bones, and skull and producing changes toward masculinization (eventuating in puberty). The bulk of ingested semen goes to the boy's semen organ, where it accumulates as a pool. This pool is drawn on after puberty for two purposes: it produces pubescent secondary sex traits, especially muscle, body hair, and a mature penis; and it provides semen for later sexual contacts. (The first sign of surplus semen in the body comes from wet dreams.)

Girls require and are permitted no inseminations until marriage. Postmarital oral sexual contacts in cases of marriage before menarche provide a young wife's body with semen to stimulate the final changes necessary for childbearing. Men also argue, as noted above, that women need semen to create breast milk. (Some women dispute these views and say that a woman's body creates its milk; however, other women disagree.)

In sum, semen creates biologic growth directly in initiates and wives through sexual contact, primarily fellatio, whereas it creates growth indirectly in the fetus and newborn through being transformed by a woman's body into fetal tissue and milk. For spouses, then, growth and procreation are concepts that refer to different aspects of the same sexual contacts. For the offspring, as third-party semen recipient, growth is vital after birth, and long postpartum taboos prohibit marital sexual intercourse for fear the infant will be harmed (be stunted or ugly, an outcome that would shame the parents, especially the father, who would be viewed as lacking sexual restraint). In homoerotic activity, men offer boys the normative goal that

10. *Monjapi'u* is shortened by men from *pinu pungooglumonjapi.*

semen "grows" them. But from the donor's standpoint, though initiates' growth does provide vicarious long-term confirmation of the fellated's manhood, a fellator's growth is not of direct importance to a bachelor's personhood. Rather, homoerotic play takes precedence as the fellated's motive; the boy's growth is a latent social function of the bachelor's behavior (and is, I think, often a rationalization on the men's part).

STRENGTH

Strength *(jerungdu)* is one of the key concepts of insemination in Sambia culture; we shall here examine only its implications for semen transmission and thereby human maturation.

"Strength" is absolutely derived from semen and its equivalents: mother's milk and pandanus nuts. But more than those substances, semen masculinizes a male's body; there is no substitute for it. Unlike procreation or growth valuations, strength can be obtained directly only through semen. In Sambia thought, there is a tendency to play down strength and stress growth as characteristic of the breast-feeding relationship. Suckling milk makes a baby grow, but it is much less associated with strengthening it. Semen in the womb forms the skeletal fetus; nursing helps create the baby's teeth, the hardening of its skin and skull. But milk is more for growth. The strong results of milk, Sambia believe, are transformations of semen: the mother ingests semen, which her breasts convert into milk. The strong part of milk is also more crucial for male infants, but it alone will not masculinize them. Thus, strength is not intrinsically produced but is rather derived from the mother-infant relationship, itself a product of marriage. In male subjectivity, however, strength is a transactional product that makes use of the father's secret sexual acquisition of semen from other men, which he feeds to his wife, whose body, in turn, has a natural capacity to store the fluid and turn it into breast food that strengthens and matures the infant.

As with growth, a father can indirectly add small amounts of strength over the years following weaning by providing meat and pandanus nuts to children. Cassowary meat, too, which may be eaten only by males, has fat *(moo-nugu)* that sometimes is treated as a second-rate semen equivalent (Herdt 1981:110). (Other kinds of fat, e.g., from pigs or eels, are never likened to semen.) But these are small increments.

If one follows the semen cycle, we see a chain of links in which men strengthen people: husband strengthens wife through initial fellatio; father strengthens baby through mother's milk; bachelor strengthens initiate through fellatio. Symbolically, homoerotic fellatio provides the key ritualized strengthening of boys' postpartum bodies. As I have emphasized elsewhere, male insemination is chiefly seen as making a boy grow, the perceived outcome of which is strength. Culturally, the act of feeding/inseminating is equivalent to the verbal category *monjapi'u,* male nursing, the social/perceptual outcome of which is the state of being *jerungdu,* as seen in both its physical and psychosocial manifestations: large size, attractiveness, valor, forceful speech, sexual potency, and many social achievements, including progeny.

There is another secret source of strength that is important in male thought and that concerns the nonhuman sources for replenishing semen expended in sexual intercourse. Analytically, this semen valuation might be treated as separate from the "strength" concept because of its ontogenetic status in the male life cycle (adults give semen away and then must replace it to stay strong). But Sambia do not think of the matter in this way, for this replenishment is seen simply as a further extension of strength building. Yet, since this replenishment practice is learned later in ritual life and comes from trees, not men, we shall here examine it as an auxiliary strengthening process.

In semen transactions, one person's loss is another's gain: semen, which embodies strength, depletes the donor, whose strength therefore diminishes. Fear of semen depletion is an important theme in male ritual discourse and ideology. (It is registered, too, in individual sexual aberrations [see chapter 5]). Concern with too-frequent semen loss inhibits initial homoerotic contacts, bachelors being cautioned to go easy. (Here, again, fellateds and fellators are at odds.) Yet bachelors' fears are not great, and the early use of ritual mechanisms for semen replenishment in fellateds is played down. Among married men, the situation is different. A key pragmatic focus of fifth- and sixth-stage initiation ceremonies is teaching about secret ingestion of white milk sap from trees, which is believed to replace semen lost to women. (Pandanus nuts are another semen replacement, though of less importance because they are not always available.) This milk sap comes from several forest trees and vines, and the sap is referred to as *iaamoonaalyu,* "tree mother's milk."

Trees are, in general, regarded as if they and their products were female, for example, as with pandanus trees. Myth also "genderizes" them this way (Herdt 1981). There seems little doubt that the imagery and symbolization of the adult man's semen replenishment is not, then, symbolic insemination but rather that of symbolic breast-feeding. This interpretation is confirmed by men's drinking sap from long aerial roots of pandanus nut trees: the trees are ritually referred to as "females," and the roots are likened to women's breasts. We see, therefore, that semen comes at first from homo-erotic fellatio, later to be replaced by milk sap (and, to a lesser extent, by pandanus nuts and cassowary fat), and semen, in turn, is transformed into milk and fetal tissue by women. At bottom, male ideology seems to postulate that these forest trees create new semen.

SPIRITUAL TRANSMISSION

The final category of semen valuations I shall refer to as spiritual transmission, or "spirituality" for short, though it is not a marked category in Sambia culture or language. Spirituality is, in our terms, an animistic composite of both "natural" and "supernatural" elements. These elements include, most noticeably, spirit familiars *(numelyu)* of various sorts, believed to be transmitted (not transformed) through semen for males (and through blood for females). The reproduction of spiritual elements in individuals and groups is a social outcome of sexual intercourse over which individuals have little control.

Before I describe spirit familiars, two other matters deserve mention. The first is the concept of soul *(koogu)*, a spiritual aspect of personhood that is related to sexuality and parenting. There is no clearly formulated theory of the soul's origin in individual development. Some men attribute it only to the father's semen. Others say it is a combination of semen and material in the mother's womb (they do not specify which parts of semen and/or blood). Though the womb is important, some people attribute the birth of a child's soul not to fetal life but to postnatal socialization. Men normatively relate the father's semen to the child's soul in both sexes, especially boys. This ambiguity is no doubt an expression of all persons' normative blood ties to mother and matrilateral kin. Yet, since the soul survives death and becomes a ghost, forest spirit (big man), or hamlet spirit (prominent woman) haunting its clan's territory, its patrilineal origin and afterlife influence seem clear in sociopolitical organization. The skull and bones of the deceased also become powerful weapons in sorcery and are most efficacious when used by biologic kinsmen, sons especially. In both cases—souls and bones—spiritual essences of semen are thought to survive death. The other concept is "thought," or *koontu,* which I gloss as personhood. "Thought" is the totality of one's experience, beliefs, and knowledge. Personhood is mainly a product of social training; its relation to body substance and biologic inheritance is less certain. Socialization is its chief source, however, and this means that both mother and father influence personhood.

Without question the most significant semen valuation for spirituality is

the child's inheritance of spirit familiars. Transmission of familiars is ideologically clear and sex linked. Boys inherit only their father's familiars via
his semen. Girls inherit their mother's familiars through her blood.
(Mother's milk, a semen derivative, is ignored in this domain.) Genealogical inheritance of clan familiars (i.e., totems) among males seems to derive
from the semen that creates a son's body tissue. Later, males acquire other
familiars attracted to them through ritual ceremonies: the nature of this attraction again implies that father's semen is instrumental. Shamanic familiars, transmitted through semen from father to son in the mother's womb,
are a clear case of necessary patrilineal inheritance required for legitimate
performance of the shamanic role (Herdt 1977), though some women
shamans claim inheritance of father's familiars. Other familiars, both personal and clan related, ensure longevity, spiritual protection, or strength.
Male ideology generally denies women such blessings from their natal
clan familiars. Men may have their familiars stolen unwittingly by male
children, which leads to sickness or premature death. Homoerotic inseminations do not transmit familiars to semen recipients (cf. Schieffelin
1976). Finally, men's ingestion of milk sap from trees is consistent with the
perpetuation of their clan familiars (though this is not fully conscious in
Sambia thought).

Semen Value in Social Transactions

Who may and should have sexual intercourse with what categories of persons in Sambia society? What are the principles of these social transactions?
In this section I examine social action in relation to the cultural ideas of semen valuation already described. The sociology of semen transactions involves two viewpoints. First, there are direct semen transactions between
persons resulting from sexual intercourse. Second, there are indirect semen
transactions with a third party, believed to occur by transforming semen
into something else by a second party, whether the source of semen is human or nonhuman (i.e., trees), though the semen transformers are always
humans. A subcategory of indirect inseminations may be seen as delayed
exchanges between social groups, semen being returned to donor groups
via former recipients in the subsequent generation. I shall study each of
these types in turn.

DIRECT SEMEN TRANSACTIONS

All sexual contacts are restricted by exogamous taboos and social norms. Sexual contacts are permissible only between unrelated people; that is, those related through common cognatic links, especially agnates, are forbidden sexual partners. Marriage should be arranged between different clans, preferably of different villages. Statistically, though, up to 50 percent of all marriages are contracted within large, consolidated hamlets; father's sister's daughter marriage is normatively permitted in delayed-exchange marriage contracts, and mother's brother's daughter marriage, though frowned on, occurs rarely, when no alternate wife can be found (Herdt 1981). Homoerotic contacts are likewise prohibited between all clansmen, matrilateral kin, age mates, and with ritual sponsors. (Homoerotic infractions occur, however, as between matrilateral cross-cousins or distant kin not normally encountered, though these are unusual.) Male initiates' ritual sponsors are called "mother's brother," a social title, since only some sponsors are actual or classificatory mother's brother. Nonetheless a boy's sponsor becomes, in effect, a pseudo-kinsman who combines both maternal and paternal attributes, making it very wrong for any sexual contact to occur between them. In general, all sexual transactions are highly regulated and tend to occur with people of other hamlets (who are potential or real enemies), so sexual relations distinguish kin from non-kin and friendly from hostile persons.

In direct sexual transactions, all the above cultural ideas of semen value come into play, but the domain of erotic play is especially important. Erotic play is a social motive and goal that applies mainly to adult men. Their motive for erotic play is orgasm. Boy-fellators never have orgasms in homoerotic play. And men deny, in general, that women experience orgasm, though they believe women are lascivious and enjoy sexual play.

Men's enjoyment of erotic play changes through the life cycle. Some older boy-fellators do experience vicarious erotic pleasure from homoerotic fellatio, as indicated by their reports (near puberty) of their own erections while sucking a bachelor, or by certain feelings or body sensations during fellatio. Bachelors inseminate in homoerotic play to (in local idiom) "straighten their penises," that is, to reduce sexual tension/frustration, or to "feel *ilaiyu*" (here meaning pleasure) from orgasm. Men get erotic pleasure from copulating with their wives, first through fellatio, and then in genital-to-genital intercourse, which most men favor over fellatio. To repeat: male-female oral sexual contacts, like those with boys, are regarded more as erotic play.

Male social ideology defines both homoerotic and heteroerotic play as transactions in which the older male is always the inseminator. No role reversals are ever situationally permitted. The older male is viewed as the socially active party who should control the behavior interchanges that lead to the insemination. A man's control over sexual contacts is established by the social norms regulating the behavioral conditions of sexual intercourse. Men are physically bigger than boys and most women. During intercourse the man either stands over his fellator (who kneels) or lies on top of his wife (in the missionary position), methods that allow a man instant freedom to withdraw from body contact at will. Men are also usually years older than their insertees, either boys or women (even though, curiously, men regard younger wives as of like age and maturity [see Herdt 1981:177, 181]). Again, these interactions are defined as unequal: women and boys get semen; men get erotic pleasure. Most men are (consciously) uninterested in the erotic arousal of either boys or women, so direct sexual transactions emphasize the sexual excitement of the inserter.

In spite of the men's view, the concept "erotic play" admits of some social reciprocity between all sexual partners. Men recognize that women have erotic interests; for instance, sexually experienced women are rhetorically described as lascivious harlots consumed by insatiable erotic appetites (Herdt 1981:187). Perhaps this dogma is the men's response to knowing that women favor certain men over others as mates. Men also know that boys joke about fellatio among themselves and that initiates favor some bachelors over others in regard to the amount and taste of their semen.[11] Bachelors likewise favor certain boys over others: those who are more attractive to them are either more or less sexually aggressive and/or willing to perform fellatio. These reciprocal aspects thus underscore the frame of play, and they are not found in notions of sex for procreation, growth, strength, or spirituality, all of which stem from insemination.

Since semen is highly valued as a means to valuable social ends—personal strength, marriage, offspring, personhood—it should be conserved and wisely spent. Men assume that women and boys desire their semen for those social ends; no other motive is searched for in understanding why insertees engage in sexual intercourse. (We know the situation is more com-

---

11. Sambia have invented an art we could call semenology: they are fascinated with the forms, textures, and tastes of semen, which they discuss frequently, like wine tasters. Among boys, a fellated's penis size is not accorded much importance, whereas his seminal fluid, amount of flow, etc., is. (Privately and unconsciously, though, penis size is sometimes important.) Among women, the situation seems the reverse: a man's penis size (and sexual prowess) is important— women prefer men with big penises—whereas semenology is less significant, or so say men.

plex. For instance, boys must at first be coerced into fellatio, but men also know this.) The seeming personal conflict on men's part, at least in homoerotic contacts, is that they get only sexual release in return for their semen. They recognize this in idioms that depict the penis as having a mind of its own: for example, "that no-good man down there [penis] gets up and we follow its nose" (euphemism for glans penis), as if men inseminate from sexual impulse, almost against their will. Here, then, is a perceived conflict between private impulses and public norms.

This conflict is felt in two other ways. First, women are prized as sexual outlets more than boys. Women are owned: this ownership is a contributing dynamic to the sexual excitement of Sambia men. Power is a critical part of this excitement. Male-female relationships are, in general, filled with more power than are male-male contacts, for heterosexuality is more highly regulated. Sexually, women are also more powerful, for they can contaminate as well as deplete, and women deplete semen more than do boys. Moreover, sexual impulses leading to adultery are a tremendous social problem in Sambia society (see below). Second, when orgasm occurs, it is treated as being beyond conscious control. Wet dreams are the best example. For women, breast-feeding may also apply: some women report that they experience *imbimboogu,* which they liken to orgasm, when feeding, though it is not clear yet what this social labeling of their experience means (Herdt and Stoller 1990: chapter 6).[12] All these points support the conclusion that individual sexual impulses are stronger than the need for semen constraint in hetero- versus homoerotic relations

Underlying this conflict is the fact that sex for erotic play is the only sexual mode that produces no social advantage to the semen donor. Because all ejaculation is debilitating and semen is a male's most valuable resource, all sexual contacts are viewed as a "careful metering of semen" (Gell 1975:252). Seen this way, erotic play represents what Gell (1975) refers to as a "nemesis of reproductivity": it makes no sense in the scheme of things, even though it is personally pleasurable. All other categories of direct sexual transactions may be defined as work, not play, for this reason; like other forms of work (e.g., gardening), sex for procreation, growth, and so forth produces social products. One's semen is spent to reproduce heirs and perpetuate one's

---

12. Sexual behavior in the imagery of dreams is viewed as erotic play: wet dreams are pleasurable but wasteful erotic play with spirits, who may wish to harm the dreamer. Breast-feeding, even though women say they experience *imbimboogu,* is never conceived of as erotic play by women, as far as I know, though breast-feeding is apparently a common image and form of scripting for men's erotic daydreams (vis-à-vis fellatio performed on them)

clan. With this view in mind I will now contrast other cultural ideas pertaining to hetero- and homoerotic transactions.

The idea of procreation applies only to male-female sexual contacts. In native theory all heterosexual contacts, oral or vaginal, contribute to a woman's reproductive competence. In practice, however, only early marital sex is treated this way: oral sex is infrequent after a woman bears children. My impression is that both men and women in later years prefer genital-to-genital contact (and I think most women always prefer vaginal sex). Though homoerotic transactions are not procreative (but cf. individual boys' fears of becoming pregnant [Herdt 1981] and similar beliefs about male pregnancy elsewhere [Meigs 1976; Williams 1936a]), semen in boys does assist in becoming reproductively competent adults.

The concepts of growth and strength are applied to both homo- and heteroerotic transactions. In theory, boy-fellators as semen recipients use sexual contact first to grow and then to get strong. Until third-stage initiation this norm holds; youths are thereafter accorded physical maturity and may no longer serve as insertees. Growth and strength apply differentially to women as semen recipients. Essentially, all heterosexual fellatio makes a woman grow and strengthens her until she is a mother. Later oral sex does not make a woman grow, for she is viewed as biologically mature. It does replenish her strength, however—a sort of perpetual fountain of youth men must give up after bachelorhood. Indeed, men complain that women are healthier and outlive them because of this ready source of orally ingested strength. (In this sense, a wife is like a boy-fellator.) Vaginal sex is generally believed to contribute neither growth nor strength to a woman; instead, indirectly, a man's semen creates and strengthens fetus and infant.

Finally, the concept of spirituality applies unequally to direct sexual transactions. No transmission of spirit familiars occurs between males and females. None is imparted to one's wife; she is simply one source of the transmission of soul and familiars to one's offspring. Again, men believe that only sons inherit the father's familiars (either indirectly, through semen via the mother, or directly, through cult ceremonies that call forth one's father's familiars after his death). A daughter's familiars come only from her mother, but her soul is linked (the notion is vague) to her father and his clan territory, though not irrevocably.[13] Moreover, there is ab-

13. However, there is ambiguity here, since a woman who lives in another hamlet (her husband's) long enough becomes after death a ghost or hamlet spirit who may haunt there rather than return to her natal hamlet or clan territory. Even so, the souls of females are not a subject in which men place much interest.

solutely no sense that a boy-fellator acquires his familiars from any bachelor-fellated; but the idea is neither here nor there, since Sambia never consider the possibility.[14] Conceptually, though, we should underline that their folk model of spiritual transmission keeps familiars discreetly in clans and firmly embedded in the man's procreative role. Here we see a firm separation between spirituality and sexuality, on the levels both of ideology and of social action. The division between spiritual and material reproduction in marriage is especially notable (see Tuzin 1982).

There is one other notion, which we may define as spiritual, that involves direct homoerotic transactions: *kwolaalyuwaku,* a highly secret, multivalent ritual concept referring to "masculine decorations and ritual paraphernalia," which also doubles as a ritual secret pseudonym for semen.[15] (It is also close to *kweiaalyu-waku,* meaning, "sun's white grease," an alternate for cassowary fat *[kaiouwugu moo-nugu].*) The semantic referent of the semen aspect is esoteric, yet it clearly signifies a collective semen pool. This pool is perceived as the semen contained in the bodies of all men living within neighboring hamlets: it therefore reflects the ritual cult and the confederacy. The idea is that boys have access to this pool, which they can tap into through homosexual insemination, strengthening themselves. Symbolically, then, *kwolaalyuwaku* is a metaphor for the men's collective sense of manliness and their intergenerational transmission of semen in secret and political ways.

But on the individual level, the concept is bi-directional. I was long skeptical of certain men's statements that it strengthened themselves to inseminate many boys. How could this be? Men argue that just as a boy draws strength from numerous men, who deposit their semen in his reserve for future use, so men are kept healthy by having their semen safely "contained" in many boys, who are likened to a sort of magical string of semen depositories for one's substance, spread throughout society. Should a man or any of his semen recipients get sick, other recipients remain strong and healthy. And since recipients harbor parts of one's semen (strength) inside them, so, too, one is kept healthy (in sympathetic/contagious magical thought). A woman lacks this protection: she is not a cult initiate, and her semen comes

14. Cf. the Great Papuan Plateau societies, especially Kaluli (Schieffelin 1976:127–28; 1982), which have institutionalized such beliefs about homosexual insemination (see also Kelly 1976; Sørum 1984). On the individual level, Sambia boys report fantasies and beliefs that make it clear that identification is a part of their homoerotic experience, including, for instance, notions that incorporating a fellated's semen may influence his personality traits.

15. *Kwol* marks male; *aalyu,* water; *waku,* a type of strong betel nut and a cover term for certain decorations. Sometimes the term is shortened to the secret name, *kweiwaku,* which men use explicitly to refer to "the semen of all men."

from only one man, her husband. Nor is a man likewise protected by inseminating women or creating children: the concept is not extended beyond homoerotic contacts. Thus, semen not only bestows but also maintains strength, the only evidence known to me that directly explains why homoerotic insemination is felt to be less depleting than that of heterosexuality. In this ritual sense, boy-inseminating practices are placed within a spiritual framework and are opposed to heterosexuality and marriage.

All the above sexual contacts concern normatively appropriate semen transactions between donors and recipients. Illicit heteroerotic transactions (which includes all premarital intercourse and extramarital adultery) reveal the social boundary of ideas about exclusive jural claims over a man's semen. All adultery is severely condemned; a man may use violence against a wife suspected of it. Therefore, it is hidden until discovered, when the spouses fight. If a husband is accused of adultery or of wanting to take a second wife, the fight is called *kweikoonmulu,* literally "semen fight." Semen fights entail dreadful cursing and brawls. This adultery can be seen as "stealing another woman's semen," though it involves much more, of course. Accusations of a wife's adultery (which is rarer, for Sambia treat adulterous women harshly) also concern semen in two ways: fears that a husband's penis has been contaminated by intercourse with his wife's vagina after sex with another man (thought to bring him sickness), and questions about the wife's lover's semen contributions to a future child. In sum, adultery reveals that marriage bestows the right of exclusive spousal control over semen and insemination exchange as scarce resources.

What are the social effects of these direct sexual transactions on group relationships? Let us examine the most general latent and manifest functions of sexual contacts in the same generation. First, semen flow mirrors marriage transactions between groups. Semen may only be normatively transacted between persons of groups who can intermarry; that is, homoerotic contact is forbidden with matrilineal kin and clansmen. The same clan that donates a wife thus has clansmen who are appropriate homoerotic partners (cf. Kelly 1976). Affines of the same generation (e.g., brothers-in-law) are especially appropriate homoerotic contacts. The paradigm of this affinal homoerotic bond would be a young man who marries a younger woman and who can inseminate her younger initiate brother, either consanguineal or classificatory wife's brother (see Serpenti 1984; and Sørum 1984). This man inseminates his wife to make her grow and to strengthen her, and to procreate, and may (along with his fellow clansmen) inseminate her younger brother for erotic play, the effect of which is to help a boy grow and to strengthen him. These sexual transactions would define a man and his clan as semen donors, while his wife and brother-in-law would be recipients. Yet ego's clan is also a wife recipient from his younger homoerotic partner's donor clan. This set of social transactions is common in Sambia life.

Second, marital/sexual bonds tend to create closer political ties between unrelated groups. Sambia generally engage in marriage and boy-inseminating practices with propinquitous groups in the same confederacy. One does not receive or give semen to intertribal enemies. Affinal ties, in particular, create closer political affiliations for mutual defense between and within hamlets. Affinal ties also establish marriage contractual obligations and sentimental bonds that persist into the next generation, influencing alignments among hamlets.

Third, semen metaphorically defines political power: inseminators are more powerful than recipients in virtually every sense. All male persons eventually serve as both direct semen donors and as recipients. All females are always direct recipients or indirect donors—to their offspring—whereas males constitute a category of both direct givers and takers. And their sexual status, of course, flip-flops during the male life cycle. Symbolically, I think, Sambia define the administration of semen as a masculine act, whereas the taking in of semen makes the recipient into an object of desire. One of the manifest functions of the secrecy of homoerotic fellatio is to hide from women the shame men feel at having earlier performed in this feminine way (Herdt 1981: chapter 8). A latent function of homoerotic secrecy is to rationalize and disguise men's use of boys as a sexual outlet. By the same token, the ritual secret of insemination growth and strength unites all males as a category against all females. This social link, which also mystifies the nature of male-female relationships, politically reinforces male power and thereby perpetuates the men's ritual cult.

INDIRECT SEMEN TRANSACTIONS

The mode of social transaction in indirect semen transactions is based on the symbolic principle that semen is transmitted to someone whose body transforms it into something else useful to a third party. The paradigm is the nuclear family triad: father-mother-child. The alternative form of indirect insemination views men as replenishing their semen from tree sap, which their bodies turn into semen: tree-man-semen recipient. Having already described direct sexual contacts, I can easily outline these semen transformations.

We have seen that sexual intercourse between spouses involves all the cultural meanings of semen value except spirituality. Now when we examine the effects of a woman's husband's semen on her prospective infant, the woman's role as transformer is clarified at two developmental points. First, to repeat, her orally ingested semen is transformed into breast milk. This milk is stored for the infant's nourishment after birth. Subsequent semen from vaginal intercourse is stored and transformed in the woman, converted by her womb into fetal tissue, as we saw. Both the intrauterine formation of the child and its postnatal breast-feeding are indirect products of the father's semen.

In this type of indirect transaction there is a subtle application of cultural beliefs to action. Erotic play occurs between the spouses, leading to procreation, but the concept is not extended to the transformative outcome, since the father never has sexual intercourse with his offspring. Indeed the paradigm of sex as work suggests that woman, as wife/mother, is the means of production men need to effect children's adult reproductive competence. Semen is indispensable for reproduction, yet so is a woman's body (breasts and womb). Moreover, no matter how much the men attempt to claim procreation as solely of their production, a wife is vital for social reproduction. She not only gives birth but also nourishes and cares for heirs, transforming semen into the strength of clans. She also transmits her husband's spirit familiars to sons and her own to daughters. Both parents contribute to the child's personhood or thought, but men believe only they produce its soul. Following weaning, a girl is believed to mature on her own, but a boy needs more semen for growth and strength. Thus, a boy indirectly taps the semen pool of his father through homoerotic contacts with other men who substitute, in his father's place, as ritual semen donors, motivated out of sexual play. The sexual cycle is completed when this son becomes an inseminator, and his sister is traded for his wife, sister and brother having reached sexual maturity.

The other form of indirect transaction consists in men's ingesting the white tree saps. It may seem odd, here, to juxtapose this secret ritual practice with reproduction. But Sambia male ideology treats tree-sap ingestion as a part of the whole adult cycle of reproduction; and, in my experience, men directly associate tree-sap drinking as a normal and regular link in a chain of psychosexual activities that are as much a part of everyday life as their own eroticism. Drinking tree sap is not actually taught until a man's last initiation, when he is a new father. Thereafter, men regularly ingest it but always in abundance after sexual intercourse with their wives. Men are thus preserving their biologic maleness (semen) and restoring their strength. Not erotic play, growth, or procreation as cultural ideas is applied to contacts with trees. Drinking tree sap simply regenerates semen and preserves health against depletion. So this ritual practice may be considered a defensive tactic—and the more so because it is secret—yet it is more than that.

Drinking tree sap also has a latent creative function: creating new semen that flows into the societal pool of semen. Sambia men do not view it this way: to them, drinking tree sap merely replaces what they have personally lost. But, besides that, they see their society as a closed system, its resources limited for reasons I shall not here detail. Suffice it to say that their religion is animistic and their ethos dominated by warrior values that recognize adulthood as a personal achievement that is, nonetheless, carefully nurtured through a strict ritual system regulating people, marriage, sexuality, and semen. This view is predicated on a cyclical model of time (see Leach 1961); seasonal movements, ceremonies, and customary transactions unfold in the round. Sambia do not recognize that their population is now expanding or that the concomitant stress on their resources (means of production) may be increasing. Nonetheless, men believe that they expend semen and that they get more from trees. Let us now consider this view for their use of the concept of spirituality.

The trees from which men acquire sap are on clan territory. The land itself is one's main material inheritance from previous generations; it is held in agnatic corporate estate, though men own specific tracts of it, from which they exploit resources (game, pandanus nuts, milk-sap trees). Land is coveted and defended against other groups; it is central to a clan's residential and territorial organization. It is also guarded by clan spirits. Ritual practices, too, are a social heritage, customs valued in themselves and for group identity, having been handed down from previous generations. It seems obvious, therefore, that the social ideology of trees provisioning new semen through the bodies of clansmen is a latent function of the regeneration of patrilineality.

Patrifiliation thus provides land and trees, ritual practices, and the social personae needed to transform tree sap into semen. Tree sap without an adult male body is just tree sap. The male body—the product of a long process of procreation with women and homoerotic insemination from men, of magical ritual treatment making it fertile and procreatively potent—is the instrument that regenerates society. Tree sap maintains maleness and masculine personhood. It regenerates one's clan, its patriline and hamlet-based warriorhood, and thus the community itself. These social identities are conceptually placed, in time and space, through concentric social networks based on a magical notion of successive degrees of purest patrilineal substance. Hence, male ideology claims that father, son, and clansmen are of one semen substance, one common origin place, one residential location—all elements of genealogical ancestry that fans out to embrace a pool of spirit familiars and ancestral spirits, the semen sustaining all. Whether the trees are seen as beginning or finishing this process is beside the point: Sambia have a cyclic view of their system that makes tree sap pivotal in a greater chain of being. What is the nature of semen value in this whole system?

DELAYED EXCHANGE

The final category of indirect semen transactions concerns exchanges across generations between groups. This subject is very complex indeed, so I shall merely sketch the contours of the system of intergroup relationships. What do groups give and receive? And do their exchanges of semen balance out across time?

The key principle of delayed exchange is that groups who exchange women also exchange semen through homoerotic contacts. Group A takes a woman from group B. They become affines. Their initiated males of different cohorts at different life-cycle stages engage in homoerotic intercourse both ways (giving and receiving semen). Children of groups A and B become matrilateral kin in the following generation. In delayed-exchange (infant betrothal or bride-service) marriage, group A later returns a woman to group B. In direct exchange (sister exchange) they will not. Marriage between generation 2 of these groups is frowned on, except in the case of delayed-exchange infant betrothal to father's sister's daughter, that is, a daughter of group A goes back to group B. Yet actual father's sister's daughter marriage (addressed as "sister" by her mother's brother's son) is also disliked; more commonly this woman is traded for another woman from a different group. Homoerotic contacts between generation 2 are also forbidden. In effect, generation 2 shares ties of blood and semen: boys of group A were formed from the blood of a woman of group B, and their body tissue came from their father, some of whose own semen may have come from males of group B. These boys (of group A) must turn to a third, unrelated group, to take both a wife and semen.

What do groups A and B exchange? Group A gets a woman as garden producer and maker of babies. She produces heirs to perpetuate group A. Group B gets food gifts and a promise of a return woman (possibly her daughter) in the next generation. Boys of group A get semen from bachelors of group B and vice versa. Homoerotic insemination ensures masculinization and adult reproductive competence. Boys of groups A and B may receive ritual sponsors from each other's group (in purest form, mother's brother). This man is the boy's guardian and teacher in sexual matters (remember, they are forbidden to have sex). So each group provides boys of the other group with semen and sexual tutorship. In generation 1, a man may copulate with both his wife and her younger brother. The man gets a wife and another homoerotic transitional sexual outlet. His wife and her younger brother both receive semen—growth, strength. And the younger brother (or, if not himself, his sons or clansmen) will eventually receive a return wife, the brother-in-law's daughter, which the latter's semen created and nourished.

What does intermarriage do to social relationships? First, marriage transforms groups from unrelated enemies to less hostile affines. Where homoerotic practices occur with groups who are politically hostile, and between which warfare and masculine competition are common, marriage places affines in a set of productive relationships where none existed before. Second, they exchange women as resources. It is in the wife-givers' best interests to ensure that the marriage is productive in every way, so that they receive a woman in return. Marital sex for procreation is productive social work; it outweighs erotic play in homoerotic contacts and results in social sanctions against adultery and barrenness. Third, women and semen thus become circulating commodities. Unrelated groups exchange semen, on both sides, with the wife-donors getting a wife out of the bargain. The initiated boys of both groups require semen to complete their personhood, while the men need wives as sexual outlets and procreators to step out of the transitional stage of homoeroticism into the adult stage of marriage and family. Semen, therefore, though a crucial commodity, is secondary to women as a commodity: without wives men cannot attain full personhood. Even though semen is needed to attain manhood and it strengthens the new warrior recruits a village requires to protect and expand itself, this warriorhood goes for naught unless women are available for the group's economic and biologic reproduction.

Finally, the value of semen as instigator of social reproduction at both the individual and group levels pits males against one another in symmetric competition. This competition takes two forms, intragroup and intergroup transactions (Forge 1972). The one is intrahamlet individualized competition for homoerotically procured semen in order to grow and have first pick of wives needed for reproduction later. Here, boys as age mates try to outperform one another in a contest to achieve maturity first. (In fact, older brothers encourage their juniors toward this end.) The other competition is between hamlets and, in a wider sense, between a confederacy of intramarrying hamlets vis-à-vis the other confederacies of Sambia society. Men aspire to make their confederacy outdo others in war and overall productivity. Hamlets also act together to find women for their bachelors so as to produce more children—potential warriors and females for the marriage trade—compared with other groups. A race is on; its outcome is social reproduction. Conflicts within hamlets erupt over men competing with one another for wives and resources. Fights with peers over women in other hamlets also occur, sometimes precipitating warfare. But intrahamlet competition is overshadowed by the normative stress on achieving social maturity in concert with the best interests of one's own village group. Ultimately, social survival requires competing neighbors too, for they provide women and semen, and are the best defense—strength in numbers— against enemies elsewhere.

Summary

The creation and regulation of semen, through a variety of structural transactions, and as measured by their valuations from several points of view, are pivotal to the production of Sambia sexual culture. What may seem esoteric, vulgar, and trivial now seems complex and symbolically significant in understanding how the Sambia construe sociality, the body, and their own folk concepts of sexuality in the structure of social relations and modes of production. Erotics belongs to this symbolic field and cannot be understood, either subjectively or objectively, except in relation to the meaningfulness of this field over time.

Until recently anthropology ignored erotics and its meanings, especially in constructing comparative models of social organization and culture. Even heteroerotic activities have, in general, scarcely been studied, and the meaning of the temporal and symbolic structuring of heterosexuality has not been accorded much analytic value beyond the vague category "sexual antagonism," which has been implicitly used to support whatever explanatory model an author advanced (Herdt and Poole 1982). The fluids of sexual and reproductive acts—semen, blood, and milk—have been too narrowly studied as entities or artifacts in exchange, or as parts of the growth process in reference only to individual development or societal functioning. They have been interpreted less often as symbolic objects and commodities, expressed through concepts and social transactions, whereby the natives reproduce the identities of persons, social roles, clans, and intergroup relationships across generations. Here, Marilyn Strathern's (1988) work is foundational and has changed the field.

Past analyses of semen and blood as culturally constructed concepts in New Guinea belief systems, for instance, reveal this structural-functional emphasis. These fluids have long been viewed as important in native notions of sexual temperament and gender (e.g., Mead 1935). The great interest in procreation beliefs shown, first by Malinowski (1913) among Aborigines, and then in Trobriand descent ideology (Malinowski 1929, 1954), illustrates this importance. Writers questioned whether natives were ignorant of procreation and what such purported ignorance of conception meant (Ashley-Montagu 1937; and see Bettelheim 1955; Leach 1966; Spiro 1968). Denial of semen valuation in kinship and ritual dogma belongs to a broader cultural discourse on social regeneration and reproduction (Weiner 1978, 1980).

In New Guinea Highlands studies, since Read's (1951, 1954) work, ethnographers have noted blood and semen as cultural signs of the body, sex, and gender. Accounts of the norms of sexual contacts, dogmas about conception, sterility, and reproductive competence, and ideas about exchange of menstrual blood and semen between people as patrilineal kin and affines all illustrate how ethnographers functionally related body fluids to sociosexual relationships and the positioning of people in networks of social groups (e.g., see Berndt 1965; Glasse and Meggitt 1969; Langness 1967; Meggitt 1964; Newman 1964; Reay 1959; A. Strathern 1972; M. Strathern 1972; Wagner 1972). Preoccupation with the exchange of sexual fluids between groups addressed Western individualist concerns with "discrete acts of giving and receiving" (Weiner 1980:71; cf., e.g., A. Strathern 1969, 1972). Classical social theory has gone beyond exchange constructs, or structural models that view body treatment merely as reflections of society's divisions and boundaries (Douglas 1966), to interpret semen, blood, and other entities as the culturally valued materials out of which gender and reproductivity are symbolically perpetuated (Gell 1975; Herdt 1981; Lindenbaum 1972; Meigs 1976; Panoff 1968; Poole 1981, 1982; M. Strathern 1988; Weiner 1980).

With the Sambia, we are dealing with people whose cultural systems use sexual relationships and fluids as objects and commodities to recreate social order in successive generations, for these are among the scarcest and most vital resources in this process. Semen and other body fluids are not just things that are: they have a value beyond themselves for extending one's personhood—that is, existence—beyond the present. No doubt many experiences of these material things (e.g., fluids, sex, and others' bodies) entail this transcendent attitude. Sambia spiritual concepts speak to this issue directly, just as the conflict between sex as work and sex as play addresses it indirectly. "Religion is an art of making sense out of experience, and like any other art, say, poetry, it must be taken symbolically, not literally," Firth (1981:596) has said, a view germane to the ritual meanings of semen.

The social fact of semen for Sambia is that it is a scarce resource that circulates through time. Its material and phenomenological attributes make it usable as commodity that can be consumed, stored, and given away. Its perceived use-value derives from the fact that (1) semen can be "contained" indefinitely in bodies and (2) then be seemingly passed, from person to person, without changing its essence or efficacy; (3) it represents an investment of labor (food, care, procreation of children) acquired through direct individual sexual transaction or indirect transformation (semen into milk), which can be given or received; (4) in being transmitted semen extends its transformative value to make the recipient more reproductively and socially competent; (5) these recipients, in turn, will produce more wealth and future individuals, who will fill productive roles and fill out social groups; and (6) by so doing, semen transactions recreate social links between the living and the dead, the worldly and the spiritual realms, between ego and others, and between the divisions of the society.

In Sambia imagination, individuals are born and die, but semen flows through them (along with blood) to recreate society. Individuals pass on. Growth as an aspect of these individuals dies with them. But strength persists: in the form of bones and skin tissue in offspring; in spirit familiars; in ghosts and spirits; and in the deceased's bones, which after death may be used for sorcery. Erotic play passes on too, but is useless except insofar as it has effected growth, strength, and procreation. Sex as work is far more productive, if less exciting: family and heirs result. In this model, a woman's body as sexual-procreative property belongs to her husband as much as his semen belongs only to her. Her blood, after marriage, belongs to his clan, through his offspring, which must be paid for in birth ceremonies. Both fluids are necessary for procreation, but it is semen that men own and control best. The natural fact that semen can be drunk (passed on) like any drinkable fluid sustains the view that it is a circulating, valuable, unchanging resource that must be, nonetheless, internally transformed in certain ways by certain persons to achieve certain ends.

The most powerful social fact of boy insemination is that it may only occur between potential enemies who may become affines (generation 1) and then kin (generation 2). Semen transactions not only define who is related and in what salient ways, but homoerotic contacts predicate the partners' relationship as prospective affines in their generation, which makes their children matrilateral kin in their own. Structurally, social ties based on blood and semen should not be mixed via sexual relationships: semen relates non-kin, who in turn, through women as links, have descendants sharing semen and blood. (A male ego may receive semen from his brother-in-law, whose children, that is the ego's sister's children, possess her husband's semen and her blood.) Ties of semen and blood (via women traded) flow in the same direction. The seeming exception is marriage to actual (not classificatory) father's sister's daughter, a marriage Sambia frown on. Such marriages are acceptable only when this woman cannot be traded for another, but in these rare marriages spouses share no blood, though they may indirectly share semen via their fathers' homoerotic contacts with each other's groups. Thus, the cultural principle not to mix blood and semen is contravened, and people resist such marriages. In general, this cultural linkage (blood and semen) makes heteroerotic relationships more socially important and multiplex than homoerotic contacts. Both men and women, their bodies and fluids, are needed to achieve biologic and social reproduction in this model (cf. Lévi-Strauss 1949; see Pettit 1977:70–72).

The practice of boy-inseminating rites is embedded in a cyclical tradition of semen transactions that made one's mother and father and will define one's own future relationships with boys and women. Identities follow from this semen flow. The tempo of such an ancient practice is to be found not only in this or that day's contacts but also in the last generation and the next. The system sets rigid constraints, but individuals and groups follow strategies around broad time posts to maximize the value of themselves and their resources. Sambia sexual culture, in this model of cyclical time, does not forget who gave and who received semen.

THREE

Fetish and Fantasy in Sambia Initiation

All cases of Fetishism, when examined, show that the worship is paid to an intangible power or spirit incorporated in some visible form, and that the fetish is merely the link between the worshiper and the object of worship.

—A. C. HADDON (1921:70)

Central to the ethos of Sambia male initiations are secret bamboo flutes of great and mysterious power. Sambia men come to "worship" those flutes with an ambivalent mixture of fear and affection. Perhaps we should expect this of a male cult whose ritual instruments personify a compelling need to separate boys from their mothers and reinforce masculine authority traumatically, thereby creating a hierarchy of dominators over underlings. Beyond these political facts, though, there is a paradoxical side of the flutes which is as puzzling with regard to Sambia as it is when found in other New Guinea societies: the conviction that these flutes—paramount symbols of maleness—are animated by an eroticized female spirit. Men's ritual attachment to this Janus-faced fetish and its relationship to a cultural fantasy system is the key problem of this chapter.

More than two generations have passed since K. E. Read (1952) established male initiation as the primary mechanism for conscripting boys into the *nama* male cult he so skillfully sketched among the Gahuku-Gama tribe of the Eastern Highlands. Read's landmark study was the first to map out, systematically, a range of interrelated anthropological interests associated with such initiatory cults. Social organization and social structure were highlighted, but the belief system was also worked into his analysis. The sacred flutes were always viewed as the dominant symbol of the men's cult.

Read's work evinces four research interests in men's cults. The first, and certainly the most timely interest in its day, was sociological: the flutes were conceptualized as a "symbol of unity" representing the "solidarity of males" as kinsmen and cult members (Read 1952:7). Here, as Read granted, his

89

work was frankly Durkheimian in its concern with how the social functions of the cult assisted in "the regulation, maintenance and transmission of sentiments upon which Gahuku-Gama society depends" (1952:1). From this functional viewpoint arose another, expectable political interest: the cult's significance both as an "index of male dominance and (as) an institution serving to maintain the status quo of male hegemony" (1952:15). By means of political "deceit" and "conscious falsification" (1952:9), the flutes sanctified masculine authority. Read implicitly argued that the cult was therefore a one-sided species of Durkheim's religion: society worshiped only males.

This male hegemony opened up a third thematic interest in male cults: their rampant misogyny and resulting "antagonism" between the sexes. Here, Read served notice of a basic tension existing between men's dogmas and their rituals: "In the final analysis, the idea which men hold of themselves is based primarily on what men do rather than on what they have at birth. They recognize, indeed, that in physiological endowment men are inferior to women, and, characteristically, they have recourse to elaborate artificial means to redress the contradiction and to demonstrate its opposite" (1952:14). It was those ritual "contradictions"—and what they meant for the "idea which men hold of themselves"—that gave rise to the last, and most neglected, of these themes.

This represents the multivalent meaning of the flutes themselves: how they always appeared in the three grandest pageants of masculine life—initiation rites, pig festivals, and intermittent "fertility rites" (Read 1952:2); how they were linked to powerful, male-controlled, mystical spirits; how their sounds were meant to excite men and frighten women; and how, oddly enough, the material shell of a flute was not in itself sacred (1952:4) but was easily replaceable. Read never forgot these aspects of the *nama* cult, as his writings show (1951, 1952, 1955, 1965).

Subsequent investigators have confirmed the widespread importance of initiatory cults like those of the *nama* throughout the Central Highlands (cf. Berndt 1962; Lindenbaum and Glasse 1969; Langness 1967, 1974; Lawrence and Meggitt 1965; Meggitt 1964; Newman 1965; Salisbury 1965; Watson 1960, 1964). In many areas these secret societies are so central that an understanding of New Guinea social organization and culture is impossible without an understanding of the cults (see Allen 1967; A. Strathern 1969, 1970). Further, many workers have followed Read's Durkheimian lead in studying the cults. This approach poses difficulties, as Langness (1967, 1974) and others (e.g., Koch 1974) have noted. For example, a researcher taking such a structural-functional perspective on the cult would concentrate on "the solidarity of the male community," but only by understanding that it emerges "at the expense of females" (Langness 1974:200). This theoretical inadequacy, as we shall see, is of telling importance for interpreting Sambia ritual.

A narrow sociological paradigm no longer seems adequate. Read himself was clear in stating, from the start, that there were "many other problems" associated with male cults, elements that he had "chosen to exclude" (1952:1). These earlier studies were thus restricted, in scope and selection of data, by their focus on social-structural considerations. Of course, their contribution was still substantial; their perspectives also helped scholars manage the unenviable complexities of studying symbolic behavior; and all research, we assume, adheres to accepted conventions of disciplinary focus. Nevertheless, these restrictions have resulted in a gap in our understanding of the cultural and psychological elements of New Guinea cults (see Langness 1976). (Indeed, Read's [1965:95–140] last description of the now-vanished Gahuku-Gama ritual initiations and their subjective aspects remains superlative.) We now need an expanded anthropological approach that encompasses those other dimensions of ritual meaning and adds new perspectives to the structural-functional studies already in hand.

Of Read's "many other problems" still unstudied and unsolved, I wish to examine the symbolic behavior surrounding the ritual flutes of Sambia. In various parts of Melanesia, male secret societies apparently depended on flutes (and other sound-making instruments) as the foundation of a mystical institution. Among the Gahuku, in fact, as Read showed, the term *nama* (after which renamed their male cult) came from the word for a "mystical bird-like creature," whose cries were secretly produced by flute players. Now there is much of the exotic in Highlands ritual. This symbolic pattern, though, is altogether something more: the dogma and fantasy that powerful and fantastic beings are summoned up and brought to life through those wooden fetishes women and children hear yet must not look upon. Through the following observations I try to extend our understanding of this symbolic pattern in a direction that Read, like Bateson (1958) and Mead (1935) before him, first explored: the ritualized development of male gender identity.

The gender symbolism of men's cultural and personal constructs carries that work into the arena of collective initiation. My contention is that the efficacy of Sambia flute symbolism derives simultaneously from subjective meanings based on individual developmental experience and from the flutes' culturally constituted patterns of significance. To explicate this relationship between individual subjectivity and flute-oriented behavior requires concomitant studies of Sambia gender identity and eroticism. There are several reasons for this emphasis on sex and gender. First, the flutes are used as a political weapon vis-à-vis the social and sexual suppression of both women and boys. Second, the flutes' secret embodies the greatest of all mysteries for Sambia: the origins and divergence of maleness and femaleness. Third, the Sambia initiatory cult prescribes male homoerotic activities that inform the ritual developmental cycle of all males. Fourth—and the point to which this chapter is directed—Sambia men transmit to initiates a fantasy system concerning the flutes and their sounds, some of whose components are explicitly erotic. The Sambia flutes thus elucidate a pervasive symbolic complex known throughout Papua New Guinea, and one to which I shall later allude: namely, the identification of men with their masculinized ritual cults, flutes, and fantasy female beings.

If, as I suggest, such a fantasy system underlies collective flute-oriented behavior, then other psychosocial processes are no doubt complicating the ritual process too (see Turner 1964). How can we know? Part of the answer, I think, hinges on how we define the above research interests and on the fact that their conceptualization assumes a slant on anthropological theory and method.

A first principle: The flutes are an imaginative and multivalent fetish. They constitute more than a material instrument, a collective representation, or a cultural symbol. The flutes are man-made ritual paraphernalia capable of creating evocative effects that become adored and feared. This religious power, associated with other societal phenomena like kinship affiliation or ethnic identity, we anthropologists know well enough. Nevertheless, there is that other dimension of the Sambia flutes, too: their capacity to excite ritually, to stir erotic interest, or to signify such subjective experiences or their opposite—repression. The flutes embrace a panoply of various psychosocial domains, and yet to make this admission is tantamount to opening up that discarded Pandora's black box, the mind.

By this I mean not the "collective mind" of certain structuralists, psychoanalysts, or poets but rather the subjective processes and contents of the minds of flesh-and-blood individuals with whom I talk and interact in the routine course of each ethnographic workday. It is from such observations that we can attempt to apprehend meanings, fetishistic or otherwise. "Fetish" is an old-fashioned term nowadays, fallen into disrepute. We are uneasy handling its connotations even on those rare occasions when musty museologists use it. One reason for this uneasiness, I think, is that the impassioned ritual significances of a fetish implicates more than social custom. It implies a behavioral context, with its acts, moods, and values, as much as it implies psychological frames (Bateson 1972:177–93) orienting individual affects and intentions. The meaning of a fetish requires both types of data—on customs, and on behavior or subjectivity.

It is said of the late Evans-Pritchard that he always advised his students to study the grain of a culture, to concentrate on those patterns, in small details or large, which cohere to form an intuitive textural theme permeating all. This is what we ethnographers are about. To describe thusly the grain of Sambia culture requires that one attend to the acts, words, and feelings of individuals—sometimes impassioned acts or erotic feelings—and the mode of interpersonal communications to which they belong. This chapter will have five parts. I shall begin with a brief description of Sambia men's idealizations of initiation, and the corresponding belief system. Second, drawing on field notes, I shall relate observations of flute-oriented behavior in first-stage initiation. Third, I shall sketch some subjective fragments of these ritual experiences drawn from longitudinal, clinical-type case studies of initiated boys. Fourth, I shall consider the meaning of these complementary dimensions of the flutes as constituents of an intersubjective fantasy system. Last, my findings shall be compared with reports from other New Guinea societies.

The Men's Idealizations

It needs stating only once that men's secular rhetoric and ritual practices depict women as dangerous and polluting inferiors whom men are to distrust throughout their lives. In this regard, Sambia values and relationships pit men against women even more markedly, I think, than occurs in other Highlands communities (see Brown and Buchbinder 1976; Meggitt 1964; Read 1954). Men hold themselves the superiors of women in physique, personality, and social position. And this dogma of male supremacy permeates all social relationships and institutions, likewise coloring domestic behavior between the sexes (cf. Tuzin 1980, for an important contrast). Men fear not only pollution from contact with women's vaginal fluids and menstrual blood but also the depletion of their semen, the vital spark of maleness, which women (and boys, too) inevitably extract, sapping a man's substance. These are among the main themes of male belief underlying initiation.

The ritualized creation of maleness is the result of initiation, and men believe the process to be vital for the nature and nurture of manly growth and well-being. First-stage initiation begins the process in small boys. Over the ensuing ten to fifteen years, until marriage, cumulative initiations and residence in the men's house are said to promote biological changes that firmly cement the growth from childhood to manhood. Nature provides male genitals, it is true, but nature alone does not bestow the vital spark biologically necessary for stimulating masculine growth or demonstrating cold-blooded self-preservation.

New Guinea specialists will recognize in the Sambia belief system a theme that links it to the comparative ethnography of male initiation and masculine development: the use of ritual procedures for sparking, fostering, and maintaining manliness in males (see Berndt 1962; Meigs 1976; Newman 1964, 1965; Poole 1981, 1982; Read 1965; Salisbury 1965; Strathern 1969, 1970). Sambia themselves refer to the results of first-stage collective initiation—my main interest—as a means of "growing a boy," and this trend of ritual belief is particularly emphatic.

As we have seen, the Sambia perceive no immanent, naturally driven fit between one's birthright sex and one's gender identity or role. Indeed, the problem (and it is approached as a situation wanting a solution) is implicitly and explicitly understood in quite different terms. The solution is also different for the two sexes. Men believe that a girl is born with all of the vital organs and fluids necessary for her to attain reproductive competence through "natural" maturation. This conviction is embodied in cultural perceptions of the girl's development, beginning with the sex assignment at birth. What distinguishes a girl *(tai)* from a boy *(kwulai'u)* is obvious: "A boy has a penis, and a girl does not," men say. Underlying men's communications is a conviction that maleness, unlike femaleness, is not a biological given. It must be artificially induced through secret ritual, and that is a personal achievement.

The visible manifestations of girls' fast-growing reproductive competence, noticed first in early motor coordination and speech and then later in the rapid attainment of height and secondary sex traits (e.g., breast development), are attributed to inner biological properties. Girls possess a menstrual-blood organ, or *tingu,* said to precipitate all those events and the menarche. Boys, on the other hand, are thought to possess an inactive *tingu.* They do possess, however, another organ—the *kereku-kereku,* or semen organ—that is thought to be the repository of semen, the very essence of maleness and masculinity; but this organ is not functional at birth, since it contains no semen naturally and can only store, never produce, any. Only oral insemination, men believe, can activate the boy's semen organ, thereby precipitating his push into adult reproductive competence. In short, femininity unfolds naturally, whereas masculinity must be achieved; and here is where the male ritual cult steps in.

Men also perceive the early socialization risks of boys and girls in quite different terms. All infants are closely bonded to their mothers. Out of a woman's contaminating but life-giving womb pours the baby, who thereafter remains tied to the woman's body, breast milk, and many ministrations. This latter contact only reinforces the femininity and female contamination in which birth involves the infant. Then, too, the father, both because of postpartum taboos and by personal choice, tends to avoid being present at the breast-feedings. Mother thus becomes the unalterable primary influence; father is a weak second. Sambia say this does not place girls at "risk" of pollution—they simply succumb to the drives of their "natural" biology. This maternal attachment and paternal distance clearly jeopardize the boys' growth, however, since nothing innate within male maturation seems to resist the inhibiting effects of mothers' femininity. Hence boys must be traumatically separated—wiped clean of their female contaminants—so that their masculinity may develop.

Homoerotic fellatio inseminations can follow this separation but cannot precede it, for otherwise they would go for naught. The accumulating semen, injected time and again for years, is believed crucial for the formation of biological maleness and masculine comportment. This native perspective is sufficiently novel to justify our using a special concept for aiding description and analysis of the datum "masculinization" (Herdt 1981:205ff.). Hence I shall refer to the overall process that involves separating a boy from his mother, initiating him, ritually treating his body, administering inseminations, his biological attainment of puberty, and his eventual reproductive competence as masculinization.

A boy has female contaminants inside of him which not only retard physical development but, if not removed, debilitate him and eventually bring death. His body is male: his *tingu* contains no blood and will not activate. The achievement of puberty for boys requires semen. Breast milk "nurtures the boy," and sweet potatoes or other "female" foods provide "stomach nourishment," but these substances become only feces, not semen. Women's own bodies internally produce the menarche, the hallmark of reproductive maturity. There is no comparable mechanism active in a boy, nothing that can stimulate his secondary sex traits. Only semen can do that; only men have semen, boys have none. What is left to do, then, except initiate and masculinize boys into adulthood?

Ritual Behavior

The first sign that a collective initiation is approaching comes in the guise of piercing, melodious cries that appear mysteriously as if from nowhere but that children are told come from old female hamlet spirits *(aatmwog-*

wambu). First from within the men's house, later near the ritual cult house being built, and eventually at the edges of the forest, the haunting sounds demandingly increase in tempo. This signal alerts women to the coming ritual preparations. Boys, whose consternation may turn to curiosity or fear, are comforted or teased (according to the person and situation) with remarks like, "The female spirit wants to get you; she wants to kill and eat you." Mother or father may smile or laugh or fall silent—responses that underscore the mounting tension that intrudes on the household of a boy whose time has come. "The female spirit protects the clubhouse; she's aged and hidden until *moku* [initiation] inside an old net bag," some fathers tell their sons. Boys differ in their responses to this scenario, of course, but whether stoically indifferent or tearful, they all experience a discomfort that turns into panic at initiation. It is the sound of the flutes that creates this discomfort, signaling as it does an unalterable transition into warrior life, as we shall see.

The great cult house goes up in a matter of weeks, and its construction is soon followed by the third-stage initiation. Two principles dictate the requirement that older bachelors' "puberty" rites precede the second- and first-stage initiations. First, following their advancement, the bachelors are expected to help organize the ensuing ritual activities. Second, as new initiators, the youths are urged (a term that conveys too weakly the elders' sense of real dedication in these matters) to demonstrate their manly feelings and behavior in particular contexts. After years of ritual ordeals, third-stage initiation once again brings nosebleedings and other tests, so bachelors have endured a great deal. Though these ordeals are necessary to build strong warriors, elders also recognize the all-too-visible frustration and anger pent up in the youths. Thus, bachelors are counseled that it is "right" for them to "pay back" their mistreatment by helping beat and nosebleed the younger initiates. Likewise, they get the go-ahead to "relax their tight penises" (proving themselves manly) by serving as dominant fellateds—for the first time—to the initiated boys, who are also encouraged to acquire the semen of youths aggressively.

The Flutes

In what follows, my primary interest shall be with ritual behavior focused on the flutes. This behavior encompasses two primary contexts: the penis-and-flute ceremony (hereafter referred to as the flute ceremony) and the new initiates' first entrance into the cult house, an event that leads to erotic encounters with the bachelors on the same evening. The ritual significance of the flutes—as symbols and signs—stems from subjective, verbal and nonverbal, and situational dimensions of meaning (see Turner 1964) set within the naturalistic flow of the ceremonies. This perspective requires an aside about the flutes as physical objects.

Sambia have several types of ritual flutes, but they lump them together under the category term *namboolu aambelu* ("frog female"). Each flute is made from newly cut bamboo and is left open at one end. The hollow tubes vary in length from one to three feet; they also vary in the thickness and species of the bamboo. Two types of flutes are blown vertically from the mouth (like a jug pipe); another type is winded horizontally through a blowhole. They are always blown in pairs. Men tell women and children that the flute sounds are the wailful cries of the old female hamlet spirit who figures prominently in folklore. The bull-roarer (*duka' yungalu*, "bird's call"), by contrast, is far less secret than the flutes and is said to produce a sound akin to a powerful, but not mystical, bird (see what Gahuku-Gama and Bena Bena report about their flutes [Langness 1974; Read 1952]). Like the various forms of grass sporrans that are made or like incorporeally owned ritual customs, ritual flutes—both their size and associated tunes— are identified with phratry membership and political alliance among Sambia hamlets. The flutes are played typically during all collective initiations: once during a clubhouse ceremony near the end of fourth-stage initiations, and during the funeral ceremonies for young adult men or bachelors only. (This implies that the flutes "belong" to the bachelors, just as the youths "belong" to the flutes.)

The flutes are secretly guarded and are hidden from women and children, who are said by the men to fear the sound. Punishment, even possible death, awaits those who might violate this code. (Men casually discuss this possibility, but they take great care to conceal the flutes, and no infractions occurred during my stay.) The bamboo tubes themselves are of little intrinsic importance; they are easily made and discarded following the rituals. They are not stored or saved; they are not rubbed with semen, pig's grease, or blood, nor are they stuffed with any material, such as pork (see Berndt 1962:55–70; Read 1952:7). The longer flutes are referred to as "male" *(aatmwul)* and metaphorically as penes. The shorter and thinner flutes are called "female" (aambelu) and are sometimes likened to the glans penis. The pairs of flutes, moreover, are said to be "married" and are called "spouses" *(kwolu-aambelu)*. We shall see how these notions are drawn on later.

The Initiatory Events

At the start of initiation, boys are taken from their mothers, sometimes forcibly and sometimes not, but always in an atmosphere of great tension. They are placed in the men's house momentarily, and from there on, the boys' ritual sponsors (*nyetyangu,* also "mother's brother") become their primary guardians until the conclusion of initiation. The sponsor-initiate relationship is usually a close one based on kinship and/or affectional bonds; the parents choose the sponsor, but he is typically the boys' fathers' nonagnatic peer and is like a "male mother."

The boys are abruptly and permanently separated from their mothers. As the novices are led into the forest for the first ritual, which will take place in the afternoon, they leave behind their mothers, women, and playmates. On the occasion I shall describe, women set up a sorrowful wail as the lads were led away. The men responded to that maternal response with pointed shouts that the boys were soon "to be killed."

On the third day of the initiation the flutes are revealed, so boys learn of their secret significance; this revelation shall be my focus. The flutes are blown at other times, too, as I noted, starting with the cult house–raising ceremonies. They are always, however, kept just out of sight, and this has the effect, as we shall see, of building up a mood of expectation for the context of the flute ceremony later that day.

The day opens with a male "stretching rite," so called because the boys are beaten with switches to "open the skin" and foster bodily growth (*perulyapi*). Several hours later the boys' noses are bled in a major ritual (see chapter 4), a powerful and traumatic experience according to the testimony of boys and men alike. Then follows another painful rite in which stinging nettles are employed to "cleanse" the skin and "stretch" it. Finally, some four hours later in the afternoon, men assemble the novices for ceremonial dressing and painting in warrior garb. This sets the stage for the flute ceremony; it is later followed by a ceremonial procession back to the dance ground, whereupon boys enter the cult house for the first time. I wish to concentrate here on actual observations of a first-stage initiation sequence in 1975, beginning with the novices' body decoration:[1] As the decorating proceeds, the men around me quietly begin to make lewd jokes about the boys and their sponsors. The jokes are directed at the lads' emerging homoerotic fellator status. The tempo of jesting reaches a peak at the fastening of the novices' new grass sporrans. This lewd joking draws on the Sambia view

1. The data that follow come from ritual field notes collected over a period of eight days and nights in the Sambia River Valley in mid-1975.

that one's type of grass sporran (of men) or skirt (of women) signals erotic status and role. The attachment of that new sporran thus dramatically distinguishes novices from the category of "neuter" children, to which they formerly belonged. The banter becomes artificial, the associated feelings finding expression in public joking and horseplay, and men characterize these risqué jokes and farces as traditional. (Still, not every individual participates, and certainly not to the same extent.)

I made the following observations of the men in my party who casually reclined on the grass watching the ceremonial decoration: A married man nearby pretends to copulate with an old tree trunk. He acts as if the tree is a new novice fellator, contorting his grinning face as if to express breathless rapture. The men around roar with laughter as he repeats this mime three times. Then they crack jokes among themselves. Another man asserts that the sponsors are starting to act "funny," for, as they are attaching the novices' sporrans, our men say, the sponsors' penes are erecting. A second time they suggest that the sponsors' penes are erecting, and this bawdy insinuation elicits huge guffaws of laughter. These men then joke about men in other groups sitting nearby on the grass: they must "smell" the new grass sporrans of the boys, for they are "smiling," and later they will coax the lads into copulating with them. More laughter follows this remark. Next comes the flute ceremony, which begins in military silence as the forty-two novices are lined up, decked out in their stunning new attire, and made to await the surprises in store for them.

Two groups, each composed of four bachelors playing flutes, arrive from the forest. They circle the boys. There is total silence but for their music. The flute players are paired: one man plays a short flute, and another blows a longer flute, their musical chords harmonizing. They continue to play for about five minutes. During this period, Karavundun, a married man, picks up a long bamboo containing a narrower flute within it. He passes down the line of novices, attempting to insert the tip of the smaller, contained flute into their mouths. Approximately half the boys refuse to suck the flute. Karavundun does not press them, and there is no angry scene such as there was at another flute ceremony, when a bachelor, Erujundei, threatened the reluctant boys with a machete.[2] When a novice refuses, Karavundun simply smiles. Indeed, he jokes about those who react with displeasure. Some men nearby openly snigger at the recalcitrant novices. On the other hand, those who take to the act, "correctly" sucking the flute, are lauded, and the spectators nod their heads in approval.

2. In a different *moku* initiation observed in the Yellow River Valley, earlier in 1975.

Then, in visible anger at the defiant boys, Kokwai, a bachelor, unexpectedly enters the scene and strikes the novices with a long flute. Another man shouts, "Hit them hard; it is not like you were fighting them to draw blood!" Another instructing elder, Merumei, then repeatedly intimidates the novices by drawing attention to the large assembled crowd of men: "You uninitiated boys like to make jokes. . . . Now, make some jokes for the crowd of men here, we want to hear them!" He commands the boys: "You *kwu-lai'u*—open your mouths for the flute, they will place it inside . . . to try it on you. All of you, look at the large group of men . . . this large group. . . . You novices put it [the flute] inside your mouths, try it!"

The flutes are thus used for teaching about the mechanics of homoerotic fellatio, and in the first references to it, the elder draws attention to the physical proof of the elders to verify his words. He does so, however, not by allusion to semen but instead by allusion to the penis. There are two groups of elders who lecture: Damei and Mugindanbu remain at one end of the line, the fight leader, Merumei, at the other.

They now soundly condemn the novices for their childish mimicking of the flute sounds. As they do so, the flute players again strike the boys' chests with the butts of the flutes, as if to punish them. Mugindanbu begins, saying, "When you were uninitiated, you all played a game of imitating this sound [i.e., of the flutes], 'Um-huh, um-huh.' Now tell us, does this sound come from your mouths?"

Damei demands, "You boys think fit to imitate the flute sounds, [so] now make this sound, show us how you produce it. Why should we elders show you how to make it! . . . All of you boys look at this elder. What do you think he has done? Heard the teaching this moment and grown to be big? All of them [the men] 'ate' the penis . . . and grew big. All of them can copulate with you; all of you can eat penises. If you eat them, you will grow bigger rapidly."

The novices are enjoined to secrecy and then told of the fatal consequences of breaking this taboo: "For if you do [reveal the secrets], they [unspecified] will kill and throw your body into the river. Sambia boys, you will be thrown away into the Sambia River. . . . Moonagu [phratry] boys, you will be killed and your bodies thrown into the lower Sambia River. The big men will not help you, they will not jail us either; they will help us hide it [the murder]. This custom belongs to the Baruya and other tribes—all men everywhere. The sun itself brought this custom which we hold! If you speak out, the stone axe and the stone club will kill you. When you were children, you saw the bodies of initiates. They are like the *inumdu* [shrub], green, smooth, and not used up. They are 'nice.' Those initiates eat the penises of men and grow big and have nice skins too. If you do not, you will not grow quickly or be handsome. You must all ingest semen."

An elder, Damei, praises the novices of the earlier first-stage initiation. He reveals that the men were pleased with those novices for their acceptance of homoerotic activities. He thus urges the boys to follow the example of their peers earlier at the Yellow River Valley: "There we performed the *moku*. Our novices—'slept' [copulated] with the men. They drank the men's semen quickly. The big men all said the same: 'Those Yellow Valley men made a good *moku!*' The boys understood the teaching; they will grow quickly. The bachelors were pleased with the novices. . . they felt 'sweet' [erotically satisfied]. The Yellow Valley *moku* was truly good . . . This flute we will 'try out' [penetrate the mouth] on all of you. Later the men will copulate with you. . . They will do the same thing."

Damei and another elder, Worangri, then spontaneously represent themselves as authorities, testifying and sanctifying the "truth" of the penis teaching. They relate that only by ingesting semen can the lads grow truly masculine: "Do you boys see us? We have white hair. We would not trick you. You must all sleep with the men. When you were uninitiated, you erected the poles for banana trees and did other things. Now we have made *moku* for you; you must work harder. When you climb trees, your bones will ache. For that reason you must drink semen. Suppose you do not drink semen; you will not be able to climb trees to hunt possum; you will not be able to scale the top of the pandanus trees to gather nuts. You must drink semen. . . . It can 'strengthen' your bones."

In the next sequence of rhetoric, semen is likened to mother's milk. Boys are taught that they must continually consume it to grow: "Now we teach you our customary story . . . and right now you must ingest semen in the cult house. Now there are many men here; you must sleep with them. Soon they will return to their homes. Now they are here, and you ought to drink their semen. In your own hamlets, there are only a few men. When you do sleep with men, you should not be afraid of eating their penises. You will soon enjoy eating them. . . . If you try it [semen], it is just like the milk of your mother's breast. You can ingest it all of the time and grow quickly. If you do not start to drink it now, you will not ingest much of it. Only occasionally . . . and later when you are grown, you will stop. If you only drink a little semen now, you will not like the penis much. So you must start now and ingest semen! When you are bigger your own penis will get bigger, and you will not want to sleep with older men. You will then want to copulate with younger boys yourself. So you should sleep with the men now!" Another man shouts that unless the boys drink semen, they will fail to blow the flutes properly: "If you do not think of this [fellatio], you will not play the flutes well. A boy who does not sleep with men plays the flute badly, for his mouth is blocked up. . . . If you sleep with men, you shall play the flute well."³

In the final sequence, the boys' old pubic aprons are dramatically cut with a machete by the elder Mugindanbu. The limp pubic coverings then become the focus of a castration threat aimed at the boys as a deadly warning against adultery. The flutes are played again for several minutes. Merumei then lectures and shouts at the boys: "When you are grown, you cannot become sexually excited over the attractive wife of another man. You can touch your own wife, that is all right. The flute wants to kill you, for if you steal a woman, she will cry out like the flute, and her man will kill you. If you touch another man's wife you will die quickly. . . they will kill you. We are trying you out now for the time later when you might steal another man's wife. Then we would not just cut your grass sporran. If your penis rises and you want to steal a woman, we will cut it off." The elder cuts the old pubic covering midway between the abdomen and the genitals. "No one will help you, we will cut off your penis and kill you." By this act, not only is homoerotic insemination enjoined, but premarital heteroerotic activities are tabooed and condemned.

Following the flute ceremony, which lasts barely an hour, the boys are carefully lined up for a last inspection prior to their ceremonial parade back to the cult house. The large group of novices and older initiates files down the hillside to the dance ground, preceded by adult men who form phalanxes around the area, separating the boys from the throng of women and children who have assembled for a last view of them. For several minutes, led by a protecting shaman, the novices are paraded around the decorated grounds. He then conducts them inside the new cult house for the first time. (They have slept in a shabby lean-to, next to the cult house, until now.) That public display is the last occasion on which women can observe the boys for some years to come.

A while later something striking occurs, for as the boys enter the great cult house, they hear the flutes being played within. The boys are again taunted: "You can't go inside the *moo-angu*," the men say. They shout, "It's the menstrual hut of women. . . . Women are giving birth to babies. . . . The babies are crying." Then another man says, "Look! an *aatmogwambu* female hamlet spirit is in the ritual house." The boys are led into the ritual

3. Tali, a ritual expert, says this is a double-entendre: first, that boys who do not suck the penis cannot wind the flutes; and second, that this is because without fellatio their throats stay "blocked up" with the contaminated food of women (like the throats of little boys).

cult-house sanctuary just the same, and an hour later something even more remarkable happens.

The novices are seated on the earthen floor of the cult house. It is dusk, and after going through days of initiation, on top of this particularly long and trying day, they look pretty worn out. The women and children outside have by now been chased off. A fire has been built (for the first time), and a smattering of men sit idly beside the hearth near the lads.

Some bachelors unexpectedly tromp inside, playing flutes. There are two groups of four flute players each, as there were in the earlier flute ceremony, but they are disguised. There is silence again except for the flutes. A man says to the boys, "An old woman spirit has come. . . . She is cold, she wants to come sit by the fire." The bachelors then squat to the floor, their hands and faces disguised by bark coverings: the youths are impersonating female hamlet spirits. A young man says, "She is an *aatmogwambu;* she has come to cry for you. . . . Go away! Not good that she swallows her spit for you.[4] You must help straighten her out.[5] . . . If you feel sorry for her, you must help her out."[6]

The men then joke about this squeamishly. The flute players waddle like ducks around behind the tense boys, playing their flutes beneath their capes. The boys are again struck on their chests with the flutes. They are told not to reveal the flutes' secrets. An elder also comments, "If you see the flutes in [your] dreams, it means that men will soon come to attack and kill you. You must think about this image."[7] The bachelors unmask themselves, and the novices are hit on the heads with the flutes, which are then thrown into the hearth fire. The lads are made to stand near the fire, warming themselves and "strengthening'" their bodies with its heat. The "formal" ceremony is over, but something else is to follow.

Several of the bachelors, including those who had cloaked themselves, now come alive. It is nightfall, and the first erotic encounters begin that result in fellatio between themselves and the novices. The bachelors begin with momentary, outlandish (and unprecedented) exotic and erotic exhibitionism, as is customary: they lift up their arse covers, exposing their naked buttocks to the boys while engaging in childish games that imitate— and thereby mock—the uninitiated boys the novices previously were. The novices are enjoined to ceremonial silence (for the breaking of which they

4. A common metaphor for erotic desire.
5. Another common metaphor, this for sucking the bachelor's penis until ejaculation, which "slackens" the penis.
6. An implicit statement that boys should serve as fellators to the bachelors.
7. Little references to dream images and their cultural interpretation are commonly inserted in ritual teachings like this throughout initiation; they usually link ritual imagery to warfare vigilance.

could be soundly thrashed with cassowary quills). The exhibitionism and masculine reversal, telltale symptoms of ritual liminality (Turner 1967), finally end with a tantalizing challenge of things to come.

What soon follows, mostly from the prompting of individual boys, is the initially awkward, insistent, sometimes frantic erotic horseplay inside the house, which finally leads to private homoerotic intercourse outside on the darkened dance-ground area. Not all the initiates and bachelors join in this, but most of them take part. And before the end of the initiation five days later, all but a handful of novices have served as fellators, not once, but twice and more.

Ritual Experience

Now I should like to explore briefly the subjectivity of ritual, focusing on selected aspects of boys' experience regarding the above ceremonial behavior oriented toward the flutes. For want of space I confine myself here to the study of the initiates, not the bachelors, emphasizing the flute ceremony and subsequent homoerotic activities. That focus unavoidably ignores many other important aspects of initiation, such as the creation of personal and social ties between ritual sponsor and initiate (see Gewertz 1982), the development of age-mate and affinal relationships, or support for the economic division of labor and its complementary relationships between the sexes— not to mention a much wider range of ritual scenarios and multivocal symbols. The flutes, however, are the first and most central secrets revealed in this context, and that powerful "insight" (to use Read's term [1952:13]) gets attached to the male ethos and individual male identity. It is also significant that many Sambia men and boys often refer back to this particular scenario in orienting other facets of subsequent developmental experience.

Methodological Note

The following material on the initiates' subjectivity derives from longitudinal case studies that characterize individual boys' experiences in the wake of initiation.[8] Since these types of data are unusual in reports on ritual, their inclusion merits a note concerning my methodology.

8. These longitudinal data were collected from a number of initiates (ranging in age from nine to fourteen years) in case studies extending from three months to fifteen months duration but concentrated in my second year of field research. In-depth studies served as a baseline from which to evaluate other superficial interviews among boys and men, including interviews of a sample of forty-two initiates which were carried out according to a structured schedule.

Studying Sambia ritual experience always meant living in close quarters with individuals. While this holds true for most ethnographic enterprises, it was for me an absolute necessity if I was to explore the psychological dimension of ritual initiation. Training in cultural and social anthropology helped further that study, but it still afforded few techniques for understanding what the experience of symbolic behavior—and this term surely implies more than simply the outwardly apparent—meant for individuals. The verbal "style" of Sambia everyday discourse lent itself to my endeavor, since men (and boys, among themselves) commonly discuss their experiences as an ordinary mode of sociality. (This discourse is distinct from the exegesis of elders in ritual teachings or the commentaries of ritual experts in private secular settings.) Given such a rich medium, my problem was to describe what Sambia did, said, and thought; so I tried, as an outsider, interviewer, and friend, to fit in.

The ability to "fit in," as Malinowski (1922) taught, rests on one's linguistic and cultural knowledge, as well as on the imponderables of particular informants, their personal histories, social networks, likes, and dislikes. Fitting in, however, also requires empathic "trust": trust in one's own understanding of fleeting communicative acts that occur with oneself or in one's presence; trust that one's capacity to translate the meanings behind individual expressions will improve as the amount of time spent with one's informants adds up; and vital trust in one's own sense of the interpersonal relationships with others on which this trust is built. Malinowski never taught that, but he might have, for his data also belonged to this same medium of trust. Whatever the motives behind his silence, such a pedagogical reluctance is understandable, as "trust" is too simple a catchword for summarizing the various empathies that nourish one's capacity to be inside of one's own skin while also comfortably sharing that moment with an outsider. Those communications—words, syntax, affects, too much silence or not enough—are still data, and their behavioral concomitants also belong in our reports. This clinical ethnography, moreover, can also be applied, mutatis mutandis, to the behavior and experience of ritual, including observations of individuals' subjective perceptions of the events after the fact (see Geertz 1968:107–14, and 1977:481–82; Herdt and Stoller 1990; Obeyesekere 1990; see also LeVine 1973:249 ff.).

SUBJECTIVE ASPECTS OF RITUAL

Initiation begins with and occurs through maternal separation; the effects of this separation are visible and no doubt profound. Novices often refer to that trauma, expressing feelings of loss and sadness after the separation.

That subjectivity changes as they age, however, for marriage and personal autonomy rearrange social relationships and individuals' needs. Nevertheless, even old men have spontaneously remarked of their initiations, "I felt sorry to lose my mother." That sorrow and longing permeate the mood of subsequent ritual experiences in various ways, small and large. During initiation, moreover, boys may interact only with other males—fellow novices, older bachelors, and occasionally their fathers—but not with their mothers or other females. The awareness of the finality with which boys are separated from and prohibited from being with their mothers must, indeed, count as a tremendous component in an initiate's response to these other males, to ritual, and, ultimately, to himself. With this idea in mind, let us return to the flute ceremony.

Less than five hours after they have been subjected to ritual beatings and nosebleedings, novices are shown the flutes. The flute players appear, and in their presence, to the accompaniment of the wailing flutes, some powerful secrets of the male cult are revealed. The setting is deeply awesome. (Awesome means: a great crowd waiting in silence as the mysterious sounds are first revealed; having one's mouth physically penetrated; obediently lining up for threatening review by elders; being told that secret homoerotic fellatio exists; being taught how to engage in it; and, throughout it all, hearing at close range the sounds one has associated since one's earliest years with collective masculine power and pride.) The flutes were unequivocally treated as phalli. The ritual intent of their revelation is clear enough. Nonetheless, there is something more than mere pedagogy in the experience and related homosexual teachings. I have observed the flute ceremony during two different initiations, and while my Western experience differs greatly from that of Sambia, one thing was intuitively striking to me: men were revealing the erotic components of the mouth and penis—penile erection, sexual impulses, semen, homoerotic relations in particular, and genital eroticism more broadly. These revelations come as boys are enjoined to become fellators, made the sharers of ritual secrets, and threatened with death if they tell the women.

Novices' comments indicate that they perceive several different social values bound up with the expression of homoerotic instruction in the flute ceremony. Let us begin with an obvious value: childhood training regarding shame about one's genitals. Here is Kambo, who reveals a construct about earlier socialization: "I thought—not good that they (elders) are lying or just playing a trick. That's [the penis is] not for eating. . . . When I was a child our fathers said, 'This [penis] is not for handling; if you hold it you'll become lazy.' And because of that (at first in the cult house) I felt—it's not for sucking."[9] Childhood experience is a contributing source of shame as regards ritual fellatio: children are taught to avoid handling their own genitals. In a wider sense, moreover, Kambo's remark pertains to the alleged sexual naïveté of children and the boys' prior lack of knowledge about their fathers' homoerotic activities. (This deception and ignorance surely influence boys' early gender role behavior, since boys "know" only of their fathers' visible heteroerotic actions.)

Another key subjective construct concerns the nutritive value of semen. A primary source of this idea is, as we saw, men's ritual exegetical equation of semen with mother's breast milk. Novices seem to take up this idea quickly in their own subjective orientations toward fellatio. (Pandanus nuts, too, are regarded as another equivalent of semen.) This remark by Moondi is a typical example of such semen identifications in the teachings of the flute ceremony: "The 'juice' of the pandanus nuts, . . . it's the same as the 'water' of a man, the same as a man's 'juice' [semen]. And I like to eat a lot of it [because] it can give me more water, . . . for the milk of women is also the same as the milk of men. It [breast milk] is for when she carries a child—it belongs to the infant who drinks it."[10] The association between semen and the infant's breast food is also explicit in this observation by Gaimbako, a second-stage initiate: "Semen is the same kind as that [breast milk] of women . . . it's the very same kind as theirs, . . . the same as pandanus nuts too. . . . But when milk [semen] falls into my mouth [during fellatio], I think it's the milk of women."

Another experiential construct touches on revulsion and, again, shame regarding fellatio. This is a powerful reactive attitude: I am "eating a penis" that is quite like my own. Kambo related this thought as his immediate response to the penis teaching of the flute ceremony: "I was afraid of penis [*sic*]. It's the same as mine—why should I eat it? It's the same kind, [our penes are] only one kind. We're men, not *different* [his emphasis] kinds." This supposition is fundamental and implied in many boys' understandings. The cultural frame of this attitude is decisively important, since its underlying premise (i.e., the penes are the "same kind") is a symmetrical one. Kambo is privately asserting, then, that males are of one kind, that is, "one sex," distinct from females. This implies tacit recognition of the complementary, sexually asymmetrical character of the homoerotic dyad. Remember, too, the coercive character of the setting: the men's attempt to

9. Kambo was, at the time of these remarks, a twelve-year-old initiate who had never been out of the Sambia River Valley.

10. Moondi was a fifteen-year-old youth whose comments were made not long before his third-stage initiation, which I observed.

have boys suck the flutes is laden with overt hostility, much stronger than the latent hostility expressed in the homoerotic jokes made during the preceding body decoration. The boys are placed in an erotically subordinate position, a fact that is symbolically communicated in the idiom that the novices are "married" to the flutes. (Novices suck the small flute, which resembles the mature glans penis.) Men thus place boys in an undesirable state of subordination, which the boys may sense as being like that of a woman and wife (see Bateson 1958:131–32). This evokes panicky responses of both fear and shame.

Nearly all novices perform their first act of fellatio during *moku* initiation, and their constructs of that experience are tremendously important to our understanding of subsequent masculine development. Let me cite several responses of Moondi to this highly traumatic act: "I was wondering what they [elders] were going to do to us. And. . . I felt afraid. What will they do to us? But they inserted the bamboo in and out of the mouth; and I thought, what are they doing? Then, when they tried out our mouths, I began to understand . . . that they were talking about the penis. Oh, that little bamboo is the penis of the men. . . . My whole body was afraid, completely afraid, . . . and I was heavy, I wanted to cry.

"At that point my thoughts went back to how I used to think it was the *aatmwogwambu* [flute spirit], but then I knew that the men did it [made the sounds]. And . . . I felt a little better, for before [I thought that] the *aatmwogwambu* would get me. But now I saw that they [the men] did it.

"They told us the penis story. . . . Then I was thinking intensely, quickly. I was afraid—not good that the men 'shoot' me [penetrate my mouth] and break my neck. Ay! Why should they put that [penis] inside our mouths! It's not a good thing. They all hide it [the penis] inside their sporrans, and it's got lots of hair too.

"'You must listen well,' they said. 'You all won't grow by yourselves; if you sleep with the men you'll become a strong man.' They said that; I was afraid. . . . And then they told us clearly: semen is inside—and when you hold a man's penis, you must put it inside your mouth—he can give you semen. . . . It's the same as your mother's breast milk.

"'This is no lie,' the men said; 'you can't go tell the children, your sisters.' . . . And then I tried it [fellatio], and I thought, 'Oh, they told us about *aamoonaalyi* [breast milk; Moondi means semen]—it [semen] is in there.'"

What becomes of these sentiments in later weeks and months and years? Many things could be added. For instance, despite great social pressures, some boys evince from the start a low interest, and they seldom participate in fellatio; on the other hand, some novices feverishly join in. Those are the extremes: the great majority of Sambia boys regularly engage in fellatio for years, as constrained by taboo.[11] Boy-inseminating activities are a touchy subject among men for many reasons. They begin with ceremony, it is true, but their occurrence and meaning fan out to embrace a whole secret way of life. What matters is that boys become purveyors of this hidden tradition, and we should expect them to acquire powerful feelings about bachelors, fellatio, and semen, as indeed they do. One mundane example can stand for many: one day, while I was talking idly with Kambo, he mentioned singing to himself as he walked in the forest. I asked him what he sang about, and from this innocuous departure point, he said this: "When I think of men's name songs, then I sing them: that of a bachelor who is sweet on me; a man of another line or my own line. When I sing the song of a creek in the forest I am happy about that place. . . . Or some man who sleeps with me—when he goes elsewhere, I sing his song. I think of that man who gave me a lot of semen; later, I must sleep with him. I feel like this: he gave me a lot of water [semen]. . . . Later, I will have a lot of water like him."

Here we see pinpointed the male conviction of "accumulating semen" already established in young Kambo's thought. Even a simple activity like singing can, at least for him, trigger a mood of subjective association with past homoerotic experiences and that particular chap. Thus, Kambo's last sentence contains a wish: that he will acquire abundant manliness, like the manliness of the older friend of whom he sings.

The men's flutes come to embody a whole lifetime of experiences like these. It cannot be doubted that initiation sets in motion a certain "line of development" (Freud 1965) with discernible consequences for a boy's sense of himself and his maleness. On the other hand, those ritual experiences come to clothe, like a suit of armor, an earlier experiential core that has already been firmly established: what a boy felt in his prolonged, luxuriant relationship with his mother. It is my contention that the ritual cult's imposed "life design" for creating a warrior's adult identity rests upon a psychological frame—of merging male and female fetishistic attributes associated with the flutes, whose meaning admits of first homoerotic and then heteroerotic subjectivities.

This thesis points to the last context of flute-orienting behavior, the bachelors' impersonation of the female hamlet spirits. Here we confront a thick symbolic field of institutional ceremony, semiotics, and personal mo-

---

11. Fellatio activities are constrained by incest taboos similar to those surrounding heterosexuality. All collateral kinsmen, age mates, and ritual sponsors are prohibited as sex partners. In fact, however, male cousins sometimes illicitly violate the rule prohibiting them from engaging in fellatio.

tives. For any who doubt the last factor, consider only the obvious question: why do only certain bachelors, and not others, volunteer for this impersonation? Consider this point: Gaimbako recalled that the bachelors presented themselves on that night as "wailing old women spirits." He noted that the men told "stories" about the "milk" of the flutes: "This flute isn't crying out for just anything—it wants the milk [semen] of men. You must all drink the milk of men." This comment was unsolicited; in the course of talking about bachelors and fellatio, Gaimbako spontaneously associated back to the bachelors' ritual impersonation. And this significance is suspended within a paradoxical fantasy: despite being used by bachelors as phalli with which to teach fellatio, the vessels that cry out for milk are also linked with boys' mouths.[12] The flutists prevail on the novices to serve as erotic orifices; the boys should also look to the bachelors for the semen that masculinizes.

Take note, however, that it is the bachelors who put this fantasy into action: some of them present themselves with naked buttocks, while others come wrapped in capes, blowing flutes, hazing the boys, all of which communicates that the bachelors possess what boys need: warrior maleness (i.e., semen) and the culturally sanctioned power to inseminate. Toward this goal, bachelors take the guise of cult female spirits who are erotically excited by the boys, and not by the whole person of a novice but specifically by his mouth. Why the flute-oriented behavior subsumes this precise subjectivity is the subject of my interpretation.

Fetish and Fantasy

Because the flutes symbolically preside over the collective initiations of the Sambia male cult, it is with the meaning of their mysterious voice that we are chiefly concerned. Their power is enigmatic. The flutes are kept "secret" from the women, but it is the open, violent threat of men which prevents women from "knowing" about the inner mystery of their uses. The flutes also embody the mysteries of maleness and femaleness. Last, the flutes are paradoxical representations of orthodoxy and subversion (Leach 1972): they imply the building of maleness and masculine behavior at the expense of the maternal bond.

I choose here to examine their earliest experiential theme, of maternal loss and sorrow, rather than their later meaning of bravado and heteroerotic

---

12. Recall the men's previous allusion to the flutes as being babies crying in the cult house. Here, novices are being identified with the "crying" flutes that want milk.

autonomy among men. This focus entails examining the meaning of the flutes in first-stage initiation for boys. It is essential, however, to recognize that the novices' and bachelors' dispositions toward flute-oriented behavior really represent only different phases of a single dynamic process, masculinization, comprising maternal detachment, subordination, and then sexual domination, all of which lead to a ritually defined sense of male gender identity and competent adjustment to the masculine role. These developmental phases do not simply mirror one another; they complement and interact (see Allen 1967:24–27). Indeed, the symbolic efficacy of the flutes as the men's fetishistic "vehicle of communication" (Haddon 1921:72)—with their cult of peers, spirits, and their women—derives from fundamental developmental conflicts associated with the flutes but probably never resolved.

A developmental perspective must be anchored in the power context of the men's cult, the politics of which ultimately concern social reproduction. Men and women are generally antagonistic. Boys are closer to women than to men; women are polluting and, hence, so are boys (see Meigs 1976:401–2). Boys are detached from women only to become the relatively helpless subordinates of men, both sociopolitically and sexually. Eventually, however, the lads must become proud warriors fully in command; otherwise, how shall these little boys achieve the masculine performatory competence expected of them by women and by their peers, in warfare and in ritual? Masculinity is thus a psychosocial dialectic (Chodorow 1974), perhaps more so among the Sambia and other Highlanders than elsewhere (see Herdt 1981; Lidz and Lidz 1977; Young 1965). We must not forget, then, that cultural values, socialization, and the successive stages of ritual experience all produce a feedback effect on male development. Understanding the complexity of the flutes this way helps us avoid the one-dimensional "nothing but," the useless arguments that ritual symbolism is nothing more than a product of economics, or social structure, or psychodynamics—instead of a system that is constrained by all those factors, like a true "cybernetics of self" (Bateson 1972:309–37).

One of my contentions is that we have too long ignored the subjective impact of initiation on gender differentiation, which is especially unfortunate because the symbolic focus of many New Guinea ritual cults overtly concerns masculine development. Finding a place for the flutes in the male life cycle thus invites us to reexamine the first-stage rites during which they are introduced. After analyzing the behavioral context of the flutes, I will concentrate on boys' experience of the flute ceremony and bachelors' impersonations, finally leading to an interpretation of the culturally constituted fantasies surrounding the psychodynamic origins and identity functions of the flutes.

The flutes defend the secrets of ritualized masculinization, but they harbor their own mystery for women and boys. One riddle concerns how men manage to transform puny boys into virile warriors. Other questions concern the flutes' mysticism—what the sounds are, who or what animates them, and how men control the spirit being. It is not just that the flutes are a political weapon used to frighten and mystify women and children, who are supposed to fear and hide from them. The flutes are a primordial fetish: their bamboo tubes, when men blow them, are thought to be empowered by a being, a female spirit, who is, like men, hostile to women.

We have seen how the flutes' semantic attributes pinpoint—yet exaggerate, merge, and redefine—the vicissitudes of masculinity and femininity. The flutes are always played in pairs; they are thought to be "married." Men say they are like phalli. The longer pipe is referred to as male and as a penis; the shorter one is female and is compared to the glans penis. The flutes become the instrument for teaching about fellatio. What boys suck, in the flute ceremony, is the tip of the shorter "female glans penis bamboo," which protrudes from outside of the longer "male bamboo." The flutes are blown in rhythmic chords of two or three notes, their vibrations a synchrony among the flutists. Those orchestrated sounds—precious symphonies of human breath—broadcast the spirits' presence to excluded women and children. (In a few years, and at third-stage initiation, the boys-become-youths will learn that the flute sounds also signify the alluring, dangerous erotic moans of a woman; so life, death, and reproduction are eventually tied to the fetish.) The initiates become partners to the flutes; the bachelors are their appropriate mates. Flute players act as fellateds for the flute-sucking boys, the fellators becoming a vessel for accumulating maleness, manliness. Boys have all other erotic activity prohibited, and they must scrupulously avoid females. Hence, initiates are tabooed from blowing flutes or serving as homoerotic fellateds, while bachelors become their superordinates.

Novices relate three emotions related to flute-oriented behavior: maternal loss, fear, and shame. As a background to that subjectivity, boys know that their fathers and sponsors—gender role models—are the instigators of initiation and that ritual treatment is said to stimulate growth and thus to masculinize them.

The phenomenology of the flute ceremony begins with the cry of the flutes, a haunting, fearful sound. It is crucial to stress that a novice, like his mother (with whom he is invidiously identified), has associated the flute sounds from his earliest years with a secret power known only to his father. The sound commences whenever men hold their rituals. The music of the flutes is awesome, and whatever else children tend to feel about it, I suggest that they also fear it. Women, of course, are physically threatened by men, who guard the "secret of the flutes." This fact is itself significant; Bowlby (1973:185ff.) has noted how children as young as two years of age come to acquire the particular fears of their mothers (reinforced by siblings or others), whether or not these fears are "reality oriented." Moreover, it is plausible to assume that a boy comes to perceive the flutes as a real danger to both his mother and himself. This dangerous mystery is no doubt a source of the fearful and fascinating ambivalence of the flutes, which are finally revealed to the boys in the initiation ceremony.

The first appearance of the flute players is an omen of the hostile behavior that follows. The flute-sucking "test" is begun in silence; like the lewd joking during the preceding body decoration, it involves aggressive, intimidating behavior. The flute sucking, a goal-directed action, tacitly communicates the intentions of the elders: they seek to dominate novices through threats and seductive pleading. Human behavior is not usually so one-dimensional (see Bateson 1972:387–402), but the flute-sucking act is aimed primarily at traumatizing boys, reducing them to tears. Though a lad seems to have a choice between orally submitting to and refusing the flute, his sucking behavior reduces him to being a subordinate and, eventually, a fellator, for men clearly state that the act simulates the mechanics of fellatio and indicates a boy's willingness to fulfill his erotic role later. Conversely, a novice's refusal signals his defiance of men's authority. We saw how Kokwai responded to this: he entered the ritual scene, followed by several men, all of whom pounded the boys with flutes, making them cry. This "infantile" response was the desired outcome, I think, for the aggressiveness then ceased. There, as in secular life, boys who suck the flute are lauded and praised, whereas individuals who reject "it"—authority, status subordination, or fellatio—are scorned, and their resistance induces the men to behave in a hostile manner toward them.

Reducing boys to that helpless state thus creates a certain mood for the emotionally charged teaching that follows. The dominating acts of men, I suggest, excite the boy but strike panic; and such authoritarian coercion, exacerbated through careful pleas or threats of death and castration (by authority figures), may engender an awareness that personal choice (e.g., in gender behavior) is being utterly withdrawn, perhaps forever.

Extraordinary erotic information is also transmitted. These suggestions—in the powerful context of the flute ceremony—lead to information processing of hitherto unknown possibilities: about one's father, one's mother, and oneself. There is however, no immediate recourse to action or escape, an experience that stimulates hyperemotionality (Pribram 1967). In this manner, I propose, a boy's conscious experience of the flute ceremony may be infused with primary-process (unconscious) thought.

I wish here to describe that first ritual experience as a primordial traumatic act in relation to an individual's alternate state of consciousness triggered by the flute-oriented behaviors. There are three main reasons for doing so. First, this is the initial experience in which men actually reveal the flutes boys have long known from their titillating sounds. Second, novices evince traumatic responses—for instance, fear, shame, and awe—but without having recourse to their mothers as primary protective figures. Third, men make powerful erotic demands in the form of homoerotic practices (and, later, fantasies), sanctioned by death threats. This experiential bedrock, I contend, becomes the base for the accumulating panic of the experience.

Further, let us think of the flute ceremony, directly followed by the bachelors' ritual impersonations and associated homoerotic encounters, as engendering—and objectifying—a primordial mood (see Geertz 1966:90, on "long-lasting moods"). This mood state (or psychological frame) is emotion laden and is comprised of both conscious intentionality and elements of primary process; for, as Bateson (1972:377–78; see also LeVine 1973:237–39) argues, information processing in deeply moving experiences, like this one, tends to create an isomorphism between ritual symbolism and the inner objects of fantasy. If this pseudotrance state (Lex 1979) is a goal entailment of the ritual, then its affective dimensions are as anthropologically significant as the social facts that evoked it (Needham 1967; Sturtevant 1968). Clearly, the basis for this mood state is culturally sanctioned trauma and what is done with that trauma—how it is socially channeled, is ritually reinforced, and continues to live on in a boy's sense of himself and maleness. And to unravel that developmental complexity in the male ethos, we need to explore the constellation of cultural fantasy embedded in the primordial experience of the flutes.

The flute-orientated behavior involves several interlocking fantasies of enigmatic significance in which the novices' later subjective experience is suspended. The principal drama occurs in the cult house on the evening of the flute ceremony. The flute-playing bachelors—the impersonators—present themselves to the novices as (1) old female hamlet spirits, (2) wailing for the boys, (3) having lots of "water" (i.e., semen), and, the men asserted, (4) if the boys felt "sorry" for those beings, (5) they ought to "help them out" (i.e., relax the bachelors' penes by acting as their fellators), since, to take the native idiom, (6) the flutes (like helpless infants) are "crying out for milk" (i.e., semen). This last point apparently concerns how the flute— as a fetish—bonds the flutist bachelor (who blows it) with the novice (who sucks it) and, specifically, links the penetrating penis with the cavity of the mouth.[13] If this fantasy system, with its convoluted roles of flute players and flute suckers, seems as baffling to the reader as it first appeared to me, then reconsider its consequences.

The ritual behavior, first of all, imaginatively effects an identification between the impersonating bachelors and the female spirits. In the cult-house context, youths are dressing up as spirits. That masquerade is more than simply a metaphoric "cultural performance" (Wagner 1972:9–10); it is also a psychologically exciting disguise, a kind of pseudo-transvestite identity similar to that of female impersonators. Why initiation motivates the impersonation of specifically female cult spirits is not hard to understand if we bear in mind the primordial traumatic act of maternal detachment and loss.

Here is a hypothesis: the female hamlet spirits are thinly disguised surrogates for the mothers of boys, who have been "lost" and left behind. The impersonating flute players are their proxy. Remember, though, that it is the bachelors who dramatize and act out the figures of "wailing spirits." It is they who demand attention from the displaced boys by objectifying and then transferring back to the novices hostile images of loss and care following maternal separation. The flutes are rueful, then, because their spirits have "lost their sons." This is not, however, all of what bachelors communicate. Permeating the melody is the hint of erotic seduction: that the impersonators have "lots of water." (Do the speakers mean semen or mother's milk—or is the difference, at that moment, really important?) In other words, semen is contextually equated with breast milk as the bachelor's phallus is equated with the mother's breast. The ritual fantasy tries to transfer boys' attachments to their mothers into being inseminated by the bachelors.

The ethnography of the flute ritual confirms that a fantasy isomorphism is created between the flute player and maternal figure and between the flute sucker and infant figure. This intersubjective fantasy postulates some kind of primary-process association linking the child's experience of suckling at

13. The use of this idiom ("to cry out for") in regard to the flutes is multivalent; not only are the flutes playing, but their sound is said to represent the female spirits' cries as well. A common idiom (among men) for being sexually frustrated enough that the penis secretes drops of pre-ejaculatory seminal fluid (see Pierson and D'Antonio 1974:48–49) is that the "penis is crying out for an erotic release" (i.e., for "its food").

his mother's breast with the novice's act of sucking the bachelor's penis. One element of this complex appears to be that the bachelor has a mature glans penis and semen. He can engage in sexual intercourse; the novice cannot.

At the bedrock of this extraordinary fantasy system, I think, is a piece of deep scripting: the ultimate complementary acts (and relationships, i.e., mother-son, husband-wife) are maternal breast-feeding (see Mead 1949:88) and fellatio intercourse. In the primordial mood associated with the flutes, one suspects the men are transferring a powerful metacommunication: "Forget your mother and wanting to be like her; you'll soon have a penis that gives milk as ours do." To what extent is that belief internalized among boys?

Now we are in a better position to tease apart the mechanisms by which flute-oriented behavior radically alters the novice's maternal attachment relationships (Bowlby 1969). Culturally, the flutes are ritually gendered and registered as a symbolic substitute for the boy's mother. Psychodynamically, in a context of traumatic maternal separation, Sambia ritual attempts to use the flute as a detachable phallus and a substitute for the female breast (cf. Bowlby 1973:268). The bachelors' impersonation of female hamlet spirits illustrates but one of various attempts to shift the boys' core gender identity (Stoller 1968). The flutes release feelings of helplessness and fear and thus supplant the mother as the preferred attachment figure by offering the culturally valued penis and homoerotic relationships as sensual substitutes for the mother's breast and for the mother as a whole person (see Bowlby 1973:316; Bateson 1972:238, 299). In behavioral terms, ritual utilizes psychophysiological techniques of "brainwashing" (Sargent 1957:92–95), such as extreme aggressive behavior, to redirect the child's attachment away from the preferred maternal figure and compel it toward male figures.

Here is, in sum, a partial interpretation of the flutes' initial effects on masculine development. The secret of the flutes becomes an unspoken understanding between a boy and his father vis-à-vis his mother. It also becomes a bond among male peers in opposition to women. With the novices living under threat of castration and death, any heteroerotic tendencies are blocked for years, and ritualized homoeroticism becomes the royal road to unblocking them. A shame-provoking secret of male development is obviously that masculinization occurs under the hegemony of continual asymmetrical fellatio. Ritual secrecy—defended by the fearful flutes—prevents women from "knowing" that homoerotic relationships transform their fledgling sons into handsome youths (Herdt 1981). It is the flutes that become their other "mothers" and "wives."

It is likely, however, that the redirection of maternal attachment is never quite successful. Such bonds are, after all, the foundation of character structure, and while they may be modified, the underlying feelings of loss are perhaps handled as much by denial and repression as by anything else. Moreover, homoerotic bonds may indeed be powerful, but they are transient. It is essential to underline this viewpoint, for it helps to account for men's ambivalence toward the flutes and boy-inseminating in general. Indeed, it is apparent that death threats are necessary for men to accomplish their task: maternal separation and ritualized masculinization are not actions that boys would themselves initiate. If the boys do resist, though, as I think occurs, then how does ritual eventually produce its desired psychological transformation?

I propose that the primordial traumatic act and mood state of the flute ceremony establish a symbolic equation (Róheim 1942:348; Segal 1957) in the thought of boys, whereby the flute is eventually felt to be both a penis and a female breast. We should recall the psychodynamics of a symbolic equation: the symbolic substitute is treated as if it were an "internalized object" (e.g., maternal attachment figure) without a change in affect (Segal 1957:392–95). Ultimately, the experiential source of this subjective state is hypothesized as arising from the early conflictual nature of the child's tie to his caretakers. Certain elements of the underlying thoughts and wishes of the child, elements that are projected toward his attachment figures, may come to be repressed. Segal (1957:395) argues that the formation of a symbolic equation issues from the "capacity to experience loss and the wish to recreate the (maternal) object within oneself." Hence, the symbolic equation increases in importance after separation from mother, and the need to deny the loss of her; its subjectivity helps satisfy a need to feel secure with a maternal surrogate.

The origin of a symbolic equation, Segal (1957:396–97) contends, follows from a basic "disturbance in differentiation" between a person and his or her internalized objects, a fusion of a symbol and its designata associated with "early unresolved conflicts." We are fortunately in a position to do more than simply speculate about why Sambia males might be prone to fuse the penis and the breast in their experience of the flutes. A basic aspect of all the boys' reports about their earliest initiation experiences concerns feelings of longing for their mothers. Moreover, in the course of later development, boys become involved in significant, sometimes sustained liaisons with bachelors—the outcomes of which can only be, of course, the end of the relationship. These take on aspects of substitute maternal attachment, even as boys tend to identify consciously (including notions of literal introjection; see Kambo's remarks above) with the masculinity of bachelors.

Here I wish to stress the process whereby a shared symbolic representation may be subjectively converted into a personal symbolic equation. Segal notes that when any symbol is used as a defense mechanism (i.e., of projective identification) against depressive anxieties, it can revert back to a motivating equation (Segal 1957:396–97). This may be what occurs in the experience of homoerotic contacts. Perhaps, at first, a boy adopts fellatio practices because he will be rewarded with ritual approval and social praise and because he fears punishment; his curiosity may overcome his shame, and he also faces a strong element of coercion. Mixed in with those events is the use of fellatio as a defense against maternal loss and against, sooner or later, his negative feelings of shameful subordination, exploitation, and helplessness, all understandable reactions to his situation. In various ways, then, being inseminated by a bachelor partially substitutes for nurture by the whole mother: a valued penis for her breast. (The success of that adjustment in individual development remains to be seen.) What this interpretation of the initiatory symbolism stresses is the child's tie to his mother.

To reiterate, my view is that cultural values and institutions interact as elements in a system that includes actual behavior and subjectivity. My work differs from that of Róheim (1942), for instance, on this very point: culture cannot be reduced to unconscious processes (and vice versa); and the inferences must be drawn from observation, not theory. I underline this point to state that my speculations about the mother-infant bond are not offered as the only explanation for the precipitating of Sambia masculinity or ritual.

However, we might think of the roots of flute-oriented behavior, focused upon the fantasized equation penis = breast, as resulting from a kind of prolonged "symbiosis" (Mahler 1963) between mothers and boys in the antagonistic setting of Sambia relationships between the sexes. The ethnography supports this idea in the way boys act: they are most closely attached to their mothers, and they long especially for them, not their fathers, following ritual separation. Cultural belief and ritual action also uphold the urgent need to separate mothers and boys (not girls) and to masculinize the boys. Initiation arises from a pervasive conviction that biological maleness is tenuous and not a "natural" product, that mother's pollution threatens it, and that ritual insemination is the only means to obtain it. My perspective is that this "symbolic complex" is a culturally constituted response to the situation of most individual Sambia males' needs to sense themselves unambiguously and to perform competently as masculine men in the ways demanded by their communities. Ritualized masculinization is a necessary means toward that adult outcome.

Bettelheim's classic 1955 study, *Symbolic Wounds,* ended with a similar viewpoint, which has found increasing support over the years. Concentrating on the early maternal attachment of "pregenital fixations," of envy and identification with one's mother, Bettelheim (1955:17, 124n) sought to challenge the perspectives of Freud, Reik, and Róheim that the manly initiators merely wanted to "castrate" their sons and "create sexual anxiety . . . to make the incest taboo secure." Emphasizing boys' identity conflicts in accepting their prescribed adult gender roles, Bettelheim (1955:264) concluded that initiation rites enabled a boy to acquire "the role he wishes to play in society or which society expects him to fulfill." Here is where anthropologists need to confront the psychosocial issues of gender differentiation (Money and Ehrhardt 1972), critical-period "learning," and sex typing (Luria 1979; Maccoby 1979) in more creative ways. Mahler (1963) believes that "separation-individuation"—the critical development phase for early gender differentiation—must be established for all infants to achieve an unambiguous sense of self and body boundaries, to feel themselves distinct from their mothers. The mother can help or hinder this pre-Oedipal process, and the father's role is also crucial. Gender conflict may emerge if either the mother or the infant is reluctant to separate (thereby prolonging the symbiotic relationship). For males, unlike females, there is an added difficulty (Lidz and Lidz 1977): boys must not only disidentify (Greenson 1968) with their mothers (break the symbiotic union) but also identify with available masculine figures. If this dual process is blocked, males are at risk that any of several basic male gender disorders can result. (Primary male transsexualism is the most spectacular [see Stoller 1968, 1975.)

The anthropological significance of these perspectives is great for core gender-identity formation in the sexually polarized societies of New Guinea. Mead (1935), Whiting, Kluckhohn, and Anthony (1958), and Young (1965) reached early insights. In modern clinical studies, Stoller (1973:314) has most recently noted that core identity is "fairly well formed by a year and a half or two years" and is "almost irreversible by around age five or six." Only if a boy can "grow beyond the feminine identifications that resulted from his first encounters with his mother's female body and feminine qualities" can he become a "separate masculine individual" (Stoller 1968:98). The absence—or psychological aloofness—of the father has a lasting effect on this process (see Whiting and Whiting 1975). In Melanesian communities, with their chronic warfare, exogamous patrilocal organization, antagonistic male-female relationships, postpartum sex taboos, and separate sleeping arrangements, it is not surprising to find gender concerns at the center of the social reproduction of male cult activities (Allen 1967; M. Strathern 1988). Sambia initiation belongs to this set of cultural traditions.

To what extent is Oedipal conflict another, developmentally later motivational source of these culturally constituted concerns with gender formation? We need more data to know. Clearly, this factor is important; perhaps initiation is an "alternative" to the Oedipal transition (see Lidz and Lidz 1977). My own review of the New Guinea literature (Herdt 1981:303–25) indicates, however, that pre-Oedipal development seems as basic and pervasive as the status-envy and post-Oedipal conflict factors postulated by Whiting and his colleagues. The impetus of Sambia folk psychology concerns the generalized difficulty of the male's separation-individuation from his mother and traumatic adjustment into the highly ritualized masculine gender role.

Conclusion

This study has pursued a line of inquiry first envisioned by K. E. Read's early study of the *nama* cult but generally ignored since then. Like Read, I was led to consider the consequences of male belief and ritual for masculine solidarity, politics, and sexual antagonism. In addition, however, I have attended to the symbolic complex of the flutes as revealed through observations of behavior, subjectivity, and symbolic processes in Sambia first-stage initiation. These elements form a system; an adequate understanding would have to confront them all. Sambia differ, of course, from Gahuku-Gama and other Highlands peoples, belonging to their own time and place. Their use of ritualized boy-inseminating practices makes their initiation special. And that tradition appears to separate the Sambia from initiatory cults elsewhere in the Eastern Highlands—at least on the surface.

In other parts of New Guinea, though, ritualized boy-insemination has long been reported from widely scattered areas. To name only a few instances: the Trans-Fly (Williams 1936a) and Kiwai Papuans (Landtman 1927:237); the Marind-anim tribes (Van Baal 1966:834, and passim); the Great Papuan Plateau tribes—Etoro (Kelly 1976), Kaluli (Schieffelin 1976:124–26), and Onabasulu (Kelly 1976:16); and somewhat closer to Sambia, the Baruya Anga (Godelier 1976). Schieffelin's study (1976) provides an important instance of a system of ritualized homoerotic practices less wedded to initiation. This listing is only a small sample, yet it cannot be doubted that these groups represent a remarkable symbolic pattern neglected in the anthropology of Melanesia. Let us again concentrate on the flutes.

The flutes are arch symbols of Sambia manhood. They are identified with the normative ritual conventions of masculine performance—what we cover by the term "ritual cult." The flutes thus ensure a measure of be havioral continuity between the past (both individual and societal) and the present contexts their sounds signify: male initiation. The complementary dimensions of the flutes' meaning therefore embrace a whole way of life, and we can agree with Glick (1972:822), who states that they "are a key to understanding culture and society" in New Guinea.

It seems apparent, moreover, that the flutes are of tremendous significance for individual identity as well. We have seen this significance in highly emotional rituals, seen its expression crystallized in male fantasy and beliefs, identified it in subjective expressions, and inferred it from the interactions of boys and men and women. All of that we have explored. But what we do not know from the literature and cannot discover otherwise is what experiencing the flutes means precisely for particular individuals' sense of themselves at particular moments in their lives. And here anthropologists have unfortunately forgone precious historic opportunities for describing the living meanings attached to the now-disappearing flutes.

We look to K.E. Read's *The High Valley* (1965:115–17) for the most sensitive observations—a good place to begin the comparative ethnography of the flutes.

> Later, back in my house with the flutes carefully laid on the floor, the men were like contestants in a game that tested their strength and concentration to the limits of their endurance. They were almost drunk with excitement, balanced on the edge of exhaustion, their nervous energy so recently strung to its highest pitch seeking to return to its normal level through incessant talking.
>
> Hunehune's [the informant's] eyes were bright with feeling. His voice trembled perceptibly, like his hand, which rested lightly on a pair of flutes, while he tried to make me understand and share the wonder of the sound we had heard. . . . Hunehune turned to Bihore and remarked that his [flute] playing had so deranged him that if he had been a woman he would have come to Bihore's house. There was no mistaking the implication of his words, the attribution of sexual qualities to the *nama*. Male sexuality was a manifestation of power, the very force of life, the basis of existence; the flutes not only symbolized power . . . but also linked it to the structure of relationships that bound each man to his fellows.

With this superb sketch, let us turn to other reports and adduce some general points of comparison with Sambia flute-oriented behavior.[14]

14. For an incisive survey of the ethnomusicology and symbolism in the Melanesian literature on sound instruments, particularly bull-roarers and flutes, see Gourlay (1975). As Gourlay (1975:1–19) shows, the function and meaning of the flutes vary in different culture areas of Melanesia; in the Eastern Highlands of Gahuku-Gama and Sambia, the flutes are by far the more important instruments, though the bull-roarer is present too.

SECRECY OF THE FLUTES

The flutes are secret. Throughout the Eastern Highlands and in other parts of New Guinea, ritual flutes embody a "tension": they are regarded as secret, but they are semipublicly played and used. One of their "secrets" concerns the powers that animate them: men talk rhetorically as if they were mystical spirits; women and children allegedly fear such. Still, many ethnographers have qualified this secrecy: "How secret are the instruments in reality?" (Gourlay 1975:101). The answer is complex. In various groups, men clearly perceive secrecy as a means of ensuring their status-quo dominance over women (and children) through the contrivance of the flutes' mysticism (see Bateson 1958:169; Godelier 1976:275; Hogbin 1970:113–14; Mead 1935:15; Nilles 1950:30; Read 1952:6, 14; Salisbury 1965:71; cf. also Williams 1936 b:41, on bull-roarers). Merely excluding others gives one a mystified "superior power" (Bettelheim 1955:228) in social control, a point emphasized by Langness (1974). Another question concerns the extent of women's knowledge about the inner core of men's secret rites. Here we are on even weaker ground because no matter what part of the mystique surrounding the flutes is fiction, they are still dangerous, not a sham: their threatening guardians are armed warriors. Not surprisingly, it has been difficult to ascertain what women actually do and do not know about the flutes (see Gourlay 1975:102–18).

Like Langness (1974:209–10), I am convinced that some women see through at least part of the surface facade, the contrived content, of men's dogma and activities surrounding the flute. Among Sambia, however, women "understand" that certain contexts of ritual secrecy disguise other things—which they carefully avoid—but my guess is that women still remain ignorant of the inner sanctum of masculine ritual. What matter then, are the visible, disconcerting contradictions between the private, public, and secret facets of male and female interactions, the "charade which is not a charade" that so fascinated Read (1952).

Our analysis must be sensitive. There is a great difference between screaming secrets and whispering secrets, and we are far from understanding the behavioral intricacies of this pervasive contrast in Melanesian cultures. In particular, we have virtually ignored the interface of mystification (Barth 1975), duplicity, and complicity regarding what men believe women and youngsters do or do not really know, though there are scattered hints in the archives (Allen 1967:37; Bateson 1958:169; Hogbin 1970:72; Lawrence 1965:205; Nilles 1950:30, 46; Van Baal 1966:475–478; Whiting and Reed

1938:192; Williams 1936a:184). (One suspects that the preponderance of male ethnographers has contributed to the situation; see, e.g., the anecdotes by Camilla Wedgwood [1938:187] and Marie Reay [1959:170].) In short, there are contrasting forms of secrecy and mystery and different ways of understanding and communicating forbidden knowledge, the point being that we should probe more carefully than before, discriminate more finely than with the gross labels "secret" and "public."

THE SPIRITS OF THE FLUTES

The flutes are animated by female spirits. The literature is stimulating but sketchy on this point. The flutes are, in general, identified with ancestral spirits of uncertain sex (Allen 1967:58; Glick 1972:821–22; Gourlay 1975:75n; Nilles 1950:46; Read 1952:8; Tuzin 1980). In certain instances, the beings focused upon are fierce or carnivorous birds (Bateson 1958:162; Reay 1959:170; Salisbury 1965:60–61) or animals—for instance, crocodiles (Wirz 1959:11–17). Read (1952:10ff.) connected the flutes to pig feasts and communal "fertility rites," invoking ancestral blessings (also see Newman 1964:265–66).

Aside from Sambia, however, there are several peoples who clearly treat the spirits of the flutes as female. The Keraki (Williams 1936a:187, 197ff.) are closest to Sambia in this respect: initiates are led to meet an "old woman" whose name (Ause) also represents the flutes, which are said to be the "wives of the bull-roarer." (Note Williams's [1936a:201] link between the flutes and ritualized homoerotic sex.) Berndt (1965:89) says that Eastern Highlands women refer to the flutes as a "flute woman." The neighboring Siane refer to the spirits as birds, but the key figure is called the "Mother of the Birds," which initiates have revealed to them (Salisbury 1965:60–61). Read (personal communication) likewise feels that the *nama* creatures were female.[15] And Lindenbaum (1976:6) remarkably notes that "Fore initiation involves males playing on sacred flutes (symbolic penises) which they tell women . . . are the voices of Kabuwei, literally 'wild women,' a word that by 1970 had also come to mean a female prostitute" (see Lindenbaum and Glasse 1969:169). In these cultures, at least, the flutes are empowered by female beings of supernatural dimensions (see also Strathern and Strathern 1968: 197–98).

15. I am indebted to the late Professor Read for his kind reading in 1981 of this chapter. Part of his personal communication concerning the Gahuku-Gama *nama* cult flutes should be cited here: "The 'carnivorous bird' is simply the explanation put out for 'female consumption.' Or at least if the spirit is thought to be bird-like, it is also 'female' and 'hostile' and 'erotic.'"

IMPERSONATION OF SPIRITS

Men impersonate the spirits. Here, however, we are on thin ice because the data are not fine enough to give us a clear picture of what occurs. The ceremonial impersonation of spirit beings more generally is, of course, widespread (Epstein 1969:239–42; Mead 1935; Tuzin 1980). One suspects that more is at work in cases where initiates are secretly introduced by young men impersonating those spirits (Gourlay 1975:69; Holmes 1924:121, 164). Wogeo (Hogbin 1970:72ff.), with their *nibek* monsters, and Keraki (Williams 1936a:158, 187), who speak of the "old women" spirits in the context of institutionalized sodomy, more closely approximate the Sambia symbolic complex.

HOSTILITY OF THE FLUTES

The flutes are hostile to women. This element of the flutes seems nearly universal in New Guinea (Berndt 1962:51; Hays and Hays 1982:214; Hogbin 1970:101; Newman 1965:67; Nilles 1950:30, 46; Salisbury 1965:60ff.; Whiting 1941:90–91). Many questions arise, such as: How do men and women experience that hostility? What does that do to relationships between the sexes? And how much of a reality are men's threats in sanctioning their secrets? For instance, in reviewing this vast literature, Gourlay (1975:102ff.) points out that while everywhere women could be punished by maiming or death if they were to penetrate the flutes' secret, only one case of ultimate penalty (on hearsay at that) is actually known. This does not mean that the male cults aren't serious about defending their fetishes; it rather implies that the psychological significance of the flutes lies in their ominous presence, which keeps the sexes distant.

FLUTE CATEGORIZATION

The flutes are polarized into "male" and "female" types. Here is another widespread symbolic principle governing the meaning of flutes. As with Sambia, we find elsewhere a polarization of the paired flutes into both "male" and "female" categories (Berndt 1962:70; Mead 1935:76; Oosterwal 1961:28), and in certain places the more precise identification of a "male" longer flute and "female" shorter flute (Glick 1964:85; Hogbin 1970:73; Whiting and Reed 1938:190; Williams 1930:185). Once again, there are hints that the flutes are elsewhere labeled "spouses," "co-wives," or "age mates" of initiates or bull-roarers (Bamler 1911:50; Berndt 1965:89; Williams 1936a: 186; see also Newman and Boyd 1982:259–60.

FLUTE REVELATION

The flutes are the key "revelation" of the initiation. This point was underlined by Read (1952:13), who felt that whatever else the initiation entailed, the revelation of the flutes was its mysterious high point. The revelation dramatically bonds initiates "together with a spiritual force" (Lindenbaum and Glasse 1969:169). That holds equally true for Sambia (cf. Newman and Boyd 1982:263).

EROTIC ELEMENTS OF THE FLUTES

The flutes are eroticized. This notion concerns my final point, and it bears especially on the Sambia cult. Although we can go only so far in analyzing the implications of the available data, this theme invites attention, since workers have long ignored the psychosexual significance of the flutes.

The previous elements inferred from the literature—secrecy, female spirits, ritual impersonation and hostility, sexual polarity—add weight to the viewpoint that the flutes, and their culturally constituted fantasy system, play a major role in the ritual construction of male gender identity in various New Guinea societies. (I do not doubt that bull-roarers, either alone or in conjunction with flutes, carry a homologous symbolic "load" in still other groups [see Dundes 1976; Van Baal 1963; Williams 1936b].) All of this seems obvious and acceptably in line with the trend of anthropological research following Read (1952). Gender roles, sexual antagonism, gender ideology, and pollution: so much of that surface discussion preoccupies the literature. Nevertheless, in spite of that long interest, data on erotic behavior (both for females and for males)—which sex and gender are surely also about—are not to be found. Why that gap matters, as noted, is that the flutes represent more than symbols, a male cult, bamboo objects, or spirit beings: they pinpoint an erotic relationship between bachelors and initiates, the eventual outcome of which is a particular kind of erotic excitement in heterosexual relationships.

Taken together, the above points suggest that aside from being ritual symbols, the flutes—like an erotic fetish—may bear an "assignable relation" (Freud 1962:19) to men's object choices in their erotic life. It is the nature of the flutes' fetishistic qualities and the male fantasy system that most concerns us. The flutes stand for a lifetime of developmental experiences that have the effect of energizing and channeling masculine eroticism along certain lines.

The job of the flutes is to convert small, puny boys, too attached to their mothers, into virile and aggressive warriors (Hogbin 1970:101). That in itself is no small task. But added to it is a more monumental challenge: the creation of a gender identity that makes men erotically excited first by boys and then by women, and not just any sexual excitement, but a kind built around rigid, untender rules. In certain ways, still as yet to be understood, the flutes are connected with—can evoke—early experiences and fantasies I believe begin in infancy. The culturally constituted fantasy system of the flutes disguises all this by means of its ritual form, homoerotic relations, and impersonations. Those cultural disguises are critical for understanding the entire complex. Their part concerns mainly the surface, however, while the bamboo tubes by themselves are nothing: "The fetish is merely the link between the worshiper and object of worship" (Haddon 1921:70). What is the nature of the underlying object?

Freud first noted that there was a close nexus between an erotic fetish and what anthropologists call a religious fetish, in which it is felt that the "gods are embodied" (1962:19). The precise character of that relationship undoubtedly varies from person to person and from one cultural context to another. Without individual studies, of course, we cannot infer to what extent the meaning accorded the flutes "passes beyond the point of being merely a necessary condition" culture requires of masculine character structure and into erotic "pathological aberrations" (Freud 1962:20). This is the murky borderland revealed by Read's observations of the Gahuku-Gama. (One wonders about the sensual smearing of pig's grease or blood on the flutes and on oneself [Sambia do not do this], or the stuffing of bamboos with pork fat [Read 1952:10ff.] and the like: is this indicative of a fetishistic element linking the religious and erotic in New Guinea male cults?) Indeed, all of the formal criteria by which Stoller (1979:8) identifies the creation of an erotic fetish can be inferred from these data on the flutes, but despite that, the flute behavior of Sambia is not perverse fetishism.

A finer distinction, between fetishism and the diffusely erotic, is provided by Stoller's (1979:100–101) recent work. Sambia (unlike fetishists) are not sexually aroused by the flutes irrespective of context; the flutes do not count that much. Nonetheless, after years of powerful, sensual associations, the flutes can become erotic: their sounds can muster the fantasized drama that women and boys—curious but traumatized by the need to hide from the tempting flutes—become excited, as men had been themselves when, as boys, they were in the overpowered audience hiding from the flutes (see Newman and Boyd 1982). Perhaps in this way the flutes become a sign of men's achievement of mastery over women, real-life challenges, and themselves. And, through the primordial mood assisting that sign to the self, past "frustration and trauma are converted to triumph" (Stoller 1979:9).

This developmental scenario provides a new perspective for understanding the pervasive "sexual antagonism" of New Guinea societies. Langness (1967) felt that such cultural patterns were a response to the warring conditions of Highlands communities: ritual practices had to deny men's dependency on and desire for women. On a cultural level, I agree with this model that denies dependency, but on the individual level—the level of male gender identity and its preservation—I believe that we can go further. The psychological distancing mechanisms present in Sambia ritual (e.g., female avoidance, secrecy, ritualized boy-inseminating), as elsewhere, imply even more about male identity and character structure. In all facets of one's existence, as the flutes reveal, the differences between maleness and femaleness are fetishized, exaggerated, and blown up. This symbol structure suggests that in male erotic life, constant hostility is often needed to create enough of a distance, separateness, and dehumanization of women to allow there to occur the ritually structured sexual excitement necessary for culturally tempered heterosexuality and the "reproduction" of a society.

The flutes provide that symbolic funnel of polarity. Melanesians, however, are not the only ones to have known that, for the magical flute is, after all, a very old human symbol. The ancient Greeks, in their own way, also "worshiped" flutes, and the myth of the creation of their instruments seems timeless. Their maker was Pan (see Bulfinch 1967:35–36), the god of flocks and shepherds, who was fond of music but whom the Greeks nevertheless dreaded by association with the gloom and loneliness of his dark forests. He desired the beautiful and much-loved nymph Syrinx and one day intercepted her as she returned from the hunt. Pan attempted to pursue her, but she became afraid: she ran away, without stopping to hear his compliments, and he followed till she came to the bank of the river, where he overtook her, and she had only time to call for help on her friends the water nymphs. Pan threw his arms around what he supposed to be the form of the nymph, and found he embraced only a tuft of reeds! As he breathed a sigh, the air sounded through the reeds, and produced a plaintive melody. The god, charmed with the novelty and with the sweetness of he music, said, "Thus, then, at least, you shall be mine." And he took some of he reeds, and placing them together, of unequal lengths, side by side, made an instrument which he called the Syrinx, in honor of the nymph.

From this lovely tale the Greeks identified the origins of their Flutes. Is it not oddly disconcerting, though, that among lonely travelers, "sudden fright without any visible cause was ascribed to Pan, and called a Panic terror" (Bulfinch 1967:193)?[16] Plaintive melody and Panic fear: even the ancient Greeks knew the Janus face of our flutes.

16. After completing this manuscript I discovered the works of Hiatt (1977) and von Felszeghy (1920), whose discussions of similar phenomena—Mozart's *Magic Flute,* secret cults, and Pan—provide interesting contrasts with my arguments here.

FOUR

Sambia Nosebleeding Rites and Male Proximity to Women

Since the early work of Bateson (1958) and Mead (1935), New Guinea cultures—especially those in the Eastern Highlands studied by K. E. Read (1951, 1952)—have been identified with various initiatory rituals, among which none have proved as symbolically complex or theoretically controversial as those of bloodletting. In spite of considerable cross-cultural variation in the practices, researchers have not only drawn on these data but have also reached divergent conclusions about their meaning. Furthermore, each of the proposed interpretations implied different slants on the developmental context of the rites that were seldom explicated, let alone demonstrated. It is remarkable, then, that after these many years of theoretical interest no ethnographer since Read (1965:127–33 had published detailed observations of these ritual behaviors until recently (see Lewis 1980; Poole 1982; Tuzin 1980:72–78), and none has systematically described the behavioral experience or cultural context of bloodletting in the male life cycle of a Highlands people. It is these problems—in relation to the cultural structure of nosebleeding and the ritualization of proximity to women throughout the developmental cycle—that I shall examine among the Sambia.

New Guineasts have tended to view bloodletting rites from several analytic perspectives. Read's (1952) emphasis on the social solidarity effected by the cult context of such rites has been widely supported (Berndt 1962; Newman 1965; Strathern 1969). Others have also concurred with Read (1952) that bloodletting is a form of "psychological conditioning" associated with the male warrior ethos (Allen 1967; Hogbin 1970; Mead 1935;

Tuzin 1980; Whiting 1941). Meggitt (1964) saw consistent correlations between types of sexual activity (e.g., "lechers" and "prudes"), purificatory
cults, and intergroup hostility vis-à-vis affines (see Allen 1967:11–12, 52–53).
Langness (1967) went further, arguing that "sexual antagonism"—within
the warring Highlands environment—arose as a culturally constituted response to deny men's dependence upon women. Lindenbaum (1972, 1976)
contended that rites like male bloodletting operate as systemic ecological
controls on women and their productivity (see Chowning 1980). Langness
(1974) further added that the secrecy of cult rituals effects male solidarity
and power in regulating strategic female domains in which male social
control needs "supernatural" aids. Moreover, many New Guineasts have
emphasized native ideas that expurgations of maternal substance or "pollution" are needed to develop and maintain masculinity (Bateson 1958;
Berndt 1965:92–94; Herdt 1981; Hogbin 1970:103ff.; Lewis 1980; Mead
1935:85; Meigs 1976; Newman 1964; Poole 1982; Read 1951, 1965; Whiting
1941:64ff.). In sum, however, studies have taken a synchronic viewpoint
stressing the adult outcome of rituals for the functioning of social groups
and institutions.

Here I take a diachronic perspective on Sambia sexual polarity and ritual
that will, I hope, offer fresh questions and answers about ritual bloodletting
by attending to the developmental context in which it emerges. Let me begin by stating several analytic points about the Sambia sociocultural system
(see Herdt 1981, 1982). The first point concerns a societal imperative: before
pacification (1964–65), Sambia communities needed to create tough, aggressive fighters to fill and replenish the ranks of their warriorhood. Next, I
believe that the production of this type of "warrior personality" among
males anywhere was not easy or "natural" (Mead 1935; Schwartz 1973);
moreover, its difficulties were exacerbated by the Sambia developmental
cycle, which results in the presence of too much mother and too little father,
thus stunting the male's early separation from his mother in childhood.
Last, the accommodation of these early childhood experiences, and core
gender identity (see Stoller 1968), to the demanding behavioral environment of adult male character structure, established special, enduring,
psychosocial needs for autonomy that could be symbolically sustained
through ritual mechanisms—for example, nosebleeding behaviors—enabling competent adjustment to, and performance of, the adult masculine
gender role throughout life. Although these psychosocial needs arose as un-
intended social consequences of Sambia socialization, their symbolic expression has been culturally transmitted and reproduced to filter those
needs. The symbolic structure specifically "filtered out" mother and all that

she stood for, and "filtered in" father, aggressivity, and ritu:
to women; and these "symbolic filters" (Herdt 1981) came t(
their own—as "internal discourses" for the institution and
cault 1980:28) of bloodletting. Viewed in this way, th(
nosebleeding binds the ideological and sensory poles of me;
ignata of dominant symbols (Turner 1967) in Sambia rit(
male warrior ethos and worldview a dynamic product of th_ _____ _____
opmental context.

It is obvious and has been well reported that cutting the body in bloodletting is painful. It is also known that these "mutilation rites" are, throughout New Guinea, first administered forcibly by elders on groups of boys in
collective initiation. Bloodletting is often said to be necessary for "male
growth," so one can understand, in terms of the native model, why bloodletting should be done until maturity has been achieved. But what motivates those ritual behaviors afterward, on into old age? Unless one assumes
(as I do not) that these painful operations are intrinsically pleasurable or
satisfying, we must examine the cultural and social psychological factors
that compel subsequent adult operations: beliefs, self experiences, and
ever-present audiences that are sufficiently approving or fearsome to result
in the painful repetition of such self-inflicted acts. Here we anthropologists
have not met the challenge of Bettelheim's (1955:14) question: What is "the
function of mutilations regularly inflicted"?

The Sambia ritual cycle of initiations emphasizes four broad developmental themes in males' relationships to women that define the context of
nosebleeding throughout the life cycle. They emerge as follows: (1) Boys
must be physically separated from their mothers, and then nosebled to rid
them of female pollutants that block "male growth" (a concept that is, as we
have seen, complex). (2) The behavioral and cultural content of secret rites,
especially nosebleeding, is organized violently so as to effect psychological
detachment of boys vis-à-vis their mothers and avoidance of all females. (3)
This ritual aggressiveness, furthermore, effects attachment to masculine
figures through obedience to them as authorities, who train the boys to
become warriors—social outcomes that help explain, but also require
changes in, the cultural context of nosebleeding ritual following the initiates' social elevation to the upper ranks of the ritual cult hierarchy. (4) After
marriage, nosebleeding acts are transformed from being involuntary public
rituals to voluntary private events: men must (while alone) induce nosebleeding on each occasion of their wives' menstrual periods, into old age.
And they also become initiators. Thus, initiation nosebleedings are a social
control mechanism of the male cult which effects the collective regulation

boys, whereas among adult men, private nosebleedings become a means of one's autonomous self-regulation in contacts with women. The meaning of nosebleeding thus changes with successive ritual initiations, and, among adult men, those layers of meaning (concepts of manhood) are fixed within the developmental transformations in male character structure that enable one's self-regulation to come about. From these points there follows my thesis: psychosocial (and physical) proximity to women is the key variable in predicting the occurrence of nosebleeding behavior; changes in the cultural definitions of proximity, at different points in the male life cycle, precisely regulate the shifting temporal sequence, ideological teachings, sociocultural context, and the affective intensity of the bloodletting experience.

Each one of these developmental themes bearing on nosebleeding and proximity to women shall be examined in turn. A related and somewhat disconcerting pattern in the Sambia system will also be tackled. Sambia believe that a boy must be nosebled to "grow" and attain reproductive competence. But once married and fully initiated, men no longer offer that rationale for the private practices—not until middle age, that is. Among those older men, who have long since married once, twice, or more, and reared families, many again begin offering the pat statement that unless they nosebleed themselves, they will "stop growing." The thick connotations of that sense of "growth" must be interpreted, since they involve the end point of psychosocial autonomy and contacts with women.

The Context of Gender Relations

As I have already outlined in previous chapters, opposite sex relationships among the Sambia are sharply polarized along the lines of a misogynist male belief system depicting women as polluting, depleting inferiors a man should distrust and keep distant. Most unrelated, sexually mature women are regarded as potentially contaminating relative to their menstrual and vaginal fluids. But these ideological stereotypes (see M. Strathern 1972) do shift somewhat, according to particular individuals and situations. For example, men fear contamination mostly from their wives, not their sisters. Like Tuzin (1982), I have noted a disparity between male ritual rhetoric and the steadier domestic relationships between the sexes, including spouses. Sambia customarily expect the spouses to cohabit within a single domicile, and this pattern also affects men's ritually constituted misogyny. Nevertheless, one should not wish to push the significance of these constraints too far: men are in full charge of public affairs; women are relegated to heavy, dirty garden work and the polluting business of childbearing; ritual secrecy remains an enduring political and psychological force that suppresses women and children; most men are constantly mindful of female contamination and semen depletion through sexual intercourse; and abusive language, squabbling, and wife-beating, as well as suicides resulting from some such incidents, are pervasive in Sambia life.

The developmental cycle of children thus occurs in the context of open hostility or, at the least, ambivalence in men's behavior toward their wives. Children are involved in this familial conflict. By custom, infants are exclusively cared for by their mothers; other female caretakers later help out. Fathers remain aloof since both mother and child are regarded as one in their polluting potential, especially following birth, and also because postpartum taboos strictly forbid close interaction between the spouses, since that would lead to sexual intercourse, harming both mother and infant. Boys and girls remain closely attached to their mothers until two or three years of age (and sometimes longer, according to particular circumstances, e.g., widowhood). Girls become their mother's companions, and they continue residing with their parents until marriage, usually around the time of the menarche (c. up to nineteen years of age). Thereafter, the young women reside with their husbands or parents-in-law, which often removes them to another hamlet. Boys spend more time with their mothers and playmates than they do with their fathers. This style of maternal attachment continues relatively unchanged until first-stage initiation. But boy initiates are thereafter sanctioned for any contact (e.g., talking, looking at, or eating) with women, including their mothers. They reside exclusively in the men's clubhouses with other unmarried initiates and bachelors. Not until ten years and more later, after marriage and the strict deritualization of these avoidance taboos, may youths begin interacting with women again.

Men worry about the effects of the mother's prolonged contact with children, but especially with their sons. This concern is more than ideological rationalization, as one sees in actual case studies (Herdt 1981). Men regard the attainment of adult reproductive competence as far more problematic for males than females. Maleness is thought to depend on the acquisition of semen—the stuff of "biological" maleness—for precipitating male anatomic traits and masculine behavioral capacities (e.g., fighting prowess). Femaleness rests on the creation and circulation of blood, which is held, in turn, to stimulate the production of menstrual blood, the menarche, and final reproductive competence. A girl's menarche is celebrated in secret events that simply recognize socially her "natural" achievements. In girls, who possess a self-activating and functional menstrual-blood organ *(tingu),* maturation is thus viewed as an unbroken process leading from birth and maternal bonding into adulthood. In boys, however, two kinds of obstacles block male growth: their mother's pollution, food, and overall caretaking, which at first nurture but then stifle growth; and their innate lack of semen, since the semen organ *(kereku-kereku)* can only store, not manufacture, sperm—the key precipitant of manly reproductive competence.

Beliefs about Blood

At various levels of meaning, blood and its secular and ritual designata are identified with the vitality and longevity of women and femaleness. Females, unlike males, are believed to be gifted with an endogenous means of producing blood that hastens the development of female growth, the menarche, and the menses; it is also the provider of womb life for the fetus. The male and female parts in reproduction are clearly defined: a man's semen enters the womb and becomes a pool that eventually coagulates into fetal skin and bone tissue, set within the female blood of the womb. Fetal blood, supplied only by the mother's womb, becomes the circulatory blood needed by all babies and adults.

For all humans, circulatory blood is thought to be an elixir—within limits—that stimulates body functioning and growth, and the ability to withstand sickness or injury. The limits of this idea are embedded in several constructs through which Sambia perceive blood. First, there is a tacit distinction that amounts to the difference between circulatory blood and menstrual-womb blood. Both males and females possess circulatory blood *(menjaaku),* but only females have menstrual blood *(chenchi),* categorized with all female contamination *(pulungatnyi).* Second, Sambia speak of reproductively competent humans (and also trees and animals) as being fluid or "watery" *(wunyu-tei),* not "dry" *(yaalkoogu),* that is, either sexually mature or old and "used up." In females, fluidity stems from having circulatory and menstrual blood, vaginal fluids, and that part of her husband's semen a woman "ingests" through sexual intercourse. Males, by contrast, are fluid only through their original circulatory blood and, later (artificially ingested), semen. Children and old people are "dry," but girls are more fluid than boys; adults—unless sickly or sexually depleted—are fluid. Third, blood is said to be "cold," whereas semen is "hot." Since Sambia see sickness and plagues (*numbulyu-oolu:* pathway of sickness) as incorporeal active agents attracted to "heat" and repelled by "cold," this temperature difference counts heavily in body functioning: the more blood, the less sickness; the more semen, the greater chance of illness and debilitation. Fourth, menstrual periods are likened to a periodic sickness that rids female bodies of excess *tingu* blood and any sickness that manages to penetrate them. Ironically, then, women bounce back from their periods with greater vitality vis-à-vis this "natural" expurgative function males lack (see Mead 1935:106). The female capacities to create and discharge blood are thus designata of the structure and functioning of women's bodies, the embodiments of birth giving, procreative fluidity, and health, so men reckon that their bodies account for why women typically outlive men.

Now what matters for ritual nosebleeding is that menstrual-womb blood, although a life-giving female elixir, also represents the sine qua non of lethal fluids for male body functioning. By implication, all male circulatory blood originates from the mother's womb, so the collective initiatory nosebleedings try to purge it. Other female substances like skin flakes, saliva, sweat, and especially vaginal fluids, are also classified as *pulungatnyi* and are felt to be inimical to men. (Male illness resulting from female sorcery usually hinges on the conviction that a man has incorporated menstrual or vaginal fluids.) But menstrual blood is dreaded most. Children take in these substances through birth and, later, through feeding and touching. Women definitely evince concern not to contaminate themselves or others, especially their children, with menstrual fluids during their periods. Neither their public statements nor activities, however, reveal the intense anxiety easily aroused in men. Contrary to girls, boys are definitely at risk: menstrual-womb blood can thwart the "biological" push into masculine maturity. Men are even at greater risk since menstrual blood, in particular, can penetrate the urethra during coitus, bringing sickness and turning back the manliness that has been so hard won. For this reason, men say, they must remain cautious about contact with their children, too, since the latter may unwittingly transmit (see Meigs 1976) and infect men with traces of female pollution.

The most harmful effect of women's verbal behavior during childbearing is pinpointed on the boy's nose, which is, next to the mouth, the body's main port of entry. Here, mother's speech and harangues have a lethal power. A woman's airstream emitted while speaking is thought to emerge from her blood-filled caverns. If it is directed—particularly at close range during anger—toward boys, the boys are believed harmed. Simply by inhaling those insults and air (see Meigs 1976), a boy is defiled: the nasal orifice absorbs and stores the contaminants, henceforth blocking the free movement of circulatory blood and other fluids from the nose throughout the body. (Likewise, women pollute boys simply by lifting their legs in proximity to them, emitting vaginal smells that boys can breathe in; and, for this reason, men keep their noses plugged during coitus, avoiding incorporation of the vaginal smell they describe as most harmfully foul (see also Devereux 1937:515). Nosebleeding is the critical means of egesting these incorporated materials from the male body, since Sambia practice no other form of bloodletting.

Despite these necessary expurgations, however, nosebleeding is unmistakably risky, even dangerous. The reason is simple: blood loss from cuts or wounds in general is dangerous, a process that, if left unchecked, would rob one of circulatory blood and of life itself. Large cuts are handled as quickly as possible, and even with minor scrapes men are anxious about placing bindings to stop any blood loss. (The greatest single expense in my fieldwork medical budget was for bandages—for which people constantly asked.) Blood is "vital stuff" (Lewis 1975:203); like ourselves, Sambia view the containment of blood loss as a critical symptom of life risk and a prognostic indicator for recovery. Birth giving and menstrual bleeding also carry a risk, but one of a different sort, since the female body is thought to control blood flow "naturally." Thus, even though women use native medicines to reduce menstrual flows, they appear to be relatively unconcerned about their periods. Male nosebleeding is another matter. Nosebleeding is painful and the blood loss disliked: it is done to remove female contaminants. Indeed, it is unlikely that Sambia would ever use medicinal bloodletting as did our ancestors, or as other New Guineans do (Barth 1975:139; Williams 1936a:342). Here, I think, is a major clue about the psychosocial difference between nosebleeding and menstrual periods or medicinal bleeding: a man initiates a temporary bleeding inside a ready orifice to remove poisonous female matter, and it is he who tries to control the amount of blood loss (see Lindenbaum 1976:57).

These elements of belief, namely women's innate production of blood, its association with reproduction, the contaminating potential of female blood for males, and the riskiness of blood loss, are the background factors that generally influence—color, crystallize, constrain—the actual experience of secret nosebleeding. In their particulars, however, secular beliefs combine with subsequent ritual teachings that are introduced through transitions in the ritual life cycle. Successive stages of initiation teaching draw on more secret, explicitly sexual elements that reinforce the aggressive ethos of the Sambia warriorhood.

Ritual Nosebleeding Behavior

The nosebleeding (*chemboo-loruptu: chembootu,* nose; *loropma:* a verb meaning "to cleanse and expand") act is the single most painful ritual technique, by common assent of initiates and men alike. (In contrast, mere piercing of the nasal septum is a benign secular ceremony occurring in childhood for both sexes.) That feeling is understandable. Physically, nosebleeding is a penetrating trauma of the nasal mucous membranes. The psychological effect of nosebleeding is enhanced by secrecy; so its forcible administration by men upon boys—and by surprise, at that—turns into a violent assault having effects probably close to producing authentic trauma. Boys themselves often hark back to the nosebleeding with expressions such as "I feared they were going to kill me." The ritual efficacy and subjective dynamics of collective nosebleeding are highly focused on the actual blood flow. The body of assembled initiators always concentrate on a generous but controlled blood flow—the sight of which is greeted triumphantly with a unified ritual/war chant. That collective action amounts to a forcible penetration of a boy's body boundaries, for aside from its surprise and ostentatious context, the psychological impact of nosebleeding assumes greater power when it is understood that Sambia place tremendous personal emphasis on the nose, second only to the genitals, and the nose is second to none in matters of body appearance, notions of beauty, and their manifestations in gender symbolism.[1]

Sambia recognize two different procedures for nosebleeding that are associated with phratry affiliation. These techniques are hidden from all women and children and from younger initiates until their ritual revelation at successive initiations. Traditionally knowledge of the different practices was partially hidden from men of the two opposing phratries of the Sambia Valley since the procedures are incorporeal property ritual customs—trademarks—of the respective groups. Following pacification, however, these practices were shared with the opposite sides. Nowadays men have some choice in the type of nosebleeding utilized in collective or private ritual.[2] The most common technique consists simply of thrusting stiff sharp

1. The generic term for nose is *chembootu;* the penis is called *laakelu;* the glans penis is *laakelu chembootu*—which male idiom jokingly labels "that no-good man down there (i.e., the pubic area) without teeth." Nose and penis associations like this one are not only consciously generalized in everyday discourse (see Herdt 1981:61–62) but also unconsciously elaborated in individual dreams and cultural products like ritual and folklore.

2. This report uses the ethnographic present of 1974–76, when these data were mostly collected. Sambia say that they stopped practicing cane swallowing (see Berndt 1965:84; Salisbury 1976:65) of their own volition shortly before pacification (about 1964–65). Pacification has

cane grasses into the nose until blood flows (see Langness 1974:194; Read 1965:131). The other technique, forcing extremely salty liquid up the nose, is also painful, but there is less severe penetration since no hard projectile is involved. In the latter instance a beastly saline solution is made from soaking water in native vegetal salt that is sponged into the nostrils as the face is held upwards. Most times, blood instantly flows following that action, profusely so in some cases

The cane-grass technique was used in the first-stage and third-stage collective initiations by all the Sambia groups in which I observed nosebleeding. That practice is regarded as more dangerous than the water technique largely owing to men's perception that there is always a chance that the cane grasses might break off and lodge in one's nose, risking death—the prime reason men offer in explaining why Sambia themselves abandoned "cane swallowing" (to induce vomiting) before pacification. Following third-stage initiation, the choice of bloodletting technique is made on the basis of phratry membership in individually oriented fifth- and sixth-stage initiations. In private nosebleeding, however, personal needs and public glory are also involved; for example, the cane-grass technique is the riskier, more daring routine and is identified as among the most masculine of activities. Here men's subjectivity seems to be pinpointed on the need—and pseudo-risk—of a hard physical projectile actually penetrating the nostrils to achieve the painful and desired inward-to-outward effect of blood release. And to repeat that penetrating thrust of cane grass seems to be necessary for culturally accomplishing the first acts of efficacious nosebleeding within collective initiations.

First-Stage Initiation

Nosebleeding occurs on the third day of first-stage initiation as but one part of a longer sequence of manly ordeals. It is preceded by purificatory rites, collective dancing, fasting, beating rites, and a state of fatigue born of sleeplessness and constant, frighteningly unpredictable surprises. On the morning of its occurrence the novices' mothers are contemptuously informed

---

brought formerly hostile Sambia hamlets close together, social changes that have also resulted in sharing certain clan or phratry ritual secrets (e.g., about nosebleeding) with affines or age mates, creating more choice in these matters. During fieldwork in 1979, I noted that most Sambia men still privately nosebled, according to their self-reports. In contrast, however, those same men say that cane swallowing was simply too dangerous, painful, and messy (they feared that the canes would break off in their stomachs and kill them); nosebleeding is much preferred.

that their sons are to be killed, so women begin a sorrowful wailing, which is genuinely tearful or ritually stylized, according to their personal situations. The novices too are threateningly warned to watch out because of what lies in store. Here the mysterious power of the flutes (heard but not yet seen) comes into play, building on and infusing the novices' growing expectations about the elders' authority over the supernatural and themselves (see Herdt 1982). The initiates are first taken from their mothers and lodged in the ritual cult house; several hours later they are removed to the forest at the edge of the cleared land, where the unexpected nosebleeding occurs.

Initially, the boys confront a massive vibrating wall of thick green foliage, a fence of young saplings tightly woven together. Pieces of red headband (a ceremonial garment) are tied up in the green mass, while inside (invisible to the novices) a chorus of bachelors shakes the trees, emitting an eerie sputtering sound associated with ritual ordeals. The effect is calculatedly bizarre: from the approaching distance one is made to experience the green mass itself as if blood were dripping from the branches. The novices plunge into that disturbing morass through a small opening at its center, literally tied to the backs of their ritual sponsors. Some scream and cry; some try to escape. But all are carried through the barricade into a muddy inner chamber that leads only one way—into a cage-like passageway of naked saplings, tied together like a fence on both sides. (The passage was barely wide enough for me to walk through.)[3] Lined up, outside and next to the passageway, are numerous warriors holding wild ginger stalks, and as the sponsor/initiate pairs walk the gauntlet of the enclosure, they are pounded on their legs and backs. Most of the boys cry; indeed, by the time they exit into the forest clearing (twenty feet away), many look terrified, and some scream for their mothers as the men look on.

The initiates are then grouped around the ritual site of a small brook flowing down from a thicket. A huge crowd of men assemble, fencing in the initiates. The nosebleeders themselves take center stage: several of them are wearing upturned pigs' tusk noseplugs (worn with the tusk points turned upward only during war and during these rites). The men are serious, and even as their bodies strain forward to convey their tension, some of the men

3. It is with such imagery of ritual paraphernalia—like this "blood raining down," a dark, cavernous entrance, and a tight narrow passageway leading into a flowing stream (where blood is expelled)—that Jungians delight in interpreting womb and birth symbolism: "unconscious universal archetypes." But notice, too, that the ritual site, like a good Hollywood director's stage set, is constructed so that its subliminal perceptual effects build mystery, sanctity (Freud 1964:67), and fear, experiences that heighten and funnel subjective excitement along this particular line to a psychosocial outcome: trauma (for the novice) or triumph (for the initiator). I am indebted to Robert J. Stoller for this suggestion.

actually grimace. A "strong" man, a former war leader, steps forward and silently plunges cane grasses down his own nose: in full view of the initiates blood streams down his face into the water. Somewhere, still out of sight, the flutes hauntingly serenade his feat. The men respond with a piercing ritual/war chant: a signal that they want more.

The first boy is quickly grabbed. He struggles and shouts but is held down by three men. None of us can catch his breath before the initiator rolls up cane grasses and, as the novice's head is held back, pushes them down repeatedly into the boy's nose. Tears and blood flow as the boy is held, and then relaxed forward, over the water. Next, one and then another boy is grasped and bled. One lad tries to run away but is grabbed; as a punishment, he is bled harder and longer than the others. The next initiate resists fiercely, so four men lift him up off the ground, and, while suspended there, he is nosebled. Another boy is penetrated until blood flows profusely; and after each instance of this, the men raise the ritual/war chant time and again.

Many of the previous first-stage initiates (from an initiation held several months earlier) are also nosebled again. They stand in the wings of the group. Some resist; others do not. But few of them resist as fiercely as the novices. Soon the act becomes almost mechanical for the initiators—the boys' clansmen, cross-cousins, and matrilateral kin.

The reactions of the boys, however, are the opposite. At first the novices do not resist much. But after several boys defy the bleeders, others resist more. Some struggle and cry; some must be forcibly bled. The men have little pity for the lads. Those who resist are even more severely dealt with by prolonging the action and thereby brutalizing it. All of the novices (they numbered forty-two) are bled. Afterward, the boys remain standing over the stream to let the blood flow. The water ensures that women will not later discover any signs of blood, and it also allows the boys to wash themselves off. Then sponsors (who did not serve as bleeders) dab the boys' noses with ferns, wiping the face clean of any remaining traces of blood. An elder collects the leaves.[4]

---

4. These bloodied leaves have but one, dramatic use, vis-à-vis older men's harangues of women somewhat later, back at the dance-ground site. The initiates' mothers are cursed for their "bad" treatment (e.g., cursing) of the boys, which is said to have thwarted masculine growth and required that men "kill" the boys. The red-stained leaves are held up as evidence of the boys' deaths. On one occasion I witnessed a remarkable display: a young man, holding some of the bloody leaves, became excited and agitated and, quite beside himself, ran up to and assaulted one of the mothers nearby, forcibly stuffing some of the leaves in her mouth. He fled, and immediately a large group of women turned on the men, denouncing the assault. This anecdote graphically illustrates how the nosebleeding context—for one adult initiator, at least—precipitated a flurry of aggressive behavior that was permitted to be directed toward a boy's mother.

SAMBIA NOSEBLEEDING RITES *141*

Following the bleeding, the boys are lined up by the stream for the ritual teaching. The rhetoric describes the nosebleeding as punishment for the insubordination of novices toward their fathers and elders. Pollution is also mentioned. Merumie (a respected fight leader and shaman) does the rhetorical teaching; he begins by telling the novices to learn hospitality: "If a man visiting your hamlet comes and asks you for water, you must offer him some. You must not hide your water vessels. He ought to be given water; if there is none, you must fetch it even if it is dark and raining."

Next he reprimands the boys, saying that when they were children, they made "bad talk," sassing ritual initiates. He further asserts that if the boys defy or disregard their elders' instructions to fetch water or betel nut, they will be nosebled again, as punishment. For those acts, Merumie says, "We now pay you back." The boys are told to "change their ways."

Merumie then lectures the boys on their mothers' harmful effects and the value of letting blood: "You 'novices' have been with your mothers. . . . They have said 'bad words' to you; their talk has entered your noses and prevented you from growing big. Your skins are no good. Now you can grow and look nice."

A teaching about warrior aggressiveness was also performed until the first-stage initiation in 1973, at which time it was abandoned.[5] Elders stressed that nosebleeding could help novices become more fearless during warfare. Boys were told to be "strong" and unafraid on the battlefield. They were upbraided: having been nosebled themselves, henceforth they must not fear the sign of their age mates' or comrades' spilled blood on the battlefield. In fact, elders stressed, the sight of blood itself was to have been regarded as a challenge—to seek revenge against the responsible enemies for the loss of blood on one's own side.

Second-Stage Initiation

Nosebleeding is not performed at this event, several years later. (Likewise, no nosebleeding occurs at fourth-stage initiation.) Boys do not know that, of course, until afterward; in each subsequent initiation they are always left wondering about that fearsome possibility, until the last. Men say that the

5. Elders say that this warriorhood aspect of first-stage nosebleeding teaching was abandoned in the early 1970s because it was anachronistic. Its counterpart in third-stage rites, however, is still taught. This seeming discrepancy involved the fact that third-stage initiates are older—they still remembered warfare—and, moreover, the bachelors are required to perform socially as warriors, even though war is gone.

initiates, having been bled once and long separated from their mothers, are protected by other external "cleaning" rites, like those which painfully scrub the body through use of stinging nettles. However, individual second-stage initiates may be bled at the behest of their clansmen during subsequent first-stage nosebleeding rites. In addition, and somewhat inexplicably at that, men say that the boys, who are fed pandanus fruit (ending a taboo imposed earlier at first-stage initiation), are spurred enough by its ingestion and the smearing of its crimson juice on their skins to further "grow them." Women are expressly forbidden to see those events—whose secrecy also seems to help offset the need for another nosebleeding till the next initiation.

Third-Stage Initiation

This event is the last collective initiatory performance of nosebleeding performed on boys as a regional set of age mates. Later instances are individually oriented rites. This may be one reason the context is severe, almost cruel, in its violence and physical threats. This time, however, there is a greater element of voluntary action on the part of the youths, who, having attained puberty, are accorded the status of "young men" to be betrothed. As new warriors, they are expected to be brave, self-disciplined, and emotionally steadfast, even though some cannot live up to that demand. After two days of the initiation (which lasts a week), youths are assembled by means of a signal (not dragged into line on their ritual sponsors' backs, as occurred the first time). Many of them (they told me later) suspected they were to be nosebled. While lined up, military fashion, they are thus "attacked" by older men. A line of warriors, soot-blackened and garbed "like ghosts, like enemies," encircle them, plucking bows and arrows, hooting, shouting, and feigning an ambush. There, on a hidden hillside (away from the hamlet women), without a stream, they are grasped by sponsors and men and forcibly nosebled again (see Newman and Boyd 1982; Tuzin 1980). Although youths are not supposed to flinch, struggle, or cry, some of them do: the terror of the experience is greater than the strength of certain individuals to submit passively to nasal penetration (see table 1 on the bilaterality of choice in this situation). No stream should be needed for that reason: if the youths are "manly enough" they will effortlessly and with sober-faced calm allow themselves to be neatly nosebled. Their blood should carefully fall onto leaves provided for their own cleansing and disposal.

The teachings of third-stage nosebleeding convey to youths, for the first

Table 1

Cultural and Behavior Characteristices of Nosebleeding Rites in the Male Life Cycle

Initiation Stage	Focus of Ritual Teachings				Behavioral Context: Audience			Physical and Societal Constraints			
	Physical growth	Mother's pollution of ego	Warrior's aggressiveness ethos	Wife's pollution of ego	Directing authorities	Collective ritual	Solitary private ritual	Voluntary nose-bleeding	Involuntary nose-bleeding	Other-induced	Self-induced
First stage (7–10 years)	X	----	X ----	X	Elders	X			X------	X	
Second stage (11–13 years)											
Third stage (13–16 years)				X	Elders	X		X	X------X (Bilateral)	X	
Fourth stage (16 years +)											
Fifth stage (16–20 years)			X------X		Elders Peers	X		X		X	
Sixth stage 20–30 years)			X------X		Elders Peers	X		X		X------X (Optional)	
Wife's menses	X (Old Age)		X------X		Self		X------X			X	

time, some dangers of sexual contact—physical intimacy—with women. But that is not why elders tell them they are bled. After all, initiates must strictly avoid women, so the thought of illicit heterosexual intercourse is not even mentioned. Instead, youths are warned about three things: first, they must be vigilant and always ready for enemy attack; second, sexual contact with women will debilitate them and make them vulnerable to death in battle; and third, they must avoid women and know that death from the angry husband and his cohorts awaits adulterous transgressors. The first element is graphically impressed on the novices by the mock attack of men posing as tribal "enemies" who administered the nosebleeding. The second element is left ominously vague, for the future. The third aspect is sanctioned by, and indexed toward, the flutes, whose cries—during the ritual—are said to represent a woman's sensuous moans as she adulterously copulates with an unwary youth. The unsuspecting youth will be killed by the cuckold and his age mates, elders warn: Obey us or suffer that fate. In other words, nosebleeding is a powerful social sanction to constrain the youths' sexuality, ruling out premarital sex with women and ruling in homoerotic activities. Indeed, it is the youths' first act of being an inseminator to the boys, at the conclusion of third-stage initiation, that is culturally regarded as essential in gaining manhood.

Fifth-Stage Initiation

The events of the fifth stage are triggered by the occurrence of menarche for the youth's young wife. Nosebleeding is its final ritual. The novice and his married age mates engage in days of collective hunting in the forest (for possum-meat prestations bestowed on the wife's cognatic kin) while adhering to strict ingestion taboos. Bloodletting then becomes the focus of essential teachings that finally reveal the full dangers of genital-to-genital intercourse, vaginal pollution, and the dangers of wives' menstrual periods.

The novice himself is first to be nosebled as his elders and cohort look on. There is absolutely no question here of voluntary submission to the act. The youth is expected to be willing, even eager to be bled; most remained unflinching and frozen during the actual procedure. Any sign of fear or reticence is regarded as unmanly and inappropriate, and my observations revealed no visible reticence. Either cane grasses or the saline solution is an acceptable technique, depending on one's phratry identification, but that decision is a matter for elders, not youths, to decide. Older men actually nosebleed the youth. Afterward, when blood flows, the characteristic ritual/war chant is raised by the whole chorus of men. The novice's age mates are then bled too. Older men may choose to bleed themselves or to be bled. (Younger initiates, of course, are excluded from this secret ritual advancement.) Older men, particularly graying elders, do not usually take part, and nothing is said about this. (I have, however, seen such men on occasion spontaneously ask to be bled.)

Elders emphasize the youth's erotic/procreative relationship to his newly menstruating wife in the following teachings. More than at fourth-stage initiation, ritual knowledge of purificatory techniques is taught so youths can protect themselves against the lethal effects of female sexual contact. Examples: special leaves may be eaten and muds smeared on the skin to strengthen the body; other leaves can be used to plug the nose; and tree bark can be chewed (and later spit out) during coitus to eliminate from one's mouth traces of female body odors and breath. The youths are especially warned to be conservative in all ways about heterosexual intercourse, and they are taught how to replace depleted semen "lost" to their wives (see Herdt 1981:249). Once again, the youths are enjoined not to be adulterous, and they are warned of the fatal consequences if that rule is broken. And all of these warnings are set within the ritual prescription that, henceforth, the young man must take personal responsibility for privately nosebleeding himself alone in the forest after each of his wife's menses (regardless of whether he recently had coitus). The deadly blood must be avoided and eliminated at all costs, with scrupulous measures taken before and after each menses to avoid its contagious power.

Fifth-stage teachings also explicate a theme of hostility to women that was earlier implicit. This theme concerns making men responsible, autonomous warriors, by redirecting onto women some responsibility for the "pain of nosebleeding." It is an unmanly sign of weakness *(wogaanyu)* for the youth to sit idly by while his wife menstruates. Since she is "reproductively active," elders say, a man must be "ritually active" in a way germane to her body's release of menstrual blood into his world. Men add that they have no other orifice with which to bleed except that of the nose. Elder authorities challenge that since the youth now has (a sexual relationship with) a wife, he must prove himself stronger, manlier, on the battlefield. That message is then referred back ominously to domestic life: since it was because of the wife's harmful menses that the youth had to "feel pain," he must never forget his suffering on her account. She must bear responsibility for his pain; she must learn to respect him for the warriorhood ordeals he has endured to be fully masculine for her. So, if a wife is sassy or insubordinate, or under any hint of suspicion that she is being unfaithful, a man must not spare the rod in demonstrating his power over this creature who is responsible for his smarting nose.

Sixth-Stage Initiation

This nosebleeding occurs in conjunction with the birth of a man's first child. The rite again follows ceremonial hunting and other purificatory rites. It confirms final initiation into the male cult hierarchy, although the rites and feasting are repeated again for the next birth or two—confirming full status as a masculine person. The teachings center on the birth fluids and their polluting potential, and a man's need to adhere to postpartum taboos by keeping distant from the mother-infant pair. The nosebleeding behavior is somewhat different: as competent, manly adults, men are now autonomous and responsible for the maintenance of their own health. Indeed, the behavioral shift from being bled by others to bleeding oneself may actually occur in this initiation since novices have no choice with regard to nosebleeding themselves. (The same also applies to the initiate's age mates, who are also bled.) What matters is the greater stoic demand to nosebleed oneself self-consciously as a secret, masculine response against the immediate danger at hand: one's own wife's birth contaminants released into the close quarters of the hamlet environs. Following this initiation, most men do not nosebleed themselves again until they resume coitus with their wives following the child's breast weaning (some two to two-and-one-half years later). Whether induced by oneself or others, then, this nosebleeding is a "voluntary" act, applauded again by the ritual/war chant accompanying the released blood.

Private Nosebleeding Acts

I have already mentioned the normative injunction that a man is personally responsible for "cleansing" his body through nosebleeding after each of his wife's periods. Here I shall simply sketch the context of those private rites that follow after fifth-stage initiation and into old age.

Private nosebleedings are highly personal acts performed alone. The morning on which a man's wife disappears to the menstrual hut (and she will never even mention this to her husband or other men), the husband also quietly leaves the hamlet compound for his own forest preserve. There he nosebleeds himself according to the ritual procedure of his phratry. He ingests certain leaves and tree milk saps and also rubs the milk saps on his body to "strengthen" it at those points he contacted his wife (penis, abdomen, navel, etc.) during coitus. Then he smears red mud on his torso and limbs. This oddly sympathetic body painting obviously communicates to the community that he has done something secret in the forest; men themselves say the red mud merely "hides" the underlying white tree sap smeared on the skin from the probing eyes of women and children. Here, of course, we have arrived at the final regime of bloodletting behavior, and one in which the action is completely private, is "voluntary," self-induced, and is performed—or so one thinks—for the independent audience of oneself. At the same time, though, private nosebleeding depends on personal initiative and is publicly unobserved, so we should thus expect individual variation in its behavior and experience.

This last point raises difficult questions about the experience of adult bloodletting—a subject that constitutes a fascinating "internal discourse" in male life precisely because it is so much avoided. Most men are timid and tight-lipped about private nosebleeding, even among their peers. Younger men even evince some embarrassment about it. Such reticence seems striking and puzzling, for among their cronies men will sooner or later touch on their night's dreams, and wet dreams, body fluids (both male and female), sexual conquests or needs, and even, with repugnance, female contaminants—all ritual domains except personal bleeding. (To get detailed information, I had to elicit personal accounts from informants, and usually while alone with them.) The silent message seems to be that a powerful, but vulnerable, piece of the self is secreted in that private act—an idea to which I shall later return.

What emerges from ritual rhetoric and private conversations is the view that private nosebleeding is both burdensome and painful, necessary and cathartic. All adult men are believed to let blood regularly as described above, but their emotionality differs somewhat. The fight leaders and self-conscious elders are undemonstrative and matter-of-fact about their bleedings; younger newlyweds are more exuberant, but also more squeamish. Weiyu, a close, married informant in his early twenties, deplores the fierce pain of nosebleedings, grudgingly submits to it only when absolutely unavoidable, in public, where he uses cane grass on himself, but in private he uses the salt solution because it is less dangerous. Imano, an older, quieter, comfortable man, over thirty years old, who has two wives and definitely enjoys coitus with them, is also known as a faithful nosebleeder; he feels that it keeps him healthy, and he generously lets blood in regular synchrony with his wives' periods. Sambia men thus engage in private bleeding for many years, till they halt coitus or their wives undergo menopause and stop having periods. In between, one hears many comments about the value of nosebleeding, but the earlier idioms about "male growth" disappear. Then, among seniors in their late thirties and forties, men again offer, in explanation of their own continuing bloodletting, the pat remark: "I am still growing."

Men are quite explicit about the conscious intent of that idea. My informant, Tali, for instance, has said: "The woman expels her blood, and you, her husband, must also expel it. If you don't, your stomach will become no good, it will swell up" (see Meigs 1976). For that reason, he noted, "Old men continue nosebleeding until their wives stop menstruating." Unless they do, he said, they "won't grow anymore." And here is Weiyu: "It's [menstrual blood] not men's blood, but the bad talk and menstrual blood of a man's "sickly" wife. It [blood] doesn't belong to us, it belongs to the women. . . . We say their [women's] blood and bad words enter our skin and lodge their, so we expel it [blood] from the nose."

> GH: But what can you replace the blood with?
> WEIYU: Nothing. We don't replace it. It's the contamination *(pulun-galunyi)* of women, we expel it; it shouldn't be replaced.

But eventually, as Tali said elsewhere, "Old [i.e., senile] men don't [need to] perform nosebleedings on themselves—his [*sic*] skin is fastened to his bones. [He thinks to himself:] 'I won't grow anymore.'" To understand that belief and the developmental transformations that lead to its expressions in adult behavior, I must interpret the whole system of ritual nosebleedings that shape male character.

Ritual Transformations in Male Character Structure

Although it seems clear that forcible bloodletting—administered collectively to boys—eventuates in the adult social outcome that men will voluntarily and, in private, let their own blood, the psychosocial mechanisms underlying this shift remain implicit. Nor is it clear why ceremonial bloodlettings throughout New Guinea involve extensive "ritual violence" (Tuzin 1982), "male dominance" (Langness 1974), or "ritual aggression" (Berndt 1962), and even, as among the Gahuku (Read 1965:129), "ritual exhibitionism . . . of the sexual aspects of male strength." To understand these issues in the Sambia material, I shall analyze the above data with reference to several theoretical perspectives that help account for the influence of forcible nosebleeding on male personality development. Four developmental themes involving nosebleeding as cultural and behavioral controls on proximity to women (see table 1) will be examined: (1) maternal detachment, (2) ritual aggression and obedience, (3) ritual reversals, and (4) heterosexual autonomy.

MATERNAL DETACHMENT

The great impetus of Sambia initiation concerns the physical separation of boys from women and children, followed by their irreversible insertion into exclusive male associations. This dual process is well known from the literature (Allen 1967; Poole 1982; Whiting, Kluckhohn, and Anthony 1958). But, with few exceptions (Róheim 1942; Tuzin 1980), writers have tended not to view the behavioral experience of initiation in the context of the nature of the boy's tie to his mother (Bowlby 1969). In New Guinea societies like that of the Sambia this tie amounts to an "exclusive attachment" (Bowlby 1969) to mother and the female domain. Initiation is the most radical means of breaking that bond in order subjectively to create a new identity in the boy. This conclusion—which is not news to New Guineasts—is novel only in its psychosocial stress: boys must be traumatically detached from their mothers and kept away from them at all costs, else the vital identity transformation will not take place.

The severity of this ritual detachment remains a measure of the qualitative strength of the mother-child bond in traditional Sambia life before pacification. Admittedly, the data to support this view are retrospective and, at best, thin (but see Mead 1935; Whiting 1941). Nor does space allow an extended presentation of ethnographic material on postpacification Sambia (see Herdt 1981). But even today, from birth on, Sambia infants still experience profound and constant sensual involvement with their mothers, not their fathers, for several years and more. Babies are attached to their mothers, who meet their basic biosocial needs—food, warmth, cleanliness, stimulation, quieting, protection. In the warring environment, fathers were removed from their infants for long periods. They are still weakly involved in infant caretaking, on an hour-by-hour basis, compared with mothers or older siblings. The polarity of the sexes—in the division of labor, domestic discord, and ritual arenas—exacerbates the struggle for security in the child's developing sense of self. Were this a different historical tradition, the outcome might be left to chance.

Initiation begins with boys' being taken from their mothers in a way that guarantees anxiety in the novice. They are kept in the dark about whether or not they will be initiated. It is true that most boys "know" (at some level of awareness) that they will be initiated eventually. It is also true that initiation is associated with male pride and glory, that is, parading in ritual regalia, and that it is boys' only means to "grow up." Parents and others communicate attitudes of this sort, overtly or covertly, according to the family situation. But remember that Sambia boys are only seven to ten years old, that initiation is designed as a surprise, and that its symbolic messages are coded to create anxiety in the boy's wrenching from hearth and family: feelings of loss arising from the irreversible awareness that the initiate cannot "be with"—touch, hold, talk to, eat with, or look at—his mother.

First-stage rituals make use of this traumatic reaction in precise ways designed to radically resocialize the boy. Both parents are removed from the scene; a substitute ritual sponsor is introduced; boys undergo days of ordeals, hunger, thirst, sleeplessness, fatigue, and alarming surprises—including great revelations (e.g., about the flutes and ritual fellatio). Thus, following physical separation, a different form of attachment—"anxious attachment," in Bowlby's (1973:196–97, 201–3) terms—is stimulated. It arises from fear and the inability to predict what will happen next, while the boy is denied access to his protective attachment figure, mother. Detachment results: despair, crying, searching behavior, including depression or its suppressed counterpart, anger (see Poole 1982). Sambia rituals play upon such feelings by making familiar persons or surroundings seem alien, bizarre, and even terrifying. (Róheim [1945:249] referred to such a process as "separation anxiety.") In the wake of these experiences new male attachment figures and sentimental bonds are introduced. The ritual sponsor, for instance, is the primary guardian and maternal substitute; and boys who called for the parents, who sobbed or clung to their sponsors, for example, in nosebleeding, were carried, and offered solace and comfort, by their sponsors. Sharing in ordeals also forges lasting ties between novices as age mates (Turner 1967), and this peer-group identification also tends to mitigate maternal loss and detachment.

Forcibly inserted into secret male rites—in this mood state—nosebleeding thus becomes a most powerful means for penetrating inside a boy's body and identity. Mother is removed; blood becomes a sign of and for her, in the all-male context. Further, cutting the nose releases the mother's blood. In ritual experience this blood is not simply a "symbol" of female essence; it is isomorphic with one's (incorporated) femaleness and what that means—womb, nurturing, mother's goodness, softness and curses, and the femaleness that cannot become maleness. Ritual attempts to identify all those aspects as contained within the part of self which is removed with the blood. For as Marilyn Strathern (1979) has argued, New Guinea societies often make the body/skin surface an analog of what we call the self. Nosebleeding violates one's body boundaries, removing the "female" blood, so that one's body (self) literally becomes an object of reclamation by the ritual cult. It is only the completion of this act that paves the way for appropriate homoerotic fellatio, which "fills up" boys' insides with se-men—"biological maleness"—"displacing" the female essences.

But the critical experiential precedent is this: a male learns to nosebleed in order to eliminate femaleness from his body—an act which for boys sep-arates "me" from mother and all femaleness—and this act becomes a sign to the self that one's identity is clearly male.

Ritual Aggression and Obedience

Forcible nosebleeding belongs to a power play. Viewed in developmental perspective, nosebleeding is one of many social control mechanisms used to create and maintain the social hierarchy of the ritual cult. The hamlet-based warriorhood, into which boys are conscripted, supports this cult hierarchy. Elders are at the top of the ritual status ladder. Fully initiated married men dominate bachelors, who dominate initiates. Women and children are ex-cluded from cult rites, to which they are nonetheless politically subordi-nated. Men (including the boys' fathers) utilize initiation to separate boys from their mothers and natal households, thereafter ensuring masculine gender differentiation, conformity to adult male gender role norms, and the maintenance of cult secrets. Initiation thus effects immediate and total physical separation from all females. But what about the later nosebleed-ings, for example, those at third-stage initiations? Why is it necessary to nosebleed youths violently years after they have been detached from their mothers, have avoided women, and have conformed to ritual conventions as residents of the men's clubhouse?

To answer this question, we must understand the political context of rit-ual domination. The presence of a cult-based warriorhood in every Sambia hamlet is a function of certain societal imperatives that clan elders direct. These imperatives can be briefly stated as follows: (1) perpetuation of so-cioeconomic stability in the community, (2) requiring control and expro-priation of the products of women's bodies and labor, that is, sexual services, babies, breast milk, garden food, and domestic services (cooking, baby-sitting), (3) authority over sons, whose allegiance as ritual supporters and young warriors is vital for the maintenance of elders' authority and hamlet defense, and (4) control over female children—daughters, sisters, nieces, cousins, granddaughters—who are needed as a commodity to obtain future wives for the bachelors, whom elders control further by abrogating all responsibility for exchanging these females and arranging marriages for youths. The eventual success of all these political moves, however, is bound up with first separating boys from the female realm and making them dependably fierce warriors—obedient to "the cult," in the persons of the elders, "agents of external authority" (Milgram 1974:62).

Seen in symbolic terms, this last requirement is by no means easy or "natural." If we cast Sambia relationships in the conceptual paradigm of Bateson's (1958, 1972) ideas about "complementary" versus "symmetrical" ties, elders are faced with a dilemma that initiation resolves. As uninitiated boys, males are in complementary relationships to their mothers, who are their primary superordinates. Initiation transfers this relationship to elders and bachelors: boys become their subordinates. Initiates are removed from direct interaction with females. Age mates take up symmetrical relationships with one another, matching masculine performances in hunting and fighting. Even ingesting semen becomes a "race" between initiates to see who grows faster. By puberty, then, bachelors are superordinates of initiates but subordinates of elders. Women are tantalizingly nearby but still stringently roped off and out of reach. Ritual violence is reintroduced and then perpetuated.

Nosebleeding, periodically performed as a secret surprise of later initiations, is the most powerful social sanction for reinforcing boys' obedience to authority. Next to threats of death (which are also used), nosebleeding can be seen as an act of raw aggression (Tuzin 1980:74) over budding youths. This domination comes first in late childhood, when boys would be prone to sexual experimentation; it comes next at puberty—when a powerful inhibitor is again needed to ensure heterosexual repression. As a kind of "symbolic castration," or perhaps "phallic aggression" (Vanggaard 1972: 101–12), violent bloodletting is a very efficient but traumatic means of funneling youths' sexual and aggressive impulses along a particular developmental line—away from women and elders, respectively—toward initiates (fellators) and enemies. Adjustment to ritual cult life takes that form: being involved only in homoerotic relationships, avoiding all heteroerotic impulses and contacts with women until marriage; and performing as efficacious hunter/warriors, directed by war leaders and elders. Ritual beliefs about the deadly contaminating power of women's bodies, with their greater depleting power compared with that of boy-fellators, further rationalizes youths' fears and avoidance of women. Thus, through

these powerful conditions of ritual aggression, initiates learn fear and obedience of male authorities, bravado in war, and avoidance of women.

Ritual Reversals

A dramatic transformation occurs in nosebleeding behavior between first
initiation and the attainment of adulthood years later: the shift from being
forcibly nosebled to bleeding oneself "voluntarily." This reversal involves
many other changes—psychosexual and cultural—as well as sociopolitical
advancements in ritual roles and statuses. On the surface, this shift suggests
fundamental alterations in one's behavior, from being a helpless (not passive) victim of violent nosebleeding assaults to becoming a victorious initiator fully in charge of his own ritual actions and bodily functioning.
Psychodynamically, however, self-bleeding requires developmental changes
in character structure that Sambia identify with the esteemed traits of the
proven warrior. Being a trustworthy cult member and being self-controlled
in proximity to women are among these traits. Here, we must be chiefly
concerned with identity transformations that are psychologically entailed
by cultural and contextual shifts in the performance of nosebleeding itself.
(The gross characteristics of these changes are represented in table 1.)

   First there are changes in the societal constraints governing the cultural
context of nosebleeding. The general rule is: The more immature and less
obedient the initiate is to male authority, the more violence accompanies
bloodletting. At the start of the ritual cycle, the greatest force is used, implying that only males who must be forcibly separated from women require
physical assaults. Thereafter "voluntary" choice enters into bleeding. From
third-stage initiation on, one should stoically submit to the ordeal others
perform on oneself. The cult standard is clear: The manliness of one's identity is judged by the initiate's willingness and capacity to be bled without
fear or other "female" emotions. This reversal occurs simultaneously with
performative acts that signify one's accountability to all ritual conventions—
and without others having to regulate the initiate's activities, as, for instance, with new novices who are distrusted. From the start to the finale of
the ritual initiations it is the initiate's relationships to women that are most
visible and scrupulously monitored in this respect. A novice's avoidance of
all females is watched at first. The youth's continuing avoidance, his absti-
nence from premarital heterosexual contacts, and his patient obeisance to
his elders in regard to his eventual marriage contract are next. Later, the
signs of self-accountability in a married man are judged by his ritual regula-

tion of sexual relations with his wife, and by his adherence to postpartum taboos, purifications, nosebleedings following coitus, and avoidance of adultery.

Second are the changes in cultural beliefs surrounding nosebleeding. The general theme of ritual rhetoric stresses the dual idea that the creation and preservation of maleness ("growth") goes hand in hand with becoming an aggressive warrior. Ideologically, first-stage nosebleeding is a punishment for boys' childish insolence to men, represents the idea that mothers' blood has blocked boys' masculinization, and embodies the notion that boys must become tough and learn to master their fear of blood on the battlefield. Initiates, here as always, are made beholden to their elders for ensuring their masculine "growth." Following puberty, however, the concern with "growth" turns upon the fear of menstrual contamination. Rhetoric about "mother" is dropped. Instead, from fourth-stage until old age, beliefs about female contamination are transferred from mother onto men's wives, only sexual intercourse—not mere nurturance—becomes the perceived danger to maleness.

Throughout this transformation the only elements that remain constant are women as dangerous and the cultural beliefs about the aggressive warrior's ethos. Not only do repeated nosebleedings condition one to the sight of blood, but their initial traumas are supposed to be converted into bold prowess—leading and killing in battle without compunction. The social significance of this aggressive stance is, without doubt, later inserted into domestic life too. One who is an accomplished killer is to be feared by his wife and respected by peers. Consequently, elders constantly stress the initiates' obedience to authorities as well. Nosebleedings are timed in the life cycle to ensure that elders retain social control over bachelors—after puberty—until such time that youths are married and thereby become adult members invested in the cult. Then, of course, they can be relied upon for perpetuation of established controls over women and initiates.

Third, a number of highly structured and ritually organized reversals in sexual behavior are correlated with the meaning of bloodletting acts at various levels of significance. Ultimately, all these transformations bear upon physical proximity to women. Sexually, these changes issue from first being a passive homoerotic fellator to being a dominant fellated; thereafter sexual behavior switches from exclusive homoerotic contacts to brief bisexual encounters—secret fellatio with boys and private fellatio with one's bride— and then, finally, to exclusive heterosexual relationships in marriage. Moreover, several important symbolic attachments to ritual agents—such as the fantasized female hamlet spirit animating the ritual flutes—are fostered as transitional objects in boys' identity changes from childhood to manhood, which attachments lend transitional homoerotic practices their own excitement (see chapter 3). Changes in nosebleeding behavior then, from one ritual stage to the next, are followed by new sexual rights and duties.

Last, the composition of the nosebleeding ritual audience undergoes symbolic changes of various sorts. At first-stage initiation, novices are classed together against all older males. As age mates, these boys are placed in competition with one another, partaking in nosebleeding and doing other acts with which their masculine performance is compared and judged. They are made subordinates of all elder males, who substitute for the boys' superordinate mothers in complementary relationships to initiates. Boys' fathers are in the audience of initiators; physical presence here counts as a primary sign of the politico-ritual division between fathers and sons. Nevertheless, both generations are made privy to the all-male secret rites, compared with the mothers—who are left wailing helplessly behind in the village. But mother is symbolically inserted into the context— through the designata of nose blood, "female contamination," which insidiously links boys and women. Never again is that comparison between boys and women made. In subsequent nosebleedings, then, mother is a part of the distant background, whereas the father becomes an emerging ritual teacher, and one's peers and adult men emerge as the key audience. The ritual sponsor's role declines after marriage, until it is perfunctory. Elders remain prominent until adulthood, since they sanctify ritual teachings, but they, too, increasingly take a back seat as their physical power wanes. After puberty, moreover, the frightening attacks halt: no need to remind bachelors who are their enemies, for they are identified with other groups who kill (whose initiates drain off one's semen and whose women— potential wives—can pollute and sorcerize), not just nosebleed bachelors, as their elders do to "help" them.[6]

The final transformations occur following marriage and fatherhood. One's wife now displaces mother as the focus of contaminated blood that must be expelled owing to sexual contacts. But the bloodlettings are self-induced and private, acknowledging the marital bond and the particular periodicity of men's wives. Men do not perform for their peers or compete

6. I think that workers have tended to play down the subjective terror of this experience, for Sambia males are virtually unanimous in expressing the feeling that they believed they were to be killed on the spot at nosebleeding, and one finds similar reports elsewhere, spread between Australia (e.g., Herdt 1982) and New Guinea (Read 1965:132; Watson 1960:144–45). Tuzin's (1980:74ff.) important work well illustrates a positive example.

with them in bloodletting. They are, obviously, competing now with their wives, but this symmetrical "contest" is solitary and secret in a very special sense. That mode of self-control concerns my final argument.

Heterosexual Autonomy

Sambia manhood rests on the above ritual transformations—the fusion of which is necessary for, and "carried" in, the psychosocial elements of painfully performing private bloodlettings on oneself. That act, to reiterate, represents marriage and fatherhood: full manhood. It signals also the "acceptance" (socialization, internalization, habitualized reinforcements, etc.) of masculine rhetoric, secret beliefs, and comportment regarding self and significant others: in a word, self-autonomy. Two pervasive cultural assumptions must be kept in mind. One is that in a man's willingness to bleed himself Sambia recognize the completion of the phallic warrior. The other assumption is that only men who are married and having sex with their wives privately bleed themselves. (Analogically, then, Sambia "read" private bloodletting as meaning that one is engaging in heterosexual coitus, the most privileged sexual act.) Most of all, we must analytically underline the context of these assumptions: once again—for the first time in years following maternal separation—the individual man is placed alone intimately with a woman.

Contained within the passages leading to this heterosexual union we can see several remarkable contradictions in masculine experience. Full masculine adulthood is denied without marriage. Children—heirs—are necessary for full personhood. Cohabitation and coitus are thus necessary for social esteem and the "reproduction" of the family and society. Ironically, physical and especially sexual proximity to women is the key threat to masculine health and vitality: it saps one's semen and "paints the penis" with female contaminants. And what about heterosexual pleasure? While most men regard coitus with some trepidation, and the act itself is laden with shame (see Herdt 1981:164ff.), Sambia men generally regard it as intensely exciting and pleasurable (and no less so because it is dangerous). Mixed in these contradictions is also the great imperative that one must not become too intimate for fear of revealing ritual secrets.

There is another dynamic which we can see as a dilemma but which Sambia themselves un-self-consciously act upon. The ritual rhetoric regards women as men's inferiors. Men are supposed to be "on top," in complementary dominating relationships with women—in domestic interaction, in economic routines, in ritual, and in sex. (Never mind that women don't always or easily bow to men in public.) However, after marriage, men's private nosebleeding acts amount to quite a different symbolic pattern: symmetrical responses to their wives' periods. On the one hand, men define the husband-wife relationship as complementary: men hunt, women garden; the more womanly a wife becomes—producing babies and garden food—the more manly the husband is perceived (as genitor). On the other hand, ritual convention requires that a man match his wife's "natural periods" with "cultural periods" of nosebleeding. Otherwise, he is seen as *wogaanyu* (weak, feminine). The implicit idea is that a woman's periods are evidence that she is still growing, is still fluid, not dry or "used up." She must not "win" over her husband, Sambia say. As an instance of the "Jones effect," private nosebleeding matches female with male "growth" in terms of an equivalent (not identical) act. (Sambia do not say nosebleeding is the same as menstruation [cf. Bettelheim 1955:177–78; Hogbin 1970; Lewis 1980:128–31; Lidz and Lidz 1977; Róheim 1945:169–71].) Regular nose-bleedings thus ritually frame the marital relationship as special compared with symmetrical peer ties or other complementary relationships (subordination to elders, dominance over initiates, and dominance over wives in public). In short, the marital bond is the one enduring relationship that has both symmetrical and complementary aspects because of regular "bleedings" in both spouses.

My point is that private nosebleeding is the key ritual context in which men live these contradictions. Custom demands that men live with their wives, have sex, rear children, and yet avoid interpersonal closeness; that is, they should stay aloof (Whiting and Whiting 1975). In both public and private situations, in sex and in battle, the ritual cult depends upon a man's personal control—autonomy, vigilance, self-regulation—as well as hostility (aggressiveness) toward wife and enemies, real or potential. Of course men do not treat their wives as real enemies, and in some Sambia marriages one finds expressions of care, respect, and, in this sense, love. But the rhetoric of ritual discourse ignores these complications (Faithorn 1975) by expecting visible aggressiveness toward the world.

By culturally structuring proximity to women in terms of nosebleeding, the ritual cult has ensured that even in adulthood men will sustain these expectable contradictions. Privately, men nosebleed to eliminate their wives' femaleness from their bodies. This act compulsively repeats, time after time, the separation of the male "me" from other aspects of self (conscious, unconscious): mother, wife, father, elders, one's earlier identities. Its affects—fear, disgust, phobic reactions to red fluids, shame—suggest that the bloodletting experience has unconscious elements that utilize "conversion-reaction" as a culturally constituted defense mechanism (Spiro 1965) in the service of ego. Its solitariness also allows for the ripe experience of personal, not just collective, fantasies (Obeyesekere, 1990). For instance, that one's nose blood contains some part of mother—circulatory blood (can it be otherwise?).[7] Private nosebleeding signifies to the self that one is still male and masculine despite heterosexual union. It thus aids heterosexual virility and maintains controlled proximity in a double sense: to one's wife and to one's secret ritual (secret identity).

But what about the anomaly of old men still "growing"? This idea of Sambia folk psychology requires an answer that is both symbolic and psychological. First there is a semantic point: What does the native concept of "growth" mean? I hope it is clear that for Sambia its connotations extend beyond mere physical maturation (though the natives often couch their answers in this form when responding to posed questions).Male "growth" entails "strength" (*jerungdu,* another thick idea) and personality traits such as aggressiveness and autonomy, as well as attitudes and behavioral acts involving interpersonal ties. On these grounds "growth" has a psychological sense that is similar to our own concept of "separateness" (see Mahler [1963] on separation-individuation). We must remember that boys' first experience with "growth" is what elders collectively teach. So when men say, in middle age, that they are now privately nosebleeding because they are still growing—and their situation involves physical, erotic, and psychological proximity to their wives—then we may postulate a psychosocial conflict requiring painful ritual acts which relieve that conflict. Psychologically, I think, the resurrection of the notion of "growth" to account for their bloodletting, despite their age, social respect, wives and children, seems to suggest there is a characterological identity conflict in Sambia males that never really goes away; it just lies dormant for a time. Symbolically, growth through nosebleeding is always available as a sign for elders again to clarify the separateness of their body boundaries and sense of self as being clearly masculine.

From this viewpoint there is no puzzle about why elders say they must still nosebleed to "grow." Their own physical powers are waning. Death is

7. Here are several clues to why men avoid discussing private nosebleeding. Private nosebleeding means one is engaging in coitus. Since coitus is shameful (even when men privately discuss sex with their cronies, they tend to speak abstractly rather than refer to personal experience), private bleeding is tinged with shame (see Whiting's [1941:64] related anecdote). I suspect that men's heterosexual excitement is another factor, since sexual desire for women implies loss of control and intimacy, two areas that I have stressed above (see also Tuzin 1980:76).

ahead. They have outlived some of their peers and enemies, but their wives are still there. And they still menstruate until menopause. They still engage in sex and perhaps—as some of them say—they enjoy it more. *(Hors d'affaire?)* But their fighting days are long gone, and their hunting is negligible. They garden, visit, spin tales, and still direct ritual. In short, their phallicness is defused, they are more with their wives—upon whom they become increasingly dependent—and the old boundary between masculinity and femininity in the marital bond grows fuzzy. The main result is that they may slip into a new complementary relationship, subordinated to their wives as they were once dominated by their mothers. Nosebleeding is still a ready means to defend against this loss of autonomy in old age, for it is the best revitalizing act available. It also serves as a sign—to self and community—that the elder remains sexually active and is matching his wife's periods.[8]

Conclusion

The violence of Sambia initiation is tied to the exigencies of its behavioral environment, which used to be defined by constant war. Nosebleeding, regularly inflicted, is but one of the mechanisms that require and create an especially aggressive kind of masculinity, whose model—the idealized phallic warrior—was suited to this environment. Moreover, the rites are the most powerful regulator of male interaction with females. Consecutive initiations effect both these outcomes: males begin as infants long sheltered in their mother's world, but they must wind up as warriors capable of killing, perpetuating painful initiations, and living and copulating with potentially hostile women. The contrast between those two opposing developmental epochs is the difference between being traumatically conscripted into the ritual cult versus internalizing its "inalienable" fierce temperament (Mead 1935:265), between being forcibly bled versus painfully bleeding oneself. However much boys resist this psychosocial transformation, they cannot be allowed to circumvent it, for individual and community survival depends upon its successful outcome.

The degree of ritual violence and radical resocialization which characterizes Austro-Melanesian cults like that of Sambia is a measure of the profound psychosocial obstacles against which men must work to initiate boys.

8. Perhaps we should carefully examine again the connotations and contexts in which ideas about male "growth" are cited in Highlands societies (see Meigs 1976:399; Read 1951:162; Salisbury 1965:61).

The scale of institutionalization and the affective intensity of bloodletting rites are correlated with a configuration of fragile family dynamics virtually unmatched elsewhere in the tribal world (except, perhaps, the Amazon Basin [see Murphy 1959]). The effects of warfare arrangements on the family can be seen in intense, prolonged maternal attachment, and distance from father. And too little father and too much mother inhibit a boy's easy, rapid, conflict-free transition into the warrior mold. Mead (1952) was correct: aggressiveness is not an easy condition for humans to create. Freud (1930:34, 50) should have visited New Guinea![9]

The corresponding developmental issues are twofold. First, how to check boys' earliest pre-Oedipal identifications and wishes to merge with, and depend upon, their mothers (Mahler 1963). Thus, the "primary femininity" in a boy's core gender identity (Money and Ehrhardt 1972; Stoller 1976) must be drastically halted, for Sambia scarcely allow softness in men. Second, how to get boys to identify primarily with their fathers, with masculinity and the cult at large, thereby forcing them to conform to the psychosocial (and Oedipal) demands of war, ritual, and "hostile" women. No exceptions to universal initiation are allowed (see Barth 1975:47), which mocks the naïveté of early armchair writers (Bettelheim 1955) regarding personal choice in ritual. In short, a fierce "push" and a pride-filled "pull" by the men's organization are needed to effect maternal detachment and masculinization in boys (Lidz and Lidz 1977; Stoller and Herdt 1982). Repeated nosebleeding is essential to the culturally desired outcome.

It is the precise psychocultural definition of proximity to women at each point in the life cycle that governs the vicissitudes of Sambia nosebleeding. Let us accord full recognition to the native point of view: being close to women is a social problem of magnitude at various levels—political, sexual, psychological, ritual. For males, female proximity always remains a power-laden issue, it embodies the culture dilemma mentioned before—it

---

9. "Teenagers in pre-literate societies are probably relatively more able to meet adult tasks than are adults in our society; hence they feel less dependent on or overawed by adults. These adolescents would certainly be able to resist rites inflicted on them by old men if they wanted to do so" (Bettelheim 1955:92). Clearly, we can see Oedipal dynamics at work in the fierceness of initiation, both for fathers and sons. Indeed, it could be argued (Róheim 1942) that it is not until men fully act as initiators for their sons that they have attained the status of manly persons. How valid is Reik's (1946) contention that these fathers are mainly motivated to traumatize their sons out of hostile, Oedipal wishes? We still do not know, of course, though whatever their intrapsychic motives, there remains plenty of other socially sanctioned reasons for allowing men to believe they are acting out of necessity for the welfare of themselves and their sons. Nevertheless, there is far too much violence, trauma, and even genital threats in penis bleeding (see, e.g., Salisbury 1965:56ff.; Tuzin 1980:69–70), such that we should dismiss the Oedipal argument out of hand (cf. Bettelheim 1955; Langness 1974:204–5; Lidz and Lidz 1977:29; Young 1965).

involves conflict, domestic and ritual, intrapsychic and interpersonal, as seen most dramatically in initiations, where nosebleeding mediates between individual "life crises" and the social order.

How does nosebleeding regulate proximity? There are four domains of constraints based on ritual custom and belief. (1) Symbolic identifications: nearness to women is believed always to impart femaleness to males and, hence, pollution (demasculinization). In ritual, boys are identified with mothers, and husbands with wives. The rule is: Female contacts make one less masculine, so avoid them. Later, symbolically, one must match one's wife's periods with private bleedings to ensure that one is as clearly male and as productively masculine as she is productively feminine. (2) Cultural timing: enforced nosebleeding checks personal choice at critical junctures in attachments to women: separation from mother, puberty and sexual maturation, marriage and cohabitation, birth and postpartum "distance," and encroaching aging, which threatens overdependence on one's wife. (3) Sexual access: nosebleeding is the greatest sanction supporting boys' female-avoidance behavior, youths' taboos on premarital heterosexuality and adultery, homoerotic practices, and men's self-regulation in sexual activities with their wives. (4) Secret identity: nosebleeding experience, concealed by ritual secrecy, appropriates a vulnerable piece of the self that is primarily feminine and thus must be bounded and kept hidden from women. This last point means that nosebleeding is not only a culturally constituted bundle of defense mechanisms (cf. Bettelheim 1955; Stephens 1962; Whiting, Kluckhohn, and Anthony 1958). It is also a creator of that complex experience: selfhood.

Seen this way, nosebleeding is a system of identity contexts which layer upon one another in the life cycle. Each successive initiation introduces changes in the bloodletting act—roles, scripts, signs, and audiences which unfold and transform the social organization of experience. To balance childhood experience against the demands of adult roles (with all that entails) constitutes the "internal discourse" of private nosebleeding for men. This discourse concerns the objective dilemma that one live and be sexually intimate with a woman while staying aloof from her, being secretive, fierce, and manipulative, according to warfare and ritual designs (initiate sons, trade daughters in marriage). The formula of self-bleeding ensures this fragile holding pattern. That solitary act subsumes layer upon layer of past experience and identity. Its audiences include the inner representations or fantasized "voices" of mother and father, one's earliest objects, as well as one's elders and peers present through memories of past initiations, with their trauma, separations, violence, cutting of flesh, manly pride, respect, and autonomy. The ritual cult thus reinserts itself, time and again, into the self and the marital relationship. And this is how it must be: enjoying women and sexual release in coitus is a self-initiated threat to manhood. Bloodletting becomes a habitualized style for checking one's affections and lust, one's self-doubts about being alone with, and inside of, a woman again. It is humanly impossible for men, without coitus, to create children and reap the rewards of hard-won sexual success and manhood, but they take their lives into their own hands each time they do so. Private nose-bleeding therefore enables a man to maintain lifelong proximity to his wife—with some intimacy—by serving as a sign that he is separate and po-tent (it keeps him "heterosexually masculine") and a vigorous warrior. This thick compound of meanings is embodied in the adult sense: "I am still growing."

If my interpretation is correct, than we should expect that the end of warfare will bring an end to nosebleeding. As a system of identity contexts, bloodletting is a part of the behavioral environment that included war and other material consequences for the sociocultural system and family arrangements. Pacification has indeed changed the whole system, but the parts of the system are not changing in equal measure. In fact, cane swal-lowing was abandoned first, the warriorhood aspect of nosebleeding teach-ings was halted in 1973, and, finally, nosebleeding itself was entirely dropped from the most recent Sambia initiations in the late 1970s. Family arrangements are changing slowly, although there are no longer the tremendous pressures on males to always be seen as fierce warriors. Initia-tion persists (see Gewertz 1982). Men, reared with war, still privately bleed themselves. But, in another generation, nosebleeding will be known only as a social memory to the Sambia.

Three generations of Sambia women and their children, 1976

Initiation time, 1975: A small troop of new and older bachelors, fully dressed for the ceremonial parade (Moondi is second from left; Weiyu third from right)

Mother and children in Sambia bush hut, 1979

A pre-initiate boy, age six, 1976

Man and patrimony, Sambia village, 1975

Gilbert's house, Sambia village, with informants and friends, 1979

Senior woman, late forties, Sambia village, 1976

Pre-initiate, 1975

Sambia second-stage inititate, age thirteen, in the concentrated repose of "great-man-
to-be"

Two Sambia men, both fathers in their mid-forties, who once were homoerotic partners. (*Left*, shaman in Cassowary headdress)

Sambia first-stage initiation: Elders prepare the boys

Sambia elder, at center of attention, lectures and orates during initiation, 1975

Revealing the flutes to first-stage initiates, 1975

Presentation of the flutes (and machete), first-stage initiation, 1975

Sambia great cult house and dance ground (fenced), 1975

The new crop: first-stage initiates on the dance ground, 1975

Second-stage initiation: feasting on taro

Tali, a ritual expert, directing a pig feast, 1993

First-stage initiates adorned in their new warrior garb, 1975

Tali, Gilbert, and Weiyu, old friends. Sambia Valley, 1993

FIVE

Semen Depletion and the Sense of Maleness

The psychosocial phenomenon of semen depletion—a culturally transmitted belief that men's sexual contacts rob and empty them of semen, maleness, and eventually life itself—is known from premodern and preliterate societies, including our own. However, in New Guinea, the complementary forms of this belief system are intense and pervasively associated with male secret societies and ritual polarity between the sexes (see Herdt 1981; Hogbin 1970; Kelly 1976; Lindenbaum 1972; Mead 1935; Meggitt 1964; Read 1954; Schieffelin 1976; Whiting 1941). All of these studies have examined semen depletion from an institutional perspective: the beliefs are thought to symbolize aspects of the social structure; or they rationalize rituals, create solidarity and power for male groups; or, more recently, they serve as cultural metaphor of the category of personhood to which a man has been assigned and through which he thus defines himself. Such normative perspectives on social roles and cultural institutions are important, and others have studied them (see Allen 1967; Keesing 1982; Langness 1974). By contrast, no one has described the ethnopsychology of semen depletion as a subjective conviction—either in clinical or quantitative studies—so we remain ignorant of its subjectivities.

This chapter concerns this neglected problem and its psychological implications for the development of male gender identity among Sambia: How is semen depletion experienced? How is it associated with the emergence and preservation of gender identity? Are its anxious consequences ego-dystonic? If we grant that cultural patterns like this one also have "individual realities" (Sapir 1949:572), subjectivity contained in social acts, affects, and fantasy, then our clinical task is to describe experience at various levels of awareness. Anthropologists have taken divergent positions on cultural variations in sexual meanings since the earliest work of Malinowski, Róheim, Sapir, and Mead, and it is not my aim here to review these paradigms (see Devereux 1978; LeVine 1973); I only wish to register several perspectives that have guided my work on Sambia gender identity.

The first point is theoretical: although cultural patterns are shared and transmitted by caretakers and groups, they take variable form in the psychodynamics of individual awareness, the expressions of which can be observed in interpersonal behavior. Subjective experience thus intervenes in—and is used for reasoning out—transformations in cultural structures (Piaget 1971; Schwartz 1978; Spiro 1968). The second point is methodological: only by sampling individual behavior in depth can we hope to interpret individual meanings associated with cultural patterns. There are various ways in which this kind of sampling can be done, but all of them ultimately involve clinical relationships and empathic observation, what I have called clinical ethnography (Herdt 1981). Here, of course, the question of what constitutes a representative baseline for interpreting individual experience and behavioral expression is critical. In this work my handling of that sampling problem is similar to Levy's (1973): after talking with many of the Sambia for two-and-a-half years, I qualitatively classified—made distinctions between—affects and other behaviors that are normative or aberrant statistically, normal or abnormal in the native view, on the basis of individual biography, the behavioral context, and the "evidential continuity" of narratives.

The final point concerns psychodiagnostic evaluation. Semen depletion beliefs operate at different levels of meaning in the lives of Sambia men. On the one hand, anthropologists accept such complexity as basic to all human behavior. Yet the cultural relativism that goes along with it—which treats all behavioral patterns as equally efficacious, adaptive, or ego-syntonic regardless of context—is more problematic. On the other hand, Western psychiatrists are inclined by definition to diagnose depletion beliefs as psychopathological, the associated anxieties being "symptoms" of deeper conflicts in character structure (see Lidz and Lidz 1977:17, 30). As Devereux (1980) noted long ago, the problem here concerns applying the concept of "normality" to divergent cultural settings. Should we classify all Sambia men as aberrant, even perverse, if they share in semen-depletion beliefs? I do not think so.

Consider the differential experience of depletion anxieties among Sam-

bian and American men. Sambia fully institutionalize beliefs about depletion. All males are initiated into a ritual cult that (1) prescribes transitional
homoerotic inseminations believed to masculinize boys, (2) abhors any
careless ejaculation, and (3) teaches that unregulated sexual contacts, especially with women, can deplete one's maleness and may lead to death. Such
beliefs are not, of course, institutionalized in American culture, and few
American men, one suspects, consciously entertain or are preoccupied with
such ideas. (There are still cultural murmurings, however, such as the misunderstood biblical edict not to spill one's seed, or the folklore notion that
athletes should refrain from sex before strenuous competitions.) And most
clinicians would probably regard intense anxiety about semen loss as a
symptom of borderline or paranoid psychosis. But such symptomatology is
infrequent: Western sexual aberrance takes different forms (see Stoller
1968). Since Sambia males are all taught to fear depletion, semen loss is a
normative preoccupation, and most men evince some anxiety about it. It is
the degrees and contexts of such anxiety that symptomatically distinguish
Sambia individuals. Depletion ideas act as a sexual constraint in most men,
worrying and sexually exciting, but not crippling them to the point of inhibition. Therefore, since Sambia men must register but not be paralyzed by
such anxiety if they are to inseminate boys, marry and engage in heterosexual coitus, and thereby attain manhood, we should expect to define Sambia
aberrance by virtue of the degrees of failure in achieving these psychosexual
transitions. This definition seems to help sort out the variance: men ex-
hibiting extreme anxiety are infrequent; gross aberrance, that is, as in the
avoidance of all ejaculation, is not reported.[1] Consequently, a few, rare
cases of Sambia men—at both ends of the normal population distribution
of sexual behavior—either reveal no depletion fears, or, like Kalutwo, our
subject, are psychopathologically afraid of semen loss, but only in relation
to women.

I shall examine that latter aberrance by extracting fragments from Kalutwo's case study, since his abnormal, defensive use of depletion beliefs
helps illustrate the psychopathological extreme to which the culture pat-

1. Out of my total research population, only four or five adult men are known to engage in homoerotic fellatio regularly (not merely on the sly and occasionally) with boys, even though they
are married, and it is grossly inappropriate for them to do. These deviant men are similar to Kalutwo (whom I am about to discuss)—although he has no children and is not now married. However, there is another handful of older men who look like Kalutwo, at a distance: they are older,
have failed at marriage, are quiet, conservative, unobstructive. (One of them seems mentally re-
tarded, has never been married, and engages only in homoerotic activities.) It may turn out that
those men, on closer examination, approximate the clinical profile of Kalutwo but that possibility remains to be checked.

tern tends. The data adduced here are not exhaustive or complete, being part of ongoing longitudinal investigation of Sambia gender identity. It is important to underline that Kalutwo is a rare, perhaps unique Sambia man: his personal history, underlying depressiveness, and masculinity are non-normative; in defiance of cultural ideals, he has lived predominantly as an enthusiastic participant in homoerotic activities for all his mature years; and he fears any sexual contact with women. Nevertheless, he is physically healthy, nonpsychotic, socially involved with others. And while he is considered odd and is disparaged, he has not been shut out of the institutions and relationships that enable him to feel as worthwhile as he does. In short, his gender identity deviance disturbs but does not disable him. It is the deviance in his sense of self and its relationship to expressions of depletion that I want to examine: beliefs that have helped preserve his identity in the course of development.

Cultural Meanings of Semen Depletion

An outstanding consequence of the Sambian developmental complex, as described in some detail in previous chapters, is the dread of semen depletion. Since biological maleness is based on a fantasized accumulation of a semen pool inside the body, the depletion of that precious fluid (i.e., through ejaculation) threatens not only maleness, but existence itself. Male atrophy is the (potentially ego-dystonic) phenomenon induced by ritual and suffered by men. The male body is like an empty reservoir that must be filled up; once filled, the semen organ sustains existence by supplying sperm. Yet when diminished continually without replenishment, the source of maleness—and thus, life itself—evaporates, so only debilitation and death can result. Here is contained the terrible dilemma of Sambia masculinity. Boy inseminating, heterosexual reproduction—and their erotic pleasures—require repeated ejaculations which stimulate "growth" or "babies" in others by depleting one's only reserve. Someone's loss is thus someone else's gain.

The psychological reality of depletion is difficult if not intolerable, and it has resulted in many compromises in defending one's personal fund of semen, especially regarding women. Regulation of heterosexual intercourse is a primary defense. But, as we have seen, another is also vital: adult men practice secret, customary ingestions of white tree sap in the forest. Men say that this tree sap "replaces" ejaculated semen "lost" through heterosexual intercourse. So men regularly drink tree sap after coitus in order to replenish maleness. Interestingly enough, though, most bachelors—although they worry over semen depletion—do not replace their semen "lost" through premarital homoerotic relations. Only with marital coitus are those personal anxieties reinforced through the institutionalized practice of tree-sap ingestion (see Herdt 1981:248–51).

Briefly restated, femaleness and adult feminine reproductive competence are regarded as "natural" developments, functions of female biology and a girl's unbroken relationship to her mother. Maleness, however, is not a "natural" producer of biological growth. Attainment of masculine reproductive maturity is viewed as a problematic personal achievement made possible through the ritualized avoidance of women and through homosexual activities. Semen accumulation and depletion are the psychosocial outcomes of this developmental cycle, whose psychodynamics tend to cause a dread of women. Let us now examine these psychosocial consequences by means of the study of a single case, drawing on this cultural sketch for an understanding of their most extreme forms.

Kalutwo: Intense Fear of Depletion

Kalutwo is an unremarkable looking Sambia man in his mid-thirties whom I have periodically interviewed over five years' time in the late 1970s and early 1980s. He was reared as, appears to be, and lives as a biologically normal male. People first mentioned him as a minor shaman of a neighboring hamlet with a troubled marital history. But marital problems are quite common among Sambia, and while they made fun of him, Kalutwo's peers still acknowledged him. My first impression of Kalutwo arose from seeing him too often around the clubhouse with initiates.

I first began working with Kalutwo on his shamanistic activities, in 1975, in the course of doing case studies of individual shamans. Even then I sensed him as being odd; he sheepishly discussed his healing activities and avoided his own history. Those interviews unearthed fragments of his childhood and marital background. While Kalutwo was technically "married" four times, each marriage quickly failed, and Kalutwo has been increasingly stigmatized for those failures. The elders and his peers, as usual in such matters, tried placing the blame onto the wives or greedy lovers—who managed to steal them away. Later interviews (in 1979) clearly showed that such views were largely rationalization: Kalutwo's unmanly avoidance of his wives drove them, in succession, into other men's huts. This perspective led me to reconstruct more carefully Kalutwo's family background and childhood, which began looking more and more bizarre. The final result was my awareness that Kalutwo not only feared women, but that he preferred inseminating boys and that he, unlike other Sambia, comes closest to being an adult homosexual in the Western sense of that identity.

Well before pacification, Kalutwo was traditionally reared and initiated into the male cult. Kalutwo still lives in that traditionalism, which in his case has two aspects. Though socially conservative, he is also deviant. As an initiate, he was a little too small for his age. Later, he fought in several battles but stayed in the back lines and was never much of a fighter. (Nor did he aspire to be one, according to his own reports.) Neither is he much of a hunter, and this indifference sets him apart even more from most men. Instead, he prefers and enjoys gardening, which is a respectable pursuit—but more for older men and, of course, women. Later (after 1975), he began assisting in shamanistic healing ceremonies, which he says he does because they "help" people. It is noticeable that in gardening and healing activities, however, his performance, involvement, and interest have markedly decreased over the course of five years, as his deviance compared with his age mates has been more obvious. He is also sadder. Furthermore, in other male activities and his social relationships, he visibly exhibits decreasing enthusiasm, and consequently his peers disparage him more. Here, to the uniformed observer, Kalutwo would appear to be an enigma.

Kalutwo presents himself a tough, stiff-lipped, traditional masculine man. He always wears a grass sporran, warrior bandoleers, and bark cape: the old insignia of a true warrior. In a time of increasing social change, he has never worked on the coast and does not want to, nor does he speak Pidgin. (By contrast, half the adult male population has now served as contract plantation laborers on the coast, sometimes wear Western garb, and speak some Pidgin.) Besides dressing conservatively, Kalutwo is scrupulous about keeping his beard shaven and hair short cropped (both traditional masculine features). He is physically plain, is short and stockier than most Sambia men, and is facially stark, some say ugly, by Sambia standards. He is personally stiff, often distant and even uncomfortable in public; he is secretive, avoids children, is often quiet, emotionally flat, and can be depressively broody, with dull speech, even though he is identified as having a sharp tongue and a wry, sarcastic wit. Most of these character traits fall at the extreme end but are within the range of old-fashioned Sambia masculinity.

There are other factors about him though, that mock this appearance of surface normality. First, of course, is his total and undistinguished lack of manly achievements: no battle scars or heroic deeds, no impressive hunting record, no numerous female conquests or many wives with many babies, no oratorical skills or powerful ambitions. Kalutwo, increasingly, seems shiftless. Second, there is his aberrant marital status. He lives now as an unmarried, aging bachelor, lacking erotic relationships with women in a society renowned for valuing marriage as the bedrock of adulthood. Third, and more subjective, is his physiognomy: a face that is controlled but craggy, with creases making him look older than his years (and matched by body movements that are perceptibly slow and slumped, as if he carried a weight alone), with sad eyes and facial lines that suggest conflict, as if pieces of himself were consciously at odds or in pain. And yet, despite this appearance of age, one senses something oddly unfinished about his eyes—as if a small boy still lived within. Finally, there are his personal ties: a few companions and dogged supporters; no immediate family except for a close relationship with his only remaining blood sibling—a widowed older sister—on whom he is dependent emotionally and for subsistence; and the boys he uses as fellators, an erotic outlet that becomes increasing difficult to obtain as he ages and boys tire of him.

In short, Kalutwo only appears to be an enigma; his history and identity belie his traditional masculinity. He has supporters, most of whom see him as a social failure but not as an outcast. His outward response is to dress and act like a tough phallic warrior, but he cannot quite bring off this performance since his own psychological needs undermine it. Kalutwo is thus disparaged as a rubbish man *(wusaatu)*—and not always behind his back— for, in Sambia society, merely seeming tough is not enough to prevent oneself from being stigmatized as not masculine enough.

These psychosocial assessments arise from various sorts of information, and I should mention them schematically before going further. Kalutwo did not figure in my initial research project because, among other reasons, he was not especially articulate. Although we met on the first day of my arrival in the Sambia Valley (November 1974), and the meeting stands out, I ignored him. Later, my attitude changed after interviewing him regarding shamanic activities (1975–76). Only in 1979, while actively working with him for some three months—mostly to understand his gender identity— did I become more clinically involved. That understanding produced a great shift in my empathic communication with Kalutwo.[2] (For a more detailed portrait and discussion of the linguistic and psychological aspects of Kalutwo's case study, see Herdt and Stoller [1990].)

2. Until then, along with the other men, I had chuckled un-self-consciously at Kalutwo's disgraceful marital failures, and unmanliness, when men gossiped. But after working with him, I changed. In the midst of eliciting his history and seeing his face visibly contort with pain, that unreflected distance (i.e., hostility) in myself diminished, for I understood better the sadness he carried, and the helplessness he had had to endure inside, alone.

Childhood

By almost any sociocultural indicator, Kalutwo's childhood experience had
been unusual compared with the normative pattern of most Sambia men.
His parenting was plainly bizarre. About Kalutwo's mother (who had died
twenty years earlier), little is known except that she was a conscientious gar-
dener who disliked crowds. She eventually avoided contact with men. His
mother had had three children by her first husband, and she was an older
widow by the time she became pregnant with Kalutwo by another man.
Two children died, leaving Kalutwo's eldest sister his mother's chief com-
panion. Sometime thereafter the mother began having an illicit sexual liaison with a married man of a neighboring hamlet. (It is difficult, here, to
reconstruct what such an "affair" entailed, but it may have involved only being amiable and having had sexual intercourse several times secretly in the
forest.)

That man—Kalutwo's biological father—subsequently rejected her,
for reasons still unclear, although he was already married and had several
adolescent children. This kind of rejection seldom occurs, and rarely in this
way, since the product—Kalutwo—would normally be desired and claimed
by the father, not left to become a fatherless "bastard." (There is not even a
term in the Sambia language meaning "bastard," a social fact that reflects
the strong cultural basis for heterosexuality only in marriage, and the wish
for heirs, including adoptees.) Now, Sambia, who are prudish, who honor
and even prize virginity and faithfulness in marriage, and who outspokenly
condemn sexual promiscuity, came down hard on Kalutwo's husbandless
mother when her pregnancy became noticeable. But the man completely
disclaimed any involvement or responsibility. That rejection was ominous,
for it placed an adultery stigma on Kalutwo's mother, and it meant she was
to have no economic support in rearing Kalutwo. So Kalutwo's mother was
cruelly condemned by all, and her brothers, rather than sympathizing with
or supporting her, as might have happened, openly scorned and beat her.
She thus withdrew to live in isolation with another widow at a pig-herding
hut removed from the hamlet.

This early history—of a liaison that led to a morally offensive birth,
humiliation, banishment, and bastardization—overshadowed all of Kalutwo's childhood. He grew up without a father or acceptable substitute.
Presumably out of anger toward the mother, none of his mother's brothers
stepped in to serve as an appropriate male figure. In fact, to worsen matters—and here we see the beginnings of familial guilt and conflict unfortunately structured into the child's environment—Kalutwo was told that his

father was dead, and the man's true identity was kept hidden from the boy; that is, it became a "family secret." Kalutwo's mother had been treated shabbily. From what Kalutwo can reconstruct, she understandably communicated resentment and bitterness toward all men, generally withdrawing from community life—and especially from contact with men. Kalutwo, the "cause" of this unhappiness, and a male at that, became her only remaining joy.

Kalutwo thus grew up with the sense that he had no father, or older man, who loved or had any real interest in him. The other widow living in the isolated home had two children, an older boy and a girl. That older boy might have been an appropriate male figure and "brother" substitute, but Kalutwo claims that he was often teased and hit by the boy, whom the women could not control. After the older male's initiation, Kalutwo remained in the all-female household and spent most days with his mother in her gardens. He was then her only garden helper, so his labor was also important to her. She discouraged him from playing with other children, especially boys; she discouraged him from being with men, warning that he would get "hurt" if he engaged in the other boys' pastimes, like rough-and-tumble games. The mother's attitude affected Kalutwo. For example, he hid from men when he saw them approaching on the footpaths, he says, for he perceived them as dangerous. His one source of affectionate masculine contact was his sister's husband, with whom he would—on occasion—spend enjoyable periods. Unfortunately, that man died a little later.

Near his first-stage initiation, Kalutwo says he learned (from the other widow) about the family secret: his true father was not dead but had disowned his paternity. From that time (about age seven), until second-stage initiation (about age eleven), Kalutwo would sometimes approach "that man," but he was shunted aside. Only later (at the period of Kalutwo's mother's death) did an unspoken tie develop between the two of them, enough of a relationship for Kalutwo to receive food and some attention from the man, but little else. Nevertheless, when asked how his true father responded to him, Kalutwo bitterly remarked on several occasions: "I was just a piece of shit to him," almost scowling as he said this. "He was a very bad man." By age fourteen or so, both of his true parents were dead.

Initiation

Kalutwo resisted initiation. This resistance went beyond what some boys report, for in their fears about being initiated, most initiates receive some support from their fathers (or masculine substitutes); they feel a saving desire to emulate the fathers and become proud warriors like them. Kalutwo, however, felt only that he would be harmed. And neither his father nor his mother's brothers assumed their social responsibility properly to support Kalutwo's initiation; it was his sister's husband who did that. Even so, I was surprised about Kalutwo's recollections of that period and by his uncensored response to my first (open-ended) question about what he had felt at the time: "Why didn't I want to be born a *tai* [girl] before? That's what I thought when I thought about the [ritual initiation] beatings. . . . Mother lectured me: 'The men can truly beat you before they decorate you with the yellow flower [the *mooniglu* orchid stem fiber, a reference to initiates' warriors bandoleers). They don't decorate you for just any reason. . . . They can all fight you first.' Mother, too, she thought about it [Kalutwo's fate] very hard." Here, in this self-report about being initiated, we have the first powerful indication of aberrance in Kalutwo's sense of maleness: he feared the beatings and resisted by wishing that he had been a female.

Kalutwo's initiation was unexceptional. He was put through a long series of frightening and exhausting ordeals. The key ritual experience is the penis-and-flute ceremony, wherein ritualized fellatio is revealed along with the secret of the flutes, conventions that men share in and hide from women and children (see chapter 3). Kalutwo's response to the homoerotic teachings is worth mentioning in part:

> GH: How did you feel at the penis teaching?
>
> K: At the time I thought, "Is this [penis] like the 'food' of the women, and the men, too—that they all 'eat' it?" That's what I thought and I felt shame. . . . When they taught about fellation—using the bamboo [flute]—I thought they were lying. . . . I felt afraid. . . . Not good that their huge penis—that is breaks my neck! The penises were enormous, and at first you fear them. . . . Only after practice do you think their penises are smaller. After you sucked them, fear that the neck will be broken goes away—and you feel that it's [fellatio is] easier. . . .
>
> GH: What about your shame?
>
> K: The first night he buttered up to me; a bachelor inseminated me. I wasn't truly ashamed, just a little bit. And that first night, after he inseminated me, my shame was gone.

These statements are somewhat unusual compared with those of most males in that Kalutwo claims that he "got over" his fear and shame quite quickly. For many Sambia boys, that takes much longer.

More significant, in relation to this first homoerotic experiences, we can clearly define some aberrance in Kalutwo's sense of maleness, as seen by his precocious homoerotic excitement. After working with Kalutwo a long time—and toward the conclusion of our work—he said (with reluctance, even then) that he had often had erections when sucking the bachelors. Eventually, with embarrassment, he said that he had experienced that excitement even in his first acts of fellatio.

> K: The first time the bachelor penetrated me [mouth], I [penis] got hard. . . . The second time too. . . . And the third time too. All three times I was inseminated in the cult house, I got an erection.
> GH: What did you feel about your erections?
> K: My penis is tight and later, then I [as a bachelor] can also butter up to boys; my penis will also get up.

My impression is that Kalutwo is being highly revealing; he believes he really had those erections. Whether or not they actually occurred, though, that conviction is absolutely extraordinary: no other man had described having erections during those first experiences. (Although some boys, as fellators, described having erections years later.) In other words, Kalutwo's aberrance could be defined as his early, prepubescent genital excitement, first experienced during the initiations.

What about the value of semen for biological maleness? I next asked Kalutwo about his sense of the ritual belief that equates semen with breast milk. Semen is the same as mother's milk, men said: "You boys don't throw away pandanus nuts—and you must not do that with semen. It's not urine, its name is *koonbooku* [abbreviated lexeme for semen]. They [bachelors] all only want to give a prize to your penis. . . . If you go and continue [being inseminated], you, too, can give 'water' to all the initiates. . . . But if you don't "sleep" with the men, you can spend a long time [later, copulating] but still not ejaculate "water." If you do that [fail to be inseminated], later your own penis will stay erect, like an empty cord, without "water" [semen]."

A long time later (at least a year, possibly two), as part of his adjustment to the fellator role, Kalutwo began to have more extended sexual relationships with certain bachelors. In general, Kalutwo's homoerotic activities, like those of most Sambia males, have always been promiscuous. But several relationships lasted days, weeks, and—in one instance—about two months. Here is Kalutwo on his longest relationship: "I liked his [bachelor] 'water'—[for] he had a lot. . . . He didn't come quickly, but he did ejaculate a lot. He'd butter up to me. . . . As a *choowinuku* and then as *imbutu* [first- and second-stage initiate], he'd give me food. As a *choowinuku*, I was a little afraid. . . . But as an *imbutu* I felt okay." Kalutwo admitted that at first he feared he'd become "pregnant from being inseminated." But other males advised him "not to worry." He continued thus as a fellator until puberty.

Puberty

At puberty, Kalutwo experienced a lot of difficulty in making the adjustment to third-stage initiation, and thereafter serving as a bachelor-fellated. He developmentally associated having pubic hair with his biologic readiness to be an inseminator. He experienced these secondary sex-trait changes as filled with shame. It was still very hard for him to talk about this "shame" in 1979.

> GH: What did you feel?
> K: [Blandly] I didn't feel anything.
> GH: Why can't you recall that? What do you feel now?
> K: I was ashamed. . . . (pause) I hid my body hair [pubic hair] very well.
> GH: Why were you ashamed?
> K: I saw the "penis hair" and feared that others would make fun of me.

Although Sambia boys experience some embarrassment about puberty changes, most overcome that shame. In discussing his feelings here, Kalutwo vicariously experienced that shame again—a shame that is still close to him—and such a body sense, among adult Sambia men, is considered unmanly and is remarkable. His first experience as a fellated was also somewhat shameful for Kalutwo. That act occurred while he was being initiated into the third-stage bachelorhood, as is customary.

> K: I gave him [the novice] my "water"—I felt "sweet" [sexual pleasure]. I thought that's what other bachelors felt, huh? I felt that, and then, in a little while, I felt a little shame.
> GH: What was that little shame?
> K: Not good that the boy would go and tell others [what we'd done]. . . . But I knew he wouldn't [i.e., boys fear sorcery retaliation]. . . . A month later, the same boy came back to me in the men's house. I slept and the boy awakened me. He got me up, I thought about his mouth, and my penis got very hard.
> GH: Did you worry about replacing the semen?
> K: No. [But then Kalutwo reiterated a concern that he has had about homoerotic ejaculation from the start.] Inseminating his [the fellator's] mouth was a new feeling. . . . I was pleased with his "hot water" [metaphor for mouth as sexual orifice]. But after finishing, I thought, worried a lot: not good that all the men stare at me. . . . I must forget about him [the fel-

lator]. Not good that the elders think I want him too much, and they cross me. They'd say I want to hold on to him. . . . [The elders would say:] "You've got to sleep with many boys, not just one! He's not your wife!" And I thought: you must not sleep with a boy too much, for your bone will slacken—[and] women will spit on you because you haven't enough semen to make a baby.

In summarizing this material on his early homoerotic experiences, I simply wish to underscore the obvious: that Kalutwo was already behaving unusually in several respects. He says he was genitally aroused by fellating older bachelors, and his response to his experience of being fellated was a feeling that he mustn't like it too much—an indicator of its powerful pleasure. The transition from boyhood to adolescence, and from being a fellator to a fellated, is difficult for all Sambia males. In Kalutwo's case, these transitional problems were subjectively pegged to the flow of semen—how much went inside or outside his body. He felt that the elders would be gauging that process. Semen flow had already become a symptomatic way of talking about his own maleness.

Marriage

Over the years, Kalutwo has been technically assigned in marriage to four different women in succession. The first marriage began some months after Kalutwo's fourth-stage initiation, which is unusual, since most men already have a woman assigned in marriage before the ceremony. But Kalutwo socially lagged behind his age mates. The first marriage failed; the union was never consummated. The second, third, and fourth marriages also failed: each time the women was "stolen"—lured away—by another man, which Kalutwo passively allowed. Throughout this chaotic marital history, Kalutwo says he has had sex only once with a woman—his second "wife"— and that sexual contact was an instance of fellatio that she (an experienced widow) initiated. The experience so frightened and filled him with guilt that he confessed it to his sister, who told everyone, and this disclosure, as he must have known, resulted in his humiliation. Throughout the wreckage of these marital ups and downs, Kalutwo has continued living in the men's house and engaging in homoerotic activities secretly with boys. The last attempt at marriage occurred in 1975. Since then, Kalutwo has been increasingly ridiculed by others for his marital failures and marriageless state. I cannot describe the complex history here; instead, I shall illustrate his heterosexual inhibitions by sketching events surrounding the last marriage.

The context of Kalutwo's last marriage (1974–75) was as follows: He had been "given" a young widow for his third marriage by two biological brothers who were his clansmen and who felt that she was wanton, so they declined to marry her. Kalutwo accepted her "second- hand." She resisted Kalutwo, who didn't immediately cohabit with her, as he should have, to consummate and seal the marriage. What predictably followed, under his own nose, was that the woman began a liaison with A, another married man, who got her pregnant, and whom she then joined—that is, "married." Tricked out of his "sexual property" and pushed on by the two brothers (the original donors of the woman), Kalutwo litigated against the other man who had "stolen" his "wife." It was that man, then, who "gave" another woman, W (also a widow), to Kalutwo as his fourth wife, thus avoiding fines or jailing by the locally elected councilman. W was a childless young widow of strong will; she was considered attractive—a good catch. But from the very start, Kalutwo believed that W did not want him.

K: The men told me to take her to my hamlet and [start to cultivate] gardens (sexually consummate the marriage). As we walked down the path, she said she didn't want me, she wouldn't marry me, that she would copulate with other men.

GH: What did you say?

K: Nothing... [except]: "Oh, that's your choice" [in a totally passive voice]. ... The councilman had pushed me into marrying her. ... He said that if I left her, then A [the man who bestowed her on Kalutwo following litigation] would steal her back. So I accepted her. [But] when we walked to the hamlet, I knew she wouldn't marry me; she'd run away. She'd go to M [a much older, married man, a powerful shaman, who was giving her gifts]. We went and slept with my sister in her house. We were going to make gardens [the next day]. Then, I also discovered that this women [W] had a bad spirit familiar, the *aatmwogwambu*, in a dream. I had a dream, I saw her that night.... And after that, I was "tired" of her [W]. I said: "That's fine, you can marry someone else, I'll stay single.".... For, I saw that spirit [in the dream] and I was afraid; so I told her—"That's alright," I won't die, I don't need a women [to deplete me].... Fornication isn't like food. ... You don't fornicate all the time.... And women are no good: you copulate with and give her [*sic*] your "water": can she then replace your "milk?" No. She'll take yours, for herself, and you'll age quickly....

GH: Did you try to prosecute the other man [W] for taking her?

K: No—she had the [bad] spirit; I didn't litigate. [But still] he didn't "pay" me, or replace her—none of the thieves [the men who took his "wives"] did! [some anger] M took her, he said, "I'm made of stone, I can marry her" [She won't harm me].... But later, M got very ill; he accused me of sorcerizing him. So I went and ate with him [to clear himself of sorcery accusations]. I'm glad I lost that woman. . . .

GH: Did you continue inseminating boys?

K: Yes. . . . I went back to my hamlet and slept in the men's house. Since then, I've been "alone" there. . . . There's been no more talk of giving me a wife. [The elders say:] "We've given you many women; we won't give you any more." . . . So now I'm like the other men's rubbish—they don't consider me [in marriage arrangements] now.

It was Kalutwo's inability to be the properly masculine, pushy, arrogant fornicator most Sambia idealize as a warrior figure that inhibited his heteroerotic and marital development. He both allowed other men to move in and steal his wives and, through his own passivity and fear, drove the other women away. Kalutwo is not an easy person to get along with—not because of aggressiveness but because of his frustrating ambivalence—and one senses that the women could not bear the latter. He fears women sexually; he even uses his dreams socially to defend himself against being with women. Consciously, his sexual avoidance of women is focused on semen depletion and, hence, demasculinization. But even though he is concerned about that depletion, he has continued inseminating boys.

Adult Compromises

Since the failure of his last marriage, two related psychosocial trends have been noticeable in Kalutwo's adult development. The one concerns his formal involvement in shamanistic performances. The other trend bears on Kalutwo's exclusive homoerotic activity and its underlying fetishistic fantasy system. In both of these areas, Kalutwo is, I think, still attempting to resolve developmental problems associated with adjustment to the normative context of masculine adult performance. And although his behavior is aimed at preserving his sense of maleness, his adjustment compromises have made him seem a little more desperate than ever before.

Like the rest of his developmental experience, Kalutwo's history of shamanism is splintered and convoluted. It contains too many contradictions to be considered only a role performance or dismissed merely as a defensive maneuver. Examples: Kalutwo had his first possession and trance experience around puberty, but he did not begin serving in healing ceremonies until much later. (That delay is too long and therefore aberrant.) He notably lacks the genealogical ancestry to properly claim "inheritance" of shamanic spirit familiars (usually inherited from one's father or father's

brothers). His trance states—which I have observed in healing ceremonies—seem shallow and forced compared with those of other shamans
(a fact that his peers recognize by disparaging him as a "weak" shaman), and
he cannot exorcise objects (the performative act of a full shaman, par excel-
lence). Nonetheless, Kalutwo was ritually installed as a new shaman ceremonially in the shamanic initiation in 1975 (see Herdt 1977). One suspects
that his marital problems and the failure of his latest marriage must have
been on his mind then.

On the surface, Kalutwo's shamanic status does help bolster and defend
his identity in several ways. The shaman's role makes Kalutwo stand out
somewhat from the male crowd. His spirit familiars also provide him with
supernatural powers that others should take note of, even if they don't fear
them. During healing ceremonies Kalutwo is more than usually aggressive
and exhibitionistic. He has several familiars; some are female, some are
male, and these figures—subjective "voices" that he experiences during
trance states—must appeal to dimensions of identification with femaleness and maleness that I believe remain more fully conscious in him (as in
other shamans), compared with most Sambia adult men. Kalutwo's particular shamanism, then, helps him to sustain, against formidable social pressures, his particular sense of self—of maleness—while lacking in other
manly achievements.

The other trends of Kalutwo's adjustment over the last five years I knew
him related to his exclusive homoerotic practices and their manifestations
in fantasy. We have seen that Kalutwo has had almost no overt heterosexual
experience. He has attempted marriage again and again, but each time he
suffered humiliation and defeat. There is no doubt that his last marriage, in
part, resulted from peer pressures: they wanted (and needed, i.e., in terms
of reassuring themselves about their own past identity transactions) Kalutwo to be married and less "visible." With that last failure, however, the
men seem to have given up, to have written him off, even though his deviance continues to be an embarrassment to the men.[3]

What does Kalutwo want for himself? Clearly, now as much as ever, Kalutwo prefers sex with boys, but how is this pedophilic preference also
(only? sometimes? completely?) a defense against women and fear of them?
Kalutwo's behavior reveals three patterns—or clues about fantasy—that
provide some understanding of these issues.

First, semen depletion is not only a generalized cultural belief, but it is

3. In other words, Kalutwo would be rated as a near "6" on the Kinsey scale of sexual activity
(0 = complete heterosexuality, 6 = exclusive history of homosexual activity); see Bell and Weinberg (1978:53–54).

also a dynamic element in Kalutwo's particular erotic excitement vis-à-vis boys. Here is Kalutwo talking about a recurrent daydream.

> K: I think about inseminating him [the boy-fellator]—his [mouth] hot-ness.... And, at the same time—I think of how he can truly finish off my "water" [semen]. Not good that I die quickly.... So I [think that I] must go to a different boy.... That boy is stealing [*kooku*] my bone.
> GH: What do you mean?
> K: The boy comes for my penis....
> GH: Yeah.... But what about the penis does he come for?
> K: He's thinking about his bone [male strength].... And he comes to me. The boy thinks, "Oh, this man, here, he must strengthen my bone."... He [the boy] only thinks about getting my "water."

And elsewhere, Kalutwo explicitly linked the excitement and fetishization (see Stoller 1979) of fellation to his core sexual excitement.

> K: He [the boy in a daydream] comes and holds onto my penis.... I wake up slowly, my eyes open.... Wait to awaken, as the boy holds my penis, shaking me.... And the boy says, pushing me: "Hurry-up, what are you waiting for!"... I am a little angry [at being awakened, prodded] but still pleased.... While asleep, your penis is slack.
> GH: What makes it hard?
> K: Just [him] holding my penis, for he wants to steal my bone. Once hard, the boy pushes.... He's thinking of *gami yungdu* [his bone].

Here we see, in Kalutwo's sexual daydreams, evidence of a fantasized inter-change—of giving and taking that is hostile and somewhat dangerous, for it will be depleting. The point is that, psychodynamically, the thought of having his semen stolen from him is what most excites Kalutwo.

Second, and following from the above, are the variations Kalutwo has formulated to keep from being bored in his homoerotic contacts with boys. The most obvious maneuver is his promiscuity: seeking new fellators and avoiding too much continuous contact with the same ones. Next, as he has aged and become less attractive to boys, Kalutwo has increasingly had to re-munerate, or "purchase," sexual favors from boys. But in all such cases, I think, the character of the sexual contact is socially and consciously defined as erotic—not as the "nurturance for masculinization" of ritual fellatio. And finally, there is another, more disturbing element about Kalutwo's ho-moeroticism that I can only report from hearsay. Several of the initiates with whom he has recently had fellatio report (to me, and to their friends; i.e., it is a gossiped confidence among the boys) that he has tried to break taboos and reverse roles, to suck their penises during sex. They say they refused and withdrew; the incident disturbed or amused them. In our work Kalutwo steadfastly and angrily refused even to approach the general area of these allegations. In short, the initiates say that Kalutwo wanted to suck them, which (if confirmed) would make his sexual attempt a perversion (Stoller 1975), in the strict sense of the term.[4] These factors keep homoerotic activities exciting.

Third, Kalutwo's semen depletion fears must be viewed also as a means of preserving his identity: a little fear makes homoerotic fellatio exciting; too much fear, however, creates anxiety and inhibition—and it is that kind of overwhelming danger that Kalutwo associates with women (i.e., heterosexuality).

> K: I didn't worry about losing "water" [after the third initiation]. . . . I gave "water" to them all [the initiates]. . . . The elders say that won't deplete you. [Kalutwo cites ritual teachings here to uphold his conviction that homoerotic fellatio isn't too depleting.]
> GH: But what about being married?
> K: I wasn't married yet; I hadn't finished growing. . . . [K cites ritual lore to defend his position about not wanting to be married too early.] [It's true that] I first worried about inseminating boys—losing semen—and only then. But I thought that other men also inseminated boys and didn't die, so I wouldn't either.

Later, after his first marriage and fifth-stage initiation, Kalutwo was taught about drinking tree milk sap to replace his semen. He said that he did not then worry about replacing semen. But he added:

> K: Inseminating boys isn't for making babies. Inseminating women is for that. . . . So, I'm worried about screwing women. . . . Drinking tree sap is for helping babies grow, too. . . . That's what I think: [and] women are a no good bunch. . . .

"Feeding" semen to boys is sexually exciting, "feeding" semen to a woman—especially into her vagina to "make babies," is too dangerous for Kalutwo. Homoerotic experience—the older Kalutwo controlling a boy—is a little risky and depleting, but the more exciting for it; heterosexual contact—with an adult women—is only draining and threatening.

By the time of my last period of interviewing Kalutwo, this final point had become conscious and obvious to us both. Kalutwo was finding it increasingly difficult to use boys—who resisted—as a sexual pastime. He

---

4. By definition, Kalutwo's draining a boy's semen would be defined, for the Sambia themselves, as a harmful, destructive act (as is masturbation). My impression is that these reports are probably true. Here, Kalutwo stands virtually alone in his community.

seemed more troubled, sadder, and in more pain than before. Kalutwo, I think, has been mildly and chronically depressed for much of his life.[5] From time to time he would start to ponder aloud about being married, having children, leaving heirs—before it was too late. He especially wanted children. He wondered idly and conspicuously whether the men would ever give him another wife. But there were no offers and none in sight. And perhaps that was what Kalutwo really wanted, for his behavior and life-style hadn't changed much: he wasn't that desperate, and others sensed it. But he still despaired and had come, rather unhappily, to accept the sad fate before him: social oblivion.

> K: Now, I think like this: I'll just remain with the initiates—if I die, some-time, that's alright [matter-of-factly]. Some others lived like this [as old bachelors] before, and they died [that way], didn't they? [Quieter, de-spairing] So if I stay like this and die, that's alright.

Discussion

As a Western male, and an ethnographer of Sambia, I initially experienced the men's concerns about semen depletion with mild surprise and disbelief. In time, however, that fresh impression faded. My adjustment to the local scene was spontaneous, a relativistic accommodation to *coutimes exotiques,* intellectually on a par with various other cultural elements—how yams are boiled, how ghosts are feared, how men must conserve their semen or else die—and a part of me as an observer became too comfortably detached. Though I accepted the idea that semen was limited, and could be valued as a form of commodity ("strength") along with milk or meat, I subliminally "read" men's statements as metaphor—symbolic representations that united men and expressed what it meant to be a Sambia masculine person. Only later, through individual case studies, did I realize that such an approach was inadequate, that it could not explain all the data. Then I again

5. Kalutwo's depression has been signified by a variety of signs and symptoms in this chapter, including his low repertoire of emotional expressions, and a tendency to shy away from being with and disclosing himself to others, especially other adult men. On many occasions, and in his relationship with me, he was more than passive; he also seemed genuinely to "feel nothing," as if he were "consciously empty." I'd argue, here, that Kalutwo was subliminally aware that in certain areas of social life, he must avoid probing (disclosure, insight) because it would make him anxious, so he consciously resisted discussing certain subjects (associated with unconsciously repressed and denied conflictual feelings, and their old trauma). Such interchanges in ethnographer/native awareness, and their methodological implications for transference/countertransference issues were famously discussed by Devereux (1967; see Herdt and Stoller 1990).

questioned: What part of depletion beliefs is experienced as cultural metaphor and what part as concrete conviction? Do they reveal the self-awareness, "I am a male"?[6]

I reiterate that Kalutwo is exceptional; in him, anxieties about semen depletion are symptomatic of a kind of aberrance that is rare, even among Sambia. Kalutwo belongs to a group of persons I have studied in order to understand gender formation and disorder. Clearly, his socialization has gone wrong, and though its consequences are still very much with him, his secretiveness—even as regards his peers—has made it difficult to decipher the elements of his gender subjectivity, defensive public behavior, and visible sadness. Even now, one wishes he could be helped to feel more comfortable, for he privately disparages himself as the kind of person remembered for his failures, not his successes. Finally, this chapter has said little about variation in semen-depletion-oriented behavior among normal Sambia boys and men, a subject considered elsewhere (Herdt and Stoller 1990).

In Melanesia, one can chart the variations in the cultural intensification surrounding the "metering of semen": all the way from the extreme case of the West New Guinea Dani, who (Heider 1976, if it is to be believed) only engage in sex at intervals of several years, through the "lechers and prudes" of the Western Highlands' Enga and Kuma (Meggitt 1964), on to the Eastern Highlands Gahuku-Gama (Read 1952), Fore (Lindenbaum 1972), and Sambia, who evince a lot of concern about depletion but still regularly engage in sexual intercourse, and on out to the (matrilineally based) Trobriand Islands, where Malinowski (1929) found sexual life free and easy and "nondepleting." This range of ethnographic cases is instructive: it indicates that we cannot account for "regulation theories" of body and gender depletion beliefs merely according to the presence (e.g., Enga, Trobriands) or absence (e.g. Sambia) of ceremonial exchange systems. Things are more complex than that. Only through individual case studies will we understand gender development and the desires created through these cultural ideologies.

The dynamics of male depletion beliefs raise important developmental questions about gender identity formation in these Melanesian societies. Here, Stoller's (1968) general work on identity development is helpful, and his chapter "The Sense of Maleness" provides suggestions. Arguing that the

6. In American society, we have more diffuse forms of unfinishedness in the sense of being male, as indicated by men's desires to use the right aftershave lotion, be musclemen, have big penises, be like a sexy Hollywood star, or by their fear that masturbation will lead to homosexuality (see Lidz 1975:322).

sense of maleness is "permanently fixed long before the classic phallic stage (age 3 to 5)," and that the penis contributes but is not essential to the development of maleness (1968:39–40), Stoller distinguishes between the subjectivity of early core gender identity ("I am a male") and later gender role labeling ("I am a boy, I am manly"). "Normally," Stoller continues (1968: 47), "the male external genitalia are a sign to the individual and to society that this is a male, but they are not essential to producing the sense of maleness." This last point, I think, has important implications that have thus far been overlooked in understanding New Guinea gender differentiation.

Sambia infants are definitively assigned to one or the other sex at birth. Male infants are assigned to the male sex on the basis of having a penis and testes. But prolonged maternal attachment and the father's aloofness combine to allow mother-infant symbiosis and pre-Oedipal identification. Male individuation and disidentification from the mother come late. Culturally stereotypy then lumps in initiated boys together with females. The effect, I hypothesize, is to "postpone" (Stoller 1968:73) core gender development. How do Sambia males experience that effect? The answer appears to be that boys have the awareness "I am a male, but not yet a biologically complete male." The completeness of the sense of being male is based on two signs to the self: the presence of secondary sex traits, especially pubic hair and a mature glans penis, and the conviction that one possesses and has available internal semen.

The extreme sexual polarity in Sambia society thus seems to result in a splitting up of the developing sense of being male. A precept of the core gender conviction—"I am a male"—is attached to the performative signs of semen flow in later sexual experience. First come homoerotic inseminations, a flow-into-the-body; second, ejaculation, a flow-out-of-the body; then there follow depletion fears and learning to drink in tree sap, externally replenishing the externally acquired semen. These ritual mechanisms are critical in handling the fluid state of maleness (see Meigs 1976) and its vicissitudes in social adjustment. A boy's adjustment to puberty and the performative context of ejaculation places enormous demands on the self, for it is at this juncture in adolescent development that one stops ingesting semen and must inseminate—"lose" some maleness—to demonstrate that one is, and can be labeled as, a sexually mature, masculine person who is aware that such acts are depleting. The normative success of that transition requires the individual, after having shifted his sense of maleness, to believe that he "will remain male, even when losing semen (maleness)."

Sambia culture thus extends the fixing (Stoller 1979:234–39) of the core awareness "I am a male" into pubertal sexual performance, and perhaps—through the system of depletion fears and fantasies—even into adulthood. The intrapsychic aspects of this developmental cycle remain to be fully understood, but we can conjecture. To compel boys' conformity to the rough standards of the adult masculine gender role is no mean achievement, for, among its roadblocks, is the boys' wish to stay blissfully attached to mother. (Their painful initiation demonstrates that their fathers will not allow that to happen.) The "fear of not growing up" (Whiting 1941:64), of not having semen or of losing it once acquired (e.g., castration anxiety), is transmitted to and inculcated in boys, helping them—consciously, unconsciously—to want to be like their fathers and to avoid wishing to be one with their mothers again, what Stoller (1975) calls "symbiosis anxiety." Like other identity signs, depletion beliefs function as intrapsychic barriers defending and maintaining the sense of maleness (see Stoller and Herdt 1982). This is the scenario of normal development.

Kalutwo reveals the ego-dystonic consequences of what may happen when the fine balance of male development in the Sambia family is upset. His aberrance is remarkable, even in the cultural setting to which he has adjusted (cf. Devereux 1956:114). Indeed, his sexual deviance—in Sambia terms—is rare, and on close examination, his biography and family history reveal the strange sort of picture that one would expect to find only in such extreme cases. His gender development, preceded by the cruel treatment his mother suffered owing to Kalutwo's birth, evinces too much mother and virtually no father (masculine figure). Undoubtedly, Kalutwo's exclusive homoerotic preference and fear of being depleted by women are products of this strange family background (Stoller 1968:45). One wonders whether other Kalutwos are to be found living lives of quiet desperation in other New Guinea societies where comparable gender socialization and ritualized homoeroticism occurs (see Herdt 1981). More focused research on sex and gender is needed to know.

The argument that the Sambia core sense of maleness is unfinished in adolescence differs from the social learning viewpoint (Money and Ehrhardt 1972) that sex assignment fixes gender identity during the initial three or four years of life, and that postnatal environment conditioning simply reinforces gender labeling. That model is important in helping explain the powerful effects of social training on gender behavior, but where it proves inadequate is in acknowledging the equally powerful dynamics of identification. Early childhood experience is split up at initiation; gender development is not a process of social continuity but rather discontinuity. Aspects of male gender constructs remain fluid. That fluidity is found in the adult psychological state that one can be depleted: "I am at risk of losing my identity." Maleness is not based only on being psychologically convinced—by others, by oneself—that one is "biologically" complete and contains all the elements needed to believe "I will always be male." Among Sambia males, that conviction also means that one must always have semen inside.

SIX

Father Presence and Ritual Homoeroticism: Paternal Deprivation and Masculine Development in Melanesia Reconsidered

Does father absence lead to homosexuality? The early Freud and certain later American psychoanalytic writers thought so; their perspectives were no doubt grounded in the folk models and epistemology of our culture. Recent work on ritualized homoeroticism in Melanesia (Herdt 1984) challenges this old idea. Surprisingly, in those New Guinea cultures in which the practice of boy-inseminating occurs, fathers are present in customary sleeping arrangements in childhood. Contrarily, in New Guinea cultures in which boy-inseminating is absent, there we find that fathers always live apart from their sons in childhood. The Melanesian findings suggest a revised image of father's role in child development and call for alternative ways of thinking about the effects of mother and father upon masculine personality and sexual orientation in males. Contrary to earlier approaches, I emphasize the historically conditioned material and symbolic father who is present in the development of the child. In this view, father and mother do not "cause" sexual orientation, but their social and symbolic presence and statuses help to explain systematic variations in homoerotic practices in Melanesia.

What Does the Western Theory Predict?

A long history of psychosocial inquiry into the nature of homosexuality has revolved around the differing influences of mothers and fathers in its determination. What began in the later part of the nineteenth century as a discourse on the origins of "inversion" took as its benchmark *Three Essays on the Theory of Sexuality,* wherein Freud suggested that the absence of a strong father may "favour the occurrence of homosexuality" (1962:146). Notwithstanding Freud's views on biological bisexuality (see Stoller 1975) and his later tolerance of homosexuality (Isay 1987), Freud clearly contributed to this pathologizing. In *Totem and Taboo* (1950a) he went on to explain the origins of "religion, morals, society and art" by reference to "one single concrete point—man's relation to his father" (1950a:156–57).

Subsequent writings in American psychoanalysis further pathologized this idea, rigidifying Freud's tentativeness and distorting his ambivalence on the issues, culminating in the Bieber et al. (1962:311) conclusion that "a warmly related father precludes the possibility of a homosexual son." Where Freud (1922:230) had emphasized the child's fixation on his mother, later American analysts, most notably Bieber et al. (1962), claimed that mothers were fixated on and overprotective of the child. This theory assumed that parents determine sexual orientation, pathologize parental roles, and adopt a "judgmental" attitude (Stoller 1985c:183) toward homosexual activity. The folk theory also implicitly "blamed" mothers for being dominant and fathers for being absent. Such a folk view happened to fit the general but erroneous conception of Melanesian societies as being sexually segregated, with the spouses living apart and child rearing being "mother monopolized" (the term is from Balbus [1982]). In fact, the situation is far more complicated.

Following upon Freud's ideas, the works of Rivers, Róheim, Malinowski, Mead, Whiting, Bettelheim, and, more recently, Dundes (1976), Spiro (1982), Allen (1984), Lidz and Lidz (1977), Herdt (1981), and Poole (1985), psychoanalysts and anthropologists have seen in Melanesian cultures personal symbols and cultural practices that reflect or mediate intrapsychic and unconscious processes. Initiation rites, for example, have been consistently viewed as manifestations of the Oedipal complex since the early Freud and Reik's (1946 [1915]) essay on puberty rites (Allen 1967; Bock 1980:155–58; see chapter 4 above).

Among the strong inferences that have resulted from decades of Melanesian work, perhaps none has proven more resilient than the "overmothering," "cross-sex identity" view identified with Bettelheim and the early Whiting (reviewed in Allen 1967:1–27; Herdt 1981). This theory suggests that primary attachment to mother and weak or absent father attachment are necessary antecedents for the institutionalization of cultural practices that mediate Oedipal conflict in the nuclear triangle (reviewed in Lidz and

Lidz 1977; Parker, Smith, and Gignat 1975; Paul 1976; Spiro 1982). Furthermore, ritual boy-inseminating would seem to be a prototype, perhaps even an exemplar, of how the effect of strong maternal figures and absent father figures in the unconscious produces compromise formations in cultural practices.

Are Sambia such an exemplar? Several psychoanalytic writers have interpreted the published materials on Sambia in this way, and one of them, Robert Endelman, in a 1986 paper, "Homosexuality in Tribal Societies," provides our starting point: "The [Sambia] father is psychologically absent. Individuation of the male infant is blurred. Closeness to mother classifies the infant boy with his mother, not his father. The initiation ceremonies are necessary to complete separation-individuation and masculine identity" (1986:194). Thus, strong maternal presence and paternal deprivation are thought to be predictive of certain sexual outcomes in all societies, of which the Sambia are but an extreme example (Lidz and Lidz 1989; Snarey and Son 1986). The subsequent work of Lidz and Lidz (1989) is the furthest example of the propping up of this theory.

So powerful is the Freudian folk conception that parents determine gender identity and sex-object choice in their children that a long tradition of gender research links the salience of parents in childhood with Oedipal strivings, mediating cultural factors such as initiation rites, and predictable adult outcomes such as "protest masculinity" in males who had absent fathers (Gilmore 1986; Parker, Smith, and Gignat 1975; Snarey and Son 1986; Whiting and Whiting 1975). Indeed, father absence—physical and/or psychological—is thereby strongly linked to the development of "sexual problems" in a boy's sexual identity formation. This gives rise to an even stronger inference that father absence is indicative, if not causative, of male homosexuality (Green 1987); and that, all things being equal, father presence is causative of male heterosexuality. If absent fathers are causative of homosexuality, as the reasoning of the early Freud and our folk model would have it, then we would expect that in Melanesia—where sexual segregation has long been reported—homosexual behavior would be common and its consequences for masculine development so profound as to have been historically institutionalized on a widespread scale, a point adduced by Davenport (1977:156) for South Seas societies.

The source of this folk theory of father absence in culture and personality work is not hard to find in old historical themes of sexual repression and inversion (Foucault 1980). Freud himself referenced homoeroticism as "inversion" in Ancient Greece (1962), though he recognized the difference between sexual behavior (subject) and sexual object choice (object). He could not resist the temptation, however, to conflate these and to interpret the case of Leonardo da Vinci as showing how "the presence of a strong father would assume for the son the proper decision in the selection of his object from the opposite sex" (1910:61).

Reik's (1946) work stressed castration anxiety and Oedipal conflict in the symbolism of puberty rites. Fathers are both hostile and affectionate to sons, Reik thought, with their hostility unconsciously motivated by repetition of trauma and remembered incestuous impulses directed toward mothers, for which they feared paternal punishment. The "latent homosexuality" of Laertes is often hinted at (see Lidz 1975); this became a model for much subsequent "overinterpreting" of homosexuality, everywhere (see Stoller 1985c; and for a critical review, Rycroft 1985:109–12). Bettelheim (1955:140) speaks approvingly of Freud's primal *Totem and Taboo* figure as an "all-powerful father" and as a "defense against the much more feared, *omnipotent mother* who stands at the beginning of all our lives" (emphasis in original). This trend toward Freudian universalism may have reached its peak in the writings of George Devereux, who argued that a "fantasized homosexual triumph over the father is a sine qua non stage in the resolution, or sublimation, of the boys' Oedipal complex" (1978:190; reviewed in Allen 1967; Bettelheim 1955; Endelman 1986; Herdt 1981; Keesing 1982; Spiro 1982; Stoller 1985b; Stoller and Herdt 1985; Vanggaard 1972).

A powerful dimension of this emphasis on paternal deprivation arises from certain Western assumptions about the etiology of "homosexuality." In this folk model, "homosexuality" lumps together gender identity; sexual behavior; preferred sexual, social, and emotional partners; life-style; and other correlates of same-sex behavior into the same category (Herdt 1987a; Stoller 1985b). The historical prototypes regarded homosexuality as a "disease of effeminacy," as well as a form of "psychic hermaphroditism," or a third sex (see chapter 9). These notions obscure the distinctive cultural formations of same-gender relationships to be found around the world (Herdt 1997a).

The classical study is that of Bieber et al. (1962), who analyzed 100 heterosexual and homosexual patients. Fathers were classified as warm and not detached or aloof/absent and detached. The characterizations of father-son relationships are extremely negative. This sample was a wealthy, urbanized, white population. West (1977:87) summarizes the Bieber study by stating that "four-fifths of the mothers of homosexuals were dominating, three-fifths were over-protective, three-fifths openly preferred her [*sic*] son to her husband." Over 80 percent of the fathers were completely absent or ignored their sons. Many sons hated and feared their fathers. So strong was this view that "Bieber came to believe that a warm, supportive, masculine father figure practically precluded the possibility of a son growing up homosexual" (West 1977:87). There was no sense of the historical specificity of their population as a cultural foundation for their generalizations.

Twenty-five years later, the psychoanalyst Richard Isay (1986) challenged this view and offered an interpretation that relies on the son's erotic interest in his father, not his mother, for understanding adult homosexuality. Adam (1986) suggests that homosexual conduct is far more bound to specific cultures, situations, and their attendant meanings than this Western folk model suggests. I (Herdt 1987a) have argued for the localizing effects of symbolic systems upon people's sexuality in general and homoeroticism in particular. Weeks (1985) also argues with the essentialism of Freudian and other universalizing models of sexual development. The universalism of these models ignores local meanings and symbols, particularly those in prior developmental sequelae (see chapter 7). These models ignore the social reinforcements and symbolic meanings of local gender and erotic norms and values for the person, especially in the child's struggle to be close to his father.

The theory treats father absence and mother presence in a language of Western bourgeois sexual identity development, which values the individual as a unit of analysis over the relationships in which this person establishes meaningful concepts of selfhood, gender, and sexuality. We assume that sexual contact merges desire with necessity, homosexual behavior equating to homosexual identity, subject and object merged. As Sudhir Kakar (1985), the Indian psychoanalyst, has elegantly argued in another context, our Western folk and clinical models tend to pathologize that which deviates from the perceived Western norm, including that of selfhood. To summarize: the received Freudian folk theory has overemphasized the psychopathology of father's absence and paternal deprivation in masculine gender identity development. Furthermore, too much stress has been laid on the structural rules, norms, and codes of father relationships, with less attention to the ethnographic description of father's physical and emotional presence and sleeping arrangements, his caretaking and the quality of bonds with others (see Whiting and Whiting 1975).

Melanesian ethnography has long been a stronghold of ideas about gender (Malinowski 1927; Mead 1935). Powerful images of fathers and mothers polarized by symbolic forms of sexual antagonism emerge here (Herdt and Poole 1982). Whiting and his colleagues (1958) formulated an influential early gender-identity theory regarding how overly close maternal relationships result in the functional response of male initiation rites. Covertly, they argued, initiation breaks excessively strong dependence on mother engendered during the period of postpartum taboos, thus ensuring later identification with adult males (1958:361). If father terminates the breast-feeding relationship, there should be concomitant envy and hostility in the boy, especially at puberty. In his New Guinea example, Whiting suggested that most tribal groups institutionalized "close" mother-child relationships, the infant sleeping with his mother until he is "two or three years old. The father, in the meantime, sleeps apart on his own bark slab bed" (Whiting, Kluckhohn, and Anthony 1958:362). Postpartum taboos stimulated the ather's aloofness from the caretaking scene and weakened the marital bond.

Whiting's views on this matter were influenced strongly by his own fieldwork among the Kwoma, a people of the Sepik riverine culture area, whose mothers and children sleep close together, while father sleeps separately. Only at weaning does the father displace the child, who can no longer "be permitted to sit on his mother's lap" (Whiting, Kluckhohn, and Anthony 1958:362). What Whiting could not know at this time was that the Kwoma pattern does not characterize all areas of Melanesia. Nonetheless, in the Kwoma case envy and hostility, of father toward son and vice versa, are events that "make it necessary" for the society to initiate and control boys. Societies that manifest such child-rearing practices will practice initiation rites, the intensity of the case resting on the exclusivity of mother-child sleeping arrangements, in the absence of which, Whiting, Kluckhohn, and Anthony (1958:363) concluded, there should be no such rites.

Burton and Whiting (1961) subsequently modified this theory, but not in a way that altered the picture of the father in Melanesian society. They advanced the status-envy hypothesis, by which, once again, the father's absence from childhood sleeping arrangements became "the best index of status envy during childhood" (1961:88). Changes in later identity development were contingent upon early parental proximity. "The bed seems to be the center of the child's world during the first year or two of his life," Burton and Whiting (1961:88) argued. In their sample, thirty-six of their sixty-four societies had the parents sleeping apart, but the most intense sex-identity conflict correlated with the strongest mother-son sleeping pattern, in patrilocal residential grouping (1961:90). Their prediction is supported, they argued, with thirteen societies practicing severe genital operations in initiation.

In a comparative section on Western societies, Burton and Whiting saw deleterious effects of father absence on boys. Paternal absence during World War II, they felt, resulted in "boys from father-absent households [who] behaved like girls." This was not easy or entirely possible to modify in subsequent development (1961:93), they said. Character defenses, such as protest masculinity, including Don Juanism, resulted from fears of effeminacy and homosexuality (D'Andrade 1973). This model would thus predict that extreme initiation customs, such as ritual homosexuality, would occur in societies with absolute father absence and exclusive mother-child sleeping arrangements (see Pleck 1975).

Highlands and Lowlands Societies

While the anthropological literature emphasizes striking cross-cultural variations in child-rearing customs among New Guinea peoples (reviewed in Brown 1978; Bulmer 1971; Herdt 1981; Poole 1985), a sorting of these practices suggests that when Highlands and Lowlands societies are compared, the variation is not random. This has no doubt to do with historical/material differences between the two broad regions (Herdt 1984a; Lindenbaum 1984; Read 1984). Population density, scale of grouping, productive and consumptive modes (tuber production and pig herding vs. sago production and hunting), and differences in marriage, ritual, and warfare customs tend to distinguish Highlands from Lowlands peoples (see esp. Knauft 1993).

The distinctiveness of father absence in early childhood emerges as a cultural theme in Highlands social structure. Mainstream Highlands groups, as was first hinted at in Read's (1954) survey, have distinct residential abodes for males and females, which not only constitute the sleeping quarters but also reflect the strong division of socioeconomic activities in general. Paula Brown has concluded of Highlands familial patterns: "The mother, daughters, and young sons who sleep in one woman's house at night are a close family group. The father and older boys of the nuclear family usually sleep with other males in a men's house" (1978:144).

The exact degree of social separation and psychological distantiation between men's and women's houses and thought-worlds varies from society to society of course. Langness (1967:163), writing of how Bena Bena typify sex segregation in Highlands villages, has noted: "Male solidarity involves the residential separation of the sexes and a complex of beliefs and sanctions designated to insure such separation as well as a minimal amount of contact between males and females in general." Here, too, men and women room apart, and "boys were not taken to sleep in the men's house until they were ten to twelve years old" (1967:164). Initiation was violent and traumatic, involving bloodletting of the tongue and urethra

(1967:165), the procedural form of bloodletting common to Eastern Highland groups (see chapter 4 above) and one whose underlying structural premise was to egest female substance from the male body in preparation for ritual masculinization (Herdt 1982). Meggitt's (1964) work on male-female relationships provides an unusual vantage point on the problem of boys' enculturation into the men's worldview, based on exclusive sex segregation. "Men and women generally live in separate houses," Meggitt writes, with the men's house being "a secular meeting and sleeping place" (1964:206–7). Fear of female pollution and manly disdain for early child care also culturally sanction men's aloofness from young children. Later, father's socialization provides the "local children's introduction to the subject" of relations between the sexes: "When a boy is about five years old, his father and brothers begin to warn him of the undesirability or being too much in the company of women, and they (and his mother) encourage him to spend more time in the men's house and in herding pigs with older lads. The boy, alarmed by these admonitions, is eager to associate with the men and within a year or so regularly sleeps in their house" (1964:207). Deviations from these rules are negatively framed and are punished. Subsequent masculine development involves the development of fear of female pollution, ambivalence about coitus, male pubertal seclusion and purification, and marked sexual antagonism between adults, outcomes that are understandable for men who say of themselves, "We marry the people we fight" (Meggitt 1964:218).

Langness (1974) in particular has emphasized the problematics of behavioral proximity in Melanesia and the structural design of secret male rituals which limit contact with females. Male bonding rites go beyond the putative Durkheimian function (Allen 1967) of creating patrilocal solidarity: "It is not contact with menstrual blood that is at issue . . . but, rather, any kind physical contact with females including too much mere physical proximity. Men as adults, are simply not supposed to spend time in the company of females. If they do their comrades in the men's house ridicule, criticize, and insult them. Prior to European contact I believe it would have been . . . unthinkable, for a man to stay in a house with his wife rather than the men's house. . . . After more than forty years of contact and substantial changes, sanctions are still brought to bear on men who show a preference for the company of their wives" (Langness 1974:207).

Subsequent studies have supported this insightful view of the continued residential segregation of the sexes in the face of social change (Brown 1978; Gewertz 1982; Herdt 1993; Herdt and Poole 1982; Langness 1974; Meggitt 1977; Meigs 1976; Read 1984; Schieffelin 1982; Strathern 1979).

The Melanesian Puzzle

Boy-inseminating practices are institutionalized in 10 percent to 20 percent of all Melanesian groups (reviewed in Herdt 1984a). The identified groups are shown in table 2. These are nearly all Lowlands cultures or groups descended from them. (The roughness in the estimate of the incidence results from Galton's problem and the distinctiveness of historical populations in Melanesia [Herdt 1984a:55–56].) Ritual homoeroticism (RH) is here defined by obligatory rules and asymmetric relationships, the outcome of which is not exclusive homoerotic or bisexual behavior in adulthood, an age-structured "species" of "homosexuality" distinct from our own (Adam 1986; Herdt 1987b; Murray 1984). Male ritual discourse expounds belief in this homoerotic practice as the masculinizer of boys. Clearly, homoerotic experience occurs in both Western and Melanesian contexts, though its manifestations are symbolically different for shaping male development and psychological selfhood (Stoller and Herdt 1985).

Given this natural history of homoerotic bonding in Melanesia, the Freudian folk theory would predict that father's presence should be low or even absent in these societies. Mother's salience should, conversely, be very high, with intense intergenerational bonding between mother and son (Whiting, Kluckhohn, and Anthony 1958). Concomitantly, in those Melanesian societies lacking ritual boy-inseminating practices, father figures should be stronger in childhood, thus "defeminizing" the effects of maternal bonding on subsequent masculine development (Lidz and Lidz 1989).

Herein lies the intellectual puzzle: Over a ten-year period I described and analyzed aspects of gender and ritual among the Sambia. My training was grounded in psychoanalytic thought regarding gender and selfhood. In 1981, for instance, I showed the enormous influence of secret homerotic practices performed in the context of Sambia initiation rites and their effects upon male development. I noted as well the conditions of early child-rearing and sleeping arrangements, fathers, mothers, and children dwelling in the same small, igloo-like hut (Herdt 1981:3; diagram 3 shows sleeping patterns). This confluence of psychocultural elements had always puzzled me. But it was not until several years later, after having edited works on male initiation rites (Herdt 1982), and ritual homoeroticism (Herdt 1984a), that my uneasiness changed to discovery. Upon completion of a survey of the historical literature (1862–1983) regarding boy-inseminating, I was surprised to find that many of these groups had father living close to his children (see Herdt 1984a). This is all-the-more puzzling when it is remem-

Table 2
The Distribution of Ritualized Homoeroticism in Melanesian Groups

Geographic subregion	Social Unit (referred to in test; N = 28)	Related Social Units (not referred to in text; N = 19)
I. Eastern insular Melanesia	1. Fiji 2. New Caledonia 3. *New Hebrides:* Malekula Island	
II. Northeastern insular Melanesia	4. New Britain 5. Duke of Yorks 6. East Bay	
III. Western Papua	*Lower Fly River:* 7. Kiwai Island (+ Buglai) *Trans-Fly Delta:* 8. Keraki 9. Suki 10. Boadzi	Karigare,[a] Yarne, Kaunje, Wekamara
IV. Southeastern Irian Jaya	11. Kanum 12. Yei-anim 13. Marind-anim 14. Kimam (Fr. Hen. Is.) 15. Jaquai 16. Asmat 17. Casuarina Coast	Maklew-anim,[b] Yab-anim, Kurkari-anim
V. Northeastern Irian Jaya	18. Humboldt Bay	
VI. Great Papuan Plateau	19. Bedamini 20. Etoro 21. Kaluli 22. Onabasulu 23. Gebusi (Nomad River)	
VII. Anga (Kukukuku)	24. Sambia 25. Baruya 26. Jegjuje 27. Other Highlands Anga groups 28. Lowlands Anga groups	Usarumpiu, Wantukiu Axiana Lohiki,[c] Kapau, Ivori, Mbwei, Yagwoia, Ampale, Langamar, Menya, Katje

[a]From Williams (1936c:208)

[b]From Van Baal (1966:maps)

[c]From Gajdusek et al. (1972)

bered that mainstream New Guinea societies are known for the spouses sleeping apart in sexually segregated quarters (Whiting and Whiting 1975:191). Whereas before I had treated Sambia as exceptional in the culture area, the counterintuitive co-occurrence of father closeness and ritual homoeroticism subsequently led me to review again the same corpus of data, and to reexamine my previous assumptions regarding sexual-identity development among Sambia.

A key issue concerns the measurement of father presence. Measurement here stands for good old counting and the explanation of the incidence. In the Whiting paradigm, "sleeping arrangements" are the key variable in measuring father salience. However, we cannot rely upon sleeping arrangements given the uneven data base in Melanesia. Other variables would help. A partial list of those factors relevant to measuring father salience among Sambia would include the following: (1) sleeping arrangements in the village, (2) sleeping arrangements in garden and hunting shelters, (3) postpartum taboos (duration, intensity, sanctions), (4) the amount of paternal attachment or "time on" father which occurs after weaning, (5) father's aloofness and fear of pollution transmission from children (via mother), (6) early age of initiation and father's role in selecting it, (7) severity of initiation customs, including enforced attachment to father (or his proxy or symbolic representations), (8) degree of absoluteness of avoidance of mother and women following initiation, and (9) later adolescent and adult images and responses to father (Herdt 1987a). As with all ethnographic survey studies, however, the meaning of cultural traits and their synergistic relationship to other elements of a sociocultural system must be grounded in historical and structural factors that contextualize them. The co-occurrence of ritual homoeroticism and father presence is no different; previous studies have simply ignored this.

Two points are essential to understanding the relevant Melanesian-Western comparisons. First, ritualized homoeroticism is a customary social practice with a defined role and obligatory expectations. Obviously, this institutionalized form is different from Western practice, which takes the lone individual as its focus. The identity states in the two cultural traditions are very different (Herdt 1987a, 1997a), and subject and object are not merged in Melanesia in the same way. Homoeroticism, however, may be a linking element, for though the identity states differ, homoerotic excitement occurs in the person in both traditions. Second, one must separate the ultimate and proximate causes of RH. I argue that the ultimate causes are prehistoric migrations of ancient circum-Melanesian peoples (Herdt 1984a:48–54). This autochthonous social formation is the necessary but not sufficient cause of the occurrence of ritual homoeroticism, however. For the latter we require the proximate causes of a certain configuration of parental roles, family dynamics, symbolic polarity, and marked warfare. Among these later sufficient conditions is that of father's presence in child development.

One of the central observations of this chapter is thus to show that father absence is not a discrete variable but rather a psychosocial process (see Biller 1970, 1976; Hetherington 1966; Lamb 1976; Lynn 1974:268–79; Ross 1982). The quality and quantity of father's caretaking time spent with the child provide the basis for gender and cognitive development and for the acquisition of cultural competence with regard to the men's clubhouse society. Hence the problem is not merely one of valuing children, for, as Ann Chowning (1973:63) has remarked generally of New Guinea, "offspring are a source of pride" to fathers.

What is constant in New Guinea societies—Highlands and Lowlands—is close proximity to mother in childhood. Mother is invariably the primary caretaker until weaning, and often until the child reaches age five or so. What varies is proximity to father during this period. Virtually all Lowlands peoples (west of the Fly River, including the Great Papuan Plateau societies) and those of the Mountain Anga, have residential sleeping arrangements in which father is situated in the same house as mother and children, or in different sleeping quarters of the same long-house.

We need to stress the actual physical contacts between persons, their resting and sleeping spaces, and the manner in which these real-life material conditions influence familial interaction. So much emphasis has been directed to ideal norms, rules, and institutional setups that it becomes extremely difficult to determine from many ethnographic accounts the exact behavioral and sleeping arrangements. Such data are, however, critical to an understanding of the kinds of questions stimulated and given different response by others (Ross 1982). One such question is germane to this chapter: Why do spouses bed together, or sleep in the same room, in so many societies (Whiting and Whiting 1975)? The answer lies, in part, in understanding the degree of men's authority and control over wives as sexual objects and their paternal roles with children. Spousal co-residence creates contradictions and produces ambivalence in fathers toward offspring. I agree with Michael Allen (1967:26) here, who argued that the high status of women in some societies constitutes a "threat to overt male dominance."

In an analysis of the variants of child-rearing and sleeping arrangements in societies that practice ritualized homosexuality, three distinct prototypes of father presence emerge. These three types are collated with regard to the

Table 3
Distribution of RH Societies by societal Prototype
(Breakdown of Societies)

Type I Coresidence with father (N = 14)	Type II Longhouse father proximity (N = 12)	Type III Separate but nearby (N = 2)
1	7	12
2	9	13
3	10	
4	11	
5	15	
6	16	
8	17	
14	19	
18	20	
24	21	
25	22	
26	23	
27		
28		

NOTE: See table 2 for identification of societies by number.

twenty-eight known RH groups in table 3. Type I shows the father to be in same-hut sleeping and face-to-face contact with wife and children, but with unpredictable absences. Here we find the most severe menstrual taboos and earliest initiation ceremonies as well. Type II involves father living permanently in a divided longhouse, separate from wife or children, but near enough to be a "same-house father." Type III societies have father living in a separate dwelling but one that is close to the hut of wife and children, so that constant communication is possible. We shall now examine these three "types" by describing and contrasting the relevant ethnographic data on several societies characteristic of each.

Type I Societies: Co-Residence with Father

MALEKULA "BIG NAMBAS" (VANUATU)

The Big Nambas chiefly tribe (who live in Vanuatu, formerly New Hebrides; "Nambas" refers to a penis wrapper) of Malekula Island provides one of the the best-known instances of boy-insemination in Melanesia. Among the Big Nambas, "homosexual practices between men . . . are very highly developed" (Deacon 1934:487), and chiefs have many boy lovers.

Layard (1942:489) went so far as to refer to Big Nambas as "an extreme form of patrilineal culture," with patrilineality and patrilocal residence co-occurring. Institutionalized homoeroticism and genital mutilations are also practiced.

The Big Nambas' residence pattern markedly contrasts with that of the sex-segregated Highlands. One difference is inter-island variation in same-house father-residence among neighboring groups. The Big Nambas' domestic domicile is, like the longhouse of other groups on mainland New Guinea, one large room "in which inmates sleep and the women and children spend their time when it is too wet to be in the open" (Deacon 1934:31). By day, sexual segregation occurs as a consequence of the economic division of labor; Deacon (1934:36) tells us that "men generally gather in their clubhouse." Women and children tend to spend their time in the village's "open spaces." Until weaning, children are with their mothers.

> When it is time for the adults to retire, most of the married men go to their dwelling houses, while others, who for the same reason wish or are constrained to keep apart from their wives, together with all boys and bachelors, settle down to rest in the *amel* (clubhouse). . . . The sleeping arrangements are clearly determined. In one corner the man has his mat; diagonally opposite this in another corner, is the mat of his wife, which she usually shares with a young daughter. . . . A little boy will also sleep with his mother for a time, but he is promoted to his own mat earlier than his sister, and sometimes he will take it across to the other side of the room and settle down near his father. This, however, is not usual. . . . Unlike boys, who leave the house and go to sleep in the *amel* when they are about twelve years old, girls remain living and sleeping at home until they are married and go to their husbands. (Deacon 1934:41)

In polygynous marriages, Deacon (1934:165–66) tells us, each wife has her own house, "with its pigsty at the back, but the chief wife lives always in her husband's hut." Men visit each wife in turn. Children reside with their mother, the girls till marriage and boys "until they are advanced to the men's fire, when they sleep with their father or in the clubhouse" (1934:167).

KIMAM

The Kimam of southwestern Irian Jaya provide another example of spousal co-residence, thousands of miles at the other end of Melanesia. Spouses reside and sleep together in the same hut, though they may have different sitting spaces therein (Serpenti 1965:77, 1984:295). Fathers are involved in the birth-giving process but only to a limited extent. Postpartum taboos are prolonged and here, as with the Sambia (Herdt 1981), wives retire for birth, and the father will not see wife and newborn child until it is "two or three months old" (Serpenti 1965:153), taboos designed to thwart coitus and the father's supposed magical harm to the infant. Mother's brother (MB) plays a significant role in ceremonies of the child's development, including the hair-cutting rite between ages three and four (1965:156–57). This practice breaks "off the ties with its mother" and places the child "under the father's authority," which increases thereafter. A joking relationship evolves between a son and the mother's brother as well, and eventually, during initiation, the boy is mentored by an "adoptive father," who is this same "mother's brother." Homoerotic relationships allude to this man, who is surely not a boy's "real" mother's brother but is instead his "son" (MBS) or classificatory cross-cousin (Serpenti 1984:305). Here we see a theme of structural influence of affinal relationships that enters into homoerotic activities nearly everywhere.

EAST BAY

Among the island people of East Bay, Davenport (1965:169) reports the same division of sleeping arrangements. Thus, "unmarried men and boys" sleep in the men's houses, where "married men spend much of their time during the day." Married spouses and their children, however, sleep and eat together, first in a man's older brother's or father's house (1965:175), and later in their own neolocal residence (Davenport 1977:150).

Homoerotic behavior in East Bay is relatively universal among males, but it is a phasic or transitional kind of contact that is "best seen along the life history of the individual" (Davenport 1977:155). Mutual masturbation tends to occur between adolescent peers, as nascent sexual activity. Anal intercourse is also practiced between unequals (usually married men and boys, whose ages are unspecified). An interesting feature of RH practice here, as elsewhere, concerns the boy's father's involvement in homoerotic "partnerships": "Before a boy could be induced into such a partnership, permission had to be obtained from his father. A boy complied with the arrangements out of deference to parental and adult authority, although it was expected that he would be rewarded with small presents from time to time" (Davenport 1977:155). So strong is the Western view that sex segregation leads to homoerotic behavior that Davenport, in contradiction to his own data, argues that East Bay demonstrates that sex segregation results in the ritualized practice: "One can entertain the hypothesis that in the strongly gender-segregated communities of Melanesia, when the culture also imposes effective barriers to heterosexual intercourse, there is a likelihood that institutionalized male bisexual practices will result" (1977:156). The irony is, of course, that East Bay does not exemplify sex segregation in childhood, and that contrary social systems elsewhere do not manifest ritual homoeroticism.

KERAKI

The Keraki of the Trans-Fly River delta are also a well-known early case study of boy-inseminating in New Guinea (Williams 1936a). Older and younger cross-cousin initiates engaged in anal intercourse. Previously, no one had associated this RH with residence and sleeping arrangements, but when we do so, we find customary practices that support the hypothesis of father presence in childhood.

Keraki have several types of houses, which are sketched by Williams (1936a:13), but the chief residential household unit is the *mongovivi*. Households are small and "simply constituted," Williams (1936a:108) says, and "in the majority of cases the family slept under the verandah of the *mongo* (yam house)." Keraki practice child-betrothal, so that after symbolic marriage rites occur, the girl becomes a "member of her husband's community, though the couple sleep apart: she with her betrothed's mother or elder brother's wife, he with his mates in the men's house" (1936a:145). This continues until she reaches sexual maturity, and they live together. After marriage a man may also take multiple wives, who with their husband "live together in their husband's house or share the same campfire and shelter" (Williams 1936a:150). In polygynous households, coitus occurs usually in the bush, or when a man is alone with one wife (1936a:150). Postpartum taboos hold "until the child is able to stand" (1936a:175). Menstruation among women and war raids and initiation ceremonies among men (Williams 1936a:269) interrupt co-residence, however, producing unpredictable absences in the child's caretaking.

Father's presence, in sum, seems intermittent from mid-childhood until first initiation, in spite of residential proximity. Boys are not able to influence their fathers' movements and actions effectively, particularly with regard to the men's secret society.

ANGA

The Anga peoples of Mainland New Guinea also manifest father presence and co-residence, as illustrated by the earlier reference to (Herdt 1981).

Separate clubhouses for males are utilized by unmarried initiates at all times, and by married men during certain ritual and warfare periods. Otherwise, spouses reside and sleep together, albeit symbolically separated into "male" and "female" spaces that are fully visible and within reach of one another. Marital coitus occurs usually in the bush. Godelier (1986) reports this pattern for Baruya Anga as well. However, the fact that postpartum taboos require fathers to avoid infants for some months after birth, and later to reside at times in the men's house during warfare and ritual, requires examination below.

Type II Societies: Longhouse Father Proximity

KIWAI

Landtman's *Kiwai Papuans of British New Guinea* (1927) describes a form of ritual homoeroticism that seems historically related to the Marind-anim of Southwest New Guinea, and to peoples of the Upper Trans-Fly and the Papuan Gulf (reviewed in Herdt 1984a; Van Baal 1966; and Wagner 1972). Kiwai practice anal homerotic contact in initiation ceremonies; other structural features of their ecology and culture resemble societies of the southern fringe of the Papuan Coast (Herdt 1984a:48ff.).

Kiwai culture is known for its longhouse, which links it to other non-Austronesian-speaking groups in the interior, described below. Kiwai actually had two types of traditional houses, "the *moto,* or communal longhouse, where principally women and children live, and the *darimo,* or men's house" (Landtman 1927:4; figs. 4 and 5 in Landtman are photographs showing such longhouses, one of which is 154 meters in length). On the face of it, this description would seem to obviate the hypothesized relationship between father presence and RH. Landtman (1927:7) further notes, however, that "each family has a separate fireplace, and around it dwell the members of the household." Separate men's and women's entrances to the longhouse indicate internal partitioning in the communal longhouse. Moreover, villages without a men's house permit unmarried initiated males to live in a separate section *(taera)* of the communal house (1927:7): "Women are not supposed to enter the house through the *taera,* and formerly never did so." The men's house is architecturally identical to, but separate from, the communal longhouse. Even in traditional times not every village had its own men's house (1927:8). Initiation changes the residential status of Kiwai males and females. After initiation, "a young man begins to sleep in the men's house" (Landtman 1927:237). The rule here, too, is for patrilocal residence, and for "married men [to] spend the nights in the *darimo* or in the communal house according to their own wishes" (1927:248). Social changes further support the hypothesis of strong father presence, Landtman (1927:249) notes, bringing men increasingly into nuclear family-type arrangements of the kind identified with Western culture.

STRICKLAND-BOSAVI AREA

The peoples of the Strickland-Bosavi are more prototypic of the so-called longhouse societies of Melanesia, with the sexes living together but in separate sleeping divisions of the same large dwelling. The Kaluli, as Schieffelin describes them, clearly fit this pattern (see diagram of sleeping arrangements in Schieffelin [1976:33], with explanatory text on 35 and 38). Thus, women, small children, and piglets are in long, dark passages running along the side of the longhouse, with men's sleeping quarters directly "opposite them on the other side of the partition" (1976:35). The remarkable child-rearing condition here is of father being proximate—within reach and speaking distance—but not sleeping with the small child. Unmarried youths and widowers sleep at the back of the house, while during ritual periods, boys and youths retire to forest lodges for the *bau'a* ceremonial seclusionary life that involves prolonged anal homerotic activity (Schieffelin 1982). This longhouse arrangement is virtually identical to that of the neighboring Etoro, described by Kelly (1976:37), the Bedamini studied by Sørum (1984:326), and the Onabasulu reported on by Ernst (1984:137–40). The nearby Gebusi of the Strickland Plain also reveal an identical pattern (Knauft 1985:22–23; and diagram). The ineffectiveness of the sleeping divisions here is underlined by Ernst, who notes: "The partition separating the men's section and the women's is short enough to be peered over and talked over, and women frequently do both, making their views known on most all matters" (1984:137). Though the sexes live in close proximity, they nonetheless have "little knowledge" of each others' interactions, the men withholding the significance of many of their own interactions from women (Sørum 1984:326). Customary activities within the *bau'a* hunting lodge and during male initiation rites (Kelly 1976) are generally secret, and spirit seances (Knauft 1986) performed by men are the main contexts of male bonding—and incidentally of homoeroticism.

Type III Societies: Separate but Nearby

MARIND-ANIM

Among the Marind-anim are three types of abodes: men's houses and women's houses, both being of the same size in the village, and the bachelor *gotad* house, a bigger and longer platform house under a roof or a coconut grove, built outside the village and hidden from view. Men sleep in the men's house, women and children in the women's house. Boys and adolescents, although they spend the day at the *gotad,* retire to the men's house at night (Van Baal 1966:47). "The main function of both *gotad* and men's house is that of segregating the sexes" (1966:48), which seems to distinguish the Marind-anim and their neighbors from other Lowland groups that practice boy-inseminating rites (Herdt 1984a).

Rules concerning sexual segregation are explicit, Van Baal says: "It is considered a gross violation of morals when a man enters a women's house, except in the case that he has to get something from his own wife's house" (1966:48). Thus, there is a cultural division of the sexes, with allowance for some interaction in women's quarters. This is similar to the common Highlands pattern. "The rules are all very strict," Van Baal (1966:48) has repeatedly said, and yet the segregation is "ineffective": "Men's houses and women's houses stand close together, and every word spoken in the one house can be heard in the other. Except in the rainy season, the houses are dormitories only, all other activities taking place in front of or in the space between the houses. Meals are taken separately, the men squatting round one fire, and the women and children round another. Again, a strict segregation, but one which does not keep the sexes so far apart that conversation is impossible" (1966:48). The division seems incomplete at bedtime as well, because the huts are so close together, no more than two or three meters in distance: "Though sleeping in separate quarters, the two sexes are always in earshot" (Van Baal, personal communication). To attain privacy, and whenever the men wanted secrecy, they would go off to the boys' *gotad* houses, far removed from women.

In the developmental cycle of the Marind-anim we have a most unusual case of proximity and separation with regard to sleeping arrangements. Children live exclusively with their mothers, in the women's houses, till they are older, when at ages five to six, boys begin to live with their fathers in the men's houses (Van Baal 1966:52). But not until ages ten to twelve do boys go to the *gotad* bachelor house, sleeping with their mother's brother and avoiding all contact with mother and women (Van Baal 1984:133). Even after marriage, however, Marind-anim men must continue playing the active homoerotic insertee role, which is extraordinary in Melanesia (see Herdt 1984a), because such contact usually halts after fatherhood begins. Here anal contact begins and continues for some years, until a male, having achieved biological and social adolescence—becomes a *miakam,* a marriageable man—who leaves the *gotad* and lives in the men's house (Van Baal 1966:144), near the women's.

Test Cases of Father Presence

The three prototypes sketched above are ideal-types that bear only a family resemblance to empirical reality. Nevertheless, the general prototypes highlight an insight of an earlier study by Whiting and Whiting (1975). They note that Melanesia is unusual in its high incidence of societies with sex segregation (1975:191). Furthermore, their cross-cultural analysis shows that fathers have a measurably closer relationship to their children in 50 percent of those groups where husband and wife sleep together versus only 25 percent where they sleep apart (1975:189). They also suggest that when a husband sleeps apart, he "remains aloof from [his wife] and the children" in other spheres of domestic life, which aloofness is communicated to children and results in "less intimate [relations with] and more aggressive" children compared with those cultures in which "fathers are more involved in domestic affairs" (1975:199).

The Melanesian ethnography suggests that, in general, fathers tend to be most aloof from mother and child in mainstream Highlands societies, whereas in Lowlands RH societies, fathers are more engaged and intimate because of co-residence between spouses. This is generally consistent with the Whitings's suggestion. Now, however, when we contrast the three prototypes of RH groups above, predictable variations in paternal presence emerge. Thus we find the severest postpartum taboos and ritual avoidances of mother and infant in Type I societies, such as the Sambia and the Kimam. In Type II, there are somewhat fewer restrictions surrounding birth and menstruation, with less face-to-face contact between father and child, who are segregated by longhouse partitions. And in Type III, there are virtually no postpartum or other taboos, with no anxiety about menstruation, and the least physical proximity of all. In short, our review suggests that stronger paternal proximity co-occurs with greater taboos that limit paternal intimacy; and the least paternal presence is associated with the fewest taboos constraining father-child interaction.

When these distinctions are associated with the intensity of RH, an interesting pattern unfolds. The closer the physical proximity to father, the earlier will be the boy's initiation and involvement in homoerotic practices. The stronger and more intense the physical separation from father, the later will be the son's introduction to these practices and, in the Marind-anim case, the longer they will be practiced—virtually across the male lifespan. The timing and intensity of ritual homoeroticism seem contingent upon childhood closeness to father.

Having examined these prototypes of the structural relationship between father's role and ritual homoeroticism in Melanesia, let us now "test" the theory of father's presence against two contrasting examples. First, we shall examine Malekula subregional variations in father's role and sleeping arrangements to understand the presence and absence of homoerotic activities as "outcome" variables. Second, we will reexamine father presence in the Sambia case to distill our view of local cultural meanings and folk psychology as they bear upon ritual homoerotic practice.

Example 1: Vao Island (and the related Small Islands lying off Malekula) provides the first case. Vao society is, in many of its structural features, similar to the Big Nambas of Malekula, with patriliny and patrivirilocal residence stressed, and inclusive ritual male initiation and cult membership marked (Allen 1984:88). Yet, whereas the Big Nambas have hereditary chiefs, actual homoerotic relations between initiator and novice, and circumincision of the penis (which is thereafter concealed in a large, dramatic penis wrapper [Layard 1942:481]), Vao Island society has lineage elders, symbolic "homosexual" encounters between ancestral spirits and novices (Layard 1942:503), and the penis is instead superincised and concealed in a smaller penis wrapper. The distinctiveness of Vao and Big Nambas societies has long been documented in the historical ethnography (see Layard's [1942:482–91] cultural topography of regional variation in homosexuality and genital mutilation practiced in the area).

Given such a sharp contrast, we are most interested in understanding traditional childhood sleeping arrangements and whether they conform to the hypothesized co-occurrence of father presence and ritual boy-inseminating. Vao society, unlike Malekula, has separate sex residences for the spouses: "Within the village each married man possesses an enclosure. . . . Within the enclosure are two courts. Firstly, an outer court, containing the wife's house, or, if there is more than one wife, a house for each. Here also live, in the same house with their mother, unmarried daughters as well as sons till these are able to dispense with her help. Behind this . . . is the inner court where is the husband's house. With him live sometimes a young son or two, but these are usually provided for by the erection of a communal bachelors' house shared by closely related boys and unmarried youths. . . . Cohabitation occurs only in the wife's house, never in the man's, for fear of pollution by menstrual blood, and never during the menstrual period" (Layard 1942:41). Allen (1984:117) has also picked up on the ability of higher-ranking men in the neighboring Nduindui society to achieve status and exploit their power. There, too, fathers sleep in segregated houses, and homoeroticism is absent.

To summarize: in historically closely related Vao Island and Big Nambas societies, we have marked homoeroticism and father presence in the one (Big Nambas) and the absence of homoeroticism and father absence in childhood sleeping arrangements in the other (Vao Island). Though this is a simplification of a complex ethnographic corpus, the hypothesized relationship between father presence and RH here seems to be a nontrivial and robust finding.

Example 2: The Sambia provide a very different "test" case, because my work (Herdt 1987a) better describes the behavioral forms of father-child interactions and their consequences for subsequent development. Father and child do not see each other for several months after birth, and father remains very aloof from child care until the child is a toddler. The father is present and living in proximity to the child about 70 percent of the total number of days in the first three years of life. However, the father is present during only about 25 percent of the infants' waking hours, and of these, I estimate that less than 10 percent are spent "on" the father as a caretaker and attachment figure. Between ages three and five, the father's visibility and "time on" increases, especially for sons. At about age five, the boy should "cross over" from the mother's "female place" and sleep in his father's "male place," a pattern we have already noted in Malekula Island. This is a problematic and often conflictual time for the child, who is especially subject to throwing tantrums (Herdt 1987a:89–95). Thereafter, boys are closer to their fathers, but they remain most closely attached to their mothers, which seems to mirror the Gebusi case. Fathers cannot permit sons to follow them into the men's house, nor into the deep forest to hunt. Consequently, it is same-sex, same-age peers who form play groups between ages four and seven, or until ritual initiation, a group of chums who become reciprocal socializers and "self-objects" (Kohut 1971) to one another during this time. These play groups, transitional gender objects, contextualize personal gender-identity development, apart from adults of either sex (Herdt 1987b; cf. Wiesner and Gallimore 1977). After initiation these same boys are confirmed as age mates in a lifelong cohort (see Read 1965). The key to identity changes here is increasing independence from mother, followed by more proximity to father. By the time of initiation, paternal relationships are normatively salient for Sambia boys, but subsequent life in the men's house provides alternative masculine caretakers, including homoerotic partners, displacing the boys' father.

In the developmental subjectivity of Sambia folk psychology, ritual introduces three distinctively different cultural beings ("transitional objects" [Winnicott 1971]) into boys' experience. The first is a symbolic object, the female flute spirit, called *aatmwogwambu,* to which boys are "married" in initiation (Herdt 1982). The second is the boy's ritual sponsor or mentor, his real or classificatory MB, a man who teaches and nurtures him. They are forbidden ever to engage in sex, and the behavioral taboos surrounding their dyadic interaction underscore the boy's attachment to this mentor, who becomes a substitutive "mother/father" androgynous figure. Third are bachelors, appointed as first homoerotic partners for the virgin boys. The bachelors take on aspects of paternal status and maternal care for the initiates, whose liminal and emergent sexual status is seen as "becoming masculine" (Herdt 1987b).

Adult masculine development following marriage (in late adolescence or early adulthood) requires a man's mastery of two additional ritual techniques. The first of these is nosebleeding, introduced and repeated in initiation. It is practiced subsequently as a demonstration of masculine autonomy and separateness from one's wife, for a man secretly lets blood from his nose each time his wife has a period. The second technique is white tree-sap "milk" ingestion. Following the period of active fellation, males are forbidden to reverse roles and ingest semen. Their sexual intercourse is believed to deplete them, however, and as an alternative source of "semen" replenishment, certain ritual trees are selected for their white latex sap, which is ingested following sexual intercourse, again, voluntarily and secretly (see chapter 4).

In native collective belief, blood represents femaleness and, more personally, mother, whereas semen represents maleness and, more personally, father. The thick description of male ritual discourse reveals also that semen is the producer of mother's milk (see chapter 3). These actually represent the orthodoxy of male rationalization, which tends to deny females procreative potential in its entirety (Allen 1984; Dundes 1976; Hiatt 1971; Spiro 1982). Thus, Sambia beliefs, as they hermeneutically encode ritual, embody a "language" for speaking of adult male experience. In this symbolic action, adult men are forever involved in the removal of "female" (mother) substance and the implantation of "male" (father) substance in their own bodies.

To summarize: Body substance symbolism reinforces socially and validates in folk psychology the avoidance of females and the proximity to males. As an exemplary case of the Type I societies, Sambia take in first semen and then white milk sap to bolster physical maleness, which I believe to be unconscious representations of father and, by proxy, the hegemonic local patrimony.

Interpreting Symbols of Father

The father's relationship to his children is best termed "ambivalent" in Types I, II, and III, with the intensity of ambivalence a function of physical closeness in early development. Here ambivalence means that a boy is faced with contradictory ideas and feelings that produce conflictual fantasies and action. Though father is present soon after birth, mother is the stronger attachment figure, and father remains aloof from the child until later. The father's culturally conditioned aloofness is mediated by the degrees of sexual antagonism in the society (Herdt and Poole 1982; Whiting and Whiting 1975), such that the greater the sexual polarity, the greater paternal aloofness, which the child experiences as ambivalent. Father's inconsistent daytime presence, and uncontrollable movements (warfare and hunting trips) to the men's house and "off-limit" arenas, are problematic for the boy. Hence, postpartum taboos, culturally mandated avoidance, sexual antagonism, and interpersonal hostility combine to form the basic psychological conditions of father's ambivalent bond to the child.

Whiting, Kluckhohn, and Anthony's (1958) emphases upon Oedipal conflict and later status envy (Burton and Whiting 1961) are therefore plausible interpretations of this residential ambivalence, but they provide an incomplete analysis of the boy's cultural and personal situation. For in his attempt to interact and identify with father, to spend time with and win his favor, and to take on an adult role, the boy is limited in the Melanesian context by virtue of the omnipresent secrecy of the men's ritual cult, which manifests itself in psychosocial distantiation between fathers and their wives and children. Comparison of Highlands and Lowlands groups is revealing here. Cult secrecy is also present in mainstream Highland cultures lacking RH. But take note that Highlands cultures do not have father proximate in childhood: there is intense social conflict between the sexes, yet the evidence increasingly suggests that this conflict is not internalized in the same way for children (Langness 1982). Thus, the distance between parents in Highlands groups helps to provide in sons more conflict-free idealization about their fathers.

In developmental terms, the individual boy's dilemma in Lowlands RH societies is that he feels close to his father but cannot consistently influence his father's behavior. The boy occupies a symbolic space in the women's quarters and is forbidden access to the men's house; thus, he finds it hard to control his father or hold father's attention. Inconsistent and intermittent reinforcement and attention are among the most powerful forms of reinforcement we know (Bandura 1969). Whereas mother as an agent cooperates and is sensitive to the achievement of the child's action sequences, without which the child cannot carry these out alone, the father—by virtue of his social role—in general remains apart from the boy and is unresponsive to him. The child cannot feel that he has control over important events in his father's life, including some sense of control over how such events influence his own action. Each parent must "agree" to be predictable, permitting the child to understand and anticipate his actions, making their actions dependent on what the child does (Maccoby 1980:79). Only in this way can the boy understand others' intentions, fit his plans into others' plans, and learn how to be responsive to the demands of others. Without all of this mutualistic and engaged interaction, no balanced partnership is possible. Thus the child cannot fully master father or father's role or enter into dialogue with him, but neither can he remove father, or distance him fully, which would enable idealizations to substitute for him. The effects of this ambivalent proximity are manifest in cultural symbols.

Representations of father can be identified as operating at three distinct but complementary levels of meaning in Melanesian ritual belief and action. I shall focus only on semen as a symbol for maintaining proximity to males in RH development. Whereas bloodletting rites clearly effect behavioral distance from mother and females, insemination rites have as their set goal (Bowlby 1969) maintenance of proximity to male—father substitute—attachment figures. First, there is the social-structural level of male status achievement. Attainment of proximity to older males and procurement of their semen symbolize adult masculine role competence, loyalty to father and father's patrilocal group, mastery of public competitive status positions, and responsibility for handling group resources through male solidarity. Second, there is the level of father as a cultural symbol (what Obeyesekere [1981] calls a psychogenic symbol). Here, semen (and its vicissitudes in homoerotic relationships) symbolizes father as a figure of reproduction and filial power, whose bodily essence transmits this power to the cultural self. Father's semen is transmitted via social representatives (mother's brother or MBS) culturally sanctioned to inseminate. Semen represents the dominance of the male ritual world over the female domestic world at this level too. And paternal representations, overtly and covertly, are encoded in myth and other (nonsexual) ceremonies (Van Baal 1984; see also Spiro 1982). Third, semen is a symbol of father at the personal, intrapsychic level: father is an internal representation of the idealized self as a masculine social object. Semen and its symbolic correlates—flute spirits, ritual guardians, homoerotic partners—serve as transitional objects, as noted before, mediating between mother and father, the domestic female and secret male domains. This latter indexical meaning of semen also represents the deep structure of male selfhood, whereby self as passive recipient (infant nursing at mother's breast) is transformed into the self as an active giver and procreator (man inseminating boy and wife).

These themes suggest that in the folk developmental psychology, male (semen) essence is not natural and innate in men; and as a sign of external power and village hegemony, its identification with the men's house and warriorhood suggests that it can be achieved through initiation and insemination only. In translation, this deep structure of father representations means that father is not a stable and predictable image in childhood (Stoller 1985a). Later developmental support for father as an intrapsychic object emerges and is reinforced in the homosocial company of the men's house.

Authority, Proximity, and Sexuality

Ritual homoeroticism is a major constituent of sexual culture and family relations in selected areas of Melanesia. Contained within its symbolic system are basic psychosocial mechanisms for the adjustment of interpersonal relationships and authority in these status-oriented patrilineal societies. How is the self to conform to ambivalent father figures and ambiguous sexual relationships? Boy-inseminating regimes here provide a means of solidifying internal images of father and masculinity while transferring the psychic energy of these images to secondary socialization agents, especially ritual elders and homoerotic partners.

For Type I societies, closer proximity to father in childhood is predictive of greater distance from the biological father during initiation and clubhouse life. Because of spousal co-residence, fathers remain with wives after their son's initiation, creating more space between them than ever before. Ironically, though, initiation makes them more allies and secret sharers in the clubhouse symbolic world, which father visits. Where before father was physically present in childhood, he is now usually physically absent from the clubhouse at the boy's bedtime. And indeed, he must be, for the father's presence would then cause his son to be aware of father in the conduct of homoerotic affairs. This must be avoided: to maintain homoerotic incest taboos, to avoid the shame of arousal in the presence of father, and, on a deeper level, to avoid arousing the boy's early (unconscious and preconscious) fantasies regarding father and parental coitus (see Herdt 1987b; Layard 1959). Shifting modes of physical and symbolic presence and absence of father and his substitutes obviously constitute a primary theme of daily life in these clubhouse settings. Bruce Knauft (personal communication) reminds me that agnatic co-residence is stronger in the Strickland-Bosavi, however, where questions about the generalizability of the model presented here remain to be answered.

A generalized psychosexual relationship which thus results from the practice of ritual homoeroticism is what we might call "father avoidance" in adulthood. Having followed in his father's footsteps, been initiated and involved in homoerotic activity, a man later marries. He usually will reside patrilocally (or patrivirilocally). According to Allen's (1967) model of initiation for male solidarity, and Langness's of sexual antagonism (1967) or ritual secrecy for male solidarity (1974), we should expect men to reside near one another, preferably as comrades-in-arms in the same men's house. Such a pattern is manifest for mainstream Highlands groups, but not so for those with RH. This is as we might have predicted. But now, when we examine closely the Type I societies, a further and remarkable variant appears, which is captured in this passage by Allen: "Yet another unusual though important feature or Big Nambas society, especially for a society in which the patrilineal principle is so otherwise so much stressed, is the prohibition against a man living in close quarters with either his father or his elder brothers. The rationale for the prohibition is the severity of the avoidance taboo between a man's wife and these two close patrilineal relatives. Though propriety can be maintained by hamlet co-residence, provided the houses are divided by a high fence without any opening, most men prefer to set up house in different hamlets" (Allen 1984:88; and see 1981:125). Allen speculates that this taboo is related to the practice of boy-insemination itself, in which grandfathers and grandsons—prospective sexual partners—would be brought into premature close proximity (Allen 1984:88–89) without the residential barrier. They might, we could extrapolate, experience affectionate intimacy, which would developmentally obviate a later homoerotic relationship between them (see Isay 1986).

The basic insight resulting from the recognition of paternal proximity in childhood here is that father's authority is symbolically transferred to alternative male figures during ritual. The boy's homoerotic partners, as prescribed by structural rules, show clearly that the male developmental cycle requires mentoring, including sexual bonding, in order to attain heteroerotic competence and mastery of the appropriate status positions in the social hierarchy.

Deacon noted that, while sketchy, Malekula data indicate that father has authority over his own children (1934:81). Furthermore, until initiation (boys) or marriage (girls), children regard their parents' hut as their home (Deacon 1934:81). Mother's brother–sister's son relationship is key, though Deacon points out that MB "has no real authority over his nephew," and if the latter is impertinent to his MB, it is the boy's father who will punish him (1934:82). Elsewhere we find a strong dualism pervading ritual relationships in the region of Malekula, creating an identification between fathers and sons (Layard 1942:294). The same holds true for Sambia (Herdt 1981) and Baruya (Godelier 1986), and most of the Great Papuan Plateau groups (Knauft 1986, 1987).

Structurally, however, relations of authority exercised by mother's brother (real or classificatory) are manifest and strong in other RH societies, especially those of Types II and III noted above. Clues to the difference in authority among all three types are revealed in two ways, the first rather obvious, marriage practices; the second, forms of homoerotic technique, less so.

Many if not most RH societies manifest the pattern of delayed semen transactions, as noted in chapter 2, the basic principle of which follows Lévi-Strauss's (1949) delayed exchange and direct sister-exchange models. However, a boy will take as his preferred older homoerotic partner his sister's husband if, and only if, sister-exchange marriage is the customary marital contractual form. The older male thus inseminates his slightly younger wife and her considerably younger brother: to impregnate and create a fetus in his wife and to masculinize and create a warrior in his boy-lover (Allen 1984; Kelly 1976; Layard 1959; Schieffelin 1982; Sørum 1984; reviewed in Herdt 1984a; Herdt and Poole 1982; Stoller and Herdt 1985).

Structural arrangements produce concomitant variations in other Melanesian groups with delayed exchange marriage. Among the Big Nambas of Malekula, the preferred partner was either real or classificatory paternal grandfather (Allen 1984:91), supporting, perhaps, the hierarchical chiefly system. Boazi emphasize father-in-law as preferred partner (Busse 1987). The Keraki, who also practice sister exchange, ideally emphasize homoeroticism between male cross-cousins (Williams 1936a:121), who are probably prospective older brothers-in-law, a pattern that appears frequently (e.g., among Etoro, Sambia, Baruya, Kaluli, Bedamini). On the other hand, southwestern Lowland groups emphasize mother's younger brother among Kimam (Serpenti 1984:304) and mother's brother among the paradigmatic Marind-anim (Van Baal 1966:478–80). A final analysis of these structural patterns remains to be done, but these clusters are enough to indicate the complementarity of ritual homoeroticism, which sustains marriage, sexual, and initiation customs across the lifespan.

These instances of structural influences upon the identity of the pre-ferred inseminator for a boy do not explain, however, the curious number of allusions to the involvement of "father" in these arrangements. Arve Sørum (1984:323) states of the Bedamini, for example: "The young man who will be a boy's inseminator is selected by the boy's father." Sambia evince the same tendency (Herdt 1987b). Kelly (1976:52) claims for the Etoro: "It should be noted that a father arranges his daughter's marriage (when she is about five years old) and thereby nominates his son's insemi-nator, since these are ideally one in the same." Schieffelin (1976), too, notes that a boy's father must select the homoerotic inseminator, to protect the boy from unwittingly choosing a male witch.

More puzzling, however, are the symbolic patterns in which the homo-erotic partner is identified as a father substitute. The Kimam refer to a boy's inseminator and guardian as "his adoptive father" (Serpenti 1984:304), and the Marind-anim refer to him as *binahor,* father (Van Baal 1984). The Kimam man has regular anal intercourse with the boy "to make him strong" with his adoptive father's semen (Van Baal 1984). (This man is, again, mother's younger brother.) We may wonder whether this is merely an extension of fic-tive kinship. While plausible—for, indeed, Sambia boys sometimes refer jok-ingly to their longer-term homoerotic partners as "my father"—such seems unlikely in the case of the Jaquai, neighbors of the Marind-anim. Boelaars re-ports: "A father can order his son to go and sleep during the night with a cer-tain man who will commit pederasty with him. The father will receive compensation for this. If this happens regularly between a certain man and the same boy, a stable relationship arises, comparable to that between father and son, *mo-* or anus father and *momaq,* anus son" (1981:84).

The Jaquai appear to have made physically manifest, in this rather dra-matic way, what may be an underlying structural fantasy, elsewhere merely symbolized by homoerotic acts arranged by father, or blessed by him. Fa-ther is, thus, a significant socializing agent, and a symbolic audience for these aspects of the boy's development. Equally important, moreover, is the image or psychic representation of father in the boy's experience, which is consolidated and integrated through these transitional events leading from childhood severance of proximity to mother.

The Gebusi of the Nomad River area (near the Great Papuan Plateau) provide a final poignant example that hints at an answer. Bruce Knauft (1987) reports early residential living in adjacent, but separate, compartments of longhouses. Mothers reject boys between ages four and six, which induces "trauma," resulting in the boy's move to the men's section of the longhouse (Knauft 1987:172–73). A dramatic change occurs: "By age five or six, the boy is usually so close to his father that he is apt to throw a tantrum when the latter must leave alone for extended hunting. . . . During latency, boys' sense of belonging to the collective male community intensifies. . . . In early adolescence (age 11–14) boys extend their affection to older unrelated males in the community by established homosexual relations with them—i.e., being their fellators. Rather than being based on subordination or domination, these relations tend to be coquettishly initiated by the young adolescents themselves" (Knauft 1987:172–73). Knauft also tells us that, later, "Gebusi men are strongly bisexual," with "little aversion to female sexuality." Male narratives imagine spirit women who have "sex with young male lovers, including child-lovers, who can transform themselves fluidly from suckling male infants into adult men and back again" (Knauft 1987:174). Such cultural and personal images express adult residues of boy-insemination, which draw upon shifting relationships and consolidate later transitions into being a father.

Discussion

We might have intuited that institutionalized homoeroticism would occur in contexts of the most extreme sex segregation, but this is not so. It has been demonstrated that, in Melanesia, ritual homoeroticism occurs in societies where the father is living within the same or virtually the same dwelling as the child.

The ultimate causes of this structural/ritual formation are historical (Herdt 1984a), of course. Moreover, the social classification of Highlands and Lowlands New Guinea societies is thus a product of diffusion and concomitant adaptation to the behavioral environment; of history, time, and space; of cultural, not strictly psychological, structures.

The proximate causes of this ritual homoeroticism, and its supporting psychological conditions, are social roles and sleeping arrangements and the quality of gender relationships. These are systematically related to other institutions of the culture as a whole. What is constant in caretaking is mother; what varies across Melanesia is father's presence in the natal household. All RH groups have father somewhat proximate to the child, but they differ in the degree to which father is face-to-face (Sambia), present only by voice or within reach (Etoro), or only as a distant auditory presence (Marind-anim). Sleeping arrangements are a key to understanding this configuration, with its rewards, envies, resources, and punishments. Early culture and personality work exaggerated the psychological process of identification and underestimated behavioral attachment, which thus ignored fathers' ambivalent real-life social roles and representations in the boys' inner world. In the Melanesian situation, sons suffer not from father absence and rivalry, but rather from an inconsistent presence with ambivalent, fantasized father (see Stoller 1985a:59). To be absent, something must first have been present; to be missing, it must never have been in place. Father is proximate here, but the kind of presence he manifests—which has largely to do with his social status and antagonism toward his wife—is beyond the boy's influence. The child must bridge not only the distinct gender culture of each parent, but must acquire the cultural competence of his father. The boy requires resocialization; ritual homoerotic practices are critical to this achievement (Herdt 1981).

This co-occurrence of father and RH as an outcome of ultimate and proximate causes of contemporary Melanesian societies leaves open to question anomalous cases. Why, for instance, do certain Sepik River societies, such as the Mountain Arapesh (Mead 1935) and the Ilahita Arapesh (Tuzin 1976), manifest fathers present in childhood, but no later ritual homoeroticism? The answer to such an interpretive question is obviously complex, and I have puzzled before over the Sepik situation in this regard (Herdt 1984:43–48a). In Melanesian examples we find, first, a small number of societies in which ritual homoeroticism occurs only on one occasion, and is thus limited in its developmental effects. The Ingiet secret society of New Britain (Herdt 1984:62a) is such an example. Here an elderly figure, much like that of the Malekula Big Nambas, ceremonially inseminates a boy during initiation proceedings, yet no further same-sex activity ever occurs. It is as if a certain psychological condition—for self and other—were here satisfied easily, and definitively.

A second structural formation, however, manifests homoeroticism, but only in symbolic and mythological form rather than in actual sexual contact. Vao Islands society is a strong example. The Iatmul (Bateson 1958) are another example, perhaps even a prototypic one (Herdt 1984a:43–45). The conditions of early childhood are revealing among Iatmul. Fathers are present, but not always so, and the presence of multiple wives and residences complicates living arrangements. Margaret Mead (1949:95–96) wrote that "strong taboos" explicitly prohibited homoerotic behavior among Iatmul as well. Outside Iatmul society, however, Iatmul males tend to become "active homosexuals" in aggressive interactions with males of other tribes. Mead thus suggests that desires for homoerotic contact are checked by taboos. And on the mythological level, homoeroticism is expressed as a theme of relational identity between mother's brother and sister's son. One wonders how much these ceremonial and mythological alternatives to institutionalized homoeroticism occur also in other regions of the Sepik, where father presence in child care is prominent.

A third and previously overlooked alternative social formation is provided in the example of Mountain Arapesh (Mead 1935). The famous references to Arapesh as "cooperative" and "loving" of children certainly come to mind. Fathers were not only present but also very involved in care taking. We find Mead (1935:50) suggesting that after age five, Arapesh boys "transfer their major allegiance" from mother to father and are "very dependent" upon fathers. Fathers, by and large, accept this relational attachment and have status positions which largely permit them as adults to do so. Indeed, Mead hints that Arapesh boys' strong desire for paternal dependence after weaning itself provides a shield and a comfort which facilitate the boys' transition into initiation later. Institutionalized homoeroticism is absent. This is a kind of intense and affectionate paternal presence which is rare in Melanesia, and it contrasts with both the Lowlands and Highlands models discussed above.

These structural influences on homoerotic relationships point more to a continuum or process and less to an absolute outcome of permanent "homosexual orientation" in Melanesia. Some findings related to variability in masculinity and femininity in boys as a function of paternal presence bear comparison here (Money and Ehrhardt 1972; D'Andrade 1973; Snarey and Son 1987). These processual models imply more subtle adaptations than the universalism of the Freudian model suggested. The dangers of the Freudian model are thus to overgeneralize and normalize the custom, to attribute too much emphasis to parental figures, and to place homoeroticism in an inappropriate and invalid Western framework (Herdt 1997a). Moreover, our Western folk model exaggerates rivalry, envy, individualism, and the separateness of persons—echoes of our own individualistic, Western notion of sexual development in isolation. Such folk models place the individual above relational concepts of selfhood, gender, and sexuality, as Japanese analyst Takeo Doi (1972) has observed about same-gender homoerotic relations in Japan.

Such strong inferences from our own experience are thus helpful only up to a point in understanding a phenomenon such as father presence in Melanesia. Paternal deprivation (Biller 1974, 1976) is the wrong concept to cover such meanings. Father is present in both of these traditions, and he is an authority figure as well. The RH family functions as an economic and social unit, though not one that can easily be separated from the clan village as an extended family, a corporate unit. Father's presence is both a stimulator to the child and a source of interpersonal conflict: through his mother, first of all, in her problematic marriage, and then through direct interaction with him. In the Western model, father becomes an Oedipal rival, an envied figure of power; the child who identifies with father must then disidentify with mother. In the absence of father or in conditions of familial conflict, the mother must "proxy" for the father, who often is "invisibilized," to use Chodorow's (1978:50) term. The Melanesian pattern, on the other hand, has the father present but highly ritualized in his role and actions. Father is more of an aloof presence until middle childhood, when he can become an authority, even a foe, owing to familial rivalries. Ritual homoeroticism resolves this conflict by separating father and son. Surprisingly, the residential and rooming circumstances here are closer to the psychosexual situation of our own child development than we would have thought, for closeness to other males forges bonds just through living together.

This special Melanesian pattern of identity development may seem inimical to the inculcation of masculinity in the West, but such a view rests in part upon the overgeneralizing power of our own folk model of homosexuality. The Melanesians have not merged instinct and object, as we have in our cultural ideology; to have sex with a person of the same sex does not mean for them that one is fixated on the same sex, nor that bonds with the opposite sex will not in time emerge. Instead, through a developmental process of residential change and homoerotic contact, the boy distances himself from his mother's world and forms closer ties with males and a more efficacious and stable construct of father and maleness as an internal representation (see Snarey and Son 1987:115). This inner symbolic object is reinforced by social practices, such as subsequent rites and masculine attitudes and norms in everyday life.

The latter emphasis on masculine development suggests one further implication of this study that seems surprising and counterintuitive: in Melanesian societies that lack RH but have fathers close, we find a kind of "protest masculinity" and disapproval of homoeroticism most reminiscent of Western society. Iatmul society seems to illustrate these conditions. There, inconsistent and proximate fathers co-occur with no outlet for homoerotic responses, which are "tabooed" (to use Mead's term). Thus, boys are not able to spread their image of maleness over two cultural roles (father and homoerotic partner) (see Paul 1976:347), such as Trobrianders might do. Nor can they distance themselves from father and idealize him, as occurs in Highlands societies.

An aspect of what Chodorow (1978) elsewhere called "compulsive masculinity" exists in their responsiveness to boys and aggressiveness to other men (Bateson 1958). Thus, among Iatmul we find a situation whereby closeness with fathers increases difficulties that cannot be repressed, or be idealized in his absence and would result in more hostile responses institutionalized in genital mutilations, for example (Graber 1981:421). We have in the making, then, the conditions of extreme reaction to fears of merging with Other—especially of being engulfed by mother or destroyed by father, conditions ripe for "conversion reactions" of the type associated with taboos and homophobic reactions against homoeroticism. Such responses are familiar to the Western context (Biller 1976). In this context it is significant that Gregory Bateson (1946:122) himself used the term "compensatory reaction" in defining responses to early male identification with females among Iatmul. In both Iatmul and Western father-son interaction there is an ambivalence and a presence that can cause other problems in later development. And in both instances, contrary to the case of father presence in societies with ritualized homoeroticism, the individual father's role is critical in influencing the outcome. As Kakar (1982:422) has written of India and the West: "The guiding voice of the father can become effective and the alliance succeed only if the father allows his son emotional access to him—[allowing] himself to be idealized at the same time that he encourages and supports the boy's own effort to grow up."

In Melanesia, ritual systems anticipate the effects of differential mother and father influences on masculine development. On the level of social roles, the degree of polarization expected of adult men versus women is a critical, anticipated outcome of development. Early proximity to father and male adult distantiation from females are thus the two poles between which are suspended the symbolic mediations of ritual homoeroticism. In the embedded ritual discourse of Melanesian societies, Highlands cultures emphasize sexual segregation (Western Highlands) and the letting of female blood (Eastern Highlands) to attain male growth and masculine maturity, whereas Lowland societies stress insemination to achieve the same end. These are the ritual developmental regimes. For postinitiation masculine life, the sex-segregated Highlands groups continue to emphasize pollution and avoidance of women. The RH societies, however, have spousal co-residence and the men's cults to emphasize insemination for young boys, watched over by fathers and grandfathers.

The case of Sambia again clarifies. The symbolic objects of their male cult, sacred bamboo flutes and female hamlet spirits, are unconscious symbols of mothers' breasts and of mother herself. Semen and homoerotic partners symbolize father. After initiation, males may attach themselves to female objects, but only symbolically, whereas in social interaction it is only father, homoerotic partners, and other males to whom boys have actual proximity. The partner has symbolic elements (penis = breast, semen = breast milk) that merge mother and father as internal representations. The boy's role, through ritual development, results in the construction of a less ambiguous, more stable self-adaptive object of father-male and self. This is necessary because, as an adult, a man will stop living with males and—having taken the royal road—be married and live with a woman, his wife.

After years the male is again alone with a female, albeit temporarily; then children arrive. Semen symbolizes this self-object representation by anticipating a boy's moving into the symbolic space of his father. In the unconscious language of the cultural practices of the Sambia, for instance, where the boy at age five must cross over the boundary post from female to male space, and at fifteen must "cross over" from being inseminated to being an inseminator, the boy as a man must leave the men's house completely and live with his wife and children. Here again is a critical structural difference in adult outcomes between Highland and Lowland cultures. These transformations in living and sleeping space are symbolically carried by life-cycle changes in semen as personal and collective symbol. Thus, it eventually comes to be an internal representation of self, a blend of conscious (father's semen) and unconscious (mother's milk) elements. It has also symbolized father's status position in society and has served as a transitional object that facilitates the boy's move from mother to father.

In the beginning it seemed obvious that people who institutionalize homoeroticism would epitomize the absent father syndrome. Now we find instead that the ambivalent presence of fathers creates different symbolic outcomes in development. Father presence is a richly textured, development process, not a trait to be tabulated without regard to context. Likewise, the cultural meanings and folk psychology of "homosexuality" require more careful documentation of sexuality and gender socialization than in the past. The case of father presence in Melanesia provides an alternate way for us to see around the edges of our own cultural assumptions about sexual orientation and gender. Such assumptions are powerful and change slowly, for they capture, even imprison our attention, and deflect us away from basic questions of ethnographic inquiry, such as: Where does father sleep? What does folk theory have to say about this? The Freudian paradigm provided clues, but these were also laden with baggage, and the intuitions were not sensitive to historical and local conditions and their manifestations in developmental subjectivity. In this regard, I cannot resist ending with Freud's famous quote from Goethe, that "Strong tyrants have short reigns."

SEVEN

Developmental Discontinuities and Sexual Orientation across Cultures

Anthropology has pioneered the understanding of variations in sexual practices across the spectrum of human groups on the basis of intensive ethnographic study. The speculative hierarchical taxonomies of Victorian evolutionists in the nineteenth century, for instance, gave way to the encyclopedic surveys of Havelock Ellis (1936) and Westermarck (1917), among others, in the early twentieth (reviewed in Bullough 1980; Foucault 1980; Herdt 1984a; Money and Ehrhardt 1972); this in turn was succeeded by Freud (1962). By 1925, Freud (1961), in a classical paper on sex differences, could speak confidently of "universals" in psychosexual development as if cross-cultural variations were irrelevant. The influence of the Freudians was great, and it shifted interest to the psychic level of gender meanings. Malinowski (1927) complained of this universalism, but he could not provide a counterpoint to the view that "anatomy is destiny." Margaret Mead's (1935) classic work on New Guinea, *Sex and Temperament in Three Primitive Societies,* attempted such a response, however. From the available evidence it would seem that Mead and her followers succeeded to a remarkable extent.[1] Since the 1930s many other ethnographers have provided insights on the extent to which, as Carrier (1980:100) has put it, "Intercultural varia-

1. Social scientists (including anthropologists) have been critical of Mead's findings, as she herself noted in her preface to the 1963 edition of *Sex and Temperament* (1935); the controversy of her Samoan case study has continued and renewed such criticism (Freeman 1983). But in other fields and in sex research and popular culture (Rappaport 1986), Mead's influence on gender ideas was powerful. I would point out that most textbooks still utilize Mead's 1935 study as a crucial cross-cultural example, the Katchadourian and Lundt 1980 text—a widely selling college textbook of its kind—being a case in point.

222

tions in patterns of human sexual behavior are mainly related to social and cultural differences occurring between societies around the world." While anthropology has examined cross-cultural differences in sexual patterns across societies, it has had little to say regarding another dimension of sexual socialization: developmental discontinuity in sexual behavior across the course of life.

How do sexual behavior and experience change across the developmental cycle of a person, and how do cultural practices and related psychosexual mechanisms structure such variance? This general problem area—which surely is one of the more perplexing and controversial in the study of our own society—has been largely ignored in the study of other cultures. In this chapter, I explore similarities and differences in developmental change in sexuality from an anthropological perspective. I suggest that when we sift through the considerable cross-cultural archives, we discover that change in sexual behavior and experience after childhood is a clear part of the human condition. This point regarding the potential for change is supported by accumulating evidence from life-span development studies of a wide-ranging nature in our own society (see, e.g., Honzik 1984). In a recent review that includes sexual development, Kohlberg and his colleagues (Kohlberg, Ricks, and Savarey 1984:156) suggest "that there is more change than constancy between childhood and adolescence or adulthood." Because of its exploratory nature, I will not undertake a systematic survey of all the literature here.[2] Moreover, in keeping with the focus on sexual culture, I will study issues related to understanding the structure and meaning of homosexuality and bisexuality, especially in non-Western cultures. Because homosexuality cannot in my view be disengaged from the study of heterosexuality—both forms of sexual action occur in the same ongoing social field of institutions, roles, and symbols, which take as their objects male and female experience—we must also ground our study in the historical and cultural context.

The relationship between discontinuity in sexual development and homosexuality across cultures is not, I think, fortuitous or trivial, and indeed, their co-occurrence helps explain both the absence of studies on discontinuity by anthropologists and how I have arrived at the present problem in my own work. With a few exceptions, such as Ruth Benedict's classic paper (1938), discussed below, anthropologists have not taken continuities and discontinuities in sexual development as problematic. Benedict used insti-

---

2. I will not here deal with exceptions, but I have no doubt that some could be found. These do not obviate a *general* theory, for in cross-cultural studies it is difficult to find any generalization other than the most vacuous for which exceptions cannot be found.

tutionalized homosexuality in Australian and New Guinea tribes as a key example of how, in developmental time, children in some cultures must "unlearn" cultural things so they can learn other adult cultural practices. By contrast, Benedict's student, Mead (1935), saw homosexuality as a form of "deviance" and as an unanticipated outcome of unusual temperaments that could not accommodate themselves to the heterosexual norm.

The historical treatment of sexuality by anthropologists must be seen in the broader context of functional studies of culture and personality associated with the work of Benedict, Devereux, Mead, Whiting, and others from the 1920s onward. These psychoanalytically oriented studies were holistic and largely ahistorical; they focused on adults and normative outcome variables. Homogeneity of experience and behavior was often stressed, so that in understanding particular cultural "ways," even sexuality, ethnographies presumed the equation of culture with the "basic personality" of a tribal people. Furthermore, descriptive relativism—the view that all cultural elements are meaningful in their native context—led to normative relativism: the idea that moral judgments about cultures cannot be made, because they are all of equal worth (Spiro 1989). Functionalism and relativism thus operated together in the epistemology of anthropology. Since cultures were "adaptations" and "functioned," it was argued that they must be consistent, integrated, and relatively useful accommodations— nonpathologic (see Spiro 1982; Wallace, 1969:24–25). Culture was nearly self-contained in providing the necessities of adult rational adaptations to environments (Benedict 1934). So strong was the view that cultural adjustment requires normative homogeneity in beliefs and practices shared by *all* members of a group that Margaret Mead, for example, once suggested that "cultural heterogeneity is *ipso facto* pathogenic" (quoted in Wallace 1969).[3] Added to this situation was the general trend that anthropologists avoided the study of sex per se (LeVine 1979); kinship, family, marriage, and the like were prior concerns (Vance 1991).

Thus, when it came to dealing with it, homosexuality was a strange intruder in the garden of functional anthropology. Let us take, as a case in point, Marvin Opler, an anthropologist who worked with the Ute Indians and who also wrote an early review on homosexuality in anthropological study (1965). First, Opler thought of homosexuality solely in the context of Freud's (1955) notorious Schaefer case, as a paranoid defensive manifesta-

3. A. F. C. Wallace (1969:72) quotes Margaret Mead: "In a heterogeneous culture, individual life experiences differ so markedly from one another that almost every individual may find the existing cultural forms of expression inadequate to express his peculiar bent, and so be driven into more and more special forms of psychosomatic expression."

tion of the Oedipal complex. However, he argued that Freud's model was historically culture bound to middle-class Viennese society. He suggested, contra the Freud of *Totem and Taboo* (1950), that initiation and penis mutilation have nothing to do with "castration anxieties" or erotic matters among Australian aborigines, although no evidence was adduced to support his contention (Opler 1965). Apparently Opler was unaware of institutionalized homoerotic practices among certain aboriginal societies (Herdt 1984a).[4] Following that assertion, Opler then claimed: "The point about these societies and other non-literate hunting and gathering societies is that homosexuality is generally rare and, in some instances, virtually nonexistent" (1965:111). Opler proceeded to dismiss the resilient findings of Ford and Beach (1951) on the frequency of homosexual practices across cultures, arguing that their survey data were decontextualized and unreliable.[5] (Rado [1956], however, who felt that homosexuality was situation specific to prisons and associated with "impulse-ridden schizophrenics," was more reliable, according to Opler.)[6] After suggesting further that this "deviant homosexuality"—astonishingly, the term is never defined—occurs also in "aberrant" Siberian shamans and Norwegian rats, Opler concluded: "One thing is clear: In the absence of an organic or hormonal basis, homosexuality in practically all cultures is regarded as a deviation from the majority values and norms of conduct" (1965:114). The prosecution rested, its case against homosexuality in other cultures firmly made.[7]

Is there any wonder that virtually a generation has passed and now a new generation of anthropologists have come along to disagree and reopen the case to critical inquiry (Blackwood 1986; Carrier 1995; Murray 1995; Nanda 1984; reviewed in Herdt 1997a; Lewin and Leap 1996)? It is no wonder that the development of homoerotic and bisexual behavior, their role and meanings in the developmental cycle of people, are still poorly understood.[8]

---

4. In my own survey of Australian and Melanesian societies (Herdt 1984a), I found area experts who either did not know of or ignored the evidence on forms of structural homoeroticism.

5. Ford and Beach (1951:130) found, for example, that "in 49 (64%) of the 76 societies other than our own for which information is available, homosexual activities of one sort or another are considered normal and socially acceptable for certain members of the community."

6. Had Opler and Rado forgotten that Freud himself, in the *Three Essays on the Theory of Sexuality* (1962:5), believed that homosexuality was "remarkably widespread among many savage and primitive races"?

7. Stoller (1985c:183) has recently said of psychoanalytic research on homosexuality: "We have transformed diagnosis into accusation, covering our behavior with jargon. But though it hides hatred, it promotes cruelty; jargon is judgment. It serves hidden agendas."

8. Clyde Kluckhohn, one of the great anthropologists of Mead's cohort, remarked in the context of reviewing Kinsey's work from an anthropological perspective: "One may perhaps infer that

What Did Kinsey Measure?

It was during the heyday of functional anthropology, the 1930s and 1940s, that Kinsey began his ambitious project on American sexual practices. Kinsey did draw upon anthropology in contextualizing some of his findings, as we can see in *Sexual Behavior in the Human Male* (Kinsey, Pomeroy, and Martin 1948), wherein he cited ethnographers with regard to variations in sexual norms. He used Margaret Mead's work, for instance, in comparing American practices of premarital intercourse and extramarital intercourse with those of other cultures. Kinsey's use of cross-cultural references was generally citational, not expository, however, and the references are positioned at the beginnings of chapters, usually to raise the question of the universality of sexual practices.

Kinsey's great and lasting contribution, of course, was to disengage the binary monolithic cultural categories—homosexuality/heterosexuality—from the disparaging discourse of the 1940s and 1950s by demonstrating process, variation, and continuum in sexual behavior. His empirical findings challenged the moral and political images of what was "normal," and like Freud's work, this insinuated that everyone was at one point "deviant" with regard to heterosexuality. However flawed, whether by sample, procedures, or analysis, Kinsey's insistence upon behavioral variation opened the way for far-reaching and critical cultural transformation in Americans' understanding of sexual orientation. Kinsey challenged, that is, the biological essentialist and morally flawed deficit views of human nature—in man and woman—as social and psychological prototypes in Western thought. We need not belabor the point that his critics, among them the infamous Joseph McCarthy, exacted from Kinsey and his associates a heavy price for this scientific and societal progress. Nor must we forget its scientific benefits for the emergence of the remarkable research of the 1950s and 1960s, such as the seminal contributions on sexuality of John Money and his colleagues (1956) or the later survey studies (see Bell, Weinberg, and Hammersmith 1981). Subsequent dissatisfaction with the Kinsey scale, the notion of sexual orientation, the analysis of bisexuality as a residual category, and the polarization of homosexuality and heterosexuality as psycho-

---

even anthropologists are insufficiently emancipated from their own culture to investigate sexual behavior with the same detachment and scrupulous attention to detail that they have devoted to basketry, primitive music, and kinship systems. Of course, it must in all fairness be added that, even if the individual anthropologist were emotionally free to be truly scientific, he might be realistic enough to realize that published researches upon sex were unlikely to lead to secure teaching positions or even to scientific recognition" (1955:333).

sexual prototypes distilled in a different form from that in which Kinsey found them must not overshadow the historical and cultural domains into which Kinsey and his colleagues brought genuine enlightenment.

Kinsey has been criticized on various grounds, not the least of which concerns the implied universality of his American study. Responses by anthropologists at the time ranged from the very critical (Gorer 1955) to the more positive Kluckhohn (1955). Geoffrey Gorer, a British anthropologist, felt that Kinsey exaggerated sex as behavior as a mere "device for physical relaxation. . . . Not only is sex, in Dr. Kinsey's presentation, as meaningless as a sneeze, it is also equally unproductive; after the equivalent of blowing the nose, that is the end of the matter" (1955:51–52). This point, while perhaps overinflated, raises a cultural critique agreed upon by many in gender research, including John Gagnon (1990) and John De Cecco (1990): that Kinsey studied disembodied acts, discrete behaviors, rather than meaning-filled patterns of action. As De Cecco sees it, Kinsey had four conceptions of sex: that it was a physical activity, that it developed in a mechanistic way, that robust sexual performance was to be admired, and that its chief outcome was not reproduction but erotic pleasure. These attributes all are related to the question of sex as meaning-filled symbolic expression of normative development and sexual socialization in culture. By emphasizing acts instead of symbolic action, Kinsey managed to create a field of sexual study amid a moral climate that had hindered it (Kluckhohn 1955), yet he did so at the cost of divorcing sex from the lives and meanings of whole persons (see also Stoller 1985a).

Why this is important to me is that Kinsey's work fostered a view that sexual acts can be seen apart from the developmental life-course stages in which they are studied. This implied a "steady state" view that sexual development is always based on *continuities* in cultural conditioning, if not in fact on actual *experienced* successive continuities, in people's lives. Such a preconception is based on a cultural conception of human nature as steady, constant, and unrelated to life experience, as in our own folk American view.

But to return to my own question: What Kinsey thought he measured were overt sexual experiences that indicated the individual's developmental continuity in sexual behaviors. He looked for a linear trend. Kinsey, Pomeroy, and Martin (1948) specifically believed that attitudes, fantasies, and other "subjective" materials were too introspective to be reliable measures of experience. This typically eliminated inconsistencies between acts in the head and those in the real world. Furthermore, because Kinsey scores for the same person were not aggregated, the sexual preference and behavior of the individual were studied at one point in time not as successive sequelae but as outcome variable. Cross-sectional studies of different age groups were held up as a composite picture of the "meaning" of psychosexual development in American society. But this was problematic in view of retrospective bias (Ross 1980). This approach had the effect of eliminating sexual change within the same person's life, of making the act more important than its inner experience, and therefore of concentrating on the mechanics of how, not the meanings of why, people engage in erotic intercourse.

Ruth Benedict on Discontinuity

During the start-up period of Kinsey's research, Benedict (1938) published "Continuities and Discontinuities in Cultural Conditioning," which outlined an implicit future critique of Kinsey's treatment of sexuality in cultural and developmental perspective. "All cultures must deal in one way or another with the cycle of growth from infancy to adulthood," Benedict began:

> Nature has posed the situation dramatically: on the one hand, the new born baby, physiologically vulnerable, unable to fend for itself, or to participate of its own initiative in the life of the group, and, on the other, the adult man or woman. Every man who rounds out his potentialities must have been a son first and a father later and the two roles are physiologically great in contrast; he must first have been dependent upon others for his very existence and later he must provide security for others. This discontinuity in the life cycle is a fact of nature and is inescapable. Facts of nature, however, in any discussion of human problems, are ordinarily read off not at their bare minimal but surrounded by all the local accretions of behavior to which the student of human affairs has become accustomed in his own society. (1938:160)

The "facts of nature" are not "natural" for humans, Benedict argued: between nature and human behavior, culture is a great "middle term," a mediator. Transitions in the life course involve "cultural bridges" (1938: 160). Such bridges—social practices, roles, expressive ceremonies such as initiation rites, and so on—embody underlying conceptions of human culture: what it is, how it is made, and how it changes over time (Geertz 1973). In Benedict's view, then, cultures differ in the degree of continuity of experience, task assignment, rules, norms, beliefs, expectation, goals, and roles structured across the developmental cycle from infancy to adulthood. Continuity means, Benedict wrote, "that the child is taught nothing it must unlearn later" (1938:165).

As a mundane example of continuity in cultural conditioning, Benedict cited the practice in America of eating three meals a day. By age two or three, infants achieve the adult schedule. No change in this occurs or is expected. Modesty is another illustration she used: "We waste no time in clothing the baby, and in contrast to many societies where the child runs naked till it is ceremonially given its skirt or pubic sheath at adolescence, the child's training fits it precisely for adult conventions" (1938:161–62). For examples of discontinuity, Benedict selected three domains: "responsible-nonresponsible status role," "dominance-submission," and "contrasted sex role." On responsibility, she argued that Americans and other Westerners treat the child as wanting to play, whereas the adult has to work. Child labor laws in England and the West changed a historical pattern in which, during the Middle Ages, children had been regarded as small adults who had heavy work responsibilities (Ariès 1962). Agrarian children in the United States and other Western countries also differ in this way. Benedict cited the Papago Indians as a people who treat children more like adults, including respecting them. Mead (1930), in her *Growing Up in New Guinea,* stressed discontinuity in the responsibility of Manus Island children, who shunned the concerns of adults. "The contrast with our society is very great," said Benedict (1938:163).[9]

Discontinuity in sex-role training, Benedict's third domain, is most relevant to my analysis. The discrepancy between facts of physiological maturation and cultural concepts of sexual differentiation between children and adults poses a great challenge to the adult outcome of sexual development. Is the child regarded as neuter or sexless? Are children permitted to experiment sexually? Are homosexual acts considered morally neutral or repugnant? And how is sexual variation handled in adulthood? The answers to such questions vary enormously across cultures (Herdt 1987a; Mead 1961). Discontinuity is not linked in any simple way to whether a people are prudish or sexually tolerant. Benedict (1938) noted that among the Dakota Indians, for instance, "Adults observe great privacy in sex acts and in no way stimulate children's sexual activity," so there is no developmental discontinuity because the child "is taught nothing it does not have to unlearn later" (1938:165). In such societies, sexual experimenta-

9. The village children of Manus Island in New Guinea stayed free of adult concerns until age ten or twelve: "Where the adults were a driven, angry, rivalrous, acquisitive lot of people . . . the children were the gayest, most lively and curious" (Mead 1956:110). Neisser (1962:68) states: "In these circumstances, coming of age involved drastic reorientation of the child's entire way of life. It would seem, then, that infantile amnesia among the Manus of that period should have been both deeper and longer than among ourselves."

tion is viewed as harmless because it poses no serious consequences for adult behavior. Yet in our society, in which preadolescent sexual activity is generally disapproved and sexual variations are punished, the potential for unlearning values and attitudes is very great and may be associated with a kind of emotional and cognitive amnesia of childhood (Cohler 1982; Gagnon 1971; Neisser 1962).

Societies vary greatly in their regard or disapproval of same-sex relationships. Carrier's (1980) review categorizes societies into three types: accommodating societies, which are approving; disapproving societies; and societies that do not formally sanction same-sex activity but utilize social regulations to inhibit its free expression. An important form of accommodation to homosexual practices is that of tribal initiation and secret male cults. Benedict cited two well-known examples from New Guinea, the Keraki of the Trans-Fly River (Williams 1936a) and the Marind-anim of Southeast New Guinea, both of which she referred to as "making of men" initiations: "Among the Keraki it is thought that no boys can grow to full stature without playing the passive homosexual role for some years. Men slightly older take the active role, and the older man is a jealous partner. The life cycle of the Keraki Indians includes, therefore, in succession, passive homosexuality, active homosexuality, and heterosexuality. There is no technique for ending active homosexuality, but this is not explicitly tabu for older men; heterosexuality and children, however, are highly valued" (1938:166). Benedict believed that cultural institutions can "furnish adequate support to the individual as he progresses from role to role or interdicts the previous behavior in a summary fashion" (1938:167). This problem in developmental discontinuity should be seen not as an individual difference issue, Benedict chided, but rather one of contradictory cultural "institutions" and "dogmas."

Benedict seems to have been responding to the medicalization of homosexuality. Instead of creating more dogmas about sexual neurosis, she suggested, we ought to develop new social institutions that would remove these pressures. Her plea for a new social fabric—one heard before and since—was in keeping with the cultural determinism, humanism, and relativism already outlined. Although she hinted at ideological conceptions of human nature and elsewhere indicated that these were always to be seen as ethnocentric folk models all peoples exhibit (Benedict 1934), she did not say how these were related systematically to problems of sexual discontinuity. Take note that she never defined homosexuality, though her reference to "jealous" Keraki partners implied that this was more than a ceremonial performance. Note, too, her assumption that the imposed discontinuities of ritualized homoeroticism do not create psychosocial problems either for the individual or society. Her relativism suggested that our society was "worse" than others in how it accommodated individuals to "natural" developmental changes. In spite of the differing conceptual approaches, however, Kinsey and Benedict shared in common the notion that homosexuality is not *necessarily* abnormal and may be one of many potentials we humans have for fluidity and change in our "human nature."

Developmental Changes in Sexuality

Suppose that we agree with the view that the "facts of nature" impose inevitable psychophysiological changes upon the life course of sexuality in humans. Where do we go from there? Sexual differentiation from infancy to adulthood certainly involves numerous changes in primary and secondary sex traits (Luria 1979), not all of which are developmentally or socially problematic, or even of conscious interest, to human groups (Maccoby 1979; Ortner and Whitehead 1981; Williams 1986). This potential for flexibility in sexual accommodations to culture is a "two-edged sword," Margaret Mead (1935:310) once wrote, because it allows for both positive and negative imposition of external structure and goals upon the person in development.[10]

The difficulty with Kinsey's scale of measurement in this regard was that it placed too much emphasis upon discrete acts of sex and not enough stress upon the cultural context and total developmental outcomes to which these acts are related. This is the same failure that today manifests itself in enormous quantitative sociological surveys of homosexuality that decontextualize the culture and lives at issue (Bell, Weinberg, and Hammersmith 1981). The corrective, as Benedict argued, is to view all developmental changes in the context of social structure and cultural "dogmas" of human nature that make them seem "normal and natural." What she failed to do, however, was to explicate these cultural patterns and folk concepts of human nature underlying the direction of psychosexual changes in each case. By contrast, Kinsey and colleagues took a different approach, which deemphasized the cultural and made sexual behavior primary. They seemed to have had in mind the proverbial onion analogy, in which, if one peels away the layers (cultural meanings), one finds the core, a universal of

10. Mead used examples such as the Nazis in Europe to show how social engineering could retard and regress sexual enlightenment in societies.

sexual behaviors: not a cultural but a physical nature with culture wrapped around it. However, as Clifford Geertz has suggested, humans are neither innate capacities nor discrete bundles of actual behaviors. "When seen as a set of symbolic devices for controlling behavior," Geertz (1973:52) has said, "extrasomatic sources of information, cultures provide the link between what men are intrinsically capable of becoming and what they actually, one by one, become."

The nonbiological changes that co-occur with sexual differentiation— social and psychological differentiation—are complex, while the biological transformations can be modeled as universals (the psychosocial correlates vary greatly) and must be modeled as local contingencies (Ehrhardt 1985). Such changes, to which the person must adapt, include ideas about the human-nature folk model thought to cause and result from the changes, ideas about gender roles, ideologies, rules for sexual conduct, and normative images of appropriate gender behavior that guide action in nonsexual domains—some of which are performed as cultural ideology in work and love, while others are expressed in developmental subjectivities from childhood to old age.

Although this paradigm incorporates quite a bit, it does not exhaust the content of personal and cultural experiences, which are contingent upon, among other things, early attachment, learning experiences, and their related fantasies (Obeyesekere 1981; Stoller 1979, 1985a). In this area I maintain, with Freud (1962), a "presumption of bisexuality" in human potential.[11] Although many, but by no means all (Ford and Beach 1951), human groups associate appropriate gender and erotic behavior with moral institutions (the family, inheritance, religion), other cultures do not make such assumptions or social connections. They certainly do not disapprove of them in same way as ourselves (Herdt 1997a). Departures from norms may thus be "disapproved" (Carrier 1980), but only if they are idiosyncratic, not cohort normative. Discontinuities of the type discussed by Benedict may therefore be problematic for the individual but not so for the society in which cultural guidelines anticipate developments of "human nature." This is particularly evident in cultural systems that institutionalize dra-

---

11. According to Freud: "Psychoanalytic research is most decidedly opposed to any attempt at separating off homosexuals from the rest of mankind as a group of special character. . . . It has found that all human beings are capable of making a homosexual object-choice and have in fact made one in their unconscious. . . . Psychoanalysis considers that a choice of an object independently of its sex—freedom to range equally over male and female objects as it is found in childhood, in primitive states of society and early periods of history, is the original basis from which as a result of restriction in one direction or the other, both the normal and inverted types develop" (1963:11–12).

matic change in sex-role development (Stephens 1962). Gagnon's (1971) seminal review made this point in our society, and my work in Melanesia has also illustrated this point in a non-Western society (Herdt 1981).

One means of sorting out this variance is to establish a provisional typology of societies relative to how prescribed or preferred sexual conduct is structured across the life cycle. In this model, societies socialize children in the direction of degrees of relative continuity or discontinuity, as the case may be, from the perspective of the final outcome: full adult personhood. From this perspective we can infer how underlying conceptions of human nature are felt to contribute to normative developmental changes in sexual being and sexual action. The following are thus idealized models which attempt to capture the degree and range of continuity experienced by people in regard to sexual practices and associated attitudes across the life span.[12]

LINEAR DEVELOPMENT

Linear development is the first type. It represents an unbroken developmental line (Kohlberg, Ricks, and Savarey 1984) of sexual behavior that is constructed on the basis of fully anticipated outcomes by parents and other caretakers. No dramatic change—unlearning—in sexual conduct or orientation and little discontinuity from early childhood onward are anticipated, and none should be experienced by the person. As ethnographic examples of linear sexual developmental regimes, I would cite the !Kung bushmen (Shostack 1980), the Trobriand Islanders (Malinowski 1927), and the Tahitians (Levy 1973), though others could be identified as well (see, e.g., Mead 1961).

DISJUNCTIVE OR SEQUENTIAL DEVELOPMENT

The second type, disjunctive or sequential development, is conceptualized ideally as a disjunctive and broken developmental line of sexual behavior, revealing marked and sometimes dramatic changes in anticipated outcomes between childhood and adulthood (see Money and Ehrhardt

12. Degree of discontinuity is here meant to index such variables as (1) the age at which change is introduced to the person, (2) the number of domains that change affects, (3) the radical transformations in beliefs, values, and norms involved across these domains, (4) their obligatory nature for the person, (5) the public or secretive and thus unexpected quality of the imposed change, (6) the extent to which antecedents of the change are consciously or preconsciously known to the person and his caretakers, and (7) among other things, the impact of such revisions of the perceived symbolic environment upon the self-concept of the person and the socially constructed reality in the society.

1972). Wherever one finds emotional upheaval, including traumatic developmental changes, often institutionalized by ritual or ceremony, there we can expect the interruptions of individual experience that lead to disjunctive sexuality. Variable and even discrepant norms and rules here radically transform sexual being and action from one life-cycle stage to another, perhaps in reaction or antithesis to the prior stage. One or both parents may avoid or be unaware of adult anticipated sexual practices, so that no *direct* preparatory socialization enters into childhood teaching. It is important to note that the genders, too, may vary within a society, so that girls may have a disjunctive experience, while boys develop under a linear sequence of norms, and so on.

For examples of disjunctive regimes, I would cite late Victorian England and the United States (D'Emilio and Freedman 1988; Smith-Rosenberg 1985) as a prime example, indeed, the one which Freud knew very well. For a contemporary sexual culture I would focus on white middle-class America (Fine 1988; Herdt and Boxer 1993), in which many caretakers still regard children as erotically naive and sexless, as Benedict once argued, but expect them in middle adolescence to emerge as full-blown sexual actors. American boys, especially, are culturally defined still as testosterone machines that seek sexual outlets for their "sex drives" (Gagnon 1971). In both of these historical illustrations the role of the parents is partly intentional, partly accidental, in how the culture expects them to avoid sexual discussions and sex education in regard to the child.

Sambia are a prime example of a disjunctive sexual culture, as I have elsewhere argued (Herdt 1987a). Indeed, particularly for the role of the parent, all cultures in Melanesia that institutionalize secret homoerotic contacts (hidden from women and children) are a paradigm case for understanding how the parent cannot anticipate the future. Power relations obviously are at play here, with parents, mothers especially, having little say over the future social and sexual development of their sons. Likewise, Sambia boys have the greatest degree of disjunctive experience in growing up, owing to the six stages of secret initiation. However, girls also experience later intense disjunctive experience, as they leave their natal villages and move into the homes of their husbands, who are strangers to them. The question of nonconscious or unconscious awareness of eventual sequential change is problematic and will be discussed shortly. However, my operational rule is that for inclusion in this developmental regime type, at least one and possibly both parents must disagree or be unaware of the eventual career of the child, as the anticipated changes are hidden or not spoken of by both the socializers (Herdt 1987a). Thus, disjunctive or sequential development can be analyzed as a system of serial stages or consequences that logically succeed one another toward an end that is determined by structures of power beyond the choice of the individuals involved.

By its very nature, a disjunctive sexual socialization regime is phasic or episodic, as argued by John Money (1987). Two points stand out. First, there are dramatic changes in sexual behavior not handled by the primary socialization group (e.g., the nuclear family) but rather by secondary socializing groups or institutions (e.g., ritual cults, peer groups). Again, a division of labor, and an imposition by authorities, change the rules of development beyond the reach of individuals. Second, certain elements of the sexual code may be continuous even in the face of radical change in other components of the sexual culture. To take the example of age-structured homoerotic relations in Melanesia, ancient Japan, Greece, and elsewhere, all caretakers and children seemingly share in the norm that boys and girls will marry and reproduce; this norm does not alter across the life span, in spite of the introduction and experience of homoerotic activity as a radically different change in sexual status between childhood and adulthood (Herdt 1997a). We can thus refer to phasic and nonphasic patterns of sexual and nonsexual behavior in systems of sequential development.

EMERGENT DEVELOPMENT

Emergent development refers to a more "open-ended" sexual culture in which new sexual values and practices are based upon uncertain and ambiguous futures. Emergent, as a label, implies that socializers are less sure of the absolute outcomes of sexual behavior codes in the future. This may be the product of revolution or innovation; of drastic cultural upheaval, as happens in war or conquest; or of dramatic change due to the environment or changing technologies. New values, for instance, replace or transform older ones. However, change in itself may not produce dramatic sexual change. As examples of total social systems in which dramatic change occurred, but did not fundamentally affect the sexual code, I would cite Manus Island (Mead 1956) and postrevolutionary Mexico (Wolf 1969). Societies that have undergone far-reaching change in social and sexual being and behavior simultaneously would include the Israeli kibbutz, the People's Republic of China, and the transformation of the former Soviet Union into contemporary Russia (Kon 1995).

The "sexual revolution" in the United States of the 1960s (actually the second such profound change in this century, following that of the 1920s) brought new values and behaviors into the sexual culture. The rise of feminism, changes in age cohorts and the decision to marry or have children, and the rise of the gay and lesbian movement, and later the bisexual movement, have all wrought long-term consequences and retrenchment yet to be seen (D'Emilio and Freedman 1988; Herdt 1997a). Surely the cultural concepts "gay" and "lesbian" belong to emergent developmental regimes. Thus, for the first time in history, a child may declare in early adolescence her expressed attraction for the same sex or self-expressed identity as gay or lesbian (Herdt and Boxer 1993). Nevertheless, emergent regimes have a core; not everything changes. Some deep-seated premises of sexuality endure, such as the concept of "sex drives" or the notion that "heterosexuality is biological and normal," while other surface features, including fashions (wearing earrings for men), hairstyles, and the like, may drastically change. Androgyny in dress and cosmetic styles, for example, becomes temporarily popular, as in British "punk culture" (Plummer 1989). Emergent sexual regimes are found in rapidly changing, technologically advanced societies, although emergent values and attendant social changes are rapidly occurring in the Third World (reviewed in Herdt 1997a).

Take note that being and acting gay and lesbian remain a developmental discontinuity in our society. The norms, values, and roles familiar to children are those of their "heteronormal" parents and peers. This is in line with the generalized dichotomization of human nature in Anglo-Saxon traditions, mentioned previously, to which Kinsey first implicitly directed his work. Early studies showed that self-identification as "homosexual" involved change in heteronormal cognitions and affects (reviewed in Troiden 1989). People must "unlearn" certain normative attributes and socialization orientations and learn new ones appropriate to the gay or lesbian role and life-style (reviewed in Herdt 1989a). The well-known stage models of homosexual development all assume that significant sequential changes are antecedents of homosexual "identity consolidation" as an adult outcome (reviewed in Herdt and Boxer 1993).

We would do well, however, to study "bisexuals" more, for they, in their sense of themselves and their sexual practice, may more closely approximate developmental continuity through the life cycle (Weinberg et al. 1994). As Kinsey established, exclusive "heterosexuals" and exclusive "homosexuals" (ones and sixes) on the Kinsey scale are rare; most people fall somewhere in between these extremes, when viewed across the life span and on multiple dimensions of gender and erotic measurement. Increasingly it must be wondered if this is still the case, as the enormous weight of sexual classification lines individuals up early in development, on one side or the other. Nevertheless, if bisexuality is experienced consciously as such in the face of differential social pressures and stigma that should push people to "make a choice" on one side, we are presented with a great opportunity to understand the biopsychological and cultural factors that constrain developmental continuity and discontinuity in human sexuality.

The sketch of these three types of sexual developmental regimes implies somewhat different conceptions of human nature that can only be hinted at.[13] Such cultural "dogmas," to use Benedict's term, are translatable into ideologies and sexual practices, at the collective level, and developmental subjectivities or scripts, for the individual. Suffice it to say in the present context that variability in the normative sexual "careers" of societies involves factors of sexual practice, emotion, cognition, and relationships— key variables of the Kinsey scale. But this cultural variability has not been transferred into the Kinsey scale findings (Herdt and Boxer 1993). The conception of human nature implied by linear developmental regimes is one in which the fundamentals of the expected adult normative outcome are believed to be present at birth or in early childhood and do not require additional "biological" or "social" treatment. There may be flexibility in relation to sexual experimentation, yet the consequences of this are perceived to be insignificant for the outcome. Why is this so? Because the "normal and natural" adult repertoire of sociosexual roles is limited, the requirements of adult personhood are met by marriage and parenthood, and no internal contradictions within the society challenge this or allow for major exceptions to the outcome (see Herdt 1997a).[14]

In contrast, the conception of human nature in disjunctive systems is one of unfinished requirements or prerequisites that necessitate unlearning. Additional biological essentials, psychosocial training, or sexual

13. Mead (1935, 1949, 1961) was among the few anthropologists who consistently studied sex, and she was probably the only one of the previous generation of major standing to discuss developmental aspects of sex and gender. In a major piece on cultural determinants of sexual behavior, she outlined all possible "sexual careers" in human groups (1961:1451–52), a piece that deserves fuller scrutiny elsewhere.

14. Shweder and Bourne (1984:189–90) review concepts of personhood across cultures and argue that "all cultures are confronted by the same small set of existential questions," which includes "the problem of the relationship of the individual to the group." There seem to be relatively few "solutions" to this last problem; the "sociocentric" solution subordinates individual interests to the good of the collectivity, while in the "egocentric" solution society becomes the servant of the individual; i.e., society is imagined to have been created to serve the interests of some idealized autonomous, abstract individual existing free of society yet living in society (Shweder and Bourne 1984:190). Here we have a fundamental existential contrast that could be used to differentiate linear regimes (sociocentric) from sequential (egocentric and sociocentric, in a mixture of elements) and emergent regimes (fully egocentric). This contrast, in other words, is not reducible to "traditional" versus "modern" societies, as Shweder and Bourne hint, but involves attributes of folk models of human nature only roughly correlated with technological/scientific structures in society.

experiences are necessary after childhood to attain normative adult outcomes. The boundaries of gender roles are subject to careful scrutiny and sanctioning. Fluidity of human potential is thus perceived as a preconception of developmental changes across the life span. Sexual fertility may seen as a kind of dynamic, electrical force that flows into and out of people, with children and the aged perceived to be sexually infertile, as we have seen for Sambia. This developmental fluidity must be seen in the context of important internal contradictions in historical societies of this type (Herdt and Poole 1982; Lindenbaum 1984; Vance 1991).

The emergent regime is the most complex type in its conception of "human nature," apparently involving assumptions of both linear and sequential regimes, but going beyond them. This has, no doubt, to do with the parallel existence of premodern traditional notions in Anglo-Saxon societies, such as America and England (Herdt 1994b, alongside post-Enlightenment scientific views coincident with late Victorian industrialization and market-economy images of the "individual" development (see Foucault 1980; Mead, 1961:1456–57) My sense is that Kinsey assumed the American conception of human nature to be universal, especially in its image of emergent sexual development, an assumption that now seems too simple.

Sambia Sexual Development

To round out my discussion of sexual development in cross-cultural perspective, I will conclude with a comment on the measurement of continuity and discontinuity among the Sambia. The Kinsey scale has not been used to measure sexual orientation in traditional societies. There are several reasons for this, but the facts that sexuality is such a sensitive topic and is seldom directly observed are critical (Mead 1961). Though I did not use the Kinsey scale, longitudinal study of many Sambia males, from children to the aged, makes it possible to assess them normatively and constitute sexual histories using the dimensions of a modified Kinsey scale (see discussion in Herdt and Boxer 1993).

In normative terms, there is no dimension of sexual behavior among the Sambia which remains constant across development. (For further discussion, see Herdt 1997a.) Emotional and social preferences for the same sex come closest in approaching developmental continuity, but these changes are so profound, following the separation of boys from mothers and boys' initiations in middle childhood (ages seven to ten), that I have referred to the transformation as one of "radical resocialization" (see Herdt 1981). The parents are differentially involved in these changes, of course, with the mother completely removed from the context of initiation, decisions about future ritual events, and all intimate and sexual relational matters involving her son. Boys thus come to learn of a hidden curriculum and secret paradigm of outcomes never shared with their mothers and sisters. The trauma and upheaval add weight to this sense of cognitive and emotional disjunction.

Why have the Sambia structured sexual socialization with this extreme disjunction? The answer has largely to do with warfare and preparation for stranger-marriages that follow. Sambia male sexual behavior is extremely malleable in being able to take boys and then women as sexual objects. Other ethnographers who have worked in "age-structured homosexual" societies of Melanesia have generally interpreted erotic expression in the same way (see Herdt 1984a). From what we know, Sambia erotic fantasy is also malleable (e.g., see Stoller and Herdt [1985], who describe homoerotic *and* heteroerotic fantasies in the same Sambia teenage male). Likewise, Herdt and Stoller (1990) have shown a range of diversity in the sexual subjectivities of Sambia men and women. However, this diversity does not translate into sexual identity concepts, which are foreign to the Sambia: the well-known dimensions of self-identification are either inappropriate or simply wrong for the Sambia male; they are too culture bound.

The degree of discontinuity in sexual development for Sambia contrasts with that of other Melanesian cultures in certain respects. The sheer presence of age-structured homoeroticism as a cultural form does not mean that sexual development is identical in these societies. For example, because the Sambia sanction childhood sex play, the possibility of more continuity in sexual behavior is limited compared with, say, the Kaluli people (Schieffelin 1976), to whom this seems more acceptable. Likewise, because the Sambia forbid adult homoerotic practice after fatherhood, continuity in overt sex practice is here blocked, as compared with the Marind-anim (Van Baal 1984) mentioned before, who not only permit but require older men to engage in homoerotic activity even though they are married and have children. Such variants must make us cautious in generalizing about continuity even in tradition-bound and seemingly similar societies.

What Sambia patterns can be compared with those of Melanesia as a whole? First, age-structured homoeroticism occurs in approximately 10 percent to 20 percent of all Melanesian societies, as noted above, making this a minority but significant population. Second, with the exception of Malekula Island (Deacon 1934) and possibly the Casuarina Coast (Boelaars 1981), all of these societies practice male, but not female, institutionalized homosexuality. The rarity of ritualized lesbianism, as previously noted (see Blackwood 1986), suggests that same-sex practice is more complex and more socially regulated for females. What role does developmental continuity play in this? There is no simple answer, yet females in Melanesia nearly everywhere seem to experience more generalized developmental and sexual continuity than males. This suggests the possibility of alternative sexual regimes in the same society: linear for Sambia females, sequential for Sambia males (Herdt 1987b). Third, ritual is a uniform mechanism of sexual discontinuity across the life span in these groups. Not surprisingly, male initiation is almost universal, whereas female initiation is uncommon in Melanesia (see Brown 1963; and Strathern 1988, on this correlation more widely). Fourth, change in sexual development occurs in a normative trajectory that leads to marriage and parenthood in spite of the previous and profound homosexual experience. This does not mean that marriage always excludes subsequent homoerotic activity, as we have seen in the instance of the Marind-anim and a few other Melanesian groups or, for that matter, the ancient Greeks (Hoffman 1984). The point is that heterosexual marriage and simultaneous homoerotic or bisexual relationships are not incompatible to these peoples. Therefore, they do not make an exclusive sex-object "choice" in the way defined as normative in Western culture. Fifth and last, the profound changes on these normative dimensions of sexuality defy an easy "scoring" of the kind that Kinsey made famous for Americans. This idea deserves a final comment.

How should we "rate" the Sambia in normative terms? As an exclusive "homosexual," or "6," in the Kinsey mode? No. Certainly not an exclusive "heterosexual," or "1." Perhaps we could score them somewhere in between. But to do so would require that we stipulate the exact variable at the exact developmental stage being measured: childhood, early or late adolescence, or adulthood. To do otherwise would be a serious disservice to them; it would inaccurately take account of the changes that come before or after, and it would tell us little about their sexual histories. Nor can we, in any simple way, describe the Sambia as exclusively homosexual, bisexual, or heterosexual in their overt behavior, because to do so would imply a sexual continuity that simply is not there.[15] This is what I believe the Kinsey scale implies: that people's prior behavior and experience are irrelevant to under-

15. I do not mean here merely the sense that a person has always felt "different" or has always been attracted (at some level of awareness) to the same sex (Troiden 1989). To fully meet the requirements of continuity in development, people would always have had to feel they were gay, have engaged in same-sex contact, and lived in a gay life-style as children, adolescents, and adults. I am not certain what this would entail for children or preadolescents. Although I can imagine that a few people have experienced this full inside-and-outside expression of developmentally being gay their whole lives, I know of no such examples described in the literature. There are many issues related to this problem, such as presumed biological precursors of homosexuality (Whitam

standing who they are—their whole sense of themselves and their world—today. Such an explanatory approach goes against the grain of the conception of human nature built into the Sambia developmental cycle and probably that of many other traditions too.

Conclusion

The cross-cultural archives of anthropology have often been used to demonstrate variation in sexuality across human groups. Today, this is still as valuable a general perspective in a volume of this kind as it was in 1961, when Margaret Mead (1961:1453) could state: "Sex role assignment may be far more complex in other cultures than in our own." All of us know that there is diversity in standards across cultures, yet it is easy to ignore this multiplicity in constituting representative models of *human* sexuality. The main contribution of this chapter has been to add another primary variable to such models—developmental continuity across cultures. Kinsey fleshed out his study from a skeleton based upon Western preconceptions about human nature and sexuality. Too much emphasis was placed upon assumed continuity in sexual behavior and experience. While this assumption is plausible in the biological realm, it tends to evade the psychological and symbolic reality of human development.

Kinsey's work produced the enormous benefit of opening up the study of sexuality and its potential for change in our societal discourse. He got us to think of sexual development as more a wardrobe of possibility and less a straitjacket of inevitability. Yet his conception of humans was too bound to a folk model arising from zoology: too much weight was placed on sex drive, sexual performance, sexual acts, and a single sex-object "choice." When is a sexual act a preference and when not? Only a developmental perspective that focuses upon the lives of whole persons in context can answer this question (see Cohler 1982; Gagnon 1971). Can we have more than one sexual preference? Is it possible to have multiple "sexual identities?" For Kinsey, Pomeroy, and Martin (1948), heterosexuality was a monolithic single and simple entity, unlike homosexuality, which was heterogeneous and complex. Nowadays we might more properly say that there are multiple heterosexualities and homosexualities, which are neither simple nor

---

1983) and how stigma structures parental and peer influences on adult sexual orientation (Bell, Weinberg, and Hammersmith 1981). We need to rethink the antecedents and consequences of bisexuality and homosexuality in the light of the kind of developmental social regimes outlined in this chapter.

"natural" but rather complicated developmental pathways to varied outcomes (Bell, Weinberg, and Hammersmith 1981; Bem 1996). These assumptions about human sexuality were built into the Kinsey scale and its interpretation, and we are only now beginning to unpack them.

Adding a developmental framework to our studies will go a long way in clarifying these preconceptions. There are at least three major and distinct types of sexual development regime across cultures: linear, disjunctive, and emergent. Each takes its own assumptions about human nature as "givens" or "constants" in the socialization of a young person's sexual behavior and related attributes of personhood. The development of gender identity is but one of these, though an important one (Stoller and Herdt 1982). In studying sexual organization around the world, it becomes apparent that these forms are not random; they cluster around types (Herdt 1997a). These cultural forms of homosexual (and bisexual) behavior are in turn correlated with many other psychosocial characteristics and institutions. Yet all of them, in varying degrees of occurrence, intensity, exclusion of other acts, and meaning, are associated with developmental discontinuity across the life cycle. That such peoples as the Sambia may not experience these changes as discontinuous is a significant and an as yet little-understood aspect of the argument; the degree to which they interpret the process as constant must be tested empirically, however. Whatever the final answer, the observer's point of view here—the behavioral/experiential discontinuity related to homosexual relationships—has far-reaching implications that beg for study at home and abroad.

One is reminded here of Benedict's (1938) insight that in systems of discontinuity people must "unlearn" things in order to "learn" the necessary elements of expected adult outcomes. Learning is, however, probably too rational and cognitive to refer to the process. For discontinuity involves many complexities of mind, especially the emotions and the subjectivities of desire, which sometimes are constructed by reaction to previous developmental sequences. The timing is important, perhaps critical, to the subsequent changes, as Freud and Mead and others have said, as is the severity of the early socialization regime.[16] Cultural and personal meaning, in short, is what is needed in pushing further the interpretation of sexual cultures and developmental subjectivities. When the whole person in cultural and developmental context is restored to the study of sexuality, we will have come a long way in the study of such sexual meaning systems.

---

16. "Divergence in the temporal sequence in which the components come together invariably produces a difference in the outcome" (Freud 1962:107).

EIGHT

Mistaken Sex: Culture, Biology, and the Third Sex in New Guinea

In the early 1970s, a time when issues of biological versus cultural origins of gender identity were emerging again in debates on sexuality, a group of American doctors published a study of a rare hermaphroditic disorder known as 5-alpha reductase deficiency syndrome. In brief, genetically normal males in the rural Dominican Republic were mistaken as females at birth and reared as completely "normal" girls. Then, at puberty, they were said suddenly to change gender roles—to act and identify as men. Julliane Imperato-McGinley and her colleagues (1974, 1979) claimed not only that these individuals switched their identities and desires but also that they did so without social or psychological influence from others. Furthermore, they viewed the change in gender identity as a primary effect of prenatal hormones that had "masculinized" brains, motivating the affected individuals to revert spontaneously to their "natural" sex. The doctors concluded: "In a laissez-faire environment, when the sex of rearing is contrary to the testosterone-mediated biological sex, the biological sex prevails if the normal testosterone-induced activation of puberty is permitted to occur. Thus, it appears that the extent of androgen (i.e., testosterone) exposure of the brain *in utero,* during the early postnatal period and at puberty has more effect in determining male gender identity than does sex of rearing. This experiment of nature emphasizes the importance of androgens, which act as activators, in the evolution of male gender identity" (Imperato-McGinley et al. 1979:1235–36).

Although supporters and critics of the Dominican Republic work have argued over many aspects of the study, the question of whether a third-sex   *243* category might exist in the local culture, and how this would change the explanation of these weighty issues, has been all but ignored. A study of 5-alpha reductase deficiency hermaphroditism among the Sambia (Herdt and Davidson 1988) opens an entirely different interpretation of "mistaken sex."

Among the Sambia, a group of hermaphrodites similar to those in the Dominican Republic has been described in anthropological and clinical detail (beginning with Herdt 1981). My initial work with the Sambia suggested that the construction of a third sex—the *kwolu-aatmwol*—was inevitable in their culture. Gradually, I have come to accept that the Sambia, at least, have created a historically divergent third-sex category, which is regarded as neither male nor female, based on the genitals and other characteristics necessary to differentiate among the three sexes (Herdt and Stoller 1990). However, continuing fieldwork, as well as intensive clinical interviews and detailed study of one *kwolu-aatmwol*, Sakulambei, a shaman, has led me to think that, while the Sambia recognize three sexes and at birth assign some infants to the hermaphrodite category, their worldview nevertheless systematically codes only two genders, masculine and feminine (see Herdt 1987a; Herdt and Davidson 1988; Herdt and Stoller 1990). Hence, the inherent tension or even dialectical relationship between their three-sex and two-gender systems poses a continuing problematic in their own cultural history and representation of the hermaphrodite.

Contrary to the medical doctors' view of the Dominican Republic hermaphrodites, however, the Sambia study suggests that an indigenous third-sex category has been present all along but was typically ignored by Western agents. Together with traditional pressures to conform to hierarchical gendered roles, these social facts are critical in explaining why individuals reared as biological females in both cultures might opt to "change" roles following puberty. Nevertheless, the change is not from a female to a male role, and certainly not to a male identity; the change is from female to a third sex. Also ignored in the Dominican Republic study are the difficulties faced by hermaphrodites reared in the direction of masculinity. These matters will be examined among the Sambia. Finally, the review of these studies provides new perspectives for understanding why the biologically reductionist interpretation of this hermaphroditism has been so intriguing to Western science for so very long.

Anthropology and the Third Sex

The classification and meaning of hermaphroditism is a particularly challenging topic to the anthropology of sexual cultures. In the representation
of the hermaphrodite, the order of culture seemingly clashes with the order
of nature. Indeed, as Michel Foucault once noted, "For a long time hermaphrodites were criminals, or crime's offspring, since their anatomical
disposition, their very being, confounded the law that distinguished the
sexes and prescribed their union" (1980:38). Many anthropologists believe
that much of gender is "constructed," to use the prevailing textual metaphor, a paradigm that finds its foundations in the classics of Ruth Benedict,
Bronislaw Malinowski, and Margaret Mead, among others. However, does
the metaphor extend far enough to accept the ontology of alternative three
sex/gender classifications?

Much sex and gender research in sexology and later in anthropology assumes that sexual dimorphism is the innate and essential foundation of sex
assignment and the modeling of gender-identity development across
cultures. Not only is this "order of nature" thought to be an ontological
preconception in natural species, but it is readily extended to gender antecedents of human nature across societies (Geertz 1983). Sexual dimorphism is certainly prominent in Western biological and evolutionary
thinking since Darwin, and it continues in recent work (Darwin 1871; Hall
1982; reviewed in Herdt 1994).

Perhaps sexual dimorphism seems so natural that our culture and, therefore, Western science have scarcely considered the absolutism that this
piece of common sense exercises over sex research. Feminist and Marxist
critiques have considered parallel problems in biologically reductionist interpretations of women's roles and the reproduction of motherhood (Balbus 1982; Chodorow 1978; Rosaldo and Lamphere 1974; Sanday 1981).
Generally, however, reductionism continues in studies of males, where
there appears to be a compelling match between the cultural expectations
ascribed to males and the biological fact of their maleness (reviewed in
Herdt 1981; Weeks 1985). Interpretations of hermaphroditism have likewise
tended to obey a presumed natural law of dimorphism, encoded in cultural
reasoning, that assigns all things sexual to biological types, male and female.
Even Robert Edgerton, whose sensitive study on the Kopot of East Africa
provided a critical reading of hermaphroditism, recapitulates the Western
essentialism of sexual dimorphism: "It is probably a universal assumption
that the world consists of only two biological sexes and that this is the natural and necessary way of things" (1985:77–78; see also Edgerton 1964).

Why does the Western model of sex and gender remain so heavily indebted to an assumed sexual dimorphism in human nature and development? During the past century, as sexologists and later anthropologists and social historians encountered numerous instances of fuzzy sex and gender categories of individuals who seemed to be neither clearly male nor female, feminine nor masculine, the strong central tendency has been to reduce the variations to the binary male/female. This is because, in brief, these fields emphasize reproduction rather than cultural roles or personal desires as the focus of sexuality and gender (see Herdt 1994; Weeks 1985; Vance 1991).

In explaining why persons have seemingly failed to conform to the two-sex system of male or female roles, two interpretations have typically been advanced. First, these individuals were interpreted as biologically aberrant, usually in genetic or hormonal development. I call this the deficit model of human development; it has been popular in explaining, for instance, the existence of the two-spirit (formerly "berdache") role among Native North American Indians for decades (in the functional accounts of A. L. Kroeber and George Devereux, among others: see chapter 9). A second interpretation, in the social constructionist model, searched for social and historical factors that might explain the construction of an alternate identity or role but without challenging the underlying two-sex model of Western culture and science (Whitehead 1981). In fact, these explanations do not neatly fall into these two categories, nor are they mutually exclusive (Herdt 1994).

But the relationship between cultural categories of sex and gender-identity development remains problematic in two areas. First, does a society have a two-sex or three-sex (or more) code for sex assignment at birth? The simple answer is that a variety of sexual cultures have been demonstrated to have an alternative three-sex or gender system (Herdt 1994). Those who argue for the biological primacy of sex assignment in the determination of gender identity are puzzled by ambiguous sex assignment, leading to the strong probability of hermaphroditic gender identity (Stoller 1968). Second, does a society implement a two- or three-gender code developmentally in the gender-role socialization of individuals across the course of life? The accumulating evidence suggests in general that societies do implement these developmental regimes, at least in the most visible cases (Nanda 1994). And does this coding apply as well to exceptional persons, such as hermaphrodites? The answer to that question remains unclear, but new evidence is coming in (Jacobs et al. 1997). Abundant cross-cultural evidence does demonstrate, however, the existence of third gender categories in other cultures and the inclusion of both normative and aberrant individuals in these categories, though we cannot be sure that they are socialized normatively (Herdt 1997a; Williams 1986).

A key problem concerns the ideological significance that a two-sex system such as ours places on sex assignment in childhood. As Margaret Mead once warned, "Sex assignment may be far more complex in other cultures than our own," largely because in subsequent "sex role assignments" there are stages at which gender status can change in the process of socialization during life. (Mead [1961] listed eleven forms of these across cultures.) Gender-identity theorists have emphasized the difficulty of postnatal gender change, and recent critiques have challenged the primacy of early influences. (On postnatal gender change, see Money and Ehrhardt [1972]; for a critique, see Kohlberg, Ricks, and Savarey [1984].) But none have considered the profound point that Mead has made in her suggestion about the readiness of other cultures to change sex and gender status.

In a remarkable essay, Clifford Geertz (1983: chapter 10) once argued that the Western dimorphic model is neither universally shared nor scientifically reliable when it comes to understanding hermaphroditism across cultures. His conceptual position straddled the line between Benjamin Lee Whorf and Ludwig Wittgenstein and viewed gender categories as reflecting neither individual experience nor collective representations. Rather, he saw gendered categories as the workings of a cultural system of meanings and perceptions laid upon and filtering "commonsense" formulations. Some peoples hold rather unhappy attitudes toward hermaphroditism, Geertz adduced, citing Edgerton's Pokot of East Africa, the ancient Romans, and, more extreme, contemporary America, whose natives express feelings of horror and nausea about hermaphroditism. Others, however, such as the Navajo of Native North America, hold a positive view of hermaphroditism, W. W. Hill tells us. Because of their curative powers, the Navajo berdache, or *nadle,* were "movers and shakers" who brought magical blessings to the community. The Navajo compared them to the American president Franklin D. Roosevelt. Thus, it seems that hermaphrodites were even "afforded a favoritism not shown to the other children in a family" (Hill 1935:274). The Navajo categorize transvestites and hermaphrodites together as *nadle,* although Hill remarks that their hermaphrodites dressed and acted as women: an outcome suggested by a meaning of *nadle* as "being transformed" (1935:275). How very different from Edgerton's Pokot, who, like Americans, look down on the hermaphrodite, although not with disgust. Rather, they see them as simple errors of God, like a botched clay pot, pathetic and useless.

The Greeks' mythic and ritual regard for the hermaphrodite was noteworthy, too, in part because of the divine precedent of the god Hermaphroditus (Hoffman 1984; Money 1961). Also famous in myth was Tiresias, the soothsayer, "who was born a boy, changed into a woman, and then back into a man" (Bullough 1976:113). These instances are especially remarkable because the Greeks, like the later Romans, usually destroyed hermaphrodites and other abnormal infants at birth. The Greeks apparently circumvented this taboo by "mistakenly" assigning a hermaphrodite to the female sex, a situation not unlike 5-alpha reductase hermaphroditism.

These cultural variations in sex-assignment codes and socialization attitudes suggest an alternative approach to mistaken gender. While anatomical or morphological sex is generally easy to classify, at least in a two-sex system, gender tasks and meanings are not. Category membership is harder to advance for gender; sex is a clearer and gender is a fuzzier set (Gelman, Collman, and Maccoby 1986). Cultures such as our own—which overlay sexual dimorphism in nature onto gender-identity development in humans—tend to be reductive and morally restrictive regarding conceptions of personhood and sexual conduct. Perhaps, then, the more gender is defined by the binary classification, the more disgusting and stigmatized gender anomalies will seem. On the other hand, cultures with three-sex systems tend not to advance such an inexorable and seamless fit between gender identity and sexual classification. Thus, they will tend to be less restrictive in socialization and more accepting of sexual variations, making androgyny a significant motif in cultural representations, even in the sacred (Herdt 1997a). Their permissiveness might be characterized, to use Freud's famous phrase, as "polymorphous perverse" (Freud 1962).

Underlying these two ideal types of sex and gender coding are alternative ontologies of sexual being (see chapter 9). Each ideal type is pragmatically associated with different commonsense beliefs and empirical attributions about maleness, femaleness, and hermaphroditeness in everyday discourse. Dimorphic cultures, such as that of the Euro-American tradition, define persons primarily by biological or deeper psychological essence, which is thought to be invariant through life. Polymorphous cultures such as those of the Sambia of Papua New Guinea, by contrast, define persons as more fluid and as relatively male or female, according to social and developmental characteristics such as life-span stage, socioeconomic status, and body ritual.

The Dominican Republic Case

The Dominican Republic syndrome (steroid 5-alpha reductase deficiency) is extremely rare; it occurs as a hormonal defect but only in males who seem otherwise biologically normal and is inherited as an autosomal recessive trait (Money and Ehrhardt 1972; Imperato-McGinley et al. 1974; Rubin, Reinisch, and Haskett 1981; Stoller 1975). The hormonal defect in these male pseudohermaphrodites is caused by a genetic deficiency in the enzyme 4 steroid 5-alpha reductase, which impairs the metabolism of testosterone to dihydrotestosterone (DHT). Since DHT is the prenatal mediator of the masculinization of external genitalia, such persons are at birth sexually ambiguous, with a marked bifid scrotum that appears labia-like, an absent or clitoris-like penis, undescended testes and associated hermaphroditic traits. Some of these persons are recognized and assigned as males at birth, but in other cases the ambiguous characteristics cause the individual to be categorized as female in sex, with subsequent socialization as females (Imperato-McGinley et al. 1974). This "natural experiment" in mistaken sex assignment would be theoretically uninteresting for gender research were it not that subsequent virilization occurs in these persons at puberty (Imperato-McGinley et al. 1979).

Because they are genetically normal males, with presumed prenatal exposure of the brain and central nervous system to testosterone, all 5-alpha reductase hermaphrodites begin to virilize again at puberty through the peripheral timing effects of their own plasma testosterone. Hence, the voice deepens, muscles develop, the penis grows somewhat and testes descend. Erections occur; sexual intromission is possible but without insemination, because of abnormal urethral position. The Dominican Republic research established that thirty-eight hermaphrodites were known from twenty-three extended families spanning four generations in three rural villages. The local condition is known as *Guevedoche* ("penis at twelve"). Of these subjects, nineteen were supposedly reared "unambiguously" as girls; eighteen of these nineteen were studied. "Of the eighteen subjects, seventeen had successfully changed to a male-gender identity and sixteen to a male gender role" (Imperato-McGinley et al. 1979:1234). The medical project argued that these persons changed their gender and sexual identity, through stages of "no longer feeling like girls, to feeling like men, and finally to the conscious awareness that they were indeed men" (1979:1234). The change in sex role occurred at around age sixteen, about the time that adult social status in the community was at issue. Postpubertal heterosexual maleness was indicated by some sexual interest in women, with intercourse (not in all the people) at ages ranging from fifteen to seventeen. Fifteen of sixteen living subjects have since had common-law marriages with women, though we do not know very much about their sexual histories or current sexual behavior. As "men," these former "women" took social roles as farmers and woodsmen, their wives being housewives and gardeners, which are locally normative socioeconomic routines. The medical team therefore concluded: "In a laissez-faire environment, when the sex of rearing is contrary to the testosterone-mediated biologic sex," the biological sex will prevail and "override" the social environment's gender socialization (1979:1234–35).

The Dominican Republic hermaphrodites posed a major challenge to the breakthrough theory of Money, Hampson, and Hampson (1956), which later became canonic. They argued that gender-identity development is determined by sex assignment and rearing, not by the gonads, a conclusion that Albert Ellis (1945) had exhaustively presaged in the literature on hermaphroditism. In cases of ambiguous sexual genitalia, they added a new criterion for standard clinical practice: sex assignment up to age two and a half is the best predictor of nonpathological gender development (Money and Ehrhardt 1972). Gender-identity change by clinical sex reassignment after this age is extremely risky for subsequent positive mental health (Stoller 1975). Microscopic prenatal sex hormonal research since that time has not changed the picture (Ehrhardt and Meyer-Bahlburg 1981; Ehrhardt 1985; Grumbach and Conte 1985). These theorists had always claimed, in short, that the social environment was the key to the development of positive gender-identity development. All things being equal, the classification of sex and subsequent social learning will overcome the intrinsic biological sex.

In retrospect the contested view that prenatal hormones caused identity development had wide-ranging effects on research and clinical treatment. The Dominican Republic study has been vigorously criticized by Money (1976), Meyer-Bahlburg (1982), and Ehrhardt (1985:382), who chided the work because "clinicians have become insecure and now seriously suggest assigning males with 5-alpha reductase deficiency to the male sex, despite the fact that they will grow up severely diminished and with ambiguous genitalia" (see also Grumbach and Conte 1985).

It is easy to prick holes in the study, as some critics have done. The ethnography is absent and interview data are sketchy; neither the interview schedule nor the exact psychosexual assessment procedures have ever been published (Money 1976; Sagarin 1975). Rubin, Reinisch, and Haskett (1981) have deconstructed the sample size on female-to-male sex-role change: of the eighteen subjects, two were dead, one continued to maintain an adult female identity and was married, another dressed as a female but reportedly considered himself male, while another lived alone as a "hermit" in the hills (1981:1322). Thus, thirteen rather than the nineteen subjects were actually observed to make a clear-cut sex-role change (Ehrhardt 1985; Ehrhardt and Meyer-Bahlburg 1981; Rubin, Reinisch, and Hasket

1981). These critiques raise two basic questions: Are Dominican Republic pseudohermaphrodites sex assigned and reared unambiguously as females? And is their postpubertal gender identity clearly male, so that "they consider themselves as males and have a libido directed toward the opposite sex," as claimed (Imperato-McGinley et al. 1974:1215)?

A review of the Dominican Republic study suggests that the American medical doctors never provided adequate evidence for their strong developmental claims, before or after puberty, either behaviorally or mentally. We are told that villagers are aware of the existence of the hermaphroditic condition in local villages, even though the ontology of the *Guevedoche* is never described. We are also told that the prepubertal subjects "showed self-concern over their true gender"; between the ages of seven and twelve, anatomical abnormality made them aware that they were "different" (Imperato-McGinley et al. 1979:1234). Public bathing and crowded living conditions may expose their childhood genital oddity, which seems critical to their gender socialization (Sagarin 1975). Indeed, the *Guevedoche* feel "insecurities because of their genitalia. They view themselves as incomplete persons . . . [which] saddens them. They fear ridicule by members of the opposite sex and initially feel anxious about forming sexual relations" (Imperato-McGinley et al. 1979:1234). We must also wonder at the circumstances of the two *Guevedoche* who did not convert to the male role. Finally, the fact that the sex-role change occurred as late as between ages fourteen and twenty-four, with a mean age of sixteen, seems inconsistent with the main effect, that is, the hormonally driven theory of gender identity development (Meyer-Bahlburg 1982:686). If the internal biology is so strong, then why does it take so long to kick in?

A critical reinterpretation of this study requires two new "insider" understandings of how the *Guevedoche* cultural system works. First, the sexual culture of the Dominican Republic villages seems to code not two but three sexes. It is striking that neither the medical researchers nor their critics have noticed this simple yet profound social fact (Sagarin 1975). In the 1979 report it is noted, "The phallus enlarges to become a functional penis, and the change is so striking that these individuals are referred to by the townspeople as *Guevedoches*—penis at 12" (Imperato-McGinley et al. 1979: 1213). The anatomical differences are explicit in the local culture since the hermaphrodites are ridiculed as *Guevedoche* or *machihembra* ("first woman, then man") (1979:1235). This registers a cultural difference in the local system of commonsense sexual categories used in sex assigning and socializing *Guevedoche*. The villagers have more than a simple word for hermaphrodite; they have a triadic sexual code for classification. That the village ontology includes a third-sex category—neither male nor female, but *Guevedoche*—challenges the biological reductionism. The second understanding involves rethinking the cultural topography of the Dominican Republic. The researchers argued that the Dominican Republic works in a laissez-faire fashion with regard to gender-identity development, implying the absence of social pressure exerted on *Guevedoche* to change into a man.

Here we are stymied by the lacuna of ethnographic information on the *Guevedoche* category. Yet existence of the *Guevedoche* suggests that over generations, these villagers have historically responded to the presence of these persons through the construction of gender-related norms, rules, and attitudes that served to mediate the normative male-female dichotomy widely occurring throughout the Dominican Republic. We cannot know whether the third-gender category was adopted elsewhere. In the absence of such local knowledge, we must rely on the distal ethnographic corpus to interpret the cultural meanings of the male-female dichotomy locally (Bramfeld 1959:108; Brown 1975:323–25; Leyburn 1966:197; Weil et al. 1973:65–76).

Caribbean images of gender inequality hardly constitute the neutrality evoked by the assertion of a "laissez-faire" environment. Indeed, for the Dominican Republic as well as the broader region we are faced with a marked power system of unequal gender roles. (On Puerto Rico, see Brameld 1959:108; on Jamaica, see Floyd 1979:66; on Black Carobs, see Kerns 1983:89–103; on Haiti, see Leyburn 1966:197ff.) The fact is, anatomically ambiguous and stigmatized hermaphrodites have much to gain— and little to lose—by "switching" sex roles. Dominican men are better off than women, for they are regarded as socially superior and politically more potent, and they have wives as domestic workers, are preferred at birth, and are able to achieve higher political and economic status than women. To summarize from a recent Dominican Republic ethnography: "*Machismo* also helps explain why power is in the hands of males" (Wiarda and Kryzanek 1982:19). In cases of an unbalanced sex ratio of children in a family, children may be "adopted" as inexpensive servants, which raises the question of the desired economic contribution of the *Guevedoche* to families in rural Dominican Republic. That *Guevedoche*—either primarily female or male hermaphrodites in sex socialization—should aspire toward the ideal of *machismo* is understandable.

Contrary to the biomedical explanation, then, my hunch is that the Dominican *Guevedoche* is not primarily motivated by the subjective postpubertal developmental experience of feeling like "being a male." The developmental subjectivity may be far more ambiguous than that, more hermaphroditic. Instead, the transformation may be experienced as a shift from having grown up as female—possibly ambiguously reared—to being a male-aspiring member of a third sex, who is, in certain social scenes, categorized with adult males. To be successful, however, the *Guevedoche* must learn to pass as a man, and engage in the social performances necessary to avoid spoiling this impression and being stigmatized (Goffman 1963). This is a very different view from that of Imperato-McGinley et al., who suggest that, as the result of (testosterone-induced) "serious self-concern" over their sex, *Guevedoche* began to "feel like men" (1981:101; see also Green 1987:44). We are told almost nothing about the proximal social circumstances of this "feeling," which seems decontextualized. What are its signs, how continuous is it in development, and can it be put into action through the necessary gender performances? Nonetheless, we do know that the sexual culture category system of three sexes was always present in their development. The *Guevedoche* are not so confused as to forget that by sex assignment they were not male: that is why villagers call them *Guevedoche!*

Two important missing links in the Dominican Republic study are related to this symbolic interpretation. The first has to do with the absence of detailed clinical ethnography on the subjective identity states of those *Guevedoche* reared in the male direction, a point to which I will return. The second missing link concerns the outcomes of those two female-assigned *Guevedoche* who did not switch roles. Imperato-McGinley et al. (1981) provide anecdotal notes to fill this gap, and while their report is not ethnographically satisfying, it casts further doubt on their own biological interpretation. Subjects 4 and 25 in the study did not make the switch to the male role. In particular, subject 4 "adopted a male gender identity" (the measure or index of this is not reported) but "continues to dress as a female" (1981:100). This person has not had sex with women, denies sexual attraction to women, has worn false breasts for years, and desires a sex change to become a "normal woman." Had they been reported ethnographically, the circumstances of gender resocialization of these female *Guevedoche* could illuminate their mistaken gender and subsequent sex-role change. Suppose, for instance, that a person's sex assignment was unequivocally female, providing a stronger biological bias to femaleness or that any hint of ambiguity in sexual development was hidden from others (Diamond 1979). Or suppose that her temperament was somehow better matched to the female identity or role than that of the others (Green 1987; Money 1987). The possibilities are developmentally complex but not infinite.

Interventions by the medical research team in the Dominican Republic villages seem to have been dramatic—and may have shifted the tide. Various clinical specimens (blood and urine) were taken following physical examinations and a variety of interviews. The related psychosocial intrusions are hinted at in a statement on "materials and methods," although the full impact cannot be gleaned from the relevant reports (Imperato-McGinley et al. 1979:1234). We may have in these reports an example of "hospital culture" exported to the field and then withdrawn to the clinic, where the "clinical gaze" of sex surgery would further confound their interpretation and decontextualize gender identity and role even more (Klaus and Kennel 1976; Foucault 1973). Thus may sex research directly alter the social field in which it takes place (Gagnon 1975).

Did a two-sex Western folk model unwittingly color the Dominican Republic hermaphroditic study? From a letter in *Science* we learn that "the younger pseudohermaphrodites of the last generation are being raised as boys, and the townspeople therefore now recognize the condition" (Imperato-McGinley et al. 1976:872). If these researchers were ethnographically insensitive to the distinctions between two-sex and three-sex cultural codes and between normative males and *Guevedoche,* they may have inadvertently interpreted or even cued cultural responses so that formerly naive actors came to label *Guevedoche* as male or female, denying their own third-sex schema. This suggests that, all along, the presence of a third-sex category and role was ignored by the medical doctors, creating an erroneous view of why the hermaphrodites supposedly shifted from the female to the male sex after puberty.

The Sambia Case

The island of New Guinea and its off-lying coastal societies is home to the most ethnically diverse social field in the world. Sexual and gendered roles and practices have long been known to be extremely varied along systematic lines in economy, society, and culture (Brown 1978; Herdt 1993; Lindenbaum 1984). Nonetheless, sexual dimorphism seems historically strongly marked in these societies; further, three-sex or three-gender variations in Melanesia are rare and controversial. Only recently has hermaphroditism been studied. D. Carleton Gajdusek (1977) first suggested that hermaphrodites reported from scattered parts of Melanesia might manifest 5-alpha reductase deficiency similar to that of the Dominican Republic study. His guess has proven correct. Anthropological reports of hermaphroditism from New Guinea, such as those among the Hua (Meigs 1984) and the Bimin-Kuskusmin (identified by Poole [1985:229]), are probable cases of 5-alpha reductase deficiency. The presence of a third-sex category among the Bimin-Kuskusmin is particularly interesting in view of the marked androgyny motifs of their origin myths (Poole 1981). We may tentatively conclude that, in certain Melanesian cultures, the existence of a third sex, on the basis of the criteria of folk biology and anatomy, seems definite, whereas the existence of third-gender categories and roles is doubtful.

The Sambia institutionalize a strident form of gender dimorphism in their beliefs and practices regarding nature and culture, and yet they also recognize in both human and nonhuman species the existence of a third sex. They do not, however, seem to offer any recognition of a third gender role or practices. Anthropological fieldwork beginning in 1974 made me dimly aware of a few slightly unusual persons, whom I at first misinterpreted as transvestites, only later to realize that, when Sambia referred to them as *turnim-man,* they meant some form of biological and anatomical transformation. In short, these persons, classified in local culture as *kwolu-aatmwol* ("changing into a male thing"), are what in the Western tradition would be called biological hermaphrodites or interssexed persons (reviewed in Herdt and Davidson 1988). I have studied one of them in depth, a male pseudohermaphrodite named Sakulambei, over a ten-year period, originally because of his role as a powerful shaman and later because of his hermaphroditic gender identity (Herdt 1987a:63–64; Herdt and Stoller 1985). Sakulambei sensed himself as a third sex, albeit more in the direction of being a male, and his mildly incestuous marriage and adopted child, while creating the performance of heteronormativity, still reinforced his classification as being a *kwolu-aatmowul* in local discourse.

One aspect of Sambia beliefs and cosmology regarding the male body is critical to understanding their view of hermaphroditism. Although semen is believed to be the spark of human life and, moreover, the sole precipitant of biological maleness (strong bones and muscles and, later, male secondary sex traits), as we have seen, the Sambia hold that the human body cannot naturally produce semen. Thus it must be artificially and externally introduced (like an androgen). Hermaphrodites mistakenly assigned to the female sex are therefore deprived of semen and can never properly masculinize, even to the extent of the *kwolu-aatmwol,* who are reared in the direction of masculinity. Biological maleness is distinct from the mere possession of male genitalia, and only repeated inseminations of the boy are thought to confer in him the reproductive competence that culminates in manliness and fatherhood. This helps to explain why the *kwolu-aatmwol*—who are reared in the context of male initiation—seem to be more enthusiastic fellators than other boys. Moreover, because they are typically unmarried and show the signs of puberty later than do others, hermaphrodites such as Sakulambei continue the semen-ingesting role for a longer time than others (Herdt and Stoller 1990). In some obscure way, this may also influence the perception of their gendered relations.

Now, to summarize the ethnography of Sambia hermaphroditism: Sambia have three sexual categories, male, female, and *kwolu-aatmwol,* a word that suggests a person's "transforming into a male thing." In popular discourse, however, Sambia use another term—*turnim-man*—from neo-Melanesian Pidgin, which refers to "turning into a man." Parents and midwives know that the condition, as a historical/symbolic category in their society, causes anatomical ambiguity at birth and dramatic masculinization at puberty (Herdt 1981). Hermaphroditic infants are sex assigned as *kwolu-aatmwol* and not as male. Those assigned as female are mistakenly reared as normal females. Yet because the phenomenon has existed for generations and the midwives and mothers go to some lengths to examine the infant's body for signs of the *kwolu-aatmwol,* it is unlikely that a mistake sex assignment will occur, and only a few instances of such a mistaken assignment, as reported below, are historically known.

In their worldview, the Sambia regard hermaphroditism as a sad and mysterious quirk of nature. They see the signs of a third sex in species such as the pandanus tree and cassowary (Herdt 1981). But in human beings, it has a more unfortunate connotation. The *kwolu-aatmwol,* unless distinguished as a shaman or war leader, is quietly disparaged. When discovered at birth, the child is reared in the direction of masculinity, but not unambiguously; rather, it is referred to as either *kwolu-aatmwol* or male, because parents know that their infant will not change into a female. Sometimes the *kwolu-aatmwol* is teased as a child and humiliated by peers for having "no penis." Nevertheless, several of these people assigned to the third-sex *kwolu-aatmwol* category are well known in local history. One of them, now deceased, was famous both as a shaman and a fight leader. The *kwolu-aatmwol* is not therefore rejected or frozen out of daily and normative social contacts and may indeed rise to distinction through special achievements, as Sakulambei has done. Nor do Sambia feel disgust toward these liminal beings. Still, theirs is a sexually polarized society, and parents do not want infants to be hermaphroditic: the men believe that interssexed infants are sometimes killed at birth by women (Herdt 1981). If it passes as female, however, it is sure to survive. Consequently, at birth, women check the infant's sex carefully to ensure that it is not *kwolu-aatmwol.*

In 1983 I was visited in the field by Julian Davidson, an endocrinologist from Stanford University, who analyzed blood samples from the Sambia pseudohermaphrodites, confirming our hunch that 5-alpha reductase deficiency syndrome was present (see Herdt and Davidson [1988] for review). I have since identified fourteen male pseudohermaphrodites over three generations since 1910; they derive from eight villages having a total historical population of about 1,700. Of these fourteen subjects, six are living, and five have been studied in some depth. Five of the total were reared as females. Nine of the fourteen *kwolu-aatmwol* were reared as males. Two of them are still alive. One late adolescent continues to live as a female, although she is unmarried, physically larger than a normal female and now known to be a *kwolu-aatmwol.*

The other one is an older adult who was reportedly reared ambiguously as a female. Signs of anatomical peculiarity in this individual after puberty, such as the lack of breast development, were obvious to villagers but were ignored. However, she was married in a normative marriage arrangement at nineteen to a man who then discovered that she had a small penis. The outraged and shamed husband wanted to kill her, but their relatives intervened. After this traumatic incident, the mistaken female began wearing male clothes and, taking a male name, moved far away. Today this individual passes as a male in a distant Highland town. He is unmarried, and while he dates women, he seems uninterested erotically in them and has not married. In three other historical cases the same social outcome occurred: the switch from one sexual category to another took place only after the social exposure resulting form marriage and humiliation (Herdt 1981). In these instances, however, the psychosexual change was not from female to male; it was from putatively female to *kwolu-aatmwol,* sometimes opportunistically categorized with other men for symbolic purposes strategically useful to the men and / or the hermaphrodite.

In certain regards one could argue that the adolescent *kwolu-aatmwol* constitutes a third-sex category for Sambia. However, it can be noted that Sambia only very rarely initiate *kwolu-aatmwol* into third-stage *impangwi* status. Typically, they remain second-stage *imbutnuku.* One definite case, that of Sakulambei, is known in which initiation from second to third stage did occur (Herdt and Stoller 1985). The circumstances of this initiation suggest that Sambia seem to recognize the importance of biological puberty as an antecedent condition of attaining social puberty. They deny social puberty to aberrant biological males because of their apparent "failure" to achieve physical maturation. One might have thought the force of consistency would influence the men's decision making, leading to a lumping together of the *kwolu-aatmwol* with biologically normal males. But a remarkable feature of the Sambia response to the developmental course of male-identified *kwolu-aatmwol* is that no further initiations, including the collective third-stage *ipmangwi* ceremony, are held for them (Herdt 1981). Because by canonical male theory all males are fully initiated into the six stages of the men's secret society, this omission seems to violate the men's own idea of the same ritual treatment applied to all "men." Indeed, the Sambia are so ideologically consistent regarding the uniformity of male ritual development that for some time I ignored asking about the subsequent initiations of the hermaphrodites.

Thus, I had observed Sakulambei initiated into the third stage in the 1970s, so my view was influenced by the apparent normative character of this event. Only later did I realize that the men, Sakulambei's father and clan brothers included, had excluded him from initiation with his own cohort in 1968. Subsequent work revealed that he had entrepreneurially engineered his own 1975 initiation in another phratry through a powerful relative's influence, an old male shaman invested in Sakulambei's career (Herdt and Stoller 1985). Later interviews and ethnohistorical work showed that all other male-assigned hermaphrodites had likewise been bypassed for "pubertal" initiation. Moreover, all cases of female-to-male sex changing occurred without subsequent initiation into the men's society, an extraordinary outcome that again challenges the internal consistency of the view that "all men are initiated," but one that the Sambia ignore.

Here, Sambia are not satisfied with being a "social" male or being socially classified as initiated and masculine: they demand that the individual be anatomically complete and able to procreate. Sakulambei's history thus supports the interpretation of a three-sex code in subsequent socialization. Biological changes in the male body anticipate the subsequent social events of third-stage puberty rites. For the person sex assigned as *kwolu-aatmwol,* ritual initiation is not enough to "activate" complete masculinization (Herdt 1981). Likewise, Sambia are being good classifiers and social constructionists in refusing to late-initiate a hermaphrodite reared as a woman. The late-adolescent transformation of the mistakenly female-assigned *kwolu-aatmwol* comes long after this person's male age-set cohort has passed into advanced normative role-status positions. Sambia believe that it is too late to change the sexuality, gender status, and social performances and memories in both types of late bloomers.

That the socialization of individuals such as Sakulambei is ambiguous can be seen both from their social behavior and from their internal identity state. They show less aggressive and assertive action and more nurturing and deferential behavior than normative males. If parents feel ashamed of or reject the child, the mental health outcome is poorer (Herdt and Davidson 1988). The *kwolu-aatmwol's* odd-looking genitals (small or abnormally

shaped phallus and possible undescended testicles) make them fearful of revealing themselves. Thus, they avoid any situation in which they must serve
as an inseminator in adolescence and they remain sexually timid as adults
(Herdt and Stoller 1985). Because Sakulambei, for instance, was not properly initiated at puberty and could prolong his practice of the homoerotic
recipient role in normative male ritual development, his history of sexual
behavior is more aberrant. There were other ambiguous features in Sakulambei's ritual development: for instance, contrary to all other male Sambia, Sakulambei has never nosebled or felt the need to let "female" blood
from his body. He feels it is a part of his core identity. It is no surprise, then,
that the *kwolu-aatmwol's* gender-identity state is neither clearly male nor
female: they have a hermaphroditic psychosexual identity that is distinctly
different, and their phenomenology reveals them to feel unique or alone in
the world (Herdt and Stoller 1990).

New Guinea systems would seem to manifest the strongest sexual dimorphism in their conceptions of the natural world and human nature. In
fact, however, we find discordance between the order of nature and the order of culture. Perceptions of androgyny in species such as cassowary and
the pandanus tree are coded into symbolic systems (Gardner 1984; Herdt
1981) In other New Guinea contexts the husbandry of hermaphroditic pigs
is popular and symbolically potent (Barker 1928). Hermaphroditism is encoded also in the primal ancestors of certain peoples (Poole 1981, 1985).

Among the Sambia, too, such a myth exists, and its hermaphroditic
theme speaks of both what to be and not to be in male development. Its revelation comes to initiates at the completion of their final initiation into full
manhood (Herdt 1981: chapter 8). The myth tells of two persons, with small
breasts and tiny penes, who began the world. The story causes concern
among some men in the audience about whether males, females, or hermaphrodites are sexually dominant. Their anxieties are played down, however, since the hermaphrodites are absent: *kwolu-aatmwol* never hear this
story, because they are not normally initiated beyond the second stage at
puberty. The myth of parthenogenesis does, therefore, "charter" Sambian
hermaphroditism in a sacred sense, but its secrecy does not repair the psychological feelings of hermaphrodites. Nor does its existence preclude
some derision of the third sex as a lower form in the order of nature. Here,
then, the Sambia attitude toward the *kwolu-aatmwol* is ambivalent: its existence is sufficiently independent as an ontological and cultural category
that, for Sambia men, and perhaps women, too, the hermaphrodite is
sometimes a useful blessing, as the Navajo seem to feel, but a mixed one, because they fear their children's being hermaphrodite. The *kwolu-aatmwol*

category thus functions largely as a major, albeit pejorative, category in Sambia culture (see also Levy's [1973] study of the Tahitian *mahu* third-gender role in the maintenance of normative Tahitian male identity).

Like other New Guinea societies, the Sambia is a gender-preoccupied culture. Males have the upper hand in public affairs, their gender hierarchy supported by the men's ritual cult. In such a world, a rational choice would favor one's being born male, in spite of its ritual contradictions and real-life dangers. Would we not, therefore, expect the hermaphrodite, belatedly discovered to be mistakenly female, opportunistically to change to "male"? And yet, this bit of common sense does not match the facts. In the four historical cases of change in sex roles, the female-defined *kwolu-aatmwol* did not convert to a different role *until* after exposure and failure as females. One of them still lives as female. In other words, social catastrophe forced them either to change or to face an unbearable and ambiguous future as no longer clearly female but not yet male-associated pseudohermaphrodites.

It is hard to see in this forced outcome, nearly twenty years after birth, strong evidence for a hypothetical effect of male testosterone-exposed brains overcoming gender-role socialization. The inclination to want the more esteemed and powerful man's role compared with the women's role also suggests a parallel with the Dominican Republic hermaphrodites. I am impressed much more by the continuity in gender development that was interrupted only by the ultimate failure of the female-assigned hermaphrodite's body sexually and reproductively to deliver what was necessary for her to fulfill her social destiny.

Obstacles to the Perpetuation of a Third Sex

I have reviewed two cross-cultural cases and demonstrated the importance of a third-sex category and role in each. What began as a critique of universals and a search for factors of cross-cultural comparison has become instead a critical inquiry into the assumptions of Western scientific models of sexuality and folk ideologies of the classification of individuals. Far from being a curiosity from the cabinet of anthropological exoticism, the third sex and gender have become a way of understanding how normal science in biology and normative inquiry in anthropology may be reshaped in a different image.

In retrospect it seems obvious that these peoples in the Dominican Republic and New Guinea would have evolved a three-category sex code while living with male pseudohermaphrodites in their midst over generations. And these beleaguered souls, such as Sakulambei, are in turn spared much of the intolerable dilemma of having to be what they are not: unambiguously male or female. The presence of a third-sex category, with sex assignment at birth and some differences in growing up, serves to mediate gender dimorphism, providing anomalous or residual, if not fuzzy, responses to their bodies and, within themselves, to their own sense of their identities. Yet there are burdens to belonging to the third sex, as we have seen, and in a culture that is stridently misogynist and dimorphic in its thought system, as the Sambia indicate, there are formidable obstacles to the construction of such a permanent social category.

This interpretive study has provided two alternative critical developmental points for explaining how Dominican interssexed males, mistakenly reared as females, become the cultural beings "men" in local discourse. One is that what counts is not anatomical sex as an objective fact but the cultural meaning of sex assignment in the symbolic world and its treatment of the person. The infant's anatomical ambiguity creates a horrific deficit only in a two-sex cultural category system like ours. In a three-sex system, with its less distinct boundaries, the person's sex and identity are reckoned in relation to a more complex sexual code and social field having three alternative socialization regimes and outcomes, each of which is known to be historically coherent: male, female and hermaphroditic. In this sense, these persons are not "mistaken females" but, rather, *Guevedoche* and *kwolu-aatmwol;* that is, third genders. The second point derives from the developmentally later effect of how a three-category system provides for greater fluidity in postpubertal gender-identity transition into adult roles. It is to the inherent social advantage of the hermaphrodite to "switch" from being a mistaken female-defined to a male-defined hermaphrodite once the person enters an adult career, because the power dynamics of gender roles in both these cultures create such motivations. However, the necessary success of such "passing" and "switching" requires the ability to marshal psychological and social resources that some individuals may lack. This interpretation suggests an entirely different hypothesis than that of the biomedical model. Only a profound inner sense that one is *inexorably female* would inhibit such persons from making the social and political sex transformation from exposed and "flawed female" to hermaphroditic male. This sense would be an identity state similar to that of the primary transsexual, one whose roots have been planted deep by the culture in the nature of the person (Stoller 1975).

The Dominican Republic study epitomizes the history of medicalized sex research, which focuses too much on the level of individual experience, taking a "lone child" model that ignores social context and ideology in gender development. In a wise and far-sighted conclusion, Mead once suggested a similar critique of the American folk model: "Early and absolute assignment of sex [and] continuous therapeutic interference with any anomalies are all highly congruent with this contemporary emphasis on the importance of every human being able to function in the same way" (1961:1476). However, the two studies examined here do not resolve the controversy over biological determinants of gender identity. The 5-alpha reductase deficiency syndrome clearly creates extraordinary prenatal hormonal effects in gender development. We cannot know for sure what is hormonally normal and abnormal in such cases or what the long-term effects of hormones on adult behavior will be (Money and Ehrhardt 1972; Ehrhardt 1985; Maccoby 1979). No biopsychic "force" can be ruled out (Green 1987; Stoller 1975). But neither has the existence of prenatal hormones as the ultimate cause of sex-role transformation been demonstrated, so it is false to think of the Dominican Republic case as a "natural experiment" for such reasons (Imperato-McGinley et al. 1974; Sagarin 1975).

Sufficient demographic instances in a local group make it plausible, and perhaps inevitable, that over time a third-sex category will symbolically emerge to classify and handle the hermaphrodite. Ambiguity in culture is best handled by creating a category for the ambiguous cases. As a cultural ideal, this category may be perceived and projected into the order of nature. Feral animal species may be classified as third sex, for example, while other animal species may be domesticated (e.g., castrated) to place them in a third sex. Because most hermaphroditism occurs in males who are competitive in public affairs and may be preoccupied with exaggerating their superiority over females anyway, this third category is inherently problematic and unstable in gender hierarchies. Where it applies purely to biologically normal males, it may be utilized as the antithesis of masculinity, as in the case of Tahitian *mahu,* where femininity is not the logical sign of what "not to be" (Caplan 1987:21). Its practical and material manifestations may be blurred in praxis, however, because cultural ideals of gender may be invoked or denied for strategic situational advantage. The point is that the third gender is a perishable category, and the historical consciousness and social practices related to it may suffer demise in encounters with Western Others, whose ideals and pragmatics are more strictly dimorphic.

A particular unconscious collusion between American folk biology and sexual ideology has evolved in gender-identity research, making it difficult to separate formal scientific from folk criteria in many cases. Beginning with Freud, it could be shown that each treatment of a gender-identity theme starts with an assumption of biological essence in or regulated by males. From this perspective, the deficit model of gender variations arises. Males are missing something inside: not enough genes, not enough hormones, not enough mother, not enough father—the cultural factors informing sex assignments and development are generally ignored (Weeks 1985). Furthermore, folk models of human nature and culture are situated in the power structure of societies so as to produce unconscious structural variations in reaction to hermaphroditism (Greenberg 1988). The polymorphous culture of the Navajo seems to have achieved a remarkable zenith in its cultural praise of the blessed hermaphrodite. For the ancient Greeks, their polytheism and gender fluidity were associated with a model of sexual polymorphism; whereas the later Romans, increasingly exposed to diverse cultural standards imported from throughout the empire into Rome, became successively more orthodox in clinging to naturalisms and more restrictions on Roman sexual citizenship (Greenberg 1988; Hoffman 1984).

For the Dominican Republic and Sambia, the historical institutionalization of a third-sex category implies a cultural transcendence of human dimorphism by investing in a more "fluid," polymorphous conception of the person. In short, the gendered socialization of the hermaphrodite is not unambiguously male or female. And the cross-cultural variations attest to the importance of gendered signs of identity as cultural and historical achievements, with implications for the emergence, in certain times and places, of a third sex.

Gender identity is not entirely a social construction, and sexual variations are not merely an illusion of culture. The felt experiences of having a certain body, including the desires and strivings of the person socially identified with that body, combine to create a powerful ontology across the course of life. Surely, some elements of sex/gender development are internally motivated or hormonally time-loaded in ways that can influence the outcome of such a life. However, we are reminded of the importance of social classification of sexual dimorphism and of the resistance to the creation of a third sex that is so enduring in Western culture. As Maccoby (1979:195) once countered: "It is not children who have critical periods with respect to gender assignments, but societies; that is, after a given age, too many people know a child, and their memories are too long to permit them to change the nature of their supportive behavior." We do not have to alienate human culture and history from biology to accept that, in some places and times, a third sex has emerged as a part of human nature, and in this way, it is not merely an illusion of culture, although cultures may go to extreme lengths to make this seem so. However, an illusion it *would be* to imagine that the answer to the problems of mistaken sex in human affairs can ever be solved without recourse to the work of sexual cultures and the elaboration of individual desires within them.

NINE

Representations of "Homosexuality": Cultural Ontology and Historical Comparison

The history of homosexuality is now well known; however, it changes daily. I am being intentionally enigmatic and not simply because of the avalanche of superb research on the social history of sexuality that has appeared in recent years. The entity called "homosexuality" has long been in dispute. What causes it? Is there an essence (inside the body) or, say, a construct (in the mind or outside in "society") that vitalizes it? Is it valid to represent these essences or constructs through the tropes of Western cultural traditions (see, e.g., Carrier 1980; Greenberg 1988; Herdt 1984a; Weeks 1985)? It is, in fact, critical to these debates to question whether there is a single "it entity" or a plurality of them. This final chapter considers the question through the deconstruction of the cultural representations, tropes, and metaphors through which we in the West have constructed boy-inseminating rituals in Melanesia.

More than a hundred years of research on ritualized "homosexuality" in New Guinea and Australia has created a basic controversy regarding erotic desire: out of this tradition of same-sex relations comes social reproduction (Herdt 1984a). Sexual relations between males of certain Melanesian societies present the history of sexuality with this problematic: these societies produce adult relationships of marriage and sex with women through having boys first experience sex and "metaphoric" marriage with older males. This cultural structure and developmental complex is prescribed by religion for all males, and it has the force of ritual beliefs and practices to support it (see, e.g., Lindenbaum 1984; Adam   *265*

1986; Knauft 1987; Greenberg 1988). Situated ontologically halfway between social conformity and sexual passion, do boy-inseminating relationships, one must wonder, express erotic desire? It is the cultural
ontology of these "homosexual cultures" with which I am concerned,
with an understanding, especially in Melanesia, of how to represent such
social practices in relation to the Western categories of "bisexuality" and
"homosexuality."

The Anatomy of Homosexual Tropes

The modifiers "institutionalized" and "ritualized" are especially powerful
tropes in anthropology for understanding traditional same-sex erotic relationships. I am especially interested in the interpretative "match" between
insiders' and outsiders' representations of the homoerotic. The deconstruction of these representations suggests that studies have tended to reduce the
total phenomenon of the homoerotic relationship in non-Western societies to sex acts or sex roles or to those domains of cultural meaning, such as
family and kinship organization, that diminish the erotic dimension of
the relationship. What are missing in these representational accounts are
deeper ontologies of the homoerotic within these traditions.

By "cultural ontology," I mean lifeways or cultural life plans in which
"culture and psyche" are made into a seamless whole (see Shweder 1989).
With few exceptions, even in anthropology, we have consistently underestimated the power of cultural ontologies of the person/self, gender, body,
and human nature in representing the homoerotic in the non-Western
world. Ultimately, of course, this slant not only informs the construction of
the "homosexual" as the Other in exotic places and times but it also conveys
an essential undervaluation of the ontology of homosexuality as a distinctive lifeway in our own cultural tradition.

Theorists of the universalistic-developmental persuasion generally subscribe to the position that there is a single "it entity." Freud, for instance,
particularly the early Freud, generally did (Freud 1962); many but not all
Freudian theorists still do so (see, e.g., Isay 1986). Stage-model theorists in
experimental and clinical psychology and sociology, writing about the development of homosexual identity and life-styles, also primarily support a
single "it entity" (see, e.g., Troiden 1989). Their representations of the homoerotic, while sometimes sensitive to the insider meanings of the person,
usually impose an interpretive schema of representations upon the text in
question. Cultural relativists, however, generally subscribe to the plurality

model, in which it is argued that there are divergent "homosexualities" (see, e.g., Bell and Weinberg 1978). For instance, by suggesting that the category of "berdache" is an essential type distinctive from others, some authors nominalize the "it entity" as "berdachehood" (Whitehead 1981). Such emphasis upon multiple forms of homosexuality is usually associated with the privileging of the representations of the insider, albeit as negotiated or translated by the anthropologist.

The history of the study of sexuality reveals many instances, however, in which it is difficult to make such a clear case for the interpretative use of representations. Alfred Kinsey (Kinsey, Pomeroy, and Martin 1948) is interesting in this regard, because although he suggested that sexuality exists on a continuum of homosexual-bisexual-heterosexual, as we saw in chapter 7, he believed that there were common biosocial origins to them all. Thus, Kinsey postulated an "it entity," but multiple sex-act prototypes through which "it" is expressed, and when it came to the representation of the diversity, his reliance upon statistics rather than his subjects' narratives privileged the outsiders' representations of the meaning of the data set. The later Freud, more hermeneutic in his concern with narrative truth, accepted the possibility of divergent homosexualities and emphasized the person's experience of them (reviewed in Herdt 1989a). Neither do disciplinary boundaries completely predict an author's interpretative "attitude" toward the question of single or plural entities. John Boswell's (1980) social history and Frederick Whitam's (1983) cross-cultural surveys share an ontological view of a single entity. Certain psychiatrists, psychoanalysts, and biologists, however, having joined anthropologists, sociologists, and historians who apparently hold a divergent ontologies view, and sometimes find themselves to be uneasy bedfellows when it comes to the issue of representing what is "normal" and "natural" in the human nature of homosexuality (Green 1987; Ehrhardt 1985). In fact, though, a close reading suggests that cultural relativists have not often disagreed with the ontological claim that there is an "it entity," but only that its shapes and sensibilities belong in the interpretation of social reality (see Carrier 1980; Read 1980).

Anthropologists have thus joined others in the social sciences and humanities in pluralizing the "it entity" into divergent types of homosexualities. Typologies of homosexualities, for complex and simple societies, now abound; they owe their modern history to the sexologists such as Havelock Ellis (1936) and Edward Westermarck (1917). A set of prototypic modifiers has emerged for the classification and interpretation of historical/cultural category differences between the plural entities across time and space. Indeed, several scholarly schemas of what we might refer to as typological "root" categories of same-sex erotic relationships are being adopted increasingly, and sometimes uncritically, in historical and anthropological writing. Typically, the category systems minimally include the following: age-structured, gender-transformed, class- or role-specialized, and modern gay/lesbian categories of homosexuality. Greenberg's (1988) work provides the most complete historical and cross-cultural review of them (see also Adam 1986; Herdt 1997a; Murray 1995; Trumbach 1977). These root types assume, among other things, a representational distinction between "homosexual identity" and "homosexual behavioral form." Furthermore, the categorical focus minimally requires "homosexual behavior" for inclusion into one of the types. Yet the cultural distinctiveness of each of these types—in regard to the question of subjective and symbolic identity—further requires the representation of ways of life (i.e., beliefs, values, norms, roles, and relational institutions) that distinguish one "identity type" from another.

The representation of these root prototypes, textually and rhetorically, suggests a conundrum of comparison of a larger kind. There is a tendency to nominalize cultural constructs as entities beyond the boundaries of a particular culture. For example, the studies examined below represent berdache homosexuality as if its application as a construct to divergent cultural groups implied the same feelings, identities, and eroticism for all persons across these groups. But there is more at stake than the matter of nominalization. The comparative study of sexuality across cultures, as in so many other areas of anthropological research, is saddled historically with the conundrum of situating entities, objects (roles, institutions), and meanings between universal processes and particular situations. For example, in addressing the question of what constitutes the origins and expressions of the berdache in local groups, various accounts invoke Western constructs, such as "sexual identity" and "sexual orientation," based upon a now widely accepted but still assumptive conventional distinction between sex (biological) and gender (cultural) elements (Money and Ehrhardt 1972; Stoller 1968; see also Greenberg 1988; Herdt 1984a, 1987a). Likewise, accounts of the homoerotic in Western societies have increasingly had to address uniformity as well as intracultural variation in factors, such as race, gender, age, and class, as these predicate sociosexual action (Gagnon 1989). The glosses on the representational problem in anthropology (now so heavily burdened with the controversies of postmodernism) are phrased in terms of insider/outsider accounts and structuralist versus subjectivist interpretative frameworks (Geertz 1973; Herdt and Stoller 1990). These issues create myriad difficulties in matching the meanings of the sexual to culture (see Strathern 1988).

Sexuality research, however, has long been entangled in another, parallel debate—actually a medically driven discourse held over by popular demand from the Victorian era—regarding "essentialism" and "constructionism." Many scholars now believe this conceptual polarity in the representation of sexuality to be outmoded, and I agree with them, though the polarity nonetheless persists. As noted in chapter 8, I reject a biological, determinist main-effect theory (hypothetical prenatal exposure of the brain to androgen) of 5-alpha reductase deficiency hermaphroditism in favor of the "third-gender category" construct of these traditions, explaining the shift from "female" to "male" sex roles as a result of cultural meaning systems. However, I am still impressed by the aberrant developmental histories and identities of these persons so influenced by their biological condition. In short, both universal and particularistic factors are necessary to interpret most cross-cultural studies, with the general proviso that one's research interest determines which elements, in what combination, are significant for understanding. The study of representations of the root prototypes of homosexualities is particularly useful here, enabling us to see around the edges of the constructionist/essentialist and universalistic/particularistic dichotomies.

The new root typologies of cross-cultural and historically salient homosexuality have thus far skirted the fundamental issue of their ontologies. Local theories of being and metaphysics of the world constitute ontologies. Folk models of ontology are concerned with the nature of being a person and of being in the time/space world with such a nature. This emphasis upon the social construction of reality often prefigures interpretative schemas of the "us" and "them" contrasts so central to the postmodern problem with Otherness. Yet these metaphysics must not overshadow an earlier concern of anthropology with the consequences of such ontologies for the culturally patterned lifeways of a people. Such local theories implicitly ask what drives, intentions, desires, and developmental pathways characterize the nature of a person. Are these characteristics found also in other persons, in entities (such as spirits), and the social and physical surroundings? The genius of culture is to create an ontological reality so compelling that what is inside and outside the person is viewed as of a piece, with no seams and patches noticeable. And thus it is with the ontology of sexuality: the distinctiveness of the berdache rests not only in the meanings of berdachehood but also in the manner in which this postulated "it entity" serves as a cultural plan for life. Our own folk model of sexuality, for instance, emphasizes the lone individual, whose sexual nature is borne in the flesh, rather apart from other entities of social and spiritual sort, and which seems immutable across developmental time. For various reasons homo-sexuality has always been a problematic representation in this Western on-tological folk theory (Herdt 1987a; see also Weeks 1985). The emergence of a new folk category—gay/lesbian—has in some ways shifted our represen-tations here, situated increasingly in gender discourse not only as a distinc-tive ontology but as a way of life (Herdt 1989a). To the anthropological eye, berdache is not the same as homosexual, which is not the same as gay. And yet we must be wary of the seemingly infinite regress of splitting and divid-ing conceptions that would result in the evasion of cross-cultural and his-torical comparison of how persons from greatly different cultural traditions might share also in the same kind of ontology. It is not my aim to show that they do or do not share identical ontologies. I want to demonstrate that comparative accounts have always had to address this representational issue by way of metaphors and tropes deriving from our own folk model of ho-mosexuality.

Note how these different modes of same-sex relations tend to map onto other areas of critical study. First, the anthropological study of these types emphasizes the culturally constituted nature of homosexuality, using the modifiers "institutionalized" and "ritualized" to suggest a total-meaning system ontology recognized within local traditions. I shall deconstruct these tropes. Second, these prototypes are distinctive of kinship-based, tra-ditional societies, where arguments concerning social change and modern-ization can be held somewhat at bay. Moreover, because these societies have been studied largely by anthropologists, we should expect a closer examina-tion of the local ontology than is permitted from, say, historical records, and it is somewhat easier for another anthropologist to criticize this work compared with scholars from other fields. Third, these homoerotic proto-types are somewhat historically bound by geographic culture area, suggest-ing that "culture and psyche" should "map" onto ontologies of sexuality better than those of complex societies. Contemporary age-structured ho-mosexuality tends to occur, for instance, in certain regions of Africa and the Southwest Pacific. Gender-transformed homosexuality tends to occur in North and South America and the Asian fringes. (Do not press me to ratio-nalize these mappings [see Greenberg 1988; Murray 1984].) Thus, for what-ever ultimate historical and structural causes, the two root forms scarcely overlap in any area of the premodern world (see Greenberg 1988; Herdt 1997a). Finally, the materials on the two homosexualities are sufficiently rich that we can deconstruct the texts of their erotic meanings to under-stand the conundrum of interpretatively matching insider and outsider cultural representations in anthropological accounts.

Here is what I mean: If, as I claim, Westerners have often misunderstood and misrepresented the ontologies of local peoples' traditions, even more so have we downplayed their erotics. Sexual feelings, ideas, fantasies, excitements, and their aesthetics—what is beautiful or ugly, luscious or nauseating, dull or titillating—have not been much attended to, Robert Stoller and I found (1990). This is a great loss because the Melanesian forms are now historically dead or dying, and it may be too late to collect the missing material on intact traditions. Furthermore, I suspect that the erotic is the royal road to understanding cultural ontology in many times and places. To privilege erotic traditions, I am emphasizing a conceptual shift in the study of sexuality. To view the erotic in its social tradition is to see its part in the whole, that is, to recognize that homosexuality is not reducible to sex acts or to cultural meanings. Our interpretative problem is to understand how the developmental subjectivity of a homoerotic form is transformed into an adult way of life within a given cultural and historical tradition. Our representations of such must then refer to the cultural realities of the erotic within that tradition, whatever our universalizing tendencies and aspirations. Emphasis upon the historical and social field of the erotic relationship thus links the study of a cultural "it entity" to the ontological meanings of body, psyche, social role, and institutional setups as these shape and are in turn shaped by erotic relationships (i.e., social reproduction) (see Herdt and Stoller 1990; Stoller 1985; Foucault 1980). Such aims are not, of course, easily attained, among other reasons because we must see past our own blind spots and recognize that the erotic is, to agree with Mead (1961), an intimate and private matter in most societies. That such is in fact attainable is, however, evidenced by the increasing number of fine and richly textured cross-cultural studies of sexuality.

The ritualized homoerotic mode in Melanesia is another "it entity," distinctive but not unique in the historical archives. The efforts of anthropologists and sex researchers to understand the phenomenon have been groundbreaking but inadequate. Its history and prehistory, social patterns and their effects upon the developmental course of the person, have been difficult to reconcile with our "it entity" nominalized homosexual. But when it was grasped, it has sometimes been rendered as a social role or practice, the eroticism removed, as if one could study dancing without the dancers. That deletion removed the local ontology too. We cannot reduce the whole to a part: sex acts, or contacts, or identities, or beliefs, or even social relationships. For none of these fully contains cultural reality, though cultural ontology must contain them all. When we begin the comparison of traditional societies, these local ontologies must become a primary object of understanding. Only then shall we begin to explicate the translation process that results in our representations of sexuality—necessary and sufficient grounds for cross-cultural comparison.

Melanesian Comparisons

In colonial Melanesia the accounts which emerged were of a very different kind of traditional homosexuality, that bounded by age. I am not as concerned with the accuracy and content of the ethnographic accounts as I am with their cultural representations of "homosexuality." This symbolic root type is best known historically from the classical literature on Attic culture, from ancient China, Japan, and some would say the whole of the Indo-European language stock (Sergent 1986; see also Greenberg 1988), and from the twentieth-century ethnographic record, select areas of northern and central Africa, the Amazon Basin, and the culture area of Melanesia (see esp. Adam 1986; Greenberg 1988; Herdt 1984a). The trope "ritualized" provides the structural scope and ethnography necessary to compare it with the canonical "institutionalized" made famous by George Devereux's (1937) study of the Mohave Indians. For instance, in cultural structure and developmental ontology, societies such as the Sambia of Papua New Guinea sequentially implement, through initiation rites, years-long sexual relations between older and younger males (Herdt 1981). They do so under the auspices of a "reproductive and growth" ideology that is impressive in its motivating purposes and legitimizing powers. It would not be accurate to suggest that their "it entity" is either cross-culturally rare or universal; however, certain features of this putative ontological "it entity" are completely absent from some culture areas, such as aboriginal North America, and widely represented in the history and culture of others.

Ritual homoeroticism as a trope is not entirely new. In Melanesian anthropology its ethnographic history can be dated from 1862 (Herdt 1984a). Similar rich material of an older nature is buried in the ethnology of kindred culture areas. "Divine bisexuality," especially as popularized in comparative religion, has an old intellectual history (see, e.g., Eliade 1958). The late nineteenth-century encyclopedic surveys of sexology and morals made much of the link between age-structured homoerotic relationships and warriorhood among archaic civilizations such as the Dorians (see, e.g., Westermarck 1917). Beginning in the nineteenth century, the ban on speaking about ancient sexual attitudes began to be lifted, culminating, David Halperin (1990:4–5) has said, in a "new era" history of sexuality inaugurated by the publication of

Dover's monumental *Greek Homosexuality.* Neostructuralists such as Foucault have since been absorbed with the representation of homoerotic desire: "To delight in and be a subject of pleasure with a boy did not cause a problem for the Greeks; but to be an object of pleasure and to acknowledge oneself as such constituted a major difficulty for the boy" (1985:221). Surely no issue has been of greater interest in the anthropology of homosexuality than this— whether we may legitimately represent the subjects and objects of the ancient Greeks and New Guinea tribesmen by our tropes for homoerotic "pleasure" and "arousal." For example, are the older partners in the ritual tradition genuinely aroused, some scholars have asked? Most decidedly, as we shall see. But what is it—attraction to the boy, excess libido, power, exhibitionism, fantasies of nurturance, and so on—that arouses the older male? And is his younger male partner also aroused? Should we represent the nature of these desires as homoerotic, not homosexual—that is, as form of desire and not just of social conformity to a sex role?

At issue in many of the relevant accounts is a text on the construction of social reality and sexual conformity, with a subtext on individual "free will." Notice, for example, the differential representations of gender-reversed versus age-structured prototypes in matters of custom and power in such societies. The berdache can only muster power by "scurrilous exhibitions of his deviation," Devereux said, whereas the older male in the ritualized tradition may be a leader with authority and resources (1937:498–527). How does ritual obligation interact with power or combine with sexual desires and fantasies of individual subjects (see esp. Allen 1984)? Indeed, can one have an erotic desire without a supporting social tradition or any intentional action that precludes personal desire? According to the more vulgar relativism, personal desire and erotic pleasure are fictions born of an ethnocentrism of bourgeois capitalism (see, e.g., Creed 1984; best reviewed in Knauft 1987, 1994; Herdt 1997a).

If being inseminated by another male is ritual obligation, and every male must participate at some stage in his development, could we represent the whole culture as "homosexual"? For comparison, we might remember that in his study of the Mohave, Devereux (1937:507), invoked the trope of "homosexual culture." It was sufficiently powerful so as to get stuck on the Mohave for decades to come. Thus, a seemingly absurd representation—that the whole of a culture is homosexual—finds credence in generalizations, both old and new, to the "homosexual societies" of New Guinea. Are these purely rhetorical representations? I think not (see Feil 1987:177–78; Lindenbaum 1987). (One finds, incidentally, the same mishandled baggage associated with the "homosexual Greeks" [see esp. Halperin 1990; also Dover 1988].)

The comparative ethnography of this "it entity" reveals two interpretative trends in its Melanesian cultural representations. First, the sexual intercourse is treated as a purely customary ritual practice, the erotics removed or excused. One finds here—as in the berdache literature—a strong tendency to ignore, dismiss, trivialize, or even invalidate the actor's homoerotic meanings and desires. A second trend, historically later than the first, acknowledges the erotic component of the ritual practice but interprets it as "bisexuality." In either case, the ontological dimension is played down, and the actor's erotic desires for pleasure with the same sex are largely dismissed. As David Greenberg has aptly summarized: "What these explanations lack is any account of erotic attraction. They simply assume that if male homosexuality is needed to strengthen male solidarity or to make marriage obligations more secure, it will spontaneously appear and be institutionalized" (1988:37). Interestingly enough, in at least one writer we find the same interpretative trend—erotic desire removed in favor of social conformity—in relation to both the berdache and the ritual homosexuality traditions (Whitehead, 1981, 1986). Both interpretative stances deodorize the erotic and peripheralize the homoerotic ontology.

The Boy-Inseminating Tradition

The comparative ethnography of age-structured male-male sexual relationships in Melanesia, while ample, is also very incomplete. Much of the literature prior to 1930 is dreadfully sparse and speculative, in some cases the fairy dust of missionaries and travelers of dubious warrant (Herdt 1984a). (We must also question the contemporary and later ethnographic accounts, but for somewhat different reasons [see, e.g., Herdt and Stoller 1990:1].) Moreover, for all practical purposes, the age-structured homosexuality of these societies, as the Dutch anthropologist Jan Van Baal (1984:128) has said, "belongs to the past." Its demise in the face of culture change and opposition from white missionaries and government officers is no less dramatic than that of the berdache in North America. And perhaps the reasons are not dissimilar. The kind of cultural ontology presented by the boy-inseminating man was reprehensible to Western agents, and soon after its discovery in most places it was stopped.[1] Some of these cultures cannot now be identified or no longer exist; it is virtually impossible to col-

---

1. See Herdt (1984a:76n13), in which the German ethnologist Parkinson is cited as saying of the Ingiet secret society and its homoerotic tradition, "The Imperial authorities are now taking steps, at the instigation of the missions, to restrain the abuses." That was in 1907.

lect new material, and thus it is very difficult to reinterpret the old. Furthermore, it is no longer possible even to query many of the original ethnographers, who are long dead. Thus, Melanesianists have for some time been involved in what was once called "salvage ethnography," the unsatisfying but necessary ethnohistorical work forced upon anthropologists in a prior generation.

Still, the Melanesian literature is younger, and much of the critical work by the relevant anthropologists—coincidentally enough, almost all trained in the European tradition or with "graduate degrees from Commonwealth or continental European universities" (Knauft 1987:157)—has been done in the past thirty years.[2] (During this time it has become more respectable and scholarly to study sexuality and homosexuality [see Read 1980]). There is a sense in which this work opened up the Nile to us, as if we had found a new kind of Other—one still alive, not frozen in the antique texts of two millennia ago. Why this contemporaneity matters is that the representations of these texts are closer to those of our present culture, closer even than the old ethnographies suggest.

The most significant result of a collection of papers published in Herdt (1984a) was to show that boy-inseminating practices were once pervasive throughout the southern Papuan coastal area of New Guinea and Australia. Together with the Highlands and coastal New Guinea examples, and off-lying islands in what was once called the New Hebrides, New Caledonia, New Britain, and the like, approximately 10 percent to 20 percent of all Melanesian cultures on which we have reliable ethnographic data once practiced ritual "homosexuality" (Herdt 1984a:6–9). It is an overwhelmingly male custom; one is tempted to represent the culture area pattern as "male ritual homosexuality," because these same-gender relations are reported for males only, with one exception (Herdt 1984:75 n.10; Adam 1986). Certainly, the kinship and secret hierarchies within these societies make male-male relationships inherently problematic. It is not simply, as the British anthropologist John Layard (1959:108) once said, that these are "men-admiring societies, not women-admiring ones." It is also that males find in insemination a cultural means of "shared identity" beyond the boundaries of their own kin group (Whitehead 1986:87).

As the news of this "traditional homosexuality" spread into the mainstream of anthropology, new renditions of and interest in the phenomenon have emerged (see Strathern 1988:57–58, 208–19; Weston 1993). And the

2. I myself received the Ph.D. degree in anthropology from the Australian National University.

heuristic—"ritualized homosexuality"—once selected as a trope to reveal the unknown and to represent the unspeakable has caught on; indeed, it threatens to insinuate itself (as Devereux's "institutionalized homosexuality" once did) as canonical (see, e.g., Feil 1987:176–86; Dover 1988). But why privilege the "ritual" aspect of these age-graded homoerotic relationships? Why not settle for Devereux's "institutionalized" trope or another modifier, such as "ceremonialized"? These are not rhetorical questions for me: I assume that each descriptor conveys cultural and psychological images to the audience that make a difference in understanding the text. The earliest Melanesian literature represents the practices as "sodomy," in keeping with the rhetoric of the day; this gave way to "homosexuality" by the 1920s and 1930s (reviewed in Herdt 1984a).

One might object that the issue of adjectives and representations is now irrelevant. Virtually all ethnographers in the Melanesian situation, myself included, have in some way nominalized the local phenomenon as an "it entity" ("homosexuality"), and we have all used the "homosexuality" trope in our accounts. And many (though not I), including Margaret Mead (who also used the trope "invert" [cited in Herdt 1984a:43, 79 n.37]) nominalized the Melanesian man's desire for a younger initiate with the representation "homosexual." The British anthropologist A. B. Deacon, for instance, early on (1934:107) refers to "a remarkable organization of male homosexuality" and to "homosexuality" as a generic categorization of the Big Nambas tribe of Malekula Island.[3] By the 1960s, Van Baal (1966:205) coined the trope "homosexual initiation rites" in reference to a vast geographic area bordering the Arufura Sea (Australia and southern New Guinea). And, again, most recently we find references to the "homosexual cultures" of New Guinea.

The ritual meaning inherent in such representations, so protean in culture, social structure, and ontology, derives mainly, I think, from a still-current Durkheimian social theory. It interprets these traditional societies as ritually constituted and reproduced by ritual. The sexual traditions bounded by ritual, as this theory represents them, are no different. Some commentators forget that the same age strictures for male-male relations apply to male-female relations; the age asymmetry is one of social structure, not merely of a desire for dominance (see, e.g., Creed 1984).

In prior work I emphasized five features of the "ritual" trope in the Melanesian situation (Herdt 1984a:6). First, everywhere in the culture area,

---

3. Deacon's work was done in the 1920s; he died in the field, and his work was published posthumously.

boy-inseminating relationships are implemented through initiation or puberty rites, which in general are collective rather than individualized ceremonies (in contrast to the berdache tradition). Second, they always have
religious sanctification, ancestral spirits or beings attending or blessing the
proceedings; hence, the homoerotic is here indelibly linked to the spiritual
development and afterlife of the whole person. Third, same-sex erotic relations are rationalized in social roles, usually age graded, that involve entry
into hierarchical secret societies. The lawful nature of these roles is specified
by cultural rules about who may occupy a status or advance up the status
ladder. Fourth, ritual beliefs motivate and rationalize insemination as the
masculine elixir vital to physical growth, social maturity, and reproductive
competence. Fifth, kinship and marriage and their related rights and prohibitions always govern the formation of homoerotic relationships for example, incest taboos mirror those of heteroerotic bonds, forbidding sexual
intercourse with certain relatives (e.g., brothers and fathers). That these
cultural ideals are sometimes broken, as they are in heterosexual incest
taboos, has been documented for the Sambia (see, esp., Herdt and Stoller
1990: chapter 4). Conversely, cultural ideals prescribe who the male inseminator should be, at least in some cases.

These and other compelling boundary conditions ultimately establish
the ethnographic and representational authority of the ritual trope as the
main category of "homosexuality" in Melanesian cultures. So compelling
are these ritual and age criteria to the constitution of cultural reality in
Melanesia that no category representation has ever been reported by anthropologists for adult men who are sexually involved with other adult
male equals.

To objectify these culture area ideals, I shall instance boy-inseminating
rites among the Sambia. As I reviewed in previous chapters, Sambia believe
that the male body is incapable of achieving maturation (or masculinization) without ritual interventions. Once boys are initiated (between the
ages of seven and ten) and their "female" traces are removed through
painful rites, they are inseminated through oral intercourse so they can
grow, become strong, and reproduce. All younger males between the ages of
seven and fourteen are inseminated by older bachelors, who were once
themselves semen recipients. The younger initiates are the semen recipients
until their third-stage "puberty" ceremony; afterward they are semen
donors to a new crop of younger initiates. The Sambia prescriptive rule allows youths, aged fifteen and older, to inseminate younger initiates for
years, until the older males marry and father a child. According to the men's
sacred lore and the dogmas of their secret society, the bachelors are "mar-

ried" to the younger recipient males—as symbolized by secret ritual flutes (themselves empowered by female spirits) (see chapter 3). Age-structured relationships are ideologically concerned with the ritual reproduction of the boys, with making them into men. With fatherhood, sexual relations with boys are to cease by ritual edict; the men's marriages and duties to their children would be compromised by boy relations, Sambia men say. This ideal life plan is borne out in most of Sambia; however, the exceptions suggest that a few males do not or cannot make the transition to opposite-sex erotic relations. In fact, more men than just Kalutwo (chapter 5) continue to prefer boys, albeit not exclusively.

Notice that the relationships between the spouses are also age bound. When men are assigned wives for marriage by the elders, these females too are always younger—some of them are premenarchal—and they are sexually inexperienced. This is because both the bride and the groom are expected to be virgins heterosexually, but the grooms have already had years of same-gender sexual relations.

The initiation of erotic relationships between bachelors and initiates is multidetermined but never one-sided. There is hazing and domination of younger boys, and sometimes abuses occur. However, the younger initiates are not without protections. Remember that Sambia is a kinship-based society, and the boys' fathers and brothers would not tolerate abuses of any abnormal degree. The boy could be favored also by a particular bachelor and protected by him—a few such relationships are deep enough to constitute what we would label "lover relationships"—and indeed, some older males promoted this closeness. Moreover, as they matured, the initiates expressed more desire for insemination, being more in control of it, and they are aggressive and flirtatious. They can refuse to have sex; generally they cannot be forced into it. Finally, they have a magical protection: if abused, they can use the men's semen to practice sorcery on them, and, while this was rare, it was always a threat and a check on the bachelors' powers.

Sambia, like virtually all tribal peoples, do not nominalize homosexuality as a category. There is neither a category term nor a cultural representation for "the homosexual" or "homosexuality," but then there are no generic categories for "sex" or "heterosexuality" either. Instead, Sambia refer to differing sexual interactions, some brief and others longer-lived, with marriage the idealized union for life. In all cases the sexual interaction is rationalized as if it produced something. For example, vaginal intercourse with women is "work" *(wumdu)* toward human reproduction, whereas oral intercourse with initiated boys is for making either "growth" in the boys or "play" (*chemonyi,* in the sense of pleasure) for the older males (as we saw in chapter 2). Then, of course, there are culturally and ontologically unimagined possibilities, such as anal intercourse, which do not exist in any form. There are no category representations for masturbation either, or for conception as a single event. And men deny that women have orgasm. Thus, Sambia cultural ontology privileges social relationships over individuals, the position of the inseminator over the recipient, and men over women, at least in certain contexts.

Sexuality, in short, is always an expression of the structure of particular relationships across time: in the case of the same sex, it is usually casual and nonexclusive; in marital relationships it is usually intense and exclusive. Semen is a major sign of how this system operates for males, a token of themselves, and how they can transmit identity to younger males. Not only ritual but myth charters their conceptions.

The experiences of same-gender, age-graded insemination, first begun in ritual, fan out into secular contexts of all sorts that create a seamless relationship between body and psyche, sexuality and sociality. It is not ritual that "grows" someone, but a man's semen; however, the ritual metaphor becomes an omnibus representation for thinking and talking about transforming a man's sexual partner into a cultural producer in all major areas of advantage: warfare, ritual, and marriage for reproduction. According to the male view of life, males and females differ in most aspects of their being, including the origins of their being in the mythological past. The sexes have, in short, different metaphysical ontologies. The ritual development of the male is designed to create and reproduce this distinctive ontology. Ritual "death" and "rebirth" are basic to it: out of the symbolic processes of initiation a new person/self is born. To be more precise: the characteristic essences and signs of masculinity are formed, among which the growth of the penis leading to the "birth" of the glans penis at puberty takes precedence over all else (see esp. Layard [1942] on this idea).

The sum of these ritual events, relationships, and their tokens, inside and outside the male, constitutes their ontological reality. It is a necessary redundancy to say that without sexual excitement—as signified by erections in the inspirer and bawdy enthusiasm in the inspired boy—these social practices would not only lie beyond the erotic but, more elementary, would not exist (see Herdt 1984a; Kelly 1976; Knauft 1987). Yet the anthropological texts of these experiences reveal their desires and excitements. It follows that relationships between youths and boys, begun in initiation but fanned out to embrace years of lived experience, are for Sambia ontologically homoerotic.

In this account of a prototypic age-structured homoeroticism and others that follow, we are struggling, of course, with the representation of cultural reality—of matching, so to speak, one intentional world of objects and categories, drives, and desires with our own. But that is not all. We tend, on the one hand, not simply to split apart subject and object, as Freud recognized long ago, but to highlight the sex of the "object" of attraction (Freud 1962:15). By spotlighting the sex of the object in Western ontology, we create the possibility of such exquisite refinements as Ferenczi's "subject homoerotics who feel like women" and "object homoerotics who feel like men" (Freud 1962:13).

The Melanesian case shows the difficult and culture-bound problematic of such subject-object distinctions. Remember that the boy-inseminating rite is developmentally age graded: first penetrated, later a penetrator. Recall also that the entire male population engages in "it." The Western subject-object split in ontology does not fit well into such traditions. For example, does a particular man desire to inseminate a particular boy, or will just any boy do? Does that man merely wish to uphold his manly honor, or donate semen to the boy's development, or use him as a convenient outlet—in all of which cases his action is role-bound sexuality or, to push the interpretation, homosexual, but not homoerotic, in my terms. Yet, if he prefers the boy over an available female sexual object—and he only has to express such a preference sometimes, not always—this would suggest that our subject has desires more properly called homoerotic.

The distinction has collective import. Simply to nominalize homosexuality, particularly at the collective level, to refer to any sex contact between persons of the same sex is to reproduce in that tradition the subject-object split in our Western self and culture. This is a false start that has led some scholars to reject the interpretation that the Melanesian practices are "homosexual" or even, for that matter, erotic.

However, some anthropologists have been willing to accept that the Melanesian rites were erotic in nature but not homoerotic. For them another trope waited in the wings: "bisexuality." Indeed, the Western notion of bisexuality provides an altogether distinctive conceptual strategy and a different egress from the problematic raised in relation to the berdache. This solution, it turns out, nominalizes boy-inseminating relations as "bisexuality" at both the cultural and individual levels (see Herdt and Boxer 1995). That this emerged from a cultural relativist effort that sought to include the native point of view while also preserving the subject-object split of Western ontology, is one of the charms of the following texts: two ethnographic papers by a significant Melanesianist. These reports were soon followed by a general sexological text that picked up on the bisexuality trope.

Because the texts in question came before the present category schemas and ritualized homoeroticism trope, my interest in their constructions is purely historical: that is, the recovery of the intellectual origins of our present representation.

East Bay

In the 1960s and 1970s the anthropologist William Davenport (1965, 1977) published two papers on the sexuality of East Bay Islanders, far off the eastern coast of New Guinea. Davenport's ethnography was already well known and respected on other aspects of the culture. His account is notable because it was probably the first "new" anthropological study of boy-inseminating rites to reach a wider scholarly audience since the 1930s. It has the merit of being more detailed and focused on behavioral interaction, unlike accounts in which it is difficult to understand who does what and where with whom. Received into the sexological literature, East Bay culture became a new source of questions and answers, as we shall see in the classic textbook of John Money and Anke Ehrhardt (1972). Indeed, Davenport felt that the erotic nature of his material was sufficiently sensitive to warrant adopting a pseudonym—the "X group"—for the whole culture (1965: 164).

The ethnographer self-consciously struggles with the question of representing same-gender sexuality as homosexuality, but concludes with the trope "bisexuality." Davenport states: "For men, homosexual relations constitute another important and socially approved substitute for heterosexual intercourse. At some time during his life, very nearly every male engages in extensive homosexual activities [which are] considered to be as normal as masturbation and marital intercourse. Homosexual activity usually begins with foreplay which consists of mutual or unilateral masturbation and ends with anal intercourse culminating in orgasm" (1965:199).

The practices occur between "good friends" or brothers, one taking the "passive" role, and the other returning the favor the next time. None of these activities is represented as homosexuality, and Davenport (1965:199, 201–2) argues instead that East Bay has "bisexual behavior." Furthermore, in a subsequent paper, he canonizes this view by referring to "institutionalized male bisexualism" (1977:156).[4] In the minds of laymen, quibbling over

4. For the disaster wrought on the concept by Freudians, see, e.g., Rado (1965). For a critical examination of Freud's conception of bisexuality, see Stoller (1975).

representing these relationships as "homosexuality" or "bisexuality" may make it seem like a case of splitting hairs. But that is precisely the point of my essay: a rose is not a rose by another name. In my own category scheme, East Bay culture is represented as an example of ritualized homoeroticism; other scholars, however, have categorized East Bay's practice as generic homosexuality (Money and Ehrhardt 1972:135). These are not the same entities, claim I: homosexuality, bisexuality, and ritual homoeroticism are like different species of roses. I worry especially that the category "bisexuality" —a residual category (i.e., in Western ontology, halfway between homosexuality and heterosexuality and therefore nowhere) if ever there was one (the psychoanalysts, e.g., long interpreted "bisexuality" as "latent" homosexuality, whereas for Kinsey "bisexuality" meant a perfect three on his six-point scale of sexual acts)—misrepresents much of what is culturally distinctive and meaningful in the East Bay system. Bisexuality in the Western folk conception is a divergent ontology from East Bay's erotic mode, both in structural form and in real-life experience. Our "bisexual" is a lone child, privatized and disparaged, whose desires and practices are shorn of the collective imprint so carefully ritualized by East Bay culture. But that is the least of the ontological difference between them and us.

Davenport (1977) legitimizes his interpretation of bisexuality by appeal to ethnographies of other Melanesian societies. He says these represent "institutionalized forms of male bisexuality" (1977:156). He writes that there are "numerous examples" in Melanesia of how "men have homosexual contact at one time or another" and "numerous examples of institutionalized male bisexualism," though no sources are named. This sociological survey metaphor—"homosexual contact"—well captures the aesthetic thematics of transience and opportunism in Davenport's account. "Contact" signifies itself without much regard to its cultural actors or surround. Davenport qualifies the permanence of the "contact" by situating "male homosexual relations . . . along the life course of the individual," these activities beginning with solo masturbation in childhood, followed in adolescence by mutual masturbation. The developmental change permits friends to have anal intercourse and "trade off playing the active or passive roles." After marriage these same-gender contacts should give way to heterosexual relationships. But then we are told—in an aside that is not critically examined—that older married men may continue to "take boys as passive partners for anal intercourse" if they so desire (Davenport 1977:155). The latter point seemingly violates his own representation of male-male sexuality as transient and opportunistic, but we shall return to it.

Three claims are made about the tendency of East Bay males to "mature" beyond boy-inseminating relations. Here, "maturity" becomes the hall-mark metaphor of normality—a requisite trope of sexual reproduction for social reproduction. In its fold we sense a hidden ontological agenda, ripe with potential for declarations of human nature. The first claim is that the same-gender sexual relationship is opportunistic and casual and therefore socially immature. There are two routes to boy-inseminating, he says. As an adolescent, "homosexual relations are considered to be a substitute for het-erosexual intercourse and a substitute that is more mature than masturba-tion" (1977:155). Later, though, men who have to avoid their wives may substitute boy-inseminating, which is socially accepted. Yet, as a man so-cially matures, the more he regards boy-inseminating as transient, sec-ondary, even boring. Sambia would agree.

The second claim concerns the loveless nature of boy inseminating. Davenport (1965) argues that "no love or strong emotional bonds are devel-oped out of the sexual aspect of the relationship." East Bay has no folk sense of a desired whole person relational attachment between the older and younger males. They are certainly "not regarded as homosexual lovers" (1965:199–200). That is, an ontological distinction between "love" and "sex" is represented, but without a discussion of what constitutes "love" or purely "sexual aspects" of relationships in East Bay. Here we are reminded again of the first claim regarding the impermanence and opportunism of boy-inseminating. Elsewhere in New Guinea, a similar argument has been made for the Kaluli tribe of the Great Papua Plateau: the male-male erotic tie is inconsequential for adult social life (Schieffelin 1976). Davenport thus implicitly suggests that to create "homosexual" love of a deeper and longer-lasting nature, a culture must provide for individualized erotic partnerships throughout life, and such a conception is our Western "homoerotic," not East Bay's "institutionalized bisexuality."

In his third claim Davenport anticipates this final issue by denying that the homoerotic could exist in East Bay. "There is no culture category," he tells us, and "therefore no recognition of the exclusively homosexual man who prefers relations with males to intercourse with females" (1977:155–56). Even more, he says, East Bay culture does not share "our commonly accepted stereotype of the 'psychological homosexual'" (1965: 202). Unfortunately, we are not told what that common stereotype of a ho-mosexual is (a rose is not a rose to everyone). Davenport's essentialism is indicated, however, by his modifier "psychological," which I interpret to mean gender inverted, perhaps in the mold of the nineteenth-century "psy-chic hermaphrodite," later to become the "subject homosexual." Indeed, a curious passage—a fragment of an anecdote in Davenport's first paper—

supports this idea. He hints that to ask about "homosexuality," he conveyed to the natives an image of an effeminate homosexual man.[5] If this was indeed the preconception that lay behind Davenport's representation of homosexuality (and why should it not? Everyone else shared it), then it becomes clear why he insisted upon a "bisexuality" interpretation. The masculinized form of boy-inseminating in East Bay could never be misperceived as an effeminate homosexuality that would mix up subjects and objects. His trope "bisexual" thus contrasts with an exclusive and adult desire for males, one that is gender reversed, and probably also one that is transvestite in nature. Take note that all of these ontological entities—cross-dressing males or males who never marry—are lacking not only in East Bay but in the whole of Melanesia.

The representation of institutionalized bisexuality in Davenport's account rests upon a subject-object split of three kinds: that of "maturity," in which an adult object must be of the opposite sex; that of sex and love, in which the adult man (object) must move beyond the former with boys toward the latter with women; and that of the categorical homosexual, which the adult man (object) must never subjectify. Given these ontological stipulations, the ethnographer could find and claim only the trope "bisexual" for these decidedly nonhomosexual people. In the absence of our Western category, he suggests, East Bay male identity cannot remain developmentally fixed as a boy (subject) with the permanent state of being an objectified "homosexual" that excludes sex with women (the objectified "heterosexual").

There is still the bothersome matter of homoerotic relations between certain recalcitrant married men and boys. They do not fit well into Davenport's ontological schema for East Bay: Why are these men not satisfied with women as objects? (Does it matter that the boy-inseminating technique is here anal intercourse [see chapter 7]?) He does not tell us exactly how the older man represents this desire, but then, neither have other ethnographers. Davenport paints a picture of the men as sexually opportunistic. The younger male, it is said, regards it as "a kind of duty to obligingly accede to the demands of an older man," and the boy will consider himself "well rewarded" with a stick of tobacco or a trade item he could not obtain otherwise (1965:200).

The obstacles to the older man's desire for a boy are emphasized. East Bay culture has two folkways that hinder a man's formation of a boy-inseminat-

5. "It will be noted that this question was phrased in the familiar American stereotype of the exclusive homosexual" (Davenport 1977:202).

ing relationship to a boy. The boy's father must first consent to his son's participation. Usually this is not a problem, we are told, since the man may be a "friend" of the boy's father. (Could such a friend have been a former semen recipient of the father?) And then, Davenport says, the boy will consent only if he is motivated by something else—either his own sexual pleasure or the "small presents" awarded by the older man. These rewards are vested in the sexual activity, Davenport thinks, not in the relationship. But how does he know? The answer hinges on the same kind of psychological essentialism as earlier: a hidden ontological preference structure. The rewards enable the boy to maintain his "existentially preferred objects of gratification" (women) while engaging in a "substitute source of gratification" (presumably receptive anal intercourse) because the boy does not subjectify a desire for the homoerotic experience within himself (1977:156). And that implication (Davenport's ideas differ from my interpretation here) is reminiscent of American male hustlers' stories that attribute their sexual intercourse with other males to economic or sexual needs but who self-identify as heterosexual or bisexual rather than as gay or homosexual.

As an aside, we know that a fair number of Melanesian societies permit married men to continue boy-inseminating. Unlike the Sambia, they do not forbid but, rather, encourage it. Thus, in cultures such as the Marindanim and the Big Nambas, the natives are content to allow older men, even grandfathers, to be married and have sexual relationships with youths on the side. Neighboring societies in New Britain provide close geographic parallels to that of East Bay, I suspect (see Herdt 1984a).

What caused boy-inseminating in East Bay? Davenport argues that "sex segregation" in East Bay ultimately explains their culturally patterned form of "bisexuality." This hypothesis is not without application to the questions of free will and "biological" inversion that underlie his account. Sex segregation, he believes, creates "analogous situations" to Western "monosexual" communities such as prisons or the army, which promote male bisexual practices as their "result." Their opportunistic specificity is thus insinuated as causative of the situational bisexuality that otherwise would not occur, at least not in a statistically frequent manner. The origin of East Bay same-gender sexual relationships, Davenport concludes, derives from the "strongly gender-segregated communities of Melanesia . . . that impose effective barriers to heterosexual intercourse," thus promoting bisexuality (1977:156).

In short, what Davenport's well-known study did was to represent East Bay same-gender relations as an "accident" of culture or, if one prefers, an interruption of human nature. Yet his account presents East Bay not as constitutive of our "it entity" homosexuality—in either the masculine/bisexual or effeminate/invert tropes—and certainly not as constitutive of East Bay cultural tradition. Rather, the "it" of Davenport's representations emerges as an essentialized and individualized sexuality, like Freud's concept of libido, the expression of which—in behavioral interaction—seeks the path of least resistance to "its" "gratification." There are echoes of Kinsey's "sex drive" in this too, the East Bay man caring less than he should about his partner's gender or orifice—if, that is, the subject-object split of Western ontology were to hold. Davenport's account portrays the age-bound relationships of East Bay males as emotionally flat and loveless, materialistic, opportunistic—in a word, unflattering. The homoerotic is an immature, bide-your-time substitute for the more truly desired heteroerotic. This must be the case, he argues, because East Bay's is a "fundamentally different phenomenon" compared with "Western preferential or exclusive homosexuality." He ascribes the difference between these two cultural forms not to the presence of something within East Bay but to the absence of the ontological homosexual of the West. The "exclusive homosexual" derives from "an inversion of the individual's motivational and cognitive organization" due to biology or early learning or both (1977:156). East Bay lacks such a subject-object identity, Davenport believes.

With this trope we see finally the representational contrast set that inspired his account: East Bay bisexuality/Western inversion. We can see the conundrum Davenport faced, writing as he did before "ritualized" homoeroticism was created as an alternative ontology; inversion homosexuality would have required, as it did in a prior generation, gender-reversed and effeminate transvestitism; and whereas the berdache delivered that ontology, East Bay men with their rites of boy-inseminating and rugged masculinity did not.

But these images are inaccurate in several ways, primarily because some—it makes a difference if the "some" is 10 percent or 90 percent—East Bay men continue to desire boys after marriage. And we are told that men form friendly and warm "relationships," not just sex contacts, with boys. The actor, the sexual subject in East Bay culture, thus represented through metaphors of our Western biological individual, can never be reconciled with, let alone seamlessly merged into, East Bay's own cultural ontology. For the latter cultural reality has different posits and subjective accounts of male-male sexuality from those of our tradition; they are neither our "invert," our homosexual, nor the residual bisexual. Where Davenport began with a whole culture and erotic system, satisfied and satisfying in its own relational modes, he ends with a textual account in which subject and object are forever split apart. I take this representational position to be an artifact of our own epistemology.

The East Bay ethnography rests upon two questionable assumptions. The first is that people (whether homosexuals, heterosexuals, or anyone else, for that matter) "learn" or are somehow socialized into their erotic lives. We clearly are trained for gender roles and acquire sexual scripts in development; our fantasies no doubt reflect the sensibilities and power structures within which we arouse. However, it is another thing to argue that people learn their desires as if they were learning how to plant potatoes. There is a problematic of cultural discontinuity inherent in societies with age-structured homosexuality. To children these secret practices are unknown, and upon initiation they are revealed but only upon pain of death. Such experience hardly facilitates simple continuity of learning, as Benedict (1938) observed long ago. Such a simple learning theory fits the developmental erotics much more poorly in Melanesia than elsewhere (as argued in chapter 7). Second, to argue for sex segregation as the ultimate cause of ritualized homoeroticism is not only to explain away the presence of one thing by the absence of another but at root it is also a deficit model of male psyche and erotics (remove the opposite sex and we find the "sex drive" of men, with its residue of opportunistic homosexuality). This is, I suspect, the "biological" essentialism of Davenport's causal model, a universal "sex drive instinct" expressing itself in "immature" ways.

Like other scholars who have interpreted initiation rites and sexuality, Davenport employs Freudian tropes that obfuscate because these confuse the developmental situation of children with that of the older initiates. East Bay men, women, and their children reside together, as do families in other Melanesian societies with age-structured homoerotic relations, as I have shown (see chapter 6). Only later, usually after initiation, are boys separated from women. By contrast, other Melanesian societies without ritualized homoeroticism have men and women always living apart. Indeed, some scholars wonder whether the latter do not have the more intense tradition of sexual segregation (see, e.g., Feil 1978). In fact, Davenport's ethnography reveals that families live together and sexual segregation begins only in adolescence (1965:169–70, 204–5). Hence, the strong inference that childhood sex segregation is causative of culturally sanctioned homosexuality is not borne out in Melanesia.

Cultural representations of homoerotic relationships in East Bay are banished to a never-never land ontology: they situate East Bay neither in our "it entity" nor in that of their own. Davenport's account has the effect of suggesting that East Bay culture lacks an authentic cultural reality of the

erotic. Perhaps, though, he would accept a heteroerotic but not a homoerotic. Boy- inseminating, Davenport hints, is a layer below "natural" sexual behavior. Thus, shorn of a symbolic space for ritualized homoeroticism,
Davenport's ethnography speaks of East Bay's not as homoerotic experiences, and certainly not as deeper social relationships involving "love."

I doubt this. Instead, I guess that through successive sexual experiences
with males and females, but at first only with males—and later perhaps
with younger boys in addition to marital sex—the East Bay man becomes a
whole social and sexual person. His same-gender relationships are developmental building blocks to being the kind of cultural person his society
desires and demands. That ontological prototype is not our homosexual
but is pretty close to the ritualized age-graded form found elsewhere in
Melanesia.

Generalizing Further

The disjunctive or sequential development of ritualized same-gender relationships raises another dimension of ontology: gender identity. In the classic sex and gender text of John Money and Anke Ehrhardt we find a
significant follow-up to Davenport's discussion of ritualized homosexuality. Their account of the age-structured prototype is compelling and concerned with the cultural context of the sexuality that links psyche and
culture. Society, they argue, constructs ontological beliefs of such power
that persons "inevitably perceive some of the dictates of that cultural pattern as eternal verities, and perhaps even as expressions of immutable natural and moral law." Such a conception neatly fits the model of cultural
ontology argued here. In New Guinea they see the same-gender erotic relationship as being not "a negation of masculinity [as] in a society like our
own" but rather as "essential to strength, virility, and growth into manhood" (Money and Ehrhardt 1972:125 ff., 139–40). So far, so good.

However, to tackle the "causes" of gender identity, they are led into biology and conscious free will. And they thus introduce sexual dimorphism as
a deep-structure determinant. "In the one case," they argue, "it is masculine
for two males to avoid getting together genitally, and in the other it is
equally masculine for them to ensure that they do get together." This "paradox," as they refer to it, is resolved over social time: "The society that prescribed homosexuality does not prescribe it for all males all of the time."
From these fine predicates, though, they conclude: "The society is, therefore, really prescribing bisexuality, for those who must follow the rule of ho-

mosexuality must also, at another phase of their lives, follow the rule of breeding" (1972:141–42).

How did they begin with these ontologically clear-minded suppositions and erroneously end with an "it entity" of bisexuality? Sex-object choice, they decide, is determined by the behavioral arrangements of societies, concurring with Davenport. The issue of choice is here based upon criteria of ontological sexuality, such as "the rule of breeding," exclusivity of sexual partners, and the obligatoriness and "facultative" choices crucial to their interpretations of Melanesian and Australian customs. Unfortunately, they lean on Davenport's East Bay ethnography, finding bisexuality and sex segregation to be key tropes for understanding boy- inseminating. Among the Marind-anim of southwest New Guinea, they find exclusive and obligatory homosexuality to be lacking, upholding their bisexuality entity. In the end they conclude that whatever the "peripheral" options and alternatives of a culture, "a well defined gender-dimorphic complementarity constitutes the nucleus—the procreative nucleus—of any system of behavior between the sexes" (1972:143–44). They feel a clear gender identity is what counts for the individual, no matter what "peripheral options" a society provides. Individuals, more or less on their own, will find such a pristine identity. They say that it is in their nature to do so.

This is but another account that finds in "bisexuality" a convenient and compelling trope for the desires of ritualized homosexuality. Is it due to a hidden Western ontology of the biological? Ontology is here again vested in the lone child. Money and Ehrhardt's study posits a deep order of nonconscious nature: the drive to phylogenetic reproduction, resulting from biological dimorphism. Gender identity is for them a product of this heritage. Bisexuality as an "it entity" emerges, as it did with Davenport, to fit a cultural ontology of same-sex eroticism into a framework that splits subject and object into separate boxes: individual drives and social tradition.

What is wrong with this model is not simply its reliance upon sexual dimorphism, though the history of sexuality is replete with wrongheaded conclusions too dependent upon dimorphism (see chapter 8). The Sambia, for example—both women and men—would agree that men and women are different in their natures: drives, intentions, and needs. It is rather the subordination of the productivity of homoerotic relations to that of heteroerotic reproduction that mismatches their ontology. Sambia, I think, would rather say that the male psyche and body require both of these to make their personal development and culture "work." The Sambia folk model is quite different from ours in its willingness to accept the same- and opposite-gender relations of the male as necessary to his development and the reproduction of society. Should we privilege that view? Such a question cannot be answered easily. In the raising of it, however, I am primarily interested in showing the distinctive ontological foundation on which life is lived here. In the Melanesian traditions, one cannot have the heteroerotic without the homoerotic, and the homoerotic is prior in the male life course. "Bisexuality" is thus too tidy a trope on which to situate their sexual ontology.

Money and Ehrhardt's allusion to ritualized gender-identity development links a long history of discourse on the relationship between these erotic practices and gender development in males (Herdt 1981). The rites "genderize" boys in the direction of "masculinity," whereas gender-reversed homosexuality, such as with the male berdache, develops persons in the direction of "femininity." Such an ideal contrast is simplistic and perhaps factually incorrect. It begs the question: What is masculine and feminine? Notice again how the ontology of gender-reversal is directed to a lone person, undergoing transformation to berdache; in the ritualized homoerotic mode, by contrast, an emphasis upon the age cohort is supreme. In Melanesian traditions a powerful discourse on genderizing boys "away" from being feminine to masculine "things" permits of cultural/ontological comparisons with the berdache. Sambia are unwilling to leave anything about this genderizing process to chance: to individual choice or, as Freud might have said, to an accidental series of events. Hence, the cultural ontology of ritualized homoeroticism implicitly codes the removal of opposite sex traits or feelings, a problematic in Melanesian ideologies of gender (see Herdt 1981; and Strathern 1988).

Western preconceptions of femininity and masculinity too easily condition our interpretation of how initiates enter into ritualized homoerotic relationships. Alan Dundes (1976), in an important review, suggests a Freudian viewpoint. The symbolism of the bull-roarer in Australian and Melanesian secret societies is replete with examples of genderized behavior that may or may not involve sexual relations. Within traditions of age-structured homoeroticism, these ritual instruments occur also, and their symbolic meanings refer to sexual and gender differentiation. Secret ritual flutes among the Sambia, for instance, represent penes and female breasts, both of which are culturally significant and erotically exciting to Sambia (see chapter 3). From his survey study, Dundes refers to "homosexual intercourse" and "homosexual acts," as well as "homosexual activity," "institutionalized homosexual relations," and "ritual masturbation," as all occurring within the relevant societies. As qualifiers, these tropes suggest a model that emphasizes universals over local symbolic meanings. Especially when it comes to gender he is tempted into the active/passive dimension to index subject-object relationships. Active/passive, consistent with Freudian theory, is a signifier for him of masculine/feminine. Thus, he refers to two ontological characteristics: the homosexual insertor is active; the homosexual insertee, passive. This is already an interpretative stance that requires justification, considering the strong folk model of Freudian theory in this regard. However, he then leaps to another, potentially alien ontological contrast, viewing the insertor as more masculine and the insertee as more feminine. He justifies this view on the grounds that certain activities of the younger initiates, such as fetching water or firewood, are "acts normally carried out by women" (Dundes 1976:234–35). More significant in ontological development, Dundes argues, ritual homoerotic acts "feminize" the boys, to help them to grow up. Certain Freudians seem prone to this kind of interpretation, whether aimed at the berdache or Melanesia.

Do not misunderstand me: I am not simply railing against Freudianism or psychoanalytic interpretations of the erotic. The issue is the understanding of traditional ontologies of the homoerotic and the tropes used to represent them. The Freudians are not the only culprits here; in fact, ethnographically, there is no question that initiates are structurally subordinate to their inseminators and, in local knowledge, their relations are situationally defined sometimes as "passive" or "feminine." But why does that matter? The Australianist L. R. Hiatt has recently written of the general issue in relation to psychoanalytic theory:

> Prolonged bachelorhood in many parts of Aboriginal Australia was required by . . . gerontocratic polygyny (i.e., the acquisition of a plurality of wives by men as they grew older). It could be said that initiation rites removed sexually maturing males from their mothers and sisters, and through a combination of violence and loving care, placed them in a situation of prolonged dependence upon senior males. . . . It is hard to escape the conclusion that man-making rites and their sequels, the ceremonial maintenance of universal fertility, were in some degree homoerotic. . . . If Freud was right in speaking of a transfer of libido from mother to wife, it would seem that Aboriginal cults siphoned some of it off before it reached its ultimate heterosexual destination (1987:97–98).

Consider for historical comparison the referential use of the term "husband" on the part of Malekula Island boys to refer to their older male lovers (Deacon 1934:261). From the account of this it might be inferred that the youth was in a passive or feminine relationship to the lover. But would such an interpretation translate into our meanings of these tropes, say, in the United States (and in gay or straight circles in the provinces or the cities)?

Not necessarily. We have no observational evidence from the Melanesian circle to suggest that ritual initiates act like girls (one meaning of the descriptor "to feminize"), and certainly none that they imitate girls (a stronger meaning of "feminine"). In fact, these boys are rather aggressive, and they are soon to become much more dangerous as adult men (Herdt 1981). That does not inhibit some of them from worrying, inside, that insemination might get them pregnant (another meaning of feminization), but I assure you that they do not broadcast that fantasy. It is confined to the extraordinary circumstances of talking with a particular ethnographer (see Herdt and Stoller 1990). Such distinctions may or may not link up to Money and Erhardt's work or have been intended by Dundes's trope. We cannot know that unless they tell us what masculinity and femininity mean; otherwise we project our own conventionalized Western meanings into the texts. And here, because of the long tradition of inversion discourse in our folk model, we are all too likely to assume that the non-Western gender/erotic ontology matches our own.

How erotic are ritualized same-gender relationships? Throughout this chapter I have approached and avoided this question for two reasons. First, the answer is ethnographically complex and cannot easily be generalized across cultures without the space necessary for an essay unto itself. Moreover, the questions raised regarding the erotic aspect require us to venture into philosophical debates: namely, is the personal erotic desire the culturally collective sexual desire? To be precise, for instance, I must again distinguish between the homosexual and the homoerotic on the grounds that intentionality (personal desires) and ontology (cultural representations) separate behavior from identity and meanings. Arousal, though usually erotic (there are, e.g., the problems of wet dreams and morning erections posed for males, which Sambia might consider erotic, depending upon their manifest dream content), does not always guarantee the full participation of a subject that we would like to ascribe to the homoerotic. But the second reason is that the comparative ethnography on these issues, though better than a decade ago, is still sparse. I should have to rely even more on the Sambia than I have done, and this would inevitably raise problems regarding the unique or general flavor of that ethnography and the critical examination of my fingerprints on it—issues of ethnographic interpretation that are valuable but tangential and too weighty to take up here. However, because I have agreed with Mead, for instance, that anthropologists have too often ignored the erotic and stressed other sociocultural dimensions of tradition that make the homoerotic very unerotic, it behooves me to have a brief look at the question. I am aided by an ontological distinction already published: that the Melanesian material sorts into two symbolic forms of homoerotic relationships (reviewed in Herdt 1984a; this volume, chapter 6). There is a Type I tradition in Melanesian male-male sexuality. It is primarily ceremonial in its ontological nature. Actual homosexual penetration or insemination may not occur; that event is subordinated to the cultural performance. The Ingiet secret society of New Britain is an example of a society in which a single instance of penetration (here, anal intercourse) seems not to lead to further same-gender relationships. Other cultures, such as the Iatmul of the Sepik River, mythologically represent the homoerotic but do not apparently express this in normative sexual behavior or ritual relationships. The Small Islands of Vanuatu provide a further contrast in that homosexual hoaxes and threats are used in initiation, but no homoerotic relations ever result from it (Allen 1984). These traditions seem to stress a kind of ceremonial ideal, but erotic male-male relationships, as in most of New Guinea, are proscribed. These examples I would like to interpret as homosexual, not homoerotic.

The Type II tradition is the most frequent and prototypic of what I call ritualized homoeroticism. Actual penetration (oral or anal) is socially recognized to legitimize the coming of age or growing up of the younger male. And because it takes two to tango, the reciprocal erotic interest and duty are recognized in the social role of the older male. The ages of the older male vary from this society to that; old men, the grandfathers' generation, certainly participate; adult men, married and fathers, such as in East Bay, are candidates in some places; but it is younger, unmarried adolescents and young adult men who are in the front line and are the most frequent troops. Sambia adolescent bachelors are the culturally idealized inseminators of this symbolic kind. In many Melanesian groups there is some flexibility for same-gender participation, according to how young a boy is when he begins and how old he is when he stops, how often he joins in, and certainly with regard to his degree of enthusiasm and gusto (see esp. Knauft 1987; Herdt and Stoller 1990: chapter 6). Even younger males are not always required to join in. Thus, we can distinguish between prescribed (Sambia and Keraki societies), preferred (Kaluli society), and acceptable (Malekula Big Nambas society) modes of participation in homosexual relationships sanctioned by ritual (Herdt 1984:a). Precisely why the cultural rules and attitudes differ across these societies is unclear. There are grounds for seeing the ultimate causes as resulting from historical diffusion and migration, as I once argued, but others have rightly pointed out the link to structural forms of social organization and, in particular, marriage exchange (see Lindenbaum 1984, 1987; Feil 1978). We could surely agree with the claim that these are transformations—historical and symbolical—of a single culture and psyche ontology. However, are they most accurately represented as "homosexual" or "homoerotic"?

Who could doubt the erotic nature of this tradition from the following ethnography, collected more than sixty years ago by the English anthropologist A. B. Deacon on the Big Nambas tribe of Malekula Island in eastern Melanesia: "Among the Big Nambas . . . homosexual practices between men are very highly developed. Every chief has a number of boy-lovers, and it is said that some men are so completely homosexual in their affections, that they seldom have intercourse with their wives, preferring to go with their boys. The bond between [them] is, however, not only a sexual one. The boy accompanies his 'husband' everywhere; works in his garden (it is for this reason that a chief has many boy-lovers), and if one or other of the two should die, the survivor will mourn him deeply" (1934:261).

And now consider, from the other end of Melanesia, the following passage from Van Baal on the Marind-anim tribe of southwest New Guinea, also collected decades ago: "As far as homosexual promiscuity is concerned . . . whereas in everyday life [the older man] has the exclusive right of using the boy [anal intercourse] any relations the boy has with others may lead to outbursts of homosexual jealousy, and there is promiscuity during the *Sosom*-rites" (1966:479). It is unlikely, in the case of Van Baal, that so clear a sentiment could have been misunderstood, or that he was inclined to place an erotic meaning on an occasion in which it was absent.

These two illustrations must suffice to establish a general point: the homoerotic no doubt contained many other dimensions of social life, as implied by Deacon's mention of chiefs who wanted boy lovers to till their gardens. That does not remove its erotic content or ontological form, which was a necessary constituent to becoming a cultural person in such societies. Nor does it remove the political or physical abuses of such practices. Comparing texts from two widely separated societies, collected by anthropologists of different nationalities during a historical period of prudishness, it is difficult to doubt the erotic authenticity of boy-inseminating rites.

It is in the nature of this ritual and age-structured form of relationships that the erotic emerges as something unlike our own conception, but not so fundamentally different that we cannot recognize it. In Melanesia, an adult man can have more than one subject-object eroticized relationship. Indeed, it is in the nature of development that he must have experienced multiple gender erotic relations. The American anthropologist Bruce Knauft, in an important essay, makes this ontological reality clear for the Gebusi tribe of central New Guinea: "In early adolescence (ages 11–14) boys extend their affection to older unrelated males in the community by establishing homosexual relationships with them—i.e., being their fellators. Rather than being based on subordination or domination, these relations tend to be coquettishly initiated by the young adolescents themselves. The ideological reason for insemination is to 'grow' the boys into men, but homosexuality appears for all practical intents and purposes to be grounded in personal affection rather than obligation" (1987:172–73). Such an affection is neither wholly nonsexual nor erotic, but it is certainly not nonerotic. In a few years, we may safely conclude, it will be erotic for most of these males as adults; perhaps for some of them it may even be homoerotic—that is, their preferred, intentional, desire.

The nature of sexuality in Sambia and East Bay and kindred places is such that one's identity includes more than one form of developmental sexual relationship and therefore multiple desired objects. Sexuality is based upon a capacity, upon which culture builds, to experience more than one kind of sexual excitement. Thus a man, when a boy, desires affection from a man, who inseminates and socially supports him, all of which guarantees desires and excitements in it. Later he "returns" the favor of such affections when as a man he enters into such relationships to donate his semen to a boy. Yet these sexual relations do not preclude interactions, including marriage and passion, with women—another kind of object—and so a different form of desire and excitement. These experiences are not partitioned in developmental and cultural ontology as we would place them. Consequently our representations of them must differ. The "homosexual" of Western culture is not their "it entity," and neither is the "bisexual" of our tradition. Both of these ontological subjects may indeed share in modes of being and desires similar to, but not identical with, those of certain Melanesians. Their developmental subjectivities are made ontologically real and necessary by their culture, which cannot "work" without having multiple sexual subject-object relationships of a transformative nature. Ours, however, are more privatized, the desires an embodiment of a folk theory of human nature that cannot imagine desires both for males and females, with males subjects and objects of other males.

Preserving Otherness

The social conditions that generate gender-reversed and ritual homoeroticism reproduce a psychological/cultural reality of a whole and satisfying nature. Such social and cultural systems belie any simple attempt to make psychopathology or population shortage or gender segregation their sole cause. What such an effort does is to argue the post facto "as if": that traditional homoeroticsm could be explained as if it were our Western "it entity," if we could only forget about the rituals, or delete the nature of semen beliefs, or ignore the extraordinary family arrangements in these societies. But such is patently absurd.

Same-gender relationships in these societies create their own conditions of cultural reality for other aspects of social life, too. For instance, they sanction social markers of the person's development, such as the dreams as omens that Mohave associate with their berdache, and they sanction social relations as well, as in the case of the Sambia boy's warmly supportive ritual guardian, a man who teaches the boy but is sexually taboo to him. The definition of social reality is forever linked to cultural and ritual traditions in such societies. Initiation is here the introduction to sexual development and erotic life. In aboriginal Australia and Melanesia, from the Papuan Gulf to the Sepik River area of New Guinea, wherever secret societies of ritual homoerotic practices flourished, the nature of all sexual interaction was generally withheld from boys until initiation. Many such societies actually disapprove of childhood sexual play. Indeed, Sambia boys are fervent in associating the awakening of the erotic in them to their initiation rites and fellatio debut with adolescent bachelor partners (see chapter 3; see also Read 1984). Thus, initiation constitutes an introduction to sexual life, as Arnold Van Gennep (1960:169) once noted, for both heterosexual and homosexual relations. We have often accepted this claim in anthropology without knowing quite what to do with it (Herdt 1984a:60–65).

Surely the structuring of cultural ontology is at issue, the stamp of the divine on the homoerotic a particular sign of a divergent ontology in these societies. Contrary to our association of the profane with the homoerotic, in Etoro culture, we are told, social reality is such that heterosexuality is "antisocial" and homosexual relations are esteemed (Kelly 1976:45). Ritual traditions present to the child what was formerly hidden in the religious and erotic folds of his society. Tradition also re-presents what is filled with power—developmental barriers to and strivings for the sensibilities of the same sex that must inevitably shape desire for first same-gender, and then opposite-gender, relationships. Yet one might object: Is this a desire for relationship to the Other (social contact, affection, power, competition, body treatment, and so on), or does the child desire for the self the associated sexual pleasures and excitements? It will be clear now that such compartmentalization is specious and false to these traditions.

The virtual absence of ritualized female homoeroticism is significant in this respect, both in terms of ethnographic reports and in cultural representations of traditional homoeroticisms. From more than a century of Melanesian ethnography we have only a handful of allusions to the female erotic side. Its tradition on Malekula Island seems reliably certain; the other possibilities are so sketchy as to raise questions about their validity. We must remember, however, that not only did anthropologists generally ignore erotic life, Malinowski and Mead to the contrary, but most of them were males, who studied other males, as did Margaret Mead. We know precious little about female sexuality of any kind in the culture area, and we have reason to believe that the dialogues between natives and ethnographers may have been susceptible to concealment rather than to disclosure when it came to female sexuality (reviewed in Gewertz 1981). Same-gender touching and close physical contact have been observed as well, and while we cannot rule out an erotic component, we cannot be sure that sexual excitement (at least consciously) is part of it.

Male power and gender hierarchy are obviously relevant here, as the complicated semiotics of female orgasm reveal (Herdt and Stoller 1990: chapter 6). Notice, for instance, that in all cases, secrecy of some degree accompanies male ritualized homoerotic relations, usually but not always as a function of an umbrella secret society. Perhaps it is the case that where local ontologies, placed in the service of gender differentiation and hierarchy, lead to the formation of secret societies, these will be almost always exclusive to and support for male power. Part of the excitement of same-gender sexuality, from that perspective, is its secrecy and devotion to privilege. In the Melanesian examples, exclusion of the opposite sex socially constructs woman as an Other whose nature not only does not require but, indeed, precludes understanding the ontology of the homoerotic in the development of the male. Whatever the case, traditional female homoerotic relations remain the great unknown.

Multiple social relationships always entail multiple desires, sexual and otherwise. Study of the formation of desires and pleasures in traditional cultures offers unprecedented opportunities for us to reconsider our own ontology of the erotic and human nature. The structuring of homosexual relations in non-Western societies obviates any simple distinction between subject and object, and even between love and sex. What is needed is a new scholarly purpose in reconsidering how humans include or exclude erotic feelings and desires for same- and other-gender relations, which—if not always available—are always on call and, in most societies, provide a major developmental route to being human.

The traditional homosexualities examined here are total meaning systems, for they encompass the history, culture, persons, bodies, and psyches of real people in real places who, in living life in those places, by necessity had to participate in the ontological traditions offered them. They had no other. We must not romanticize these Others. Their worlds were not perfect; indeed, it is lovely to read about and even think like them, but it would be a far lesser thing to have lived inside their skins and cultural realities. However, neither should we substitute our reality for theirs through the tropes of understanding them. Their ontological realities are constitutive of different entities of homosexuality than those objectified by our tradition. The fine accounts now emerging of the subjectification of the sexual and the erotic in our own society and exotic others offer hope for a richer comparative study beyond anything bequeathed to us from the Victorian and early anthropology of sexual cultures.

BIBLIOGRAPHY

Adam, B. 1986. "Age-Structured Homosexual Organization," in *Anthropology and Homosexual Behavior*, ed. E. Blackwood, pp. 1–34. New York: Haworth Press.

Allen, M. 1967. *Male Cults and Secret Initiations in Melanesia*. Melbourne: Melbourne University Press.

———. 1981. "Innovation, Inversion and Revolution as Political Tactics in West Aoba," in *Vanuatu: Politics, Economics and Ritual in Island Melanesia*, ed. M. R. Allen, pp. 105–34. Sydney: Academic Press.

———. 1984. "Homosexuality, Male Power, and Political Organization in North Vanuatu: A Comparative Analysis," in *Ritualized Homosexuality in Melanesia*, ed. G. Herdt, pp. 83–127. Berkeley: University of California Press.

Ariès, P. 1962. *Centuries of Childhood*. Trans. R. Baldick. New York: Vintage.

Ashley-Montagu, M. F. 1937–38. "The Origin of Subincision in Australia." *Oceania* 8:193–207.

Balbus, I. D. 1982. *Marxism and Domination*. Princeton: Princeton University Press.

Bamler, V. G. 1911. *Tami in Deutsch Neu-Guinea*. 3 vols. Ed. R. Neubass. Berlin: Verlag D. Reimer/E. Vohsen.

Bandura, A. 1969. *Principles of Behavior Modification*. New York: Holt, Reinhart, and Winston.

Barker, J. R. 1928. "Notes on New Hebridean Customs, with Special Reference to the Intersex Pig." *Man* 28.

Barnow, V. 1979. *Culture and Personality*. 3d ed. Homewood, IL: Dorsey Press.

Barry, H. A., I. L. Child, and M. K. Bacon. 1959. "Relation of Child Training to Subsistence Economy." *American Anthropologist* 61:51–63.

Barth, F. 1975. *Ritual and Knowledge among the Baktaman of New Guinea*. New Haven: Yale University Press.

Bateson, G. 1935. "Music in New Guinea." *The Eagle* 48:158–70.

———. 1946. "Arts of the South Seas." *Art Bulletin* 28:119–23.

———. 1958. *Naven*. 2d ed. Stanford: Stanford University Press.

———. 1972. *Steps to an Ecology of Mind*. San Francisco: Chandler and Sharp.

Bech, H. 1997. *When Men Meet: Homosexuality and Modernity*. Chicago: University of Chicago Press.

Bell, A. P., and M. S. Weinberg. 1978. *Homosexualities*. New York: Simon and Schuster.

Bell, A. P., M. S. Weinberg, and S. Hammersmith. 1981. *Sexual Preference*. Bloomington: Indiana University Press.

Bem, D. 1996. "Exotic Becomes Erotic: A Developmental Theory of Sexual Orientation." *Psychological Review* 103:320–35.

Benedict, R. 1934. *Patterns of Culture*. Boston: Houghton Mifflin

————. 1938. "Continuities and Discontinuities in Cultural Conditioning." *Psychiatry* 1:161–67.

Berndt, R. M. 1962. *Excess and Restraint: Social Control among a New Guinea Mountain People*. Chicago: University of Chicago Press.

————. 1965. "The Kamano, Usurufa, Jate, and Fore," in *Gods, Ghosts, and Men in Melanesia*, ed. P. Lawrence and M. I. Meggitt, pp. 78–104. London: Oxford University Press.

Berndt, R. M., and C. Berndt. 1951. *Sexual Behavior in Western Arnhem Land*. [Publication no. 16.] New York: Viking Fund.

Bettelheim, B. 1955. *Symbolic Wounds, Puberty Rites, and the Envious Male*. New York: Collier Books.

Bieber, I., et al. 1962. *Homosexuality: A Psychoanalytic Study*. New York: Basic.

Biller, H. B. 1970. "Father Absence and the Personality Development of the Male Child." *Developmental Psychology* 2:181–201.

————. 1974. *Paternal Deprivation*. Reading, MA: Heath Lexington.

————. 1976. "The Father and Personality Development: Parental Deprivation and Sex Role Development," in *Role of the Father in Child Development*, ed. M. Lamb, pp. 89–156. New York: Wiley.

Blackwood, Evelyn, ed. 1986. *Anthropology and Homosexual Behavior*. New York: Haworth Press.

Bock, P. K. 1980. *Continuities in Psychological Anthropology*. San Francisco: W. H. Freeman.

Boelaars, J. H. M. C. 1981. *Head-Hunters about Themselves*. [Verhandelingen van het kon. Instituut voor Taal-, Land- en Volkenkunde, no. 92.] The Hague: Martinus Nijhoff.

Bolton, R. 1996. "Coming Home: The Journey of a Gay Ethnographer in the Years of the Plague," in *Out in the Field: Reflections of Lesbian and Gay Anthropologists*, ed. E. Lewin and W. Leap, pp. 147–70. Urbana: University of Illinois Press.

Boswell, J. 1980. *Christianity, Social Tolerance, and Homosexuality*. Chicago: University of Chicago Press.

Bowlby, J. 1969. *Attachment and Loss*. Vol. 1: *Attachment*. New York: Basic.

————. 1973. *Attachment and Loss*. Vol. 2: *Separation: Anxiety and Anger*. New York: Basic.

Boxer, A. M., J. A. Cook, and G. Herdt. 1991. "To Tell or Not to Tell: Patterns of Self-Disclosure to Mothers and Fathers Reported by Gay and Lesbian Youth," in *Parent-Child Relations across the Lifespan*, ed. K. Pillemer and K. McCartney, pp. 59–93. Oxford: Oxford University Press.

Bramfeld, T. 1959. *The Remaking of Culture*. New York: Harper.

Brown, J. K. 1963. "A Cross-Cultural Study of Female Initiation Rites." *American Anthropologist* 65:837–53.

Brown, P. 1978. *Highland Peoples of New Guinea*. Cambridge: Cambridge University Press.

————. 1995. *Beyond a Mountain Valley: The Simbu of Papua New Guinea*. Honolulu: University of Hawaii Press.

Brown, P., and G. Buchbinder, eds. 1976. Introduction to *Man and Woman in the New Guinea Highlands*, ed. P. Brown and G. Buchbinder, pp. 1–12. Washington DC: American Anthropological Association.

Brown, S. E. 1975. "Love Unites Them and Hunger Divides Them: Poor Women in the Dominican Republic," in *Toward an Anthropology of Women*, ed. R. R. Reiter, pp. 322–33. New York: Monthly Review Press.

Bulfinch, T. 1967. *Bulfinch's Mythology*. Abridged ed. New York: Dell.

Bullough, V. 1976. *Sexual Variance in Society and History.* Chicago: University of Chicago Press.

Bulmer, R. N. H. 1971. "Traditional Forms of Family Limitation in New Guinea," in *Population Growth and Socio-Economic Change,* pp. 137–62. [Research Bulletin no. 42.] Canberra: ANU Press.

Burton, R. V., and J. W. M. Whiting. 1961. "The Absent Father and Cross-Sex Identity." *Merrill-Palmer Quarterly of Behavior and Development* 7 (2): 85–95.

Busse, M. W. 1987. "Sister Exchange among the Wamek of the Middle Fly." Ph.D. diss., University of California, San Diego.

Butler, J. 1992. "Sexual Inversions," in *Discourses of Sexuality: From Aristotle to AIDS,* ed. D. C. Stanton, pp. 344–61. Ann Arbor: University of Michigan Press.

Caplan, P., ed. 1987. *The Cultural Construction of Sexuality.* London: Tavistock.

Carrier, J. 1980. "Homosexual Behavior in Cross-cultural Perspective," in *Homosexual Behavior: A Modern Reappraisal,* ed. J. Marmor, pp. 100–122. New York: Basic.

———. 1995. *De Los Otros: Intimacy and Homosexuality among Mexican Men.* New York: Columbia University Press.

Chodorow, N. 1974. "Family Structure and Feminine Personality," in *Woman, Culture, and Society,* ed. M. Z. Rosaldo and L. Lamphere, pp. 43–66. Stanford: Stanford University Press.

———. 1978. *The Reproduction of Mothering.* Berkeley: University of California Press.

Chowning, A. 1973. "Child Rearing and Socialization," in *Anthropology in Papua New Guinea,* ed. I. Hogbin, pp. 61–79. Melbourne: Melbourne University Press.

———. 1980. "Culture and Biology among the SengSeng of New Britain." *Journal of Polynesian Society* 89:7–31.

Cohler, B. J. 1982. "Personal Narrative and Life Course," in *Life Span Development and Behavior,* 4:205–41. New York: Academic Press.

Collier, J., and M. Z. Rosaldo. 1981. "Politics and Gender in Simple Societies," in *Sexual Meanings,* ed. S. B. Ortner and H. Whitehead, pp. 275–329. New York: Cambridge University Press.

Corber, R. J. 1997. *Homosexuality in Cold War America: Resistance and the Crisis of Masculinity.* Durham, NC: Duke University Press.

Creed, G. 1984. "Sexual Subordination: Institutionalized Homosexuality and Social Control in Melanesia." *Ethnology* 23:157–76.

D'Andrade, R. G. 1973. "Father Absence, Identification and Identity." *Ethos* 1:440–55.

Darwin, C. 1871. *The Descent of Man and Selection in Relation to Sex.* London: J. Murray.

Davenport, W. 1965. "Sexual Patterns and Their Regulation in a Society of the Southwest Pacific," in *Sex and Behavior,* ed. F. A. Beach, pp. 164–207. New York: John Wiley.

———. 1977. "Sex in Cross-Cultural Perspective," in *Human Sexuality in Four Perspectives,* ed. F. A. Beach and M. Diamond, pp. 155–63. Baltimore: Johns Hopkins University Press.

Deacon, A. B. 1934. *Malekula: A Vanishing People in the New Hebrides.* London: George Routledge.

De Cecco, J. 1990. "Sex and More Sex: A Critique of the Kinsey Conception of Human Sexuality," in *Homosexuality/Heterosexuality,* ed. D. McWhirter, pp. 367–86. New York: Oxford University Press.

D'Emilio, J., and E. B. Freedman. 1988. *Intimate Matters: A History of Sexuality in America.* New York: Harper and Row.

Devereux, G. 1937. "Institutionalized Homosexuality among the Mohave Indians," *Human Biology* 9:498–527.

———. 1967. *From Anxiety to Method in the Behavioral Sciences.* Paris: Mouton.

———. 1978. *Ethnopsychoanalysis.* Berkeley: University of California Press.

———. 1980. "Normal and Abnormal," in *Some Uses of Anthropology,* ed. J. Casagrande and T. Gladwin. Washington, DC: Anthropological Society of Washington.

Diamond, M. 1979. "Sexual Identity and Sex Roles," in *The Frontiers of Sex Research,* ed. V. Bullough. Buffalo, NY: Prometheus.

Doi, T. 1972. *The Anatomy of Dependence.* Tokyo: Kodansha International.

Douglas, Mary. 1966. *Purity and Danger.* London: Routledge and Kegan Paul.

Dover, K. 1978. *Greek Homosexuality.* Cambridge, MA: Harvard University Press.

———. 1988. "Greek Homosexuality and Initiation," in *Greeks and Their Legacy.* Vol. 2: *Prose Literature, History, Society, Transmission, Influence,* ed. K. J. Dover. Oxford: Oxford University Press.

Duberman, M. 1996. *Stonewall.* New York: Penguin.

Dundes, A. 1976. "A Psychoanalytic Study of the Bull-Roarer." *Man* 11:220–38.

Edgerton, R. B. 1964. "Pokot Intersexuality: An East African Example of Sexual Incongruity." *American Anthropologist* 66:1288–99.

———. 1985. *Rules, Exception, and Social Order.* Berkeley: University of California Press.

Ehrhard, A., and H. Meyer-Bahlburg. 1981. "Effects of Prenatal Sex Hormones on Gender-Related Behavor." *Science* 211:1312–18.

Ehrhardt, A. 1985. "The Psychobiology of Gender," in *Gender and the Life Course,* ed. Alice Rossi, pp. 81–96. New York: Aldine.

Eliade, M. 1958. *Rites and Symbols of Initiation.* Trans. W. R. Trask. New York: Harper.

Ellis, A. 1945. "The Sexual Psychology of Human Hermaphrodites," *Psychosomatic Medicine* 7:108–25.

Ellis, H. 1936. *Studies in the Psychology of Sex,* vol. 2. New York: Random House.

Elliston, D. A. 1995. "Erotic Anthropology: 'Ritualized Homosexuality' in Melanesia and Beyond." *American Ethnologist* 22:848–67.

Endelman, R. 1986. "Homosexuality in Tribal Societies." *Transcultural Psychiatric Review* 23:187–218.

Epstein, A. L. 1969. *Matupit: Land, Politics, and Change among the Tolai of New Britain.* Berkeley: University of California Press.

Ernst, T. M. 1984. "Onabasulu Local Organizations." Ph.D. diss., University of Michigan.

Evans-Prichard, E. E. 1970. "Sexual Inversion among the Azande." *American Anthropologist* 72:1428–34.

Faithorn, Elizabeth. 1975. "The Concept of Pollution among the Kafe of Papua New Guinea," in *Toward an Anthropology of Women,* ed. R. R. Reiter, 127–40. New York: Monthly Review Press.

Federn, Paul. 1952. *Ego Psychology and the Psychoses.* New York: Basic.

Feil, D. K. 1978. *The Evolution of Highland Papua New Guinea Societies.* New York: Cambridge University Press.

Feld, S. 1982. *Sound and Sentiment.* Philadelphia: University of Pennsylvania Press.

Fine, M. 1988. "Sexuality, Schooling, and Adolescent Females: The Missing Discourse of Desire." *Harvard Educational Review* 58:29–53.

———. 1992. *Disruptive Voices: The Possibilities of Feminist Research.* Ann Arbor: University of Michigan Press

Firth, R. 1981. "Spiritual Aroma: Religion and Politics." *American Anthropologist* 83:582–605.

Floyd, B. 1979. *Jamaica: An Island Microcosm.* New York: St Martin's Press.

Ford, C. S., and F. Beach. 1951. *Patterns of Sexual Behavior.* New York: Harper and Row.

Forge, A. 1972. "The Golden Fleece." *Man* 7:527–40.

Foucault, M. 1973. *The Birth of the Clinic.* Trans. A. M. S. Smith. New York: Pantheon.

———. 1980. *The History of Sexuality.* Trans. R. Hurley. New York: Vintage.

———. 1985. *The Use of Pleasure.* Trans. R. Hurley. New York: Vintage.

Freud, A. 1965. *Normality and Pathology in Childhood.* New York: International Universities Press.

Freud, S. 1910. "Leonardo da Vinci, and a Memory of His Childhood." *Standard Edition* [*S.E.*] 11:59–137. London: Hogarth Press.

———. 1922. "Some Neurotic Mechanisms in Jealousy, Paranoia and Homosexuality." *S.E.* 18:223–32. London: Hogarth Press.

———. 1930. *Civilization and Its Discontents. S.E.* 21:64–145.

———. 1950 [1912–13]. *Totem and Taboo.* Trans. J. Strachey. New York: W. W. Norton.

———. 1955. "On the Mechanism of Paranoia," in *General Psychological Theory,* trans. J. Strachey, pp. 29–48. New York: Collier.

———. 1961 [1925]. "Some Physical Consequences of the Anatomical Distinction between the Sexes." *S.E.* 19:423–58.

———. 1962 [1905]. *Three Essays on the Theory of Sexuality.* Trans. James Strachey. New York: Norton.

———. 1964 [1927]. "The Future of an Illusion." *S.E.* 21:3–57. London: Hogarth Press.

———. 1966 [1916]. *Introductory Lectures on Psychoanalysis.* Trans. J. Strachey. New York: W. W. Norton.

Freeman, J. D. 1983. *Margaret Mead and Samoa: The Making and Unmaking of an Anthropological Myth.* Cambridge, MA: Harvard University Press.

Friedl, Ernestine. 1994. "Sex the Invisible." American Anthropologist 96:833–44.

Gadamer, H. G. 1965. *Truth and Method.* New York: Crossroad.

Gagnon, J. H. 1971. "The Creation of the Sexual in Adolescence," in *Twelve to Sixteen: Early Adolescence,* ed. J. Kagan and R. Coles, pp. 231–57. New York: W. W. Norton.

———. 1975. "Sex Research and Social Change." *Archives of Sexual Behavior* 4:111–41.

———. 1989. "Disease and Desire." *Daedalus* 118:47–77.

———. 1990. "The Explicit and Implicit Use of the Scripting Perspective in Sex Research," *Annual Review of Sex Research* 1:1–44.

Gagnon, J., and W. Simon. 1973. *Sexual Conduct.* Chicago: Aldine.

Gajdusek, D. C. 1977. "Urgent Opportunistic Observations: The Study of Changing, Transient and Disappearing Phenomena of Medical Interest in Disrupted Human Communities," in *Health and Disease in Tribal Societies. CIBA Symposium* 49, n.s. Amsterdam: Elsevier/ ExcerptaMedica.

Gardner, D. S. 1984. "A Note on the Androgynous Qualities of the Cassowary: Or Why the Mianmin Say It Is Not a Bird." *Oceania* 55.

Geertz, C. 1966. "Religion as a Cultural System," in *Anthropological Approaches to the Study of Religion,* ed. M. Banton, pp. 1–46. London: Tavistock.

———. 1968. *Islam Observed.* New Haven: Yale University Press.

———. 1973. "Thick Description: Toward an Interpretive Theory of Culture," in *The Interpretation of Cultures,* pp. 3–30. New York: Basic.

———. 1977. "From the Native's Point of View: On the Nature of Anthropological Understanding," in *Symbolic Anthropology*, ed. J. L. Dolgin et al., pp. 480–92. New York: Columbia University Press.

———. 1983. *Local Knowledge*. New York: Basic.

———. 1990. *Works and Lives*. Stanford: Stanford University Press.

Gell, A. 1975. *Metamorphosis of the Cassowaries*. London: Athlone.

Gelman, S., P. Collman, and E. E. Maccoby. 1986. "Inferring Properties from Categories versus Inferring Categories from Properties." *Child Development* 57:396–404.

Gewertz, D. 1981. "The Tchambuli View of Persons: A Critique of Individualism in the Works of Mead and Chodorow." *American Anthropologist* 86:615–27.

———. 1982. "The Father Who Bore Me: The Role of the Tsambunwuro during Chambri Initiation Ceremonies," in *Rituals of Manhood: Male Initiation in Papua New Guinea*, ed. G. Herdt, pp. 286–320. Berkeley: University of California Press.

———. 1983. *Sepik River Societies*. New Haven: Yale University Press.

Gilmore, D. D. 1986. "Mother-Son Intimacy and the Dual View of Woman in Andalusia: Analysis through Oral Poetry." *Ethos* 14:227–51.

Glasse, R. M., and M. Meggitt, eds. 1969. *Pigs, Pearlshells, and Women*. Englewood Cliffs, NJ: Prentice-Hall.

Glick, L. B. 1964. "Foundations of a Primitive Medical System: The Gimi of the New Guinea Highlands." Ph.D. diss., University of Pennsylvania.

———. 1972. "Musical Instruments in Ritual," in *Encyclopedia of Papua and New Guinea*, ed. P. Ryan, pp. 821–22. Melbourne: Melbourne University Press.

Godelier, M. 1971. "'Salt Currency' and the Circulation of Commodities among the Baruya of New Guinea," in *Studies in Economic Anthropology*. Washington, DC: American Anthropological Association.

———. 1976. "Le Sexe comme fondement ultime de l'ordre social et cosmique chez les Baruya de Nouvelle-Guinée," in *Sexualité et pouvoir*, ed. A. Verdiglione, pp. 268–306. Paris: Traces Payot.

———. 1986. *The Production of Great Men*. Cambridge: Cambridge University Press.

Goffman, E. 1963. *Stigma: Notes on the Management of Spoiled Identity*. Englewood Cliffs, NJ: Prentice-Hall.

Golde, P., ed. 1970. *Women in the Field*. Chicago: Aldine.

Gorer, G. 1955. "Nature, Science, and Dr. Kinsey," in *Sexual Behavior in American Society*, ed. J. Himelhoch and S. J. Fava, pp. 50–58. New York: W. W. Norton.

Gourlay, K. A. 1975. *Sound-Producing Instruments in a Traditional Society: A Study of Esoteric Instruments and Their Role in Male-Female Relationships*. [New Guinea Research Bulletin no. 760.] Port Moresby: Australian National University Press.

Graber, R. B. 1981. "A Psychocultural Theory of Male Genital Mutilation." *Journal of Psychoanalytic Anthropology* 4:413–34.

Green, R. 1987. *The Sissy Boy Syndrome and the Development of Homosexuality*. New Haven: Yale University Press.

Greenberg, D. 1988. *The Construction of Homosexuality*. Chicago: University of Chicago Press.

Greenson, R. 1968. "Dis-identifying from Mother." *International Journal of Psychoanalysis* 49:370–74.

Gregor, T. 1985. *Anxious Pleasures*. Chicago: University of Chicago Press.

Grumbach, M. M., and F. A. Conte. 1985. "Disorders of Sexual Differentiation," in *Text-*

book of Endocrinology, 7th ed., ed. J. D. Wilson and D. W. Foster, pp. 312–401. Philadelphia: Saunders.

Habermas, J. 1971. *Knowledge and Human Interests.* Trans. J. Shapiro. Boston: Beacon.

Haddon, A. C. 1921. *Magic and Fetishism.* London: Constable.

Hall, R. L., ed. 1982. *Sexual Dimorphism in Homo Sapiens: A Question of Size.* New York: Praeger.

Hallowell, A. I. 1967. "The Self and Its Behavioral Environment," in *Culture and Experience,* pp. 75–110. New York: Schocken.

Halperin, D. 1990. *One Hundred Years of Homosexuality.* London: Routledge.

Hays, Terence E., and Patricia Hays, 1982. "Opposition and Complementarity of the Sexes in Ndumba Initiation," in *Rituals of Manhood,* ed. G. Herdt, 201–38. Berkeley: University of California Press.

Heider, K. 1976. "Dani Sexuality: A Low Energy System." *Man* 11:188–201.

Herdt, G. 1977. "The Shaman's 'Calling' among the Sambia of New Guinea." *Journal of Societé des Oceanistes* 56–57:153–67.

———. 1981. *Guardians of the Flutes: Idioms of Masculinity.* New York: McGraw-Hill.

———, ed. 1982. *Rituals of Manhood: Male Initiation in Papua New Guinea.* Berkeley: University of California Press.

———. 1984a. "Ritualized Homosexual Behavior in the Male Cults of Melanesia, 1862–1983: An Introduction," in *Ritualized Homosexuality in Melanesia,* ed. G. Herdt, pp. 1–81. Berkeley: University of California Press.

———, ed. 1984b. *Ritualized Homosexuality in Melanesia.* Berkeley: University of California Press.

———. 1987a. *The Sambia: Ritual and Gender in New Guinea.* New York: Holt, Rinehart, and Winston.

———. 1987b. "Transitional Objects in Sambia Initiation Rites." *Ethos* 15:40–57.

———. 1989a. "Introduction: Gay and Lesbian Youth, Emergent Identities, and Cultural Scenes at Home and Abroad," in *Gay and Lesbian Youth,* ed. G. Herdt, pp. 1–42. New York: Haworth.

———. 1989b. "Self and Culture: Contexts of Religious Experience in Melanesia," in *The Religious Imagination in New Guinea,* ed. G. Herdt and M. Stephens, pp. 15–40. New Brunswick, NJ: Rutgers University Press.

———, ed. 1992. *Gay Culture in America.* Boston: Beacon Press.

———. 1993. Introduction to *Ritualized Homosexuality in Melanesia.* Rev. ed. Berkeley: University of California Press.

———. 1994. "Introduction: Third Sexes and Third Genders," in *Third Sex, Third Gender: Beyond Sexual Dimorphism in Culture and History,* ed. G. Herdt, pp. 21–84. New York: Zone.

———. 1997a. *Same Sex, Different Cultures: Perspectives on Gay and Lesbian Lives.* New York: Westview Press.

———. 1997b. "Sexual Cultures and Population Movement: Implications for AIDS/STDs," in *Sexual Cultures and Migrations in the Era of AIDS,* ed. G. Herdt, pp. 3–22. New York: Oxford University Press.

Herdt, G., and A. Boxer. 1992. "Introduction: Culture, History, and Life Course of Gay Men," in *Gay Culture in America,* ed. G. Herdt, pp. 1–28. Boston: Beacon Press.

———. 1993. *Children of Horizons: How Gay and Lesbian Youth Are Leading a New Way Out of the Closet.* Boston: Beacon Press.

————. 1995. "Toward a Theory of Bisexuality," in *Conceiving Sexuality: Approaches to Sex Research in a Postmodern World,* ed. R. Parker and J. Gagnon, pp. 69–84. New York: Routledge.

Herdt, G., and J. Davidson. 1988. "The Sambia 'Turnim-man': Sociocultural and Clinical Aspects of Gender Formation in Male Pseudohermaphrodites with 5-alpha Reductase Deficiency in Papua New Guinea." *Archives of Sexual Behavior* 17:33–56.

Herdt, G., and B. Koff. In press. *Something to Tell You: The Integration of Gay and Lesbian Youth into Families.* New York: Columbia University Press.

Herdt, G., and F. J. P. Poole. 1982. "Sexual Antagonism: The Intellectual History of a Concept in the Anthropology of Melanesia," in *Sexual Antagonism, Gender, and Social Change in Papua New Guinea,* ed. F. J. P. Poole and G. Herdt. Special issue of *Social Analysis* 12:3–28.

Herdt, G., and R. J. Stoller. 1985. "Sakulambei—A Hermaphrodite's Secret: An Example of Clinical Ethnography." *Psychoanalytic Study of Society* 11:117–58.

————. 1990. *Intimate Communications: Erotics and the Study of Culture.* New York: Columbia University Press.

Herrell, R. 1992. "The Symbolic Strategies of Chicago's Gay and Lesbian Pride Day Parade," in *Gay Culture in America,* ed. G. Herdt, pp. 225–52. Boston: Beacon Press.

Hetherington, E. M. 1966. "Effects of Paternal Absence on Sex-Typed Behaviors in Negro and White Preadolescent Males." *Journal of Personality and Social Psychology* 12:188–94.

Hiatt, L. R. 1971. "Secret Pseudo-Procreative Rites among Australian Aborigines," in *Anthropology in Oceania: Essays Presented to Ian Hogbin,* ed. L. R. Hiatt and C. Jayawardena, pp. 77–88. Sydney: Angus and Robertson.

————. 1977. "Queen of Night, Mother-Right, and Secret Male Cults," in *Fantasy and Symbol,* ed. R. H. Hook, pp. 247–65. New York: Academic Press.

————. 1987. "Freud and Anthropology," in *Creating Culture: Profiles in the Study of Culture,* ed. D. J. Austin-Broos. Sydney: Allen and Unwin.

Hill, W. W. 1935. "The Status of the Hermaphrodite and Transvestite in Navaho Culture." *American Anthropologist* 37:273–79.

Hoffman, R. 1984. "Vices, Gods, and Virtues: Cosmology as a Mediating Factor in Attitudes toward Male Homosexuality." *Journal of Homosexuality* 9:27–44.

Hogbin, I. 1970. *The Island of Menstruating Men: Religion in Wogeo, New Guinea.* Scranton, PA: Chandler.

Holmes, J. H. 1924. *In Primitive New Guinea.* London: Seeley Service.

Honzik, M. P. 1984. "Life-Span Development," *Annual Review of Psychology* 35:309–31.

Imperato-McGinley, J., et al. 1974. "Steroid 5-Alpha Reductase Deficiency in Man: An Inherited Form of Male Pseudohermaphroditism." *Science* 186:1213–15.

————. 1979. "Androgens and the Evolution of Male-Gender Identity among Male Pseudohermaphrodites with 5-Alpha Reductase Deficiency." *New England Journal of Medicine* 300:1233–37.

————. 1981. "The Impact of Androgens on the Evolution of Male Gender Identity," in *Pediatric Andrology,* ed. S. J. Kagan and E. Se. S. Hafex, pp. 99–108. The Hague: Martinus Nijhoff.

Isay, R. 1986. "The Development of Sexual Identity in Homosexual Men." *Psychoanalytic Study of the Child* 41:467–89.

————. 1987. "Fathers and Their Homosexually Inclined Sons in Childhood." *Psychoanalytic Study of the Child* 42:275–94.

Jacobs, S.-E., W. Thomas, and S. Long. 1997. *Two-Spirit: Native American Gender Identity, Sexuality, and Spirituality.* Urbana: University of Illinois Press.

Jucovy, M. E. 1976. "Initiation Fantasies and Transvestitism." *Journal of the American Psychoanalytic Association* 24:525–46.

Kakar, S. 1982. "Fathers and Sons: An Indian Experience," in *Father and Child,* ed. S. H. Cath et al., pp. 417–24. Boston: Little, Brown.

———. 1985. "Psychoanalysis and Non-Western Cultures." *International Review of Psycho-Analysis* 12:441–48.

Keesing, R. M. 1982. Introduction to *Rituals of Manhood: Male Initiation in New Guinea,* ed. G. Herdt, pp. 1–43. Berkeley: University of California Press.

Kelly, R. C. 1976. "Witchcraft and Sexual Relations: An Exploration in the Social and Semantic Implications of a Structure of Belief," in *Man and Woman in the New Guinea Highlands,* ed. P. Brown and G. Buchbinder, pp. 36–53. Washington, DC: American Anthropological Association.

Kerns, V. 1983. *Women and the Ancestors.* Urbana: University of Illinois Press.

Kinsey, A., W. B. Pomeroy, and C. E. Martin. 1948. *Sexual Behavior in the Human Male.* Philadelphia: Saunders.

Klaus, M. H., and J. H. Kennel. 1976. *Maternal-Infant Bonding.* St. Louis: C. V. Mosby.

Kluckhohn, C. 1955. "Sexual Behavior in Cross-Cultural Perspective," in *Sexual Behavior in American Society,* ed. J. Himelhoch and S. F. Fava, pp. 331–45. New York: W. W. Norton.

Knauft, B. 1985. *Good Company and Violence.* Berkeley: University of California Press.

———. 1986. "Text and Social Practice: Narrative 'Longing' and Bisexuality among the Gebusi of New Guinea." *Ethos* 14:252–381.

———. 1987. "Homosexuality in Melanesia: The Need for a Synthesis of Perspectives." *Journal of Psychoanalytic Anthropology* 10:155–91.

———. 1993. *South Coast New Guinea Cultures.* Cambridge: Cambridge University Press.

———. 1994. "Foucault Meets South New Guinea: Knowledge, Power, Sexuality." *Ethos* 22:391–438.

———. 1996. *Genealogies for the Present in Cultural Anthropology.* New York: Routledge.

———. 1998. *From "Primitive" to "Postcolonial" in Melanesia and Anthropology.* Ann Arbor: University of Michigan Press.

Koch, K. F. 1974. "Sociogenic and Psychogenic Models in Anthropology: The Functions of Male Initiation." *Man* 9:397–422.

Kohlberg, L., D. Ricks, and J. Savarey. 1984. "Childhood Development as a Predictor of Adaptation in Adulthood." *Genetic Psychology Monographs* 110:91–172.

Kohut, H. 1971. *The Analysis of the Self.* New York: International Universities Press.

Kon, I. 1995. *The Sexual Revolution in Russia.* New York: Free Press.

Kulick, D., and M. Willson, eds. 1995. *Taboo: Sex, Identity, and Erotic Subjectivity in Anthropological Fieldwork.* London: Routledge.

Lamb, M. 1976. *The Role of the Father in Child Development.* New York: Wiley.

Landtman, G. 1927. *The Kiwai Papuans of British New Guinea: A Nature-born Instance of Rousseau's Ideal Community.* London: Macmillan.

Langness, L. L. 1967. "Sexual Antagonism in the New Guinea Highlands: A Bena Bena Example." *Oceania* 37 (3): 161–77.

———. 1974. "Ritual Power and Male Domination in the New Guinea Highlands." *Ethos* 2 (3): 189–212.

———. 1976. "Discussion," in *Man and Woman in the New Guinea Highlands,* ed.

P. Brown and G. Buchbinder, pp. 76–106. Washington, DC: American Anthropological Association.

———. 1982. "Discussion." *Social Analysis* 12:79–82.

Lasch, C. 1979. *The Culture of Narcissism*. New York: Warner.

Laumann, E. O., R. Michaels, J. Gagnon, and S. Michaels. 1994. *The Social Organization of Sexuality*. Chicago: University of Chicago Press.

Lawrence, P. 1965. "The Ngaing of the Rai Coast," in *Gods, Ghosts, and Men in Melanesia*, ed. P. Lawrence and M. J. Meggitt, pp. 198–223. Melbourne: Melbourne University Press.

Lawrence, P., and M. J. Meggitt, eds. 1965. *Gods, Ghosts, and Men in Melanesia*. Melbourne: Melbourne University Press.

Layard, J. 1942. *Stone Men of Malekula*. London: Chatto and Windus.

———. 1959. "Homo-eroticism in a Primitive Society as a Function of the Self." *Journal of Analytical Psychology* 4:101–8.

Leach, E. R. 1961. "Two Essay concerning the Symbolic Representation of Time," in *Rethinking Anthropology*, pp. 124–36. London: Athlone Press

———. 1966. "Virgin Birth." *Proceedings: Royal Anthropological Institute* (1965), pp. 39–50.

———. 1972. "Melchisedech and the Emperor: Icons of Subversion and Orthodoxy." *Proceedings: Royal Anthropological Institute* (1971), pp. 5–14.

LeVine, R. A. 1973. *Culture, Behavior, and Personality*. Chicago: Aldine.

———. 1979. "Anthropology and Sex: Developmental Aspects," in *Human Sexuality: A Comparative and Developmental Perspective*, ed. H. A. Katchadourian, pp. 309–19. Berkeley: University of California Press.

Lévi-Strauss, C. 1949. *Les Structures elementaires de la parent*. Paris: Presses Universitaires de France.

———. 1966. *The Savage Mind*. Chicago: University of Chicago Press.

———. 1970. *Tristes Tropiques*. Trans. J. Russell. New York: Atheneum.

Levy, R. I. 1973. *The Tahitians*. Chicago: University of Chicago Press.

Lewin, E. 1998. *Recognizing Ourselves: Ceremonies of Lesbian and Gay Commitment*. New York: Columbia University Press.

Lewin, E., and W. Leap, eds. 1996. *Out in the Field*. Urbana: University of Illinois Press.

Lewis, G. 1975. *Knowledge of Illness in a Sepik Society*. London: Athlone.

———. 1980. *Day of Shining Red: An Essay on Understanding Ritual*. New York: Cambridge University Press.

Lex, B. W. 1979. "The Neurobiology of Ritual Trance," in *The Spectrum of Ritual*, ed. E. G. d'Aquili et al., pp. 117–51. New York: Columbia University Press.

Leyburn, J. G. 1966. *The Haitian People*. New Haven: Yale University Press.

Lidz, T. 1975. *Hamlet's Enemy: Madness and Myth in Hamlet*. New York: Basic.

Lidz, R., and L. Lidz. 1977. "Male Menstruation: A Ritual Alternative to the Oedipal Transition." *International Journal of Psychoanalysis* 58 (17): 17–31.

———. 1989. *Oedipus in the Stone Age*. Madison, CT: International Universities Press.

Lindenbaum, S. 1972. "Sorcerers, Ghosts and Polluting Women." *Ethnology* 11:241–53.

———. 1976. "A Wife Is the Hand of Man," in *Man and Woman in the New Guinea Highlands*, ed. P. Brown and G. Buchbinder, pp. 54–62. Washington, DC: American Anthropological Association.

———. 1984. "Variations on a Sociosexual Theme in Melanesia," in *Ritualized Homosexuality in Melanesia*, ed. G. Herdt, pp. 337–61. Berkeley: University of California Press.

————. 1987. "The Mystification of Female Labors," in *Gender and Kinship,* ed. J. F. Collier and S. Yangisako, pp. 221–43. Stanford: Stanford University Press.

Lindenbaum, S., and R. M. Glasse. 1969. "The Fore Age-Mates." *Oceania* 39:165–73.

Luria, Z. 1979. "Psychosocial Determinants of Gender Identity, Role, and Orientation," in *Human Sexuality: A Comparative and Developmental Perspective,* ed. H. A. Katchadourian, pp. 163–93. Berkeley: University of California Press.

Lynn, D. B. 1974. *The Father: His Role in Child Development.* Monterey, CA: Brooks/Cole.

Maccoby, E. E. 1979. "Gender Identity and Sex-Role Adoption," in *Human Sexuality: A Comparative and Developmental Perspective,* ed. H. A. Katchadourian, pp. 194–203. Berkeley: University of California Press.

————. 1980. *Social Development.* New York: Harcourt Brace Jovanovich.

Mahler, M. S. 1963. "Thoughts about Development and Individuation." *Psychoanalytic Studies of the Child* 18:307–24.

Malcolm, L. A. 1966. "The Age of Puberty in the Bundi Peoples." *Papua New Guinea Medical Journal* 9:16–20.

Malinowski, B. 1913. *The Family among the Australian Aborigines.* London: University of London Press.

————. 1922. *Argonauts of the Western Pacific.* New York: E. P. Dutton.

————. 1927. *Sex and Repression in Savage Society.* Cleveland: Meridian.

————. 1929. *The Sexual Life of Savages in North-western Melanesia.* New York: Harcourt, Brace, and World.

————. 1954. *Magic, Science and Religion and Other Essays.* Garden City, NY: Anchor.

Marx, K. 1977. "The Fetishism of Commodities and the Secret Therof," in *Symbolic Anthropology: A Reader in the Study of Symbols and Meanings,* ed. J. L. Golgin et al., pp. 245–53. New York: Columbia University Press.

Mead, M. 1927. *Coming of Age in Samoa.* New York: William Morrow.

————. 1930. *Growing up in New Guinea.* New York: Dell.

————. 1935. *Sex and Temperament in Three Primitive Societies.* New York: Dutton.

————. 1949. *Male and Female: A Study of the Sexes in a Changing World.* New York: William Morrow.

————. 1956. *New Lives for Old: Cultural Transformation—Manus, 1928–1953.* New York: William Morrow.

————. 1961. "Cultural Determinants of Sexual Behavior," in *Sex and Internal Secretions,* ed. W. C. Young, pp. 1433–79. Baltimore: Williams and Williams.

Meggitt, M. I. 1964. "Male-Female Relationships in the Highlands of Australian New Guinea," in *New Guinea: The Central Highlands,* ed. J. B. Watson. Special issue of *American Anthropologist* 66, pt. 2 (4): 204–24.

————. 1977. *Blood Is Their Argument.* Palo Alto, CA: Mayfield.

Meigs, A. S. 1976. "Male Pregnancy and the Reduction of Sexual Opposition in a New Guinea Highlands Society." *Ethnology* 15 (4): 393–407.

————. 1984. *Food, Sex, and Pollution: A New Guinea Religion.* New Brunswick, NJ: Rutgers University Press.

Meyer-Bahlburg, H. 1982. "Hormones and Psychosexual Differentiation: Implication for the Management of Intersexuality, Homosexuality and Transsexuality." *Clinics in Endocrinology and Metabolism* 11:681–701.

Milgram, S. 1974. *Obediance to Authority: An Experimental View.* London: Tavistock.

Money, J. 1961. "Hermaphroditism," in *Encyclopedia of Sexual Behavior,* ed. A. Ellis and X. Abarbanel, pp. 472–84. New York: Hawthorn.

———. 1976. "Gender Identity and Hermaphroditism: Letter." *Science* 191.

———. 1987. "Sin, Sickness, or Society?" *American Psychologist* 42:384–99.

Money, J., and A. Ehrhardt. 1972. *Man and Woman, Boy and Girl*. Baltimore: Johns Hopkins University Press.

Money, J., J. G. Hampson, and J. L. Hampson. 1956. "Sexual Incongruities and Psychopathology: The Evidence of Human Hermaphrodism." *Bulletin of Johns Hopkins Hospital* 98:43–57.

Murphy, R. F. 1959. "Social Structure and Sex Antagonism." *Southwestern Journal of Anthropology* 15:89–98.

Murray, S. O. 1984. *Social Theory, Homosexual Realities*. New York: Gaisabre Monographs.

———. 1995. *American Gay*. Chicago: University of Chicago Press.

———. 1996. "Male Homosexuality in Guatemala: Possible Insights and Certain Confusions from Sleeping with the Natives," in *Out in the Field: Reflections of Lesbian and Gay Anthropologists*, ed. E. Lewin and W. Leap, pp. 236–60. Urbana: University of Illinois Press.

Nanda, S. 1986. "The Hijras of India: Cultural and Individual Dimensions of an Institutionalized Third Gender Role," in *Anthropology and Homosexual Behavior*, ed. E. Blackwood, pp. 35–54. New York: Haworth Press.

———. 1994. "Hijras: An Alternative Sex and Gender Role in India," in *Third Sex, Third Gender: Beyond Sexual Dimorphism in Culture and History*, ed. G. Herdt, pp. 373–418. New York: Zone.

Needham, R. 1967. "Percussion and Transition." *Man* 2:606–14.

Neisser, U. 1962. "Cognitive and Cultural Discontinuity," in *Anthropology and Human Behavior*, ed. U. Neisser. Washington, DC: Anthropological Society of Washington, DC.

Newman, P. L. 1964. "Religious Belief and Ritual in a New Guinea Society," in *New Guinea: The Central Highlands*, ed. I. B. Watson. Special issue of *American Anthropologist* 66, pt. 2 (4):257–72.

———. 1965. *Knowing the Gururumba*. New York: Holt, Rinehart, and Winston.

Newman, P. L., and D. Boyd. 1982. "The Making of Men: Ritual Land Meaning in Awa Male Initiation," in *Rituals of Manhood*, ed. G. Herdt, pp. 239–85. Berkeley: University of California Press.

Newton, E. 1972. *Mother Camp: Female Impersonators in America*. Chicago: University of Chicago Press.

Nilles, J. 1950. "The Kuman of the Chimbu Region, Central Highlands, New Guinea." *Oceania* 21:25–65.

Obeyesekere, O. 1981. *Medusa's Hair*. Chicago: University of Chicago Press.

———. 1990. *The Work of Culture*. Chicago: University of Chicago Press.

Oosterwal, G. 1961. *People of the Tor*. Assen: Van Gorcum.

Opler, M. K. 1965. "Anthropological and Cross-Cultural Aspects of Homosexuality," in *Sexual Inversion*, ed. J. Marmor, pp. 108–23. New York: Basic.

Ortner, S., and H. Whitehead, eds. 1981. *Sexual Meanings*. New York: Cambridge University Press.

Panoff, M. 1968. "The Notion of the Double-Self among the Maenge." *Journal of the Polynesian Society* 77:275–95.

Parker, S., J. Smith, and J. Gignat. 1975. "Father Absence and Cross Sex Identity: The Puberty Rites Controversy Revisited." *American Ethnologist* 2:687–705.

Paul, R. A. 1976. "Did the Primal Crime Take Place?" *Ethos* 4:311–52.

————. 1980. "Symbolic Interpretation in Psychoanalysis and Anthropology." *Ethos* 8:286–94.

Pettit, P. 1977. *The Concept of Structuralism: A Critical Analysis.* Berkeley: University of California Press.

Piaget, J. 1971. *Structuralism.* New York: Harper.

Pierson, E. L., and W. V. D'Antonio. 1974. *Female and Male: Dimensions of Human Sexuality.* Philadelphia: Lippincott.

Pleck, J. 1975. "Masculinity-Femininity: Current and Alternate Paradigms." *Sex Roles* 1:161–78.

Plummer, K. 1975. *Sexual Stigma.* Boston: Routledge and Kegan Paul.

————. 1989. "Coming Out in England," in *Adolescence and Homosexuality,* ed. G. Herdt. New York: Haworth Press.

————. 1996. "Intimate Citizenship and the Culture of Sexual Story Telling," in *Sexual Cultures: Communities, Values and Intimacy,* ed. J. Weeks and J. Holand, pp. 34–52. London: Routledge.

Poole, F. J. P. 1981. "Transforming 'Natural' Woman: Female Ritual Leaders and Gender Ideology among Bimin-Kuskumin," in *Sexual Meanings,* ed. S. B. Ortner and H. Whitehead. New York: Cambridge University Press.

————. 1982. "The Ritual Forging of Identity: Aspects of Person and Self in Bimin-Kushusmin Male Initiation," in *Rituals of Manhood: Male Initiation in Papua New Guinea,* ed. G. Herdt, pp. 100–154. Berkeley: University of California Press.

————. 1985. "Coming into Being: Cultural Images of Infants in Bimin-Kuskusmin Folk Psychology," in *Person, Self and Experience,* ed. G. M. White and J. Kirkpatrick, pp. 183–242. Berkeley: University of California Press.

Pribram, K. H. 1967. "The New Neurology and the Biology of Emotion: A Structural Approach." *American Psychologist* 22:830–38.

Rado, S. 1965. "A Critical Examination of the Concept of Bisexuality," in *Sexual Inversion,* ed. J. Marmor, pp. 175–89. New York: Basic.

Rappaport, R. 1986. "Desecrating the Holy Woman." *American Scholar* (Summer): 313–47.

Read, K. E. 1951. "The Gahuku-Gama of the Central Highlands. *South Pacific* 5 (8): 154–64.

————. 1952. "Nama Cult of the Central Highlands, New Guinea." *Oceania* 23 (1): 1–25.

————. 1954. "Cultures and the Central Highlands, New Guinea." *Southwestern Journal of Anthropology* 10 (1): 1–43.

————. 1955. "Morality and the Concept of the Person among Gahuku-Gama." *Oceania* 25:233–82.

————. 1965. *The High Valley.* London: George Allen and Unwin.

————. 1980. *Other Voices.* Novato, CA: Chandler and Sharp.

————. 1984. "The Nama Cult Recalled," in *Ritualized Homosexuality in Melanesia,* ed. G. Herdt, pp. 248–91. Berkeley: University of California Press.

Reay, M. 1959. *The Kuma: Freedom and Conformity in the New Guinea Highlands.* Melbourne: Melbourne University Press.

Reik, T. 1946 [1915]. "The Puberty Rites of Savages," in *Ritual: Four Psychoanalytic Studies,* pp. 91–166. New York: Grove Press.

Róheim, G. 1942. "Transition Rites." *Psychoanalytic Quarterly* 11:336–74.

————. 1945. *The Eternal Ones of the Dream.* New York: International Universities Press.

Rosaldo, M. Z., and L. Lamphere. 1974a. Introduction to *Woman, Culture and Society,* ed. M. Z. Rosaldo and L. Lamphere, pp. 1–15. Stanford: Stanford University Press.

———, eds. 1974b. *Woman, Culture and Society.* Stanford: Stanford University Press.

Roscoe, W. 1998. *Changing Ones: Third and Fourth Genders in Native North America.* New York: St. Martin's Press.

Ross, J. M. 1980. "Retrospective Distortion in Homosexual Research." *Archives of Sexual Behavior* 9:523–31.

———. 1982. "The Roots of Fatherhood: Excursions into a Lost Literature," in *Father and Child: Developmental and Clinical Perspectives,* ed. S. H. Cath, A. R. Gurwitt, and J. M. Ross, pp. 3–20. Boston: Little, Brown.

Rubin, G. 1975. "The Traffic in Women: Notes on the 'Political Economy' of Sex," in *Toward an Anthropology of Women,* ed. R. Rapp, pp. 157–210. New York: Monthly Review Press.

Rubin, R., J. M. Reinisch, and R. F. Haskett. 1981. "Postnatal Gonadal Steroid Effects on Human Behavior." *Science* 211:1318–24.

Rycroft, C. 1985. *Psychoanalysis and Beyond.* Ed. P. Fuller. Chicago: University of Chicago Press.

Sagarin, E. 1975. "Sex Rearing and Sexual Orientation: The Reconciliation of Apparently Contradictory Data." *Journal of Sex Research* 11:329–34.

Salisbury, R. F. 1965. "The Siane of the Eastern Highlands," in *Gods, Ghosts, and Men in Melanesia,* ed. P. Lawrence and M. J. Meggitt, pp. 50–77. Melbourne: Melbourne University Press.

Sanday, P. 1981. *Female Power and Male Dominance.* New York: Cambridge University Press.

Sapir, E. 1938. "Why Cultural Anthropology Needs the Psychiatrist." *Psychiatry* 1:7–12.

———. 1949. *Selected Writings of Edward Sapir.* Berkeley: University of California Press.

Sargent, W. 1957. *Battle for the Mind.* Melbourne: Heinemann.

Schieffelin, E. L. 1976. *The Sorrow of the Lonely and the Burning of the Dancers.* New York: St. Martin's Press.

———. 1979. "Mediators as Metaphors: Moving a Man to Tears in Papua New Guinea," in *The Imagination of Reality,* ed. A. Becker and A. Yengoyan. New York: Ablex Press.

———. 1982. "The Bau'a Ceremonial Hunting Lodge: An Alternative to Initiation," in *Rituals of Manhood,* ed. G. Herdt, pp. 155–200. Berkeley: University of California Press.

Schieffelin, E. L., and R. Crittenden, eds. 1991. *Like People You See in a Dream: First Contact in Six Papuan Societies.* Stanford: Stanford University Press.

Schneider, D. M. 1968. *American Kinship: A Cultural Account.* Englewood Cliffs, NJ: Prentice-Hall.

Schwartz, T. 1973. "Cult and Context: The Paranoid Ethos in Melanesia." *Ethos* 1:153–74.

———. 1978. "Where's the Culture?" in *The Makings of Psychological Anthropology,* ed. G. Spindler. Berkeley: University of California Press.

Segal, H. 1957. "Notes on Symbol Formation." *International Journal of Psychoanalysis* 38:391–97.

Sergent, B. 1986. *Homosexuality in Greek Myth.* Trans. A. Golhammer. Boston: Beacon Press.

Serpenti, L. M. 1965. *Cultivators in the Swamps: Social Structure and Horticulture in New Guinea.* Assen: Van Gorcum.

———. 1984. "The Ritual Meaning of Homosexuality and Pedophilia among the Kimam-Papuans of South Irian Jaya," in *Ritualized Homosexuality in Melanesia,* ed. G. Herdt, pp. 292–317. Berkeley: University of California Press.

Shostack, M. 1980. *Nisa: The Life and Works of a !Kung Woman.* New York: Basic.

Shweder, R. A. 1989. "Cultural Psychology—What Is It?" in *Cultural Psychology*, ed. J. Stigler, et al., pp. 1–46. New York: Cambridge University Press.

Shweder, Richard A., and E. J. Bourne. 1984. "Does the Concept of the Person Vary Cross-Culturally?" in *Culture Theory*, ed. R. Shweder, pp. 158–99. New York: Cambridge University Press.

Smith-Rosenberg, C. 1985. *Disorderly Conduct: Visions of Gender in Victorian America.* New York: Vintage.

Snarey, J., and L. Son. 1986. "Sex-Identity Development among Kibbutz-born Males: A Test of the Whiting Hypothesis." *Ethos* 14:99–119.

———. 1987. "Sex Identity Development and the Function of Male Initiation Rites: Commentary on R. Endelman's 'Homosexuality in Tribal Societies.'" *Transcultural Psychiatric Review* 23:187–218.

Sørum, A. 1984. "Growth and Decay: Bedamini Notions of Sexuality," in *Ritualized Homosexuality in Melanesia*, ed. G. Herdt, pp. 337–61. Berkeley: University of California Press.

Spiro, M. E. 1965. "Religious Systems as Culturally Constituted Defense Mechanisms," in *Context and Meaning in Cultural Anthropology*," pp. 100–113.

———. 1968. "Virgin Birth Parthenogenesis, and Physicological Paternity: An Essay on Cultural Interpretation." *Man* 3:242–61.

———. 1982. *Oedipus in the Trobriands.* Chicago: University of Chicago Press.

———. 1989. "On the Strange and the Familiar in Recent Anthropological Thought," in *Cultural Psychology*, ed. J. Stigler et al.

Stephens, W. N. 1962. *The Oedipus Complex: Cross-Cultural Evidence.* New York: Free Press.

Stimpson, C. R. 1996. "Women's Studies and Its Discontents." *Dissent* 43:67–75.

Stoller, R. J. 1968. *Sex and Gender.* Vol. 1: *On the Development of Masculinity and Femininity.* New York: Science House.

———. 1973. *Splitting: A Case of Female Masculinity.* New York: Quadrangle.

———. 1975. *Sex and Gender.* Vol. 2: *The Transsexual Experiment.* New York: Jason Aronson.

———. 1976. "Primary Femininity." *Journal of the American Psychoanalytic Association* 24 (supp.): 59–78.

———. 1979. *Sexual Excitement: Dynamics of Erotic Life.* New York: Pantheon.

———. 1985a. *Observing the Erotic Imagination.* New Haven: Yale University Press.

———. 1985b. "Marked Femininity in Boys: An Emphasis on Fathers," in *Presentations of Gender*, pp. 43–64. New Haven: Yale University Press.

———. 1985c. "Psychoanalytic 'Research' on Homosexuality: The Rules of the Game," in *Observing the Erotic Imagination*, pp. 167–83. New Haven: Yale University Press.

Stoller, R. J., and G. Herdt. 1982. "The Development of Masculinity: A Cross-Cultural Contribution." *Journal of the American Psychoanalytic Association* 30:29–59.

———. 1985. "Theories of Origins of Homosexuality: A Cross-Cultural Look." *Archives of General Psychiatry* 42 (4): 399–404.

Strathern, A. J. 1969. "Descent and Alliance in the New Guinea Highlands: Some Problems of Comparison." *Proceedings of the Royal Anthropological Institute* (1968), pp. 37–52.

———. 1970. "Male Initiation in the New Guinea Highlands Societies." *Ethnology* 9 (4): 373–79.

———. 1972. *One Father, One Blood.* Canberra: Australian National University Press.

Strathern, A. J., and M. Strathern. 1968. "Marsupials and Magic: A Study of Spell Symbolism among the Mbowamb," in *Dialectic in Practical Religion*, ed. E. R. Leach, pp. 179–207. Cambridge: Cambridge University Press.

Strathern, M. 1972. *Women in Between*. London: Seminar Press.

———. 1979. "The Self in Self-Decoration." *Oceania* 49:224–57.

———. 1988. *The Gender of the Gift*. Berkeley: University of California Press.

Sturtevant, W. C. 1968. "Categories, Percussion, and Physiology." *Man* 3:133–34.

Troiden, R. R. 1989. "The Formation of Homosexual Identities and Roles," in *Adolescence and Homosexuality*, ed. G. Herdt, pp. 43–74. New York: Haworth Press.

Trumbach, R. 1977. "London's Sodomites: Homosexual Behavior and Western Culture in the Eighteenth Century." *Journal of Social History* 11 (1): 1–33.

———. 1994. "London's Sapphists: From Three Sexes to Four Genders in the Making of Modern Culture," in *Third Sex, Third Gender: Beyond Sexual Dimorphism in Culture and History*, ed. G. Herdt, pp. 111–36. New York: Zone.

Turner, V. W. 1964. "Symbols in Ndembu Ritual," in *Closed Systems and Open Minds*, ed. M. Gluckman, pp. 20–51. Chicago: Aldine.

———. 1967. *The Forest of Symbols*. Ithaca: Cornell University Press.

Tuzin, D. F. 1976. *The Ilahita Arapesh: Dimensions of Duality*. Berkeley: University of California Press.

———. 1980. *The Voice of the Tambaran: Truth and Illusion in Ilahita Arapesh Religion*. Berkeley: University of California Press.

———. 1982. "Ritual Violence among the Ilahita Arapesh: The Dynamics of Moral and Religious Uncertainty," in *Rituals of Manhood: Male Initiation in Papua New Guinea*, ed. G. Herdt, pp. 321–55. Berkeley: University of California Press.

———. 1994. "The Forgotten Passion: Sexuality and Anthropology in the Ages of Victoria and Bronislaw." *Journal of the History of the Behavioral Sciences* 30:114–37.

———. 1997. *The Cassowary's Revenge: Women and the Death of Masculinity in a New Guinea Society*. Chicago: University of Chicago Press.

Van Baal, J. 1963. "The Cult of the Bull-Roarer in Australia and Southern New Guinea." *Bijdragen tot de Taal-, Land-, en Volkenkunde* 119:201–14.

———. 1966. *Dema: Description and Analysis of Marind-anim Culture*. The Hague: Martinus Nijhoff.

———. 1984. "The Dialectics of Sex in Marind-anim Culture," in *Ritualized Homosexuality in Melanesia*, ed. G. Herdt, pp. 128–76. Berkeley: University of California Press.

Van Gennep, A. 1960. *The Rites of Passage*. Trans. M. K. Vizedom and G. L. Caffee. Chicago: University of Chicago Press.

Vance, C. S. 1991. "Anthropology Rediscovers Sexuality: A Theoretical Comment." *Social Science and Medicine* 33:875–84.

Vanggaard, T. 1972. *Phallos*. New York: International Universities Press.

Von Felszeghy, B. 1920. "Panik und Pan-Komplex." *Imago* 4:1–40.

Wagner, R. 1972. *Habu: The Innovation of Meaning in Daribi Religion*. Chicago: University of Chicago Press.

———. 1975. *The Invention of Culture*. Toronto: Prentice-Hall.

Wallace, A. F. C. 1969. *Culture and Personality*. 2d ed. New York: Random House.

Watson, J. B. 1960. "A New Guinea 'Opening Man,'" in *In the Company of Man*, ed. I. B. Casagrande, pp. 127–73. New York: Harper and Row.

———. 1964. "Anthropology in the New Guinea Highlands," in *New-Guinea: The Central Highlands*, ed. J. B. Watson. Special issue of *American Anthropologist* 66, pt. 2 (4): 1–19.

Wedgwood, C. H. 1937–38. "Women in Manam." *Oceania* 7:401–28; 8:170–92.

Weeks, J. 1985. *Sexuality and Its Discontents.* London: Routledge and Kegan Paul.

Weeks, J., and J. Holland, eds. 1986. *Sexual Cultures: Communities, Values and Intimacy.* London: Routledge.

Weil, T. E. et al. 1973. *Area Handbook for the Dominican Republic.* 2d ed. Washington, DC: Government Printing Office.

Weinberg, M. S., C. J. Williams, and D. W. Pryor. 1994. *Dual Attraction: Understanding Bisexuality.* New York: Oxford University Press.

Weiner, A. 1978. "The Reproductive Model in Trobriand Society," in *Trade and Exchange in Oceania and Australia,* ed. J. Specht and J. P. White. Special issue of *Mankind* 11: 175–86.

———. 1980. "Reproduction: A Replacement for Reciprocity." *American Ethnologist* 7:71–85.

———. 1992. *Inalienable Possessions: The Paradox of Keeping-while-Giving.* Berkeley: University of California Press.

West, D. J. 1977. *Homosexuality Re-Examined.* Minneapolis: University of Minnesota Press.

Westermarck, E. 1917. *The Origins and Development of the Moral Ideas,* vol. 2. 2d ed. London: Macmillan.

Weston, K. 1993. "Lesbian/Gay Studies in the House of Anthropology." *Annual Review of Anthropology* 22:339–67.

Whitam, F. L. 1983. "Culturally Invariable Properties of Male Homosexuality." *Archives of Sexual Behavior* 12:207–22.

Whitehead, H. 1981. "The Bow and the Burden Strap: A New Look at Institutionalized Homosexuality in Native North America," in *Sexual Meanings,* ed. S. B. Ortner and H. Whitehead, pp. 80–115. New York: Cambridge University Press.

———. 1986. "The Varieties of Fertility Cultism in New Guinea, Part 1." *American Ethnologist* 13:80–99.

Whiting, J. W. M. 1941. *Becoming a Kwoma.* New Haven: Yale University Press.

Whiting, J. W. M., R. Kluckhohn, and J. Anthony. 1958. "The Function of Male Initiation Ceremonies at Puberty," in *Readings in Social Psychology,* ed. E. E. Maccoby, T. M. Newcomb, and E. L. Hartley, pp. 359–70. New York: Henry Holt.

Whiting, J. W. M, and S. W. Reed. 1938. "Kwoma Culture." *Oceania* 9 (2): 170–216.

Whiting, J. W. M., and B. B. Whiting. 1975. "Aloofness and Intimacy of Husbands and Wives: A Cross-Cultural Study." *Ethos* 3:183–207.

Wiarda, H. J., and M. J. Kryzanek. 1982. *The Dominican Republic.* Boulder: Westview Press.

Wiesner, T. S., and R. Gallimore. 1977. "My Brother's Keeper: Child and Sibling Caretaking." *Current Anthropology* 18:169–90.

Williams, F. E. 1930. *Orokaiva Society.* Oxford: Oxford University Press.

———. 1936a. *Papuans of the Trans-Fly.* Oxford: Clarendon Press.

———. 1936b. *Bull-Roarers in The Papuan Gulf.* [Anthropological Report of the Territory of Papua, no. 17.] Port Moresby: Government Printer.

———. 1940. *Drama of Orokolo.* London: Oxford University Press.

Williams, W. 1986. *The Spirit and the Flesh: Sexual Diversity in American Indian Culture.* Boston: Beacon Press.

Winnicott, D. W. 1971. *Playing and Reality.* London: Tavistock.

Wirz, P. 1959. *Kunst und Kult des Sepik-Gebietes (Neu-Guinea).* Amsterdam: Koninklijk Instituut Voor de Tropen.

Wolf, E. 1969. *Peasant Wars of the Twentieth Century.* New York: Harper Torchbooks.

Young, F. W. 1965. *Initiation Ceremonies: A Cross-Cultural Study of Status Dramatization.* Indianapolis: Bobbs-Merrill.

Earlier versions of the material revised for this book appeared as follows.

CHAPTER ONE was originally published in 1988 as "The Ethnographer's Choices," in *Choice and Morality*, ed. George Appell and T. N. Madan, pp. 159–92. New York: SUNY Press. Reprinted by kind permission of the State University of New York Press.

CHAPTER TWO was published in 1990, as chapter 2 in Gilbert Herdt and Robert J. Stoller, *Intimate Communications: Erotics and the Study of Culture*. New York: Columbia University Press. Reprinted by kind permission of Columbia University Press.

CHAPTER THREE was published in 1982 in *Rituals of Manhood: Male Initiation in Papua New Guinea*, ed. Gilbert Herdt, pp. 44–98. Berkeley: University of California Press, and now under copyright to Gilbert Herdt.

CHAPTER FOUR was originally published in 1982 as "Nose-Bleeding Rites and Male Proximity to Females," *Ethos* 10 (3): 189–231. Reprinted by kind permission of the American Anthropological Association.

CHAPTER FIVE was originally published in 1980 in *Ethnopsychiatrica* 3:70–116, edited by the late George Devereux, and now under copyright to Gilbert Herdt.

CHAPTER SIX was originally published in 1989 *Ethos* 18:326–70. Reprinted by kind permission of the American Anthropological Association.

CHAPTER SEVEN was originally published in 1990, in *Homosexuality and Heterosexuality: The Kinsey Scale and Current Research*, ed. David McWhirter, J. Reinisch, and S. Saunders, pp. 208–38. New York: Oxford University Press. Reprinted by kind permission of Oxford University Press.

CHAPTER EIGHT was originally published in 1990 *American Anthropologist* 92:433–46. Reprinted by kind permission of the American Anthropological Association.

CHAPTER NINE was originally published in 1991 as "Representations of 'Homosexuality' in Traditional Societies: An Essay on Cultural Ontology and Historical Comparison," in *Journal of the History of Sexuality* 1–2: 481–504, 603–32. Reprinted by kind permission of the University of Chicago Press.